Stepping Lively in Place

Stepping Lively in Place

THE NOT-MARRIED, FREE WOMEN OF CIVIL-WAR-ERA NATCHEZ, MISSISSIPPI

Joyce Linda Broussard

The University of Georgia Press
ATHENS

A Sarah Mills Hodge Fund Publication
This publication is made possible, in part, through a grant from the Hodge Foundation in memory of its founder, Sarah Mills Hodge, who devoted her life to the relief and education of African Americans in Savannah, Georgia.

Parts of chapters 2, 3, and 4 were originally published in different form as "Naked before the Law: Married Women and the Servant Ideal in Antebellum Natchez," and parts of chapter 5 were originally published as "Stepping Lively in Place: The Free Black Women of Antebellum Natchez," in *Mississippi Women: Their Histories, Their Lives*, vol. 2, edited by Elizabeth Anne Payne, Martha H. Swain, and Marjorie Julian Spruill (University of Georgia Press, 2010).

Parts of chapters 6 and 7 were originally published in different form as "Malvina Matthews: The Murderess Madam of Civil War–Era Natchez," in the *Journal of Mississippi History* 73 (Spring 2011).

Parts of chapter 7 were originally published in different form as "Occupied Natchez, Elite Women, and the Feminization of the Civil War," in the *Journal of Mississippi History* 70 (Summer 2008).

Parts of chapter 8 were originally published in different form as "Coping with the Deluge: The Elite, Not Married Women of Postbellum Natchez, Mississippi—and the 'Other Men' in Their Lives," in *Southern Studies*, new series 17 (Spring/Summer 2010). Permission to reprint granted by the Southern Studies Institute. All rights reserved.

Library of Congress Cataloging-in-Publication Data

Names: Broussard, Joyce Linda.
Title: Stepping lively in place : the not-married, free women of Civil-War-era Natchez, Mississippi / Joyce Linda Broussard.
Description: Athens : The University of Georgia Press, 2016. | "A Sarah Mills Hodge Fund publication"—Title page verso. | Includes bibliographical references and index.
Identifiers: LCCN 2016000131| ISBN 9780820345499 (hard cover : alkaline paper) | ISBN 9780820349725 (paperback : alkaline paper)
Subjects: LCSH: Single women—Mississippi—Natchez—History—19th century. | Divorced women—Mississippi—Natchez—History—19th century. | Widows—Mississippi—Natchez—History—19th century. | Women, White—Mississippi—Natchez—History—19th century. | African American women—Mississippi—Natchez—History—19th century. | Free African Americans—Mississippi—Natchez—History—19th century. | Women—Mississippi—Natchez—History—19th century. | Sex role—Mississippi—Natchez—History—19th century. | Natchez (Miss.)—Social conditions—19th century. | Natchez (Miss.)—Race relations—History—19th century.
Classification: LCC HQ800.4.U62 N383 2016 | DDC 305.409762'26—dc23
LC record available at https://lccn.loc.gov/2016000131

To my children

Joanna, Matthew, Clinton, and Jaron . . .

My inspiration,

Forever and Always

CONTENTS

ILLUSTRATIONS

Figures

Tables

ACKNOWLEDGMENTS

I owe a special debt to my good friend and colleague Ronald L. F. Davis, who started me along the graduate school path and has been a steadfast supporter ever since. I first traveled to Natchez as a graduate student and as one of Davis's research assistants in 1992. That trip became the genesis of the Natchez Courthouse Records Project, which has continued at California State University, Northridge (CSUN), in various forms for twenty-three years and which I codirected after joining the History Department at CSUN and eventually directed after Ron retired from teaching. Ron's unique "take" on life taught me and his many students that doing history must always be a personal adventure in which the "experience" mattered above all else.

Created in 1992, the project has rescued and preserved thousands of manuscript legal records for Adams County, Mississippi, housing them at the Historic Natchez Foundation. Hundreds of CSUN and other students have participated in this preservation project as interns, producing published articles, books, and conference papers as well as numerous senior papers, MA thesis projects, and PhD dissertations. Among the many students, both mine and Professor Davis's, whose research has contributed substantially to this book are the following: Janet Aguilar, Aaron Anderson, Kashia Arnold, Justin Behrend, Darcy Bieber, Devan Brown, Janet Bruce, Jason and Erin Doolittle, Rebecca Dresser, Ed Esau, Susan Falck, Cai Hamilton (to whom I owe a special debt, as noted in chapter 2), Rebekah Harding, John Harrel, Charity Hayes, Suni Johnson, David Kibler, Wendy Machlovitz, Sheryl Nomelli, Terra Palewicz, Cody Pletcher, Darren Raspa, Julie Rowe, Beth Sadler, Tom Scarborough, Dan Shiells, Cecilia Shulman, Leslie Smithers, Kha Tara Steen, Barbara Stites, Connie Tripp, Derrick Ward, Michael Ward, Rosanne Welch, Debora White-Hayes, and Cheryl Wilkinson (as well as many others, too numerous to list fully).

When I began my PhD work at USC I was fortunate to study under Terry Seip, whose guidance in those early years helped me to focus and understand what mattered in research and writing; he is for me the exemplar of a model professor. I want to acknowledge as well the other members of my dissertation committee, namely, professors Philip Ethington, who gave new meaning to "thinking outside of the box"; Michael Renov, whose cinematic arts vision merged with my creative side; Mauricio Mazon, whose keen sense of the "irrational" enhanced my analytical perspective; and Steve Ross, whose working-class and social history angles informed my evolving work.

Along the way a number of historians have read versions or portions of my manuscript. Their comments and suggestions greatly improved my work as well, especially those of David Moltke Hansen and Noralee Frankel. My good friend Professor Elizabeth Anne Payne deserves a special word. It was she who sent me to the University of Georgia Press, and her inclusion of my essays in her edited volume, *Mississippi Women: Their Histories, Their Lives*, volume 2, provided a burst of energy and encouragement that greatly inspired and motivated me. Three readers of the book for the University of Georgia Press, one anonymous and two known, Noralee Frankel and Robert May, improved and sharpened my analysis immeasurably.

I owe much gratitude to my colleagues in the History Department at CSUN for their support and encouragement over the years. I cherish the many times my colleague and friend Tom Devine uplifted me with his humor, offered insights into the Byzantine ways of the academy, and provided heartfelt concern for my welfare. Another special colleague whose wisdom and advice I treasure is James Sefton, a veritable CSUN institution with fifty-plus years of teaching under his belt and still going strong. Charles Macune, Thomas Maddux, and Richard Horowitz, as department chairs, were incredibly supportive over the years, and much thanks goes to Dean Stella Theodoulou and prior provost Harry Hellenbrand for assisting me with travel and research monies. Importantly, I owe tremendous thanks to the two women who make everything possible in the History Department, Kelly Winkleblack-Shea and Susan Mueller. Thank you, Kelly and Sue.

I also want to acknowledge a number of archivists, archival administrators, and historians who have assisted me time and time again: Elbert R. Hilliard, Hank Holmes, and Anne Lipscomb Webster, along with their phenomenal staff at the Mississippi Department of Archives and History; Faye Phillips, Judy Bolton, and Tara Zachary Laver of the Louisiana State University Archives; Katherine Adams and Don Carleton of the Center for American History at the University of Texas at Austin; Kathleen Jenkins and Thom Rosenblum (the former park historian) of the Natchez National Historic Park; and Mary Warren Miller and Ronald W. Miller of the Historic Natchez Foundation.

Not to be forgotten are several dear friends in the Natchez community (again too numerous to mention all) that greatly facilitated my work: the late and much-loved Alma Carpenter, Angie Singleton, Beth Boggess, Joan

Gandy, Anne MacNeil, and my Natchez hero, the late Thomas Gandy. At the top of the list is Ralph Vicero, dean emeritus at csun ("Godfather of the Natchez Project"), who is currently living in Natchez; his continued hospitality and support have been there for me, Ron Davis, and our students from the start. A special thanks goes to Mimi Miller, director of the Historic Natchez Foundation. She opened the foundation archives to my students, assisting each of them through her personal mentoring, and she has helped me at nearly every step along the way with information and insights drawn from her profoundly important work on the history and material culture of Natchez. She is a living legend.

I am also very grateful to the talented folk at the University of Georgia Press. Mick Gusinde-Duffy was always ready to assist me, as was Bethany Snead. Special thanks needs to be given to my project editor John Joerschke, and a big shout-out to Joy Margheim, my copyeditor, whose close eye for detail, consistency, and context greatly enhanced the final product. Deborah Patton should be commended for her careful work on indexing. And much appreciation goes to Nancy Grayson for inviting me to submit my manuscript and for leaving me in such competent hands after she retired.

Finally, I want to acknowledge and personally thank the four most important people in my life, whom I dearly love and to whom this book is dedicated, my children, Joanna, Matthew, Clinton, and Jaron. Over the many years since I started this journey they have accompanied me on research trips to Mississippi and Louisiana and tolerated my never-ending classes and late-night writing marathons, and they have grown up to be the most amazing people in the world. Each of them is so different from the other that I often wonder how they could actually be siblings, but having them at my side and in my thoughts has given meaning to the "Stepping Lively" in the title of my book in ways that I would never have appreciated had they not been along for the ride. They always made me smile, every day, and they still do, no matter what. Thank you so very much for loving me and sticking with me on that long journey. I could never have done it without you!

A NOTE ON TERMINOLOGY

Throughout this book, I use the words "never married" and "spinster" inter-changeably to differentiate single women who never married from divorced and widowed women. Although the word "spinster" carries a negative connotation, I generally use it for clarity when talking about never-married women older than age thirty, in contrast to divorced or widowed women of similar age. When discussing widows, I make the point that widowed women were viewed culturally, legally, and socially as "ever-married" women, or women who continued to live after the death of their husbands in various kinds of relationships, often legal ones, to a dead spouse. I also refer to those women who sued their husbands for divorce as divorcing women, which better reflects their agency than the words "divorced women," words that I reserve for those women whose husbands sued them for divorce. Finally, I use the words "single women" to reference any not-married woman; these are words that I find are applicable to the total body of spinsters, divorced and divorcing women, and widows. Not included in the study are enslaved women, married or single, although the formerly enslaved who lived as not-married women after the Civil War are discussed in the postbellum sections of the book. I also use the terms "free blacks" and "free people of color" interchangeably throughout the book depending on the context, noting that contemporaries (white and black) usually referred to free blacks as free people of color.

Legally, spinsters and divorced and widowed women were grouped together by Mississippi courts as *feme soles* in order to differentiate them from *feme coverts*. A *feme sole* was always a single woman (divorced, widowed, or spinster) not married legally to a male. As a *feme sole*, a single woman had none of the legal disabilities, which I discuss at length in the book, attached to a *feme covert*, or a married woman, although she continued to carry gendered baggage that constrained her culturally, economically, politically, and socially when compared to men. These legal terms were seldom used outside the courtroom, and I avoid using them as much as possible.

It also should be noted that many of the court cases involving divorced and widowed women appeared in the various chancery courts of equity, or those courts that generally dealt with issues of equitable justice rather than strictly statute law. Of course, if litigation involved issues of debt and credit for Natchez single women, or alleged criminal actions, the cases were normally heard by circuit courts or lower judicial bodies, such as city magistrates and county officials, depending on the contested values pertaining to the dispute at issue.

Stepping Lively in Place

INTRODUCTION

In 1869, Mary Martha Gaillard, a married white woman living in Texas with her husband and two children, wrote a whispered letter to her unmarried half sister, Sinah Foster, who lived in Natchez, Mississippi, with her not-married sisters, Kate and Elizabeth, the daughters of a prominent slaveholding doctor, James Foster; women who remained single their entire lives. Mary Gaillard's letter depicts a marital scene that must have caused her sisters to wonder if the spinsterhood to which they seemed destined, what with the wartime deaths of so many potential husbands, might be preferable to marriage after all.

> My sister you can't conceive of the miserable life we lead. Mr. Gaillard has not one spark of affection for wife or children & his greatest pleasure is to curse & damn us—liquor does not cause it either. My children want me to leave him. I sleep upstairs with Minnie—they are afraid to leave me with him. Don't mention this in replying. A few days ago he choked & kicked Minnie in the stomach because she spoke to him of his treatment of me during her absence at school. Since the neighbors have heard of it he may do better. It is mortifying to us.[1]

Gaillard's tale of marital woe undoubtedly rang true to more than a few white women in Natchez, Mississippi, during the mid-nineteenth century. Although we can never know for certain how many Natchez husbands were cruel, drunken, and adulterous brutes or incompetent providers, the sizable number of Natchez divorces, legal separations, and runaway wives and husbands in the half century before the Civil War leaves little doubt but that the community's free women, as well as their families, understood the risks associated with marriage. During the 1850s, for example, at least sixteen white women in Natchez sought legally to divorce their husbands by charging them with ongoing adultery (often with prostitutes and enslaved women), extreme cruelty, drunkenness, abandonment, and habitual gambling, to the ruination of them and their families. At least five white Natchez husbands also divorced their wives during that decade for infidelity and desertion; these divorcing couples were among the several hundred Mississippians who legally ended their marriages from 1800 to 1860.[2] Nearly 40 percent of the city's twelve hundred adult white and free-black women living in Natchez in 1860 (all ages) were widows, women who had never married, and legally divorced women. Among them too were abandoned women and those who had deserted their husbands without divorcing them.[3]

Some Natchez women almost certainly remained single or never married again after they divorced or became widowed because no man wanted to marry them, for whatever reason. Others avoided marriage because they feared childbirth or an abusive husband, dreaded the family responsibilities of motherhood and homemaking even in good marriages, or found no man acceptable as a husband whom they could love and respect. Still others may have preferred women as sexual partners or nonsexual but loving companions, considered the marital contract a risky business from which there was no easy escape, or preferred their autonomy as women nondependent on husbands.

Quite likely some Natchez women had heard how Caroline Jennings, a well-known Natchez belle, discovered, moments after pronouncing her wedding vows, a set of love letters between her new husband and a mysterious woman in New Orleans with whom he planned to rendezvous. The distraught Caroline broadcast the discovery to her still-assembled wedding guests, boldly announcing that she wanted nothing to do with the "faker" who had tricked her into marriage. According to witnesses, a drunken Edward Jennings, drawing his pistol, threatened to "shoot" Caroline for her humiliating attack on his character, only to be stopped by her friends and family. Edward then left Natchez and took up with his New Orleans consort, whom he purportedly married. Caroline, in asking the court to annul her unconsummated marriage, also accused her husband of bigamy, with his third wife living somewhere in parts unknown. In her petition for annulment, she castigated her husband as "one of those characters who to the dishonor of their sex, traverses the county, winning the affection of young women, marrying them, [and] then deserting them for a new victim." The chancery judge hearing her case ruled Jennings's marriage invalid, saying that the couple had exchanged marriage vows in Concordia Parish, Louisiana, without having resided in the parish for the length of time required for a valid marriage by Louisiana law.[4]

Perhaps some Natchez free women knew about the night Jane Andre bludgeoned her violently abusive husband to death with an ax when she no longer could tolerate his beatings. At her trial, Jane claimed that rough characters, angry that her husband had prevented them from having sex with one of his enslaved women, had murdered him in the front yard of their house. The grand jury found Jane's story less than convincing because of the blood scattered throughout her bedroom, but the subsequent trial jury judged her not guilty after a lengthy hearing. Jane testified that her husband, Jacque, had been a troublesome and abusive man whose brawling ways and tendency to associate with unruly and criminal men had led to his death.[5]

Marital disputes involving the emotional torture of wives by husbands, heinous physical abuse, spousal fornication and adultery, drunkenness, and all kinds of debauchery often played out in the Adams County courts that met in Natchez, and the details were eagerly reported in newspapers or spread by alert gossipmongers. Some of the city's single, free women may have rejected marriage after reading articles and essays critical of marriage as an institution demeaning to women by writers from both North and South. Calls for reforming or abolishing marriage as an institution circulated throughout the nation as the movement for women's rights and gender equality gained momentum during the 1840s and 1850s, and it is likely (although the evidence is largely circumstantial) that literate and educated Natchez women knew about such criticisms from readily available essays and speeches, newspaper reports, periodicals, and printed tracts. In the early 1850s a wide range of publications, including periodicals and newspapers that advertised to men and women alike, were available at the Natchez Literary Depot on Main Street, and stories about women's rights issues, including but not limited to reports, mocking or not, about the infamous "bloomers," frequently ran in local newspapers and other publications.[6]

In 1839, Margaret Cox's *The Young Lady's Companion* devoted an entire chapter, for example, to spinsterhood, presenting it as a morally defensible choice for women. While supporting the ideal of marriage and motherhood, Cox warned incipient bridesmaids about the hard work and drudgery that married life entailed, cautioning young brides to prepare themselves for painful sexual encounters as married women.[7] Women's rights reformers like the South Carolinian abolitionist Sarah Grimke counseled women publicly and in print to accept marriage only when both husband and wife agreed to live together as equal companions and mutual helpers.[8] Dozens of elite Natchez white women who had married husbands from northern states, moreover, frequently traveled with their young, single daughters throughout Pennsylvania, New York, Massachusetts, and other eastern states visiting relatives and friends. These young, yet-to-be-married daughters often corresponded with their northern relatives and friends and typically welcomed them as their houseguests in Natchez. It is not far-fetched to assume that such Natchez belles discussed (at least among themselves) popular opinions critical of marriage circulating in northern states when they talked and wrote about their beaus, marriage proposals, and weddings.[9]

Perhaps some Natchez white and free-black women shied away from marriage because of the South's ideological commitment to upholding the power of males over their wives, slaves, and other household dependents, which culturally and legally empowered tyrannical husbands, if so inclined, to abuse and humiliate their wives, who had little recourse available as married women. For historian Nancy Bercaw, the very masculinity of white males in the antebellum South rested upon their mastery over a household and all its members, whether wives, children, workers, or slaves.[10] This ideology of male mastery, rooted as it was in the South's slave-based culture and political economy, affected southern marriages in ways not always found in the rest of the nation. The matter was simple enough: slaveholding husbands could, and often did, sexually exploit (within limits weakly defined and seldom enforced by local custom and law) the enslaved black females whom they owned, in blatant acts of adultery, even as they purported to uphold their marriage vows and pontificated over their wives and children as honorable men. No one better identified this marital reality as a common aspect of southern marital life than the Charleston intellectual Mary Boykin Chestnut:

> I hate slavery. You say that there are no more fallen women on a plantation than in London, in proportion to numbers; but what do you say to this? A magnate who runs a hideous black harem with its consequences under the same roof with his lovely white wife, and his beautiful and accomplished daughters? He holds his head as high and poses as the model of all human virtues to these poor women whom God and laws have given him. From the height of his awful majesty, he scolds and thunders at them, as if he never did wrong in his life.[11]

It is a good bet, too, that most adult females in antebellum Natchez understood that married women (*feme coverts*) lost their legal identities as individuals once they exchanged marriage vows with their husbands. Stripped of their legal personhood, married women in Mississippi could not sue or be sued, easily obtain custody of their non-nursing-age children in marital disputes, make contracts, post bonds, own property in their own names, or administer a dead husband's estate unless authorized in wills left by their spouses or when intervening judges occasionally appointed widows to oversee family properties and assets. Although a married woman's legal status technically improved when the Mississippi Married Women's Property Law (passed in 1839) allowed wives to own and acquire property in their own names, husbands continued for some years after its passage to manage and often control spousal properties and monies as long as they acted (in the eyes of the community and ruling judges and magistrates) in the family's best interest as head of the family household. Wealthy parents, aware that predatory or incompetent husbands might steal or waste a daughter's inherited or acquired properties, sometimes established separate estates and drew up marriage contracts for their daughters, which legally designated trustees to manage these assets, independent of a husband's authority under the common law of coverture. Even with such legal protections in place, court challenges by husbands to trustee decisions and collusion between trustees and husbands, as well as a wife's limited financial resources, often blocked married women from operating independently of husbands regarding their assets and properties, especially once their parents had died.[12]

Single white women (*feme soles*) in antebellum Mississippi, on the other hand, whether spinsters, divorcees, or widows, enjoyed, technically at least, the legal privileges and responsibilities accorded to men, except for suffrage, jury duty, the right to hold public office, and the obligation to protect through militia service the community's peace and prosperity. These single women could sue and be sued, challenge male authority in local and state courts (through male litigators they retained), pursue enterprise in their own names, and conduct themselves as though they were men within the legal arena insofar as their actions left unchallenged the basic tenets of southern life: slavery and the dominance of men over women culturally and socially speaking. In matters of business and law, a single woman (*feme sole*) stood equal, at least theoretically, to any man for her legally contracted debts and any negotiations made as a creditor, although her cultural inequality as a woman greatly limited her maneuverability and constrained how she actually exercised her rights. In most cases women, both single and married, were disallowed by custom and tradition from appearing in court even when their interests were involved. Lawyers usually handled depositions in their offices or in private homes, away from the cacophony of public trials and lawsuits, and no female lawyers or officers of the court existed in Mississippi to legally assist single or married women in pursuing their legal rights or to challenge male opponents in judicial proceedings. Nevertheless, single women, as women independent of men in the eyes of the law, were not bound by the laws and customs of coverture regarding their properties and commercial affairs.

Despite the problems associated with married life and the relative autonomy and freedom afforded single women, the prospect of a loving husband and trusted male companion nevertheless favored marriage culturally and pragmatically in the eyes of most free Natchez women. Prevailing cultural mores and evangelical and established churches in Natchez upheld marriage as an ideal for all women, emphasizing through sermons and counsel a woman's inherently gentle, nurturing nature and the sense of fulfillment and likely eternal salvation women would experience as dutiful and faithful wives and mothers. Marriage ideally promised women protective husbands; significant social, emotional, and economic support offered by family, friends, neighbors, and fellow churchgoers; and economic and physical security in a world marked by rampant epidemics, natural disasters, economic collapse, violence, crime, and a hierarchical social order that relegated women, married or single, to a subordinate status in life. And while much has been written about the often harsh reality of married life in contrast to its portrayal and promise as an expected ideal for white women in the antebellum South, there is general consensus among historians that popular thinking took for granted that women (especially middle- and upper-class women) should be married and function, if possible, as mothers.[13]

This culture of male mastery, linked as it was to marriage and motherhood for women, gave rise to a concomitant set of cultural values that glorified and honored the subordination of women as caregivers and helpmates to men and to the larger community as wives and mothers. In a slave-based culture and political economy that demanded unquestioned obedience and faithful service by the enslaved to their owners and by wives and children to their husbands and fathers, marriage enabled wives to experience (or so they were told) the honorable abandonment of self in service to their husbands, families, and the larger community. One southern writer summed up in a few words the alleged benefits accruing to women, married and single, but especially married, who embraced this "servant ideal" as a guiding principle in their lives: "Honored be woman, when with unshrinking eye she looks out upon the broad world before her, and clearly discerning her own peculiar path, walks therein with a duty-doing spirit and a humble heart. Honored be woman in all the beautiful phases of mother, wife, daughter and sister. Happy is a woman if she cannot only thus clearly define her duty, but also faithfully perform it."[14]

The prevailing servant ideal that honored motherhood and marriage promised married women a protected albeit second-class citizenship covered by the authority of paternalistic husbands, who often viewed women as wards deserving of a white man's protection and care in return for their faithful service and obedience. According to this perspective, women were destined, as were all nonwhite males and enslaved people, to live as faithful servants within a hierarchical social order that ranged from slaves at the bottom to white male masters at the top. Moral authority and self-respect as well as societal esteem followed from the degree to which individuals accepted their subordinate or superior positions and worked dutifully to fulfill their various roles within a hierarchical social structure.

This servant ideal functioned for women as a higher value within which the mother/wife ideal was but one component, and it was an ideal to which all women could aspire regardless of their married state. It rested upon a nonegalitarian perspective in which individuals were expected to submit to a higher duty, over and above their relationships to one another. The servant ideal endowed all who embraced its premise, married, single, or widowed alike, with a certain moral authority that enabled them to achieve a measure of self-esteem equivalent to, if not greater than, that afforded by those lesser dictums subsumed within it, such as the mother/wife ideal. In this context, the degree to which a woman internalized a sense of duty to the good and faithful servant ideal is the degree to which she could achieve a sense of self-esteem and value as a woman, married or otherwise, in southern society.[15]

In a world where a man's household dependents were tantamount to children legally and socially, this servant ideal conditioned wives to expect, in return for their faithful servitude, proper consideration and just treatment from their husbands in a paternalistic trade-off that defined, ideally, the relationship of all men to the members of their households. For married women, this marital code of reciprocity afforded them certain economic protections (dower rights as widows), justice in various equity court decisions (that sometimes addressed wanton spousal abuse by husbands), and community affirmation (or condemnation) when husbands acted honorably (or dishonorably) toward wives and children, workers, and the enslaved. Some historians, moreover, see the southern slaveholder's commitment to reciprocity between masters and slaves as an idealized relationship that over time became a fully articulated ideology in defense of slavery and a hierarchical social order encompassing all members of antebellum southern society.[16]

Additionally, southern popular culture often favored marriage for women by depicting spinsters, despite their legal autonomy, as aberrant and pitiful persons condemned to living unfulfilled and meaningless lives as women. In this negative view, the word "spinster" conjured up a centuries-old assault on single women older than thirty for the (assumed) soul-numbing loneliness and abject misery of their lives, which was a fate that no sane woman could or should desire. The word "spinster" originated in England in the seventeenth century. The historian Amy Froide argues that present-day demographers "use the age of 45 to 50 to define a woman as a spinster" by linking the term to a woman's ability to procreate (or lack thereof), whereas in the premodern era, once a girl reached her late teens and certainly by her mid-twenties she might "start being called a 'spinster.'" Mid-nineteenth-century American legal records in Natchez tend to support this observation, although the age when spinsterhood began in the popular mindset was probably closer to thirty. A southern male essayist writing in the 1850s captured this negative sentiment toward not-married women when he cautioned young women to "remember [that] it is an awful thing to live and die a self-manufactured old maid." He echoed the popular sentiment that so-called spinsters had no one to blame but themselves for the lonely and unfulfilled lives they lived as women who purposely eschewed marriage and the natural fulfillment that came from being a "good wife" in service to husband

and family. It was not that single women were incapable of servicing family as matronly aunts and daughters but that such service paled in comparison to what they could offer husbands and the rewards they could reap emotionally as wives and mothers.[17]

Although the wife/mother/servant ideal defined the South's culturally accepted role for its antebellum free women, countless southern women lived out their entire lives unattached to men as husbands. Single, divorced, and widowed white women in Charleston, South Carolina, and Savannah, Georgia, composed about half those cities' adult female population in 1848, and numerous free women (black and white) lived without husbands in New Orleans and Natchez on the eve of the Civil War. In New Orleans, white males often kept black and mixed-race mistresses in a uniquely institutionalized but nonmarital set of sexual relationships known as *plaçage* (perhaps more in myth, according to historian Emily Clark, than in reality). In the larger antebellum South, when rural women are taken into account, the number of women who never married possibly exceeded one-fourth of the region's population, not including divorced women and widows. If these numbers are accurate, there is little doubt but that the single life existed alongside marriage as a common phenomenon for women perhaps everywhere in the antebellum South.[18]

The surprisingly large population of single women in antebellum Charleston, Savannah, and Natchez and throughout the South raises questions about why these women remained single; how they coped with life in a culture, economy, and society rooted in slavery, with its unique form of male mastery (because of slavery); and how their communities coped with them. For historian Christine Jacobson Carter, more than a few elite white women in antebellum Charleston and Savannah chose, or were compelled, to live their entire lives as single women for all but one of the reasons that motivated many elite northeastern women to reject marriage. According to historian Lee Virginia Chambers-Schiller, numerous women in the antebellum North purposefully remained single for many of the same reasons modern women often avoid male-dominated marriages: they feared sexual intercourse and childbirth, felt bound by family obligations, found few acceptable suitors, preferred women as sexual partners or loving companions, worried about abusive relationships in marriages, could afford to live on their own, or refused to surrender their highly valued personal autonomy and liberty to would-be husbands, especially when they had the resources to survive on their own. Many welcomed what Chambers-Schiller calls the "cult of single blessedness," which grew up alongside the "cult of domesticity" and the mother/wife ideal as an acceptable alternative to married life.

The elite single women in antebellum Charleston and Savannah whom Carter

studied also feared sexual intimacy and the pains of childbirth, put family responsibilities over marriage, and rejected men whom they did not love or con-
nect to emotionally, but they seldom craved independence and autonomy from
men as a driving force in their lives or condemned marriage as an illegitimate
institution that enslaved women. Many such women in antebellum Charleston
and Savannah, Carter argues, accepted and often chose the not-married life
because the highly feminized urban culture in which they lived valued female
caregiving by both married and single women, friendship among and between
women regardless of their marital state, and the spiritual and emotional participation of women (married and single) within community-based churches,
benevolent associations, and various civic endeavors. Although Carter does not
address the servant ideal specifically, she recognizes that many of the elite white
single women in antebellum Charleston and Savannah participated honorably
and fully within a social network of service-oriented women who valued them
as dedicated servants of the larger community in which they lived.[19]

Carter and Chambers-Schiller, along with a growing body of scholarship,
highlight the commonality and cultural acceptability of spinsterhood as
a choice among some elite northern and southern women, but they largely
ignore nonelite women and the impact of class, race, and the Civil War on
not-married women's decisions to remain single or on the ways they coped
with their nonattachment to men as husbands. What specifically did it mean
to be a single woman in terms of the everyday details of navigating life for both
nonelite and elite free women in the slave-encrusted South? How did a community's free, single women handle life in a world where white males, whether
slaveholders or nonslaveholders, reigned over women as masters of households
in conformance to a slave-based paternalistic ideal that glorified marriage and
the servant ideal? By looking at the entirety of single free women in midcentury Natchez, from around the 1830s through the 1880s, this book explores how
the city's free, single women, especially those above the age of thirty, from all
walks of life coped, survived, and endured over time in a wealthy, slave-driven
community ripped apart eventually by war and its tumultuous aftermath. Few
if any spinster-aged, divorced, or widowed free women above the age of thirty
are left out of consideration, and the spectrum studied includes criminals, free
blacks, elite slaveholding women, entrepreneurs and petty businesswomen,
peddlers, prostitutes, shopgirls and clerks, teachers, and even a Catholic nun.
In exploring how the not-married, free women of midcentury Natchez maneuvered life as women sans husbands, this study discusses the legal boundaries
that governed their lives, the societal restrictions and nuanced cultural boundaries that defined how they lived, and the often complex relations between
them and the "other" men in their lives, namely, their bankers and financial

backers, business partners and customers, employees and employers, friends, lawyers, lovers, patrons, and relatives.

As its central focus and overarching theme, this book argues that the single, free women of midcentury Natchez manipulated a male-dominated social order with surprising agility by accommodating rather than challenging culturally embedded dictates governing female behavior and expectations. It shows how the city's free, single women lived often resolute lives in a variety of circumstances as they maneuvered adroitly within and around the city's male-dominated culture. The book explores (1) how these women engaged the bedrock and often unquestioned "givens" of Natchez life (slavery, the servant ideal, and male dominance over women) that held Natchez's antebellum society together as a cohesive community; (2) why their actions were tolerated and even supported by most Natchez males; and (3) some of the strategies and tactics they adopted to deal with the unprecedented tumult introduced by the Civil War and all that followed. Natchez's free, single women, aged thirty and older, tested again and again the constraints their society burdened them with as women without husbands, and they did so with amazing pluck and pugnacity, largely on their own in a world where all women were expected eventually to be linked to men inextricably as wives. How they did this depended on their individual personalities and circumstances, their good luck or misfortune, and the shifting character of the Natchez terrain over which they journeyed during slavery and in the wake of war and the emancipation of the city's enslaved people.

This study emphasizes the practical "givens" of life and the stock experiences commonly shared by individuals in their daily routine within a community. To understand the degree to which seemingly aberrant individuals partook of a social order in their everyday life is to understand the extent of their connectedness to (or isolation from) that social order. It is a conceptual framework that aims at understanding the aspects of life that were taken for granted by community members so as to identify the sources (if any) through which people obtained (if they did) a sense of security and purpose over time.[20]

In presenting the full spectrum of how the city's single women coped over time, the book profiles specific women in a series of biographical sketches; their stories reveal the complicated maneuvers and intricate steps they displayed as women both subordinate to and not dependent on males as husbands. For the most part, it is a book of stories, of personal narratives and biographical sketches that illuminate the varied spectrum of life experienced by the city's single women over several generations. It uses the "stepping-lively-in-place" motif to articulate the incredible agility with which these women engaged the steadfast cultural, economic, legal, and societal obstacles they encountered. It is a motif that helps communicate the energy with which they engaged life, the relatively slight impact their maneuvering had on a slave-based culture that supported white male dominance over all women, and the challenges they faced as single women during and after the Civil War. It helps to illuminate, moreover, why Natchez's white males, as men driven by a sense of slave-based masculinity that always placed them on top culturally speaking, tolerated the fast-paced and lively stepping of some of the city's free single women.

The Natchez women profiled in this study neither actively sought nor rejected the idea of equality with men, although their behavior, actions, and attitudes indicate that some most likely would have entertained gendered and social changes if they had possessed the resources and actual opportunity to do so. Most were simply too busy to think about such things or too pragmatic to see themselves as exemplars of, or exceptions to, the so-called servant ideal, or any other ideal for that matter. They well understood, or at least they behaved as though they understood (which is a large part of this book's contribution), that their agility as stepping-lively women could not, and must not, threaten slavery and male mastery (or the view of women as handmaidens, caretakers, and servants of the larger community) fundamentally or in any way that actually mattered to them as subordinate people or to the men they continually had to step around.

All bets were off, however, once the Civil War destroyed slavery and seriously weakened the South's white ruling class as the powerful masters of their households. Thereafter, the conventional wisdom that viewed women as incapable and inferior participants within a cohesive community dominated by men no longer so easily defined the gendered arena wherein the city's women, regardless of their marital state and race, lived and worked.[21] The number of single women in Natchez grew significantly during and after the Civil War due to the wartime deaths of husbands and sweethearts, both black and white; the addition of many formerly enslaved, not-married women to their ranks; and the paucity of competent and resourceful males as suitable husbands, given that men were devastated by the war and the economic turmoil that followed upon Confederate defeat. Although the ideology of male mastery remained a cultural norm after the war, slavery's demise sapped away much of its vitality as a strongly entrenched given of life to which all women were expected to adhere.

Chapter Contents

The book begins with a description and analysis of Natchez and its immediate plantation neighborhood as an enslaved and gendered community on the eve of the Civil War. Chapter 1 discusses the city's history from its settlement by the French in the 1720s through its transition to an enslaved and highly cohesive community sporting wealthy slaveholders and their families, thousands of enslaved workers throughout its vast hinterland, and a polyglot population of slave traders, dance hall courtesans, Catholic nuns and respected clergymen and ministers, riverboat men, merchants and shopkeepers, and a multiethnic working class, all of whom participated in an impressive urban culture (both high and low), equal in many ways to those of Mobile, Savannah, and St. Augustine. The chapter illuminates the city's atmosphere and character as a uniquely urban place that was marked by a distinct landscape, political economy, and slave-based social order and by clearly articulated gendered spaces at the time that it fell to Union soldiers in the summer of 1863.

The city's free, never-married (or spinster) women aged thirty and older are discussed in chapter 2. The chapter lays out what is known or discoverable about these women, focusing on their work, conduct, and treatment (legally speaking). An aggressively entrepreneurial and highly litigious female merchant and the spinster matriarch of a prominent banking family are profiled to illuminate how some of the city's free, not-married women engaged life as highly motivated women not dependent on husbands. The chapter discusses how the city's never-married, free women navigated life without blatantly defying prevailing cultural dictums rooted in slavery and male hegemony, why they never married, and some of the consequences they experienced from living as single women throughout their lives.

Chapter 3 discusses how and why several dozen Natchez women divorced their husbands in the two generations prior to the Civil War. It examines the divorce process over time; details the options, opportunities, and obstacles divorcing women engaged as they challenged male authority without violating the city's prevailing ideology of male mastery or the servant ideal; and profiles several divorcing females to demonstrate how some of the city's divorcing women maneuvered to exercise their individuality as well as their equity rights as married women in law and judicial precedent. The extent to which the Mississippi judicial system effectively addressed a divorcing woman's equity claims to marital justice is also discussed, examining an array of divorce cases filed in the Adams County Court (Natchez was the county seat of government) from the 1820s through the 1850s, including those brought by men against their wives.

Turning next to Natchez widows, chapter 4 addresses the laws that affected widows in matters of inheritance, property, and dower. It documents the extent of widowhood during the 1850s, the contrasting worlds occupied by impoverished widows compared to those who lived as relatively prosperous women, and the economic and legal obstacles and opportunities Natchez widows confronted after the demise of their husbands. Several widows are profiled in some depth, including one who passed for white, with descriptions and analysis of their similarities and differences and the extent to which their behavior and actions enabled them to maneuver, adroitly or not, within the confines of a male-driven social order. This chapter explores why Natchez widows, as what one historian of widowhood labels "ever-married" women, generally enjoyed a greater degree of respect within the community compared to spinsters and divorced women.[22] It also discusses why numerous widows chose not to remarry after their husbands had died and how some of the city's widows related to their children and the men in their lives.

Among Natchez women in 1860 lived several dozen single free-black females aged thirty years or older, some of whom headed households in which no males resided. Chapter 5 addresses who they were, how they survived, and the circumstances of their freedom. It discusses what set them apart from the city's married free-black and white women; their sexual relations with black and white men; and their complicated participation in the city's black and white communities on the eve of the Civil War. Several women are profiled to illuminate how and why the Natchez community generally tolerated and even embraced some free-black women who were sexually involved with, or the offspring of, some of the city's white males. The chapter highlights some of the ways in which many of the city's single free-black women exploited, dodged, and manipulated the system to obtain a measure of autonomy as racially demeaned women.

Careful analysis of extant records shows that most arrested women in antebellum Natchez during the 1850s were spinsters, divorced women, abandoned wives, or widows (approximately 90 percent). Chapter 6 discusses how the city's criminal women handled local courts and municipal authorities, moved easily between marriage and the single state, and frequently crossed racial boundaries in their sexual and lawless activities. Several personal profiles illuminate how these women managed to flaunt the behavior expected of all free women in the community and why they almost always got away with it.

The city's occupation in 1863 by Union forces, which included several thousand formerly enslaved men as soldiers, fundamentally affected the city's black and white women, married and single. Chapter 7 addresses how and why the wartime interplay among and between Natchez women and Confederate and Yankee soldiers both challenged and reaffirmed long-standing gendered conventions and behavior. It addresses the consequences for the once cohesive Natchez community when literally thousands of formerly enslaved women became free and often single women during the war. This chapter profiles the

Civil War experiences of several single women to illuminate how the city's women (married and not married) coped with the defeated and often emasculated men all around them, struggled in many cases to feminize their male enemies, and emerged from war more often than not eager to persevere in a world turned upside down. It serves as a bridging chapter for understanding what changed and what remained constant for the city's women (both married and single) with the city's occupation by enemy soldiers, Union victory, and slavery's demise.

Chapter 8 explores the aftermath of the Civil War in Natchez and the principal changes affecting the city's single women, black and white, as a result of the destruction of slavery, the reduced if not totally vitiated position in which white males found themselves as defeated warriors, and the questionable relevance of the servant ideal as a practical guide for women during the city's postwar era. It looks at the city's changing patterns of marriage and divorce during the 1870s; how the city's new political economy and laws affected its single women; and how the character of the city's female population changed with the infusion of thousands of formerly enslaved women into its ranks as free, and often not-married, women. To understand the changes in the wake of the Civil War, the chapter profiles a once elite but not-married white woman who (unwillingly) left behind her slave-derived cultural expectations to become an apparently capable businesswoman dedicated to the creation and perpetuation of the mythic "Lost Cause" memorialization of the Civil War.

Chapter 9 presents six rather detailed stories that illuminate what the city's postbellum not-married women, including the formerly enslaved, had in common and the ways in which they essentially differed; how they coped individually as not-married women; and how their experiences were shaped by their class, race, age, and personalities. It discusses how and why some of the city's not-married women, black and white, feeling abandoned by family and friends, drew on male lawyers to assist them in both their economic affairs and personal circumstances—men who often functioned like surrogate husbands, brothers, and fathers. This chapter demonstrates the incredible energy and pragmatic behaviors displayed by some of the city's not-married women as they set aside, or were forced to abandon, prewar conceptions about how women should conduct themselves, as they struggled to survive as individuals. Their stories reveal specifically how they maneuvered, coped, and endured in a postbellum world where neither slavery nor an all-powerful paternalistic hierarchy (or the servant ideal) held much relevance for them as women.

The book ends with a brief denouement or epilogue, opening with an entry from the diary of one of the city's most prominent clergymen regarding his ministry to a local prostitute and her coworkers. The passage introduces a reflection on what this book tells us about the not-married women of mid-nineteenth-century Natchez. In this final perspective, a brief summary of what is known and what is still unclear about the single women of Civil-War-era Natchez is elucidated and hopefully brought full circle.

CHAPTER ONE

Antebellum Natchez

The Place in Which They Stepped

On the eve of the American Civil War, Natchez, Mississippi, located on the eastern banks of the Mississippi River approximately 150 miles upriver from New Orleans, served as a commercial and marketing hub for the Natchez District, a plantation- and slave-based agricultural economy containing several Mississippi counties and Louisiana parishes with unusually fertile soil, spread abreast and running parallel to one another but separated by the Mississippi River. Originally settled by the French in the 1720s, the Natchez outpost was all but abandoned from around 1730 to 1760, following the uprising of the Natchez Indians, which led to their massacre and near extinction as a people by the French in retaliation.[1] In the 1760s, the French lost their holdings in the Mississippi River Valley to Great Britain and Spain, with that part of the Natchez District east of the Mississippi River going to the British. When the North American colonies revolted against Great Britain, the Spanish, who earlier had obtained New Orleans from the French, sided with the Americans and drove the British from the region, thereafter ruling the Natchez District until the United States acquired the vast lands east of the Mississippi River in 1798 (except for the Florida cession). The eastern half of the Mississippi River watershed became U.S. soil, with the rest of the Natchez District falling into American hands following the Louisiana Purchase in 1803.[2]

Both the British and Spanish authorities lavished substantial land grants on incoming Anglo-American settlers, who began moving to the Mississippi frontier after 1765, hoping thereby to win their loyalties. These Anglo-American settlers accepted British and then Spanish rule and largesse, concentrating their attention on turning the forests east of the Mississippi River into ruggedly self-sufficient indigo and tobacco plantations. The development of the cotton gin coincided with the Natchez District's official transfer from Spain to the United States in 1798, and this remarkable innovation revolutionized plantation agriculture in the southern United States by enabling the area's short-staple cotton fibers to be efficiently cultivated and ginned. Within a few years, the world's demand for cotton brought thousands of enslaved workers and white settlers to the Natchez area, but the district's pioneer families retained the lion's share of its land as planter elites to whom the title "Natchez Nabobs" accurately applied.[3]

Located at the foot of the ancient buffalo and Indian trail known as the Natchez Trace, which stretched northeastward to present-day Nashville, Natchez emerged as the most western point of the new American nation in the early nineteenth century. During those years, a regular stream of Ohio farmers floated flatboats filled with produce down the Ohio River to the Mississippi River, from whence they pushed on to the great New Orleans market, usually stopping off at the Natchez landing to supply the town's plantation hinterland. After selling their produce and their boats for lumber in New Orleans, the Ohio farmers walked upriver to Natchez, where they took the Trace northward toward home. Thousands of other migrants from points southeast and north, including those who came in slave caravans or coffles, journeyed to the Natchez frontier via the Trace from Nashville to Natchez, after which they moved or were dispersed throughout the lower Mississippi River Valley and into Louisiana and Texas. During the steamboat era, beginning in the 1820s, Natchez became a thriving riverboat city of some size. Hundreds of flatboats, steamboats, rafts, and assorted river barges and craft annually tied up at the town's waterfront. By 1825 its landing area had become world renowned as "Natchez Under-the-Hill," a place infamous for its bars, gambling, violence, whores, and riverboat characters the likes of the legendary Mike Fink.[4]

A census taken in 1787 shows the multiracial character of the town: 1,275 whites, 22 mulattos (mixed race), and 675 blacks. By 1860 the town's population numbered 2,100 slaves out of 6,612 people, including 214 free people of color. In the surrounding Adams County, of which Natchez was the county seat, lived 12,192 enslaved people and 994 whites. Across the river, in Concordia Parish, Louisiana, 12,542 black workers tilled cotton and sugar plantations and farms as enslaved chattel, and 1,479 whites lived among them as small farmers, trappers, planters, and overseers, in the main. Each of the parishes and counties adjacent to Adams County, below and above and across the river, contained a similar number and ratio of slaves and whites, although Adams County held more whites as a percentage of the county and parish populations because it included Natchez, the only city in the region.[5]

By the 1830s, plantations in Adams County began to experience severe soil exhaustion from being overworked with little attention to conservation. As a result, Natchez-area planters, while maintaining their home estates in and around Natchez, began moving their Mississippi slaves and capital to the Louisiana side of the river, where they carved out massive plantations from its fertile swamplands.[6] On the eve of the Civil War, a coterie of slave-owning elite living in Natchez and within the immediate Natchez neighborhood had

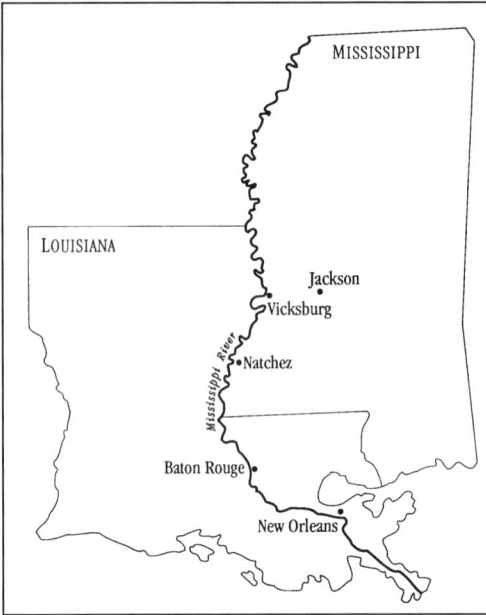

Natchez's location.
CSUN-Natchez Project
Archives, California State
University, Northridge.

erected dozens of magnificent estate houses that rivaled Bath, England, and Charleston, South Carolina, for the scale of their material culture and opulence. Surveyor's maps drawn before and after the Civil War reveal that nearly every inch of county lands surrounding Natchez had been carved up into plantation estates, each of which carried a distinctive name, such as Hollywood, Carthage, Egypt, Magnolia, Duck Pond, and Traveler's Rest, and many of which sported impressive houses and gardens.

The wealthiest of these white elite owned hundreds of slaves, cotton and sugar plantations in several adjacent counties and Louisiana parishes, and diversified investments in merchandising, western lands, eastern securities, railroads, and banking.[7] Their families competed with one another in displays of material culture exhibited in estate mansions, fine furnishings, rich libraries and wine cellars, and well-tended gardens. Some forty or fifty families, most of them with working plantations in Louisiana and adjacent Mississippi counties, lived within the Natchez neighborhood and nearby environs, thereby giving the city and its immediate suburbs an urbane atmosphere characterized by all the trappings of the very rich. Many of these elite Natchez families had intermarried by the 1860s, and their social networking, based on kinship, wealth, and a shared ideology rooted in chattel slavery, a white paternalistic social order, and the servant ideal, formed a richly endowed community ethos in which the symbols of mastery and wealth were visible at every turn. They constructed impressive churches and opera halls in the city to match their grand plantation mansions and partook of elaborate parties, weddings, balls, pageants, fox hunts, and horse-racing matches in outpourings of wealth that included their generous financial support for Natchez schools and academies, the arts, charitable societies, and impressive urban improvements, such as a bluff esplanade, monumental grave sites, several private and public gardens, and two thriving markets in downtown Natchez. And many of these truly wealthy Natchez slaveholders, with family connections in Philadelphia, New York, and other northern cities, traveled all over the nation and to Europe in frequent sojourns that greatly broadened what otherwise might have been a rather provincial outlook on life.[8]

Antebellum Natchez comprised three visible and clearly defined parts: (1) Natchez Under-the-Hill, a riverfront landing of about a mile or two in length, consisting of several dozen short streets, private docks, a racetrack, and lumberyards; (2) Above-the-Hill Natchez, which was separated from the landing by massive bluffs that rose three hundred feet above the waterfront; and (3) the Natchez suburbs, containing villa-like garden estates. During the 1850s, most of the city's middle-class white residents earned their living as shopkeepers, merchants, lawyers, doctors, ministers, teachers, bankers, and assorted retainers of the city's hinterland plantation elite; these men and women lived principally above the bluffs in houses scattered throughout the city. Interspersed among their small but relatively comfortable, although sometimes shoddy, residences were the spectacular townhouses and mansions of those elite planters who preferred to live in Natchez proper rather than in its suburbs or at their country plantations.[9]

Among the whites in Natchez were those people who did the everyday work connected with the river, the business of cotton marketing, and servicing the city's residents. This group included riverboat men, draymen, unskilled laborers, gamblers, innkeepers, saloon proprietors, dance-hall women and barmen, nuns, prostitutes, clerks, proprietors of boardinghouses and millinery shops and other stores, and those who toted cargoes, painted and repaired houses, fired bricks, staffed wood yards, sewed dresses, piloted skiffs, tended animals, built and serviced wagons, and cut hair in barber shops. By 1860, substantial numbers of unskilled Irish and Italian newcomers, who had migrated to the city during the 1840s, filled out the white population. Working-class whites generally lived as best they could at the waterfront and in upper Natchez, in rented rooms above and behind shops and stores where they worked or in boardinghouses and the let-out quarters in private homes.[10]

Amid these planters, businessmen and clerks, professionals, and working-

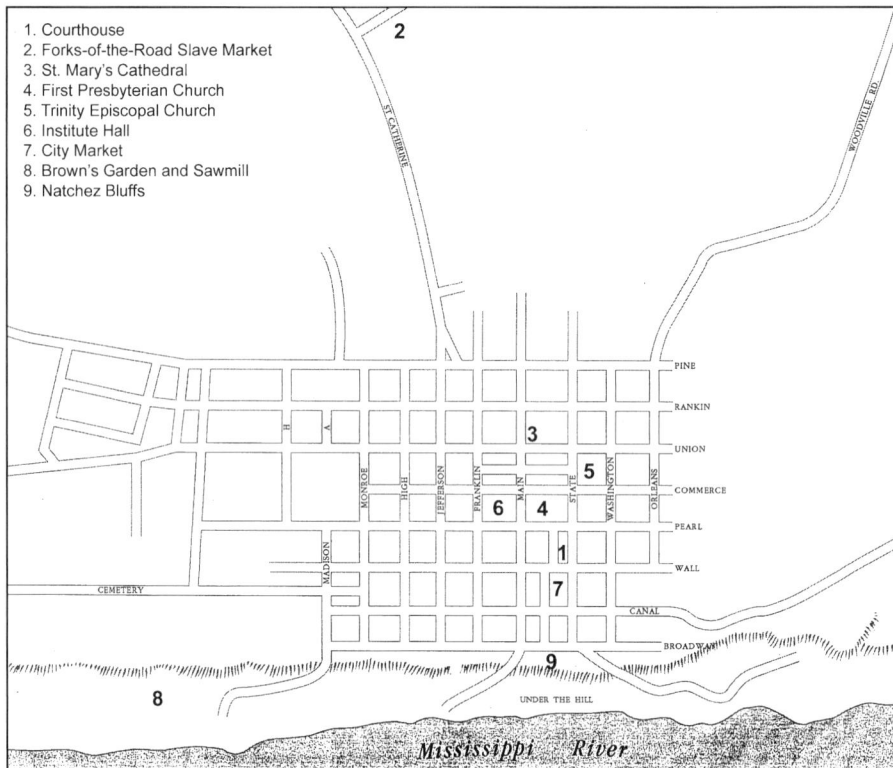

1. Courthouse
2. Forks-of-the-Road Slave Market
3. St. Mary's Cathedral
4. First Presbyterian Church
5. Trinity Episcopal Church
6. Institute Hall
7. City Market
8. Brown's Garden and Sawmill
9. Natchez Bluffs

Natchez Above-the-Hill. csun-Natchez Project Archives, California State University, Northridge.

Natchez Under-the-Hill. From Edward King, *The Great South: A Record of Journeys* (Hartford, Conn.: American Publishing, 1875). Image provided by University of Georgia Press.

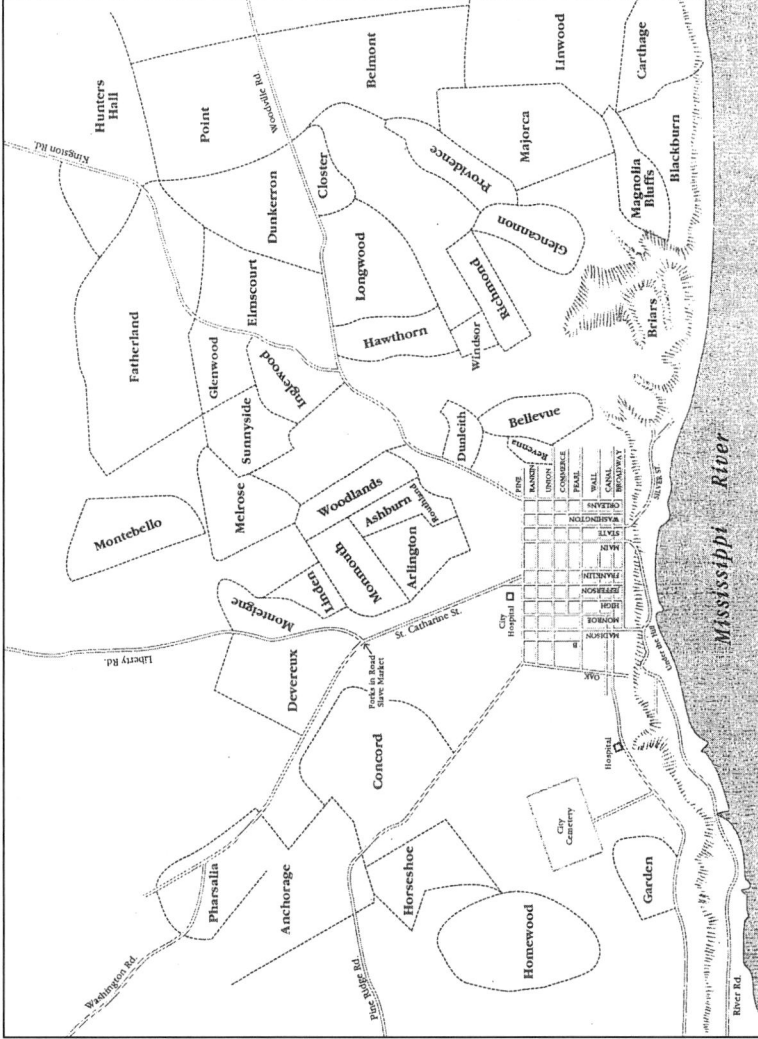

Natchez suburban estates. CSUN–Natchez Project Archives, California State University, Northridge.

class whites lived several hundred free-black hack drivers, barbers, washer-women, servants, dressmakers, lumbermen, and skilled and unskilled laborers. Most of these free people of color were the mixed-race offspring of white fa-thers (or grandfathers) who had freed them and often set them up with jobs and businesses. A few of them had migrated to Natchez as free people, and some owned slaves and property as well. They generally could move freely about the city as long as they remained deferential to whites and avoided places where only whites were allowed to congregate; Mississippi law, however, re-quired all free people of color to carry written proof of their freedom with them at all times. Not legally able to testify in court (unless against each other), most free blacks in the city enjoyed cautious but good relations with various white patrons, usually men related to them, who frequently interceded with local authorities and other whites on their behalf.[11]

These free people of color lived somewhat betwixt and between the city's several thousand enslaved people—the black men and women who drove their masters' carriages, maintained the city's impressive townhouses and subur-ban estates as gardeners and house servants, and serviced local slaveholders as domestic workers, such as cooks, butlers, waiters, personal body servants, washerwomen, nannies, scullery maids, grounds men and carriage drivers, seamstresses, and dressmakers. On Sundays and other holidays, Natchez filled up with enslaved people from the nearby countryside and suburbs who ven-tured there to market vegetables, attend church services, and congregate until the evening bell sounded their call to depart. Some enslaved males were hired out by their owners to work at loading and unloading the seventy-five thousand or more bales of cotton that annually passed through Natchez and as skilled and unskilled workers in the building trades; others were sometimes employed by the municipality in repairing roads, streets, and bridges, digging sewage ditches, and performing general city maintenance work.[12]

Few of the many thousand field slaves who lived in the surrounding country-side ever traveled to Natchez. Those who did were usually taken there by their owners to be sold in the city's Forks-of-the-Road slave market or as captured runaways and convicted lawbreakers jailed in city garrisons for murder or as-saulting whites. More frequent visitors were those enslaved people who came as wagon drivers from country plantations with loads of cotton brought to the city during harvest season in the late summer and early fall or as carriage drivers when their white slaveholders journeyed to Natchez on business or for some social occasion. Most country slaves seldom ventured beyond their plantation neighborhoods, where they typically resided and worked on large plantations with fifty or more enslaved workers cultivating cotton in arduous field labor under extremely difficult physical conditions. For them, Natchez was a mysterious place that they feared and yet were drawn to in their minds because of the stories they had heard about its great wealth, magnificent buildings, Under-the-Hill wickedness, and hated slave markets.[13]

Historian Ronald L. F. Davis has estimated that nearly two hundred thousand slaves were transported into Mississippi from the older parts of the upper South in the years between 1810 and 1860. Perhaps 60 percent were brought via the domestic slave trade rather than with their migrating owners; tens of thousands passed through the Natchez slave markets, especially its Forks-of-the-Road market, the second-largest slave depot (after the Algiers market in New Orleans) in the lower Southwest. Built in the late 1820s by interregional slave traders, including Isaac Franklin, the nation's most successful slave trader, the Natchez market gathered slaves from upper South suppliers via the Mississippi River to sell in New Orleans and a robust coastal slave trade. Others arrived overland, traveling on the Natchez Trace and along various routes through Alabama and Georgia. Traders and sellers found ready buyers among planters with lands in Arkansas, Louisiana, Mississippi, and Texas. Situated on the city's eastern outskirts, the Forks was an easy carriage ride or walk from the waterfront. Traders purchased stalls in the market, used an adjoining pond for bathing the enslaved, and displayed their human merchandise in an open viewing corral for prospective buyers.[14]

Perched atop massive bluffs (three hundred feet high) that ran nearly a mile north and south along the river, the city's neatly laid out grid pattern of streets stretched eastward from the river. Eight streets ran east from the bluffs, and nine others crossed them to form a patchwork design that made the small city easily comprehensible to newcomers. Central to the grid was the city's Main Street, a busy avenue of shops, banks, and inns. Midway up Main stood the recently completed St. Mary's Cathedral. One block north, Franklin Street served as the principal byway for traffic in cotton and for wagons destined for the commercial hub known as "cotton square," located approximately five blocks up Franklin in the city's northeast interior. One block south of Main ran State Street, which bordered a municipal square containing the city's impressive courthouse, lawyers' offices, the central market, and the jail. Farther along State to the east lay the First Presbyterian Church of Natchez; a short block to the south stood the impressive Trinity Episcopal Church. Institute Hall and Magnolia Hall, the city's free public school and opera house, were positioned between State and Main on Pearl and Commerce Streets. A city market, one of two, occupied Canal Street at the foot of Main. If a Natchez resident took a carriage ride north along Canal, the street turned into Cemetery Road, which ran out of the city to the Natchez cemetery, a powerfully visual place of interment wherein the city's dead often were buried according to their ethnicity, religion and church affiliation, family connections, and prosperity. From its highest point, living visitors to the cemetery could take in a panoramic view of the Mississippi River and its vast Louisiana floodplain, topped off by spectacular sunsets in the early evening or the ghostly haze that floated across the horizon at dawn.[15]

Among the tall spires and towers of Natchez's churches and the grid pattern of its streets, the Natchez bluffs loomed large as the city's most noticeable landmark. A beautifully landscaped and carefully tended grassy promenade dominated the city's western edge, stretching from south to north parallel to the river and high above its waterfront. The first European settlers to Natchez had erected a fort on its southern flank, which the British named Rosalie after taking it over from the French in the 1760s. Natchez residents used the town's landscaped edge as a commons or promenade, planting elegant China Grove trees amid its meandering walkways, where they gathered to celebrate holidays, listen to political orations delivered from a large mound at its center, and watch parading militia. It was a place where lovers strolled and children played; the city's residents felt safe to walk and picnic there, to enjoy and marvel at the bluffs' westward panorama and the setting sun each evening—a scene that almost certainly had captured the imagination of those Natchez Indians who once had worshipped the sun's spectacular presence as it loomed over the horizon before dropping out of sight. For the free people of Natchez, the bluffs reflected and promoted a public order and cohesiveness, culturally and socially, as a distinctively visual landscape. It was also a landscape protected by a city watch and a slave patrol that regularly policed its grounds.[16]

At three points along the bluffs, wagons, carriages, and the walking public could descend into Natchez Under-the-Hill, a lip of land that edged the water three hundred feet below. Various surveyor's maps as well as numerous artist illustrations and scores of land deeds in the Adams County mortgage record books show in some detail the waterfront's profile. Divided into four principal sections, the riverfront hugged the water with landing docks and wharves at its most southern tip; Andrew Brown's lumberyards dominated the midsection of the two-mile-long landing, an enterprise that procured lumber from as far away as Arkansas by floating cypress logs and barges of pine timbers to the yards for milling and sale. North of the lumberyards Brown had laid out a formal garden of such magnitude and horticultural detail as to be nearly as famous as the city itself, and he lived nearby in an Under-the-Hill villa estate he called Magnolia Vale. Beyond Brown's wood mill, mansion house, and garden, the waterfront became woodland and swamp, unsafe grounds occupied by a few squatter shacks and one or two farms whose owners, including a free-black family, eked out a living by growing garden crops and selling firewood to steamboats. In the city's early years, the waterfront's northern edge had been a notorious hideout for river pirates, known in legend and lore as the Devil's Punch Bowl.[17]

Silver, Main Extension, Water, and Cypress Streets linked the landing to the top of the bluffs, and all four were interconnected by alleys and side streets such as Cotton Row and Maiden's Lane. Between fifty and seventy-five lots of property fronted these streets and the water's edge, containing warehouses, shops, stables, barns, residences, coffeehouses, hotels, and taverns. At any one time during the 1840s and 1850s, a traveler to Natchez might find dozens of barges, skiffs, flatboats, steamboats, and assorted vessels at its landing docks and wharfs. In 1840, over forty river craft that were anchored at the city's waterfront sank when a tornado tore through Natchez, leaving hundreds dead in Under-the-Hill, including 250 slaves: men, women, and children shackled together in the boats waiting to be marched to the Forks-of-the-Road slave market east of town.[18]

As a general rule, the spatial divisions of larger Natchez hung together, with no clear gendered demarcations: the grid-patterned town Above-the-Hill, the suburban neighborhoods, the bluffs, Natchez Under-the-Hill, and the Forks-of-the-Road slave market. Depending largely on their personal circumstances, class, and race, Natchez free women could and did go anywhere they generally pleased within the larger Natchez scene. Nonetheless, some areas were less frequented by women than by men, or less frequented by "ladies" than by nonelite or working-class women; usually it was a question of class and custom, both cultural and social. Natchez free women, for example, might freely traverse the suburban enclaves, most of downtown Natchez, the bluffs, and the riverfront landing on their way to board a steamboat or in visiting Brown's Gardens. Shopping, visiting, attending church, and running errands regularly took the city's women to the general markets on Canal Street or near the city hall and almost everywhere in and around Main Street, but few of its elite women or even those of the middling sort who thought of themselves as "ladies" ventured unescorted for many blocks to the north or south of that central avenue.[19]

Likewise, few upper-class or refined women of the better sort ventured unescorted to Under-the-Hill Natchez; to the cotton square vicinity of Franklin Street, where wagons sat filled with cotton and the manly cotton trade business prevailed; to courthouse square in central Natchez; to the Forks-of-the-Road slave market; or to the many saloons and social clubs catering exclusively to men, where women worked as barmaids, tavern keepers, and prostitutes. Business, politics, and slavery set the pace of life in these areas, activities dominated by men and working-class women. Elite white women entered those buildings serving the city and county courts only if they were caught up in some specific litigation, and even then they usually avoided appearances at court by offering written depositions taken in their homes or given in a lawyer's office. Nonelite women, on the other hand—black and white hucksters, as well as laundresses, clerks, and shopkeepers—could be found everywhere in and around the courthouse square. For Natchez men, court days were moments of public spectacle, and the city's white men not only packed the visitors' galleries but hung around outside on the courthouse lawns, where working-class women (black and white) sold wares or offered services of one sort or another.[20]

For young Rebecca Mandeville, aged twenty-six in 1848 and the not-married daughter of a prominent banker, Natchez public spaces like the bluffs enabled her to feel contained, involved, and attached. Several typical entries in her diary are illustrative of the everyday scene:

> March 10. Walked to the Bluff with Theo, Jo, and Sissy—saw an unusual number of ladies also a neglected man who looked as if he thought himself very handsome.

> March 11. Met Lamby on the way home—who stopped with his usual pleasant smile—shook hands and chatted a little and then passed on—I do like him, there is always such a hearty friendliness in his manner to Joe and me.

> March 20. Coming up Main Street we met Bill with his hands and mouth full of cake. He stopped and insisted upon each of us taking one which we did not refuse—I squeezed mine into my bag soon as possible for there were men standing all about.

> May 3. Wore it [a straw bonnet] out this afternoon. Met Mr. P. and Jane on the Bluff. Had a long talk with them. They wanted to drive us home in their carriage. We declined, preferring to walk.

> May 4. Saw Mr. Boyd on the Bluff this afternoon. Stopped in at Stanwood's and ate ice cream. Was most ashamed too, having set there too long.

> May 5. Started out this morning to pay Miss C. a visit, thought we would stop at the ice cream saloon first, Jose went in the Bank to invite Father to go with us. While waiting on the pavement for them, I had quite an agreeable conversation with HPD. Found Miss C. at home, also her brother who talked principally to Jo.

> May 6. Sewed hard all the morning and finished my dress. Walked this afternoon—bought a hair brush. Had a visit of an hour from Maria Duncan.[21]

Mandeville felt relatively safe and unafraid to venture forth along Natchez streets as a public person, shop Main Street stores and markets, walk to church, recreate in downtown parks, and engage the city's physical domain as an extension of her personal neighborhood, always knowing where to go and what parts of town to avoid. She would never, as a refined lady, have walked unescorted to the waterfront, for example, or even much beyond the city's main streets, but given these self-imposed limits Natchez was for her and her female friends a place to be experienced for the adventure and stimulation it offered. For most Natchez residents, the city's public spaces offered a sense of security and significant intimacy on a personal level, with easily identified public and commercial avenues and buildings, courthouse squares, and the grassy bluffs palisade that served as common ground for all its citizenry, regardless of their race, class, or gender. The city's layout and historically driven character generated and encouraged among most of its antebellum inhabitants a sense of community, easily enforced and reenforced as a visually satisfying and easily perceived townscape that supported slavery and the patriarchal world slavery upheld.[22]

Yankee forces occupied Natchez in the summer of 1863, with hardly a shot being fired on either side. For the next three years the city witnessed several thousand black and white Union soldiers afoot everywhere in the community, erecting a massive earthen-walled fort at the city's northern edge and policing the city under what amounted to martial law. This occupation force, although greatly reduced in numbers by 1867, remained in Natchez until 1877, when Reconstruction ended and federal troops vacated Mississippi and the former Confederacy. During these occupation and Reconstruction years, Natchez became a hotbed of political activism wherein a new class of local and outsider black and white Republican politicos battled with reactionary local whites to control the city's political economy, a struggle that erupted in violence on more than one occasion.

In the war's aftermath, the city's once incredibly wealthy slaveholding elite, at least those who remained in the area, carried on as mere remnants of what they once had been. And while the city continued in its role as the commercial and marketing hub for a vast cotton hinterland, a new economic order quickly emerged from the ashes left behind after federal troops were removed from the area. The formerly enslaved in the city's hinterland reluctantly settled into a new kind of labor dependency known as sharecropping, in which most of the area's black farmers were soon trapped in debt to supply merchants and landowners. What is more, the new order offered them, as hopelessly impoverished people, little opportunity for political equality or economic prosperity, placing them in an economic and political box that was soon institutionalized into the standard order of the day and endured for the next hundred years.[23]

When Natchez soldiers returned home once the fighting had stopped, they found little remaining of the cohesive urban milieu they had once known. Few Natchez white women walked the city's streets with their antebellum cultural baggage comfortably intact or interacted with any sense of safety and security for their persons. Formerly enslaved and free-black women moving into Natchez from the countryside faced even greater challenges as they filled up the city, hopeful for their futures but desperately poor and unsure about what path to take forward. Urban chaos and tumult replaced the city's once apparently seamless (but rigidly enforced) tranquility as its residents strove to control their economic, political, and racial futures, a struggle that greatly constrained the city's women even as it expanded the options available to them. In these new circumstances, the city's not-married women, whose numbers had grown due to the wartime deaths and devastation among their husbands and potential mates as well as the influx of newly emancipated African American women who joined their ranks, had little choice but to step more lively, and more adroitly, than ever before. Over time, some (and perhaps most) Natchez women, especially formerly enslaved and working-class women but also many formerly elite white women, chose to cast aside as impractical and/or irrelevant their antebellum homage to, or acceptance of, slavery, patriarchy, and the servant ideal. But theirs was not a step toward women's liberation politically (words that few would have recognized) or a determinedly directed effort for gendered equality; rather, it was almost always a pragmatic stance that better enabled the city's women to cope with life as women largely on their own.

CHAPTER TWO

Stepping Lively amid Their Shadows

The Single White Women of Antebellum Natchez

In 1828, Theodosia Griffith, the widowed daughter of the Mississippi Supreme Court judge Edward Turner, wrote a beseeching note to her friend "Miss Margaret" Biggs, a longtime Natchez spinster, imploring her to consider a proposition she hoped would benefit them both as single women.

> I pray you my dear Miss Margaret to make up your mind to come live always with me. Please reflect on the loneliness of my situation and do have charity enough for that act. You shall have either of the bedrooms you prefer & shall never be molested, but it shall be yours for life or as long as I have any right to the house. You know my father wishes you to live with me. No doubt that he as well as the rest of the family will miss you. My servants, carriage, and horses, as long as I have them, would be at your service. I never have yet seen anyone that I thought I could live with on such terms of intimacy and pleasure as yourself. You are often sick, and be assured that I would always nurse you with sisterly care and affection.[1]

In making her offer Theodosia reasoned that the two women, the widow and the spinster, could craft a future based on mutual affection, companionship, and shared needs as elite women living without men in their lives as husbands.[2] Biggs, around forty years old at the time, accepted Theodosia's invitation, only to move a year later, following the young widow's untimely death from congestion, to live off and on with Judge Turner's family at Woodlands, his suburban villa located on the eastern outskirts of Natchez. Thereafter, Biggs, who, as a younger woman, may have been a governess to Turner's children, passed many of her remaining twenty-three years as a frequent houseguest of the Turner family.[3]

Although she was not a blood relative, Biggs's connection to the Turner family appears to have originated through her deceased brother William Biggs, who had owned a plantation in the St. Catherine Creek neighborhood north of Natchez, where some of the wealthiest slaveholders in the area also lived, such as Francis Surget, Alexander Dunbar, and Adam Bingaman. William Biggs died in 1822 but was survived by his widow, Ann, who passed away in the early

1830s, and their five children. Turner served as William Biggs's lawyer during his life and the lives of his heirs, and Margaret Biggs ("Aunt Maggie" to her nieces and nephews) knew Turner because of her brother's legal affiliation with him. Over the years, this legal relationship appears to have blossomed into a personal bonding between "Miss Margaret" and the Turner family.[4]

Other spinsters and single women, quite unlike Biggs, also lived in antebellum Natchez, and many of them probably crossed her path without exchanging words or acknowledging their shared status as not-married women. On the eve of the American Civil War, for example, a forty-plus-year-old single woman named Jane Mayes, who appears never to have married, headed a Natchez household on State Street that included four young white women, ranging in age from twenty-one to twenty-five. She had moved to Natchez from her Kentucky birthplace sometime during the early 1840s, and her four coresidents hailed from Missouri, New York, and Arkansas. None, including Mayes, were related to each other, listed occupations in extant records, or show up in any available source as married, widowed, or divorced women. Two enslaved women, aged nineteen and twenty-eight, along with four enslaved children, all of whom were owned by Mayes, also lived in the household.[5] Over the years, Mayes had housed various girls and women, including a three-year-old bound out to her for service until age twenty-one by her mother, Mary Ann Simmons, a known Natchez prostitute. Relatively few other domiciles in the city looked quite like Mayes's household: a racially mixed residence housing young, unmarried women headed by a more mature single woman with no apparent means of livelihood—the universal characteristics of a functioning brothel.[6]

The spinster and well-known authoress Eliza Dupuy, to offer another example, was born in Petersburg, Virginia, around 1814, one of nine children. As a young woman, she had found employment in Natchez as a governess in the country manor home of the wealthy slaveholder Thomas G. Ellis, tutoring his daughter, Sarah Ann. She later moved to the grand mansion (Dunleith) of Charles C. Dahlgren, a wealthy merchant and planter who had married Ellis's widow, Mary Routh Ellis, in 1840. Dupuy's student Sarah Ann (Ellis) Dorsey went on to publish several novels and later gained fame as Jefferson Davis's benefactress, and perhaps his mistress, after the Civil War. Dupuy also taught for a few years during the 1850s in the city's free public school, the Natchez Institute, and in several private academies in Natchez and New Orleans.[7]

Although Dupuy earned her living by teaching, she considered herself a writer first and foremost. She authored dozens of short stories and fifteen novels during her lifetime, many of which were set in Mississippi and Natchez, including *The Separation, The Divorce, Coquette's Punishment, The Country Neighborhood,* and *The Conspirator,* which dealt with Aaron Burr's exploits in the Southwest and first appeared as a serial in *New World* magazine. Her success afforded her a certain celebrity status and allowed her to pursue a somewhat eclectic lifestyle as a single woman who moved easily among the upper-class families of Natchez and New Orleans. She participated in Natchez literary salons and counted among her friends and literary compatriots well-known lower Mississippi Valley authors such as Joseph Hart Ingraham and Catherine Ware and the literarily-inclined Whig politician Seargent S. Prentiss, as well as various literarily-minded Natchez women, such as her good friend Frances Sprague, who was married to the successful Natchez attorney Sturges Sprague. Dupuy's fiction, some of which was published in *Godey's Lady's Book* and the *Southern Literary Register,* appealed to reading women and focused principally on the "domestic trials" they faced as virtuous southern spinsters or women forced to marry against their will.[8]

The White Spinsters of Antebellum Natchez

Biggs, Dupuy, and Mayes were among seventy-four identifiable spinsters, or women who had never married, aged thirty years and older who lived within the municipal limits of Natchez in 1860 (see table 1).[9] Relatively few owned real estate (25 percent) or enslaved people (30 percent). Sixteen owned one to three slaves, while another six, including Jane Mayes, held from four to nine slaves each. Most of these women held low-paying jobs, working as bartenders, cooks and waitresses, dressmakers, governesses, teachers, grocery clerks, hotel staff, hucksters, laundresses, millinery shop saleswomen, nurses, or store employees. Several owned businesses in the millinery and grocery trade. One woman managed a boardinghouse and another (Jane Mayes) most likely ran a brothel.[10] Although prostitution and bawdy houses thrived in antebellum Natchez, only a half dozen of the city's white spinsters show up in judicial records for alleged criminal activity, usually for selling liquor without a license, often to the enslaved.[11]

On the eve of the Civil War, most of the city's white spinsters lived in households headed by not-married women like themselves (67 percent), many of which contained no adult males (see table 1); such households provided these women with a male-free sanctuary of sorts. Ten lived all alone. The white spinsters and other not-married women who headed or lived in households in which no males resided were theoretically the most independent women in the Natchez area, especially those few who owned slaves and real estate, worked

TABLE I. White spinsters (aged thirty and older), Natchez and Adams County, 1860

	Natchez	Adams County	Total
Head of household	29	6	35
Living in female-headed household	21	3	24
Living in male-headed household	24	11	35
Total	74	20	94

Sources: Marriage Records, white, 1820–70, ORAC; U.S. Manuscript Census (1860), Population Schedules, Adams County, Miss., NARA.

at trades, or held reliable jobs. But living without males in their households as family members, boarders, or employees often meant impoverishment and uncertainty rather than self-sufficiency and autonomy. Male-free residential living undoubtedly affected how these women operated in the world, but to what degree living beyond the "male gaze" that was always present in mixed-gender households affected social relations among women, or influenced how women coped as individuals, is difficult to ascertain.[12]

Twenty-four white spinsters resided in Natchez households headed by white men (32 percent). Almost half were related as family ("old maid" aunts, matronly daughters, and spinsterish sisters) to the men who headed their households. The other half worked within these houses as governesses, domestic servants, and household managers, or else they lived there in rented rooms. Some undoubtedly were involved sexually with the men who headed their households, but it is impossible to know how many or the character of these relationships; none appear to have lived as prostitutes in households headed by male pimps or employers. A few of these spinsters assumed housekeeping chores as partial payment for their rent and board, while holding down other jobs.

Outside of Natchez, another twenty white spinsters lived on farms and plantations in rural Adams County and in the suburban mansions that ringed the city just beyond the municipality. Less than 35 percent of these women owned slaves, and those who did owned less than six each, although two country spinsters owned twenty-seven and thirty-seven slaves, respectively. These two women, assisted by overseers and male relatives, worked their slaves as field hands on plantations they inherited in family legacies. Nine country spinsters lived in female-only households, but only two of them lived completely alone. Unlike in the city, the white suburban and country spinsters were related by birth or marriage (sisters, daughters, and in-laws) to the males who headed the households in which they lived.

The white spinsters of antebellum Natchez and Adams County lived as legal adults (*feme soles*), equal to men in civil law, at least theoretically. Unlike married women, spinsters (as well as divorced and widowed women) could sue and be sued and could engage in contractual relationships. In matters of property, after 1839, married Natchez women shared with spinsters the legal right to own property in their own names because of the Married Women's Property Law, although married women were encumbered somewhat for a time by restrictions that empowered a husband to manage his wife's property and determine, in most cases, how it would be used to the supposed advantage of the household. Neither spinsters nor other single women faced any legal restrictions on what they could do with whatever property, including slaves, they held in legal title, unless wills or trust instruments that granted them the property established limitations governing their holdings or placed their properties and assets under trustee guidance and control. As a result, the *feme sole* spinster was legally empowered, at least theoretically, with significant autonomy as an individual. The spinster Margaret Biggs, for example, brought suits in court early in her life for an uncollected debt, bequeathed a small portfolio of stock in her will, and forgave another small loan in a deathbed gift to a close friend.[13]

On the other hand, the right to contract and own property mattered little for those single women without the resources to purchase land or slaves, negotiate contractual obligations, hire lawyers, or pay court fees. Furthermore, no Natchez spinster, regardless of her legal rights, enjoyed the cultural and political power to change laws or to participate in policy-making decisions that might affect her as a not-married woman. None could vote, hold public office, practice law, serve on juries, or bear arms (as militia members) to protect the public peace and safeguard property. As spinsters, moreover, they held no moral and legal claims to a husband's resources, such as dower rights; this mattered greatly for those poor and less-advantaged spinsters who might also suffer with little recourse the social opprobrium that followed from not being wives and mothers.

Given the diversity of their class and family circumstances and their *feme sole* legal status, many of the city's white, never-married women aged thirty years and older experienced lives much more complicated than that of the stereotypical "old maid," although more than a few certainly did fit that image perfectly well. To better understand the spectrum of spinsterhood in antebellum Natchez, and how such women coped in a place that privileged men and upheld the mother/wife ideal for women, two Natchez spinsters are profiled below: the "foul-mouthed" female entrepreneur Lydia Dowell and the elite southern "lady" Rebecca Mandeville. Their lives reveal that some of the city's white spinsters in the antebellum period (perhaps many) were strongly committed to negotiating life along remarkably individualized pathways quite unlike those taken by the married women all around them.

The "Foul-Mouthed" Lydia Dowell

The spinster Lydia Dowell appears to have had more in common with the entrepreneurial Jane Mayes than with Margaret Biggs or Eliz Dupuy. Dowell arrived in Natchez as a twenty-five-year-old woman from Philadelphia some-time around 1830, determined to make an unprecedented (at least in Natchez) go of it as a single woman in commerce and trade. During the 1840s, her male-free household included a number of young, unmarried women who lived with her as employees. By 1850, the year of her death, Dowell had amassed a substantial fortune, owning female clothing and dry-goods stores in Natchez, St. Louis, and Vicksburg; houses and investment properties in at least two of those cities; and a small number of enslaved workers at one time or another. Her probate record lists personal property, probably including slaves, valued at $3,000, and her estimated total worth came to $50,000. Although other women in midcentury Natchez ran various businesses, such as millinery stores and boardinghouses, she was the first to own and operate a commercial store in the city, and none ever matched her scope of enterprise. At least in Natchez, Dowell was ahead of her time.[14]

Although she was a young woman when she arrived in Natchez, Dowell nevertheless came equipped with some experience in the female clothing and dry-goods business and what appears to have been financial support from her father (or brother), who may have owned a similar enterprise in Philadelphia, with possible commercial connections to New Orleans.[15] Shortly after landing in Natchez, Dowell's younger sister, Ruth, joined her as a trusted store manager and advisor. Sometime during the late 1830s, Ruth Dowell married a Natchez lawyer and minor slaveholder, Christopher McClure, who often worked as Lydia's attorney. When Lydia relocated to Vicksburg in the late 1840s, McClure purchased her Natchez stores, which his wife may have continued to operate for a few years before the entire family moved to St. Louis.[16]

As a businesswoman, Lydia Dowell traveled each year to Philadelphia and New Orleans on buying trips to select materials and fabrics, sewing supplies, and various wares that she described in her advertisements as the "finer goods" for ladies. Her stores sold all kinds of material for sewing clothes and craft-ing dresses, including patterns, buttons, thread, ruffle bands, and ribbon. In addition, Dowell offered her customers blouses, chinaware and crockery in limited amounts, satin capes, coats, collars and caps, shawls, shoes for women and children, and dresses and frocks, some of which she had altered or sewn on-site using skilled seamstresses and dressmakers. She brought in fashion-able bonnets from eastern suppliers, and her workers crafted hats and advised women in creating their own designs with ribbons, real and artificial flowers, and trimmings. Dowell's store employees, as well as several enslaved women owned by her or apprenticed to her, did alterations and probably offered lessons to young women just learning to sew.

Lydia Dowell's Natchez store filled a special niche in the city's mercantile community, one aimed at the specific needs of middle- and upper-class women who lived in and around Natchez. Her female customers could shop for the latest fashions brought in from eastern sources without rubbing shoulders with male shoppers. They could try on hats and bonnets, have dresses altered and fitted, discuss fashions and gossip, exchange ideas about sewing and needlework, look through patterns, and literally let their hair down and have it made up with the latest ribbons and curls while hobnobbing with female acquaintances and friends.

Dowell also offered her female customers individual accounts with minimum oversight from husbands and fathers. The wife of Daniel G. Benbrook, for example, ran up charges of $78.28 for a cloak, combs, needles, ribbons, shoes, and yards of material she purchased in 1835; when she failed to pay her bill, Dowell sued Benbrook's surprised husband for collection. Mary Rowan's husband, in another example of an unknowing man, faced a suit for monies owed Dowell in 1842 for goods purchased by his wife on an account that she never paid. Courts usually held husbands responsible for debts incurred by their wives, although sometimes husbands contested the bills as ones they had not authorized. It is likely that many of Dowell's female customers purchased goods on accounts that were settled up periodically and willingly by their husbands or themselves.[17]

Stores owned and operated by males in Natchez sold goods for women, including the high or "fancy" sort offered by Dowell, but such general stores, staffed by male clerks, catered principally to men and boys in a masculine environment unappealing to the female shopper. Shopping in Dowell's store was an ongoing adventure for many of her female customers.[18] The young Mary McGuire, a voracious shopper, visited Dowell's store almost weekly from June through August 1835 and then less frequently once cold weather settled over the town. In another account, Mrs. George Carradine paid thirteen visits to the store in 1838. She purchased $398.61 worth of goods, ranging from corded skirts and bonnets to gloves and aprons, sewing materials, children's bonnets and dolls, buttons, and shoes. Both women appear to have been avid sewers, and they probably spent lots of time with their needles making clothes for themselves and their families in a mode of living replicated by many of the town's females, regardless of their age, class, or marital status. Sewing clothes was a necessity of life for most free women in the area as well as an enjoyable way to occupy themselves, especially for women in wealthier households with lots of idle time on their hands.[19]

As the only female merchant in Natchez until the mid-1840s, Dowell operated two shops, one located in the city center on Main and Commerce and the other at the corner of Canal and State Streets near the city market, although it is unclear whether the stores varied in merchandise and customers. Dowell lived in residences behind the stores, sharing lodging at first with her female employees before she constructed her main house at the rear of her Canal Street shop, which may have included a workroom for employees.[20]

During her years in Natchez, Dowell employed young women as clerks, seamstresses, and dressmakers. In 1840, for example, nine young women between the ages of fifteen and thirty as well as a ten-year-old girl worked in her store, and she sometimes took on enslaved or free-black apprentices sent to her by their owners or patrons to learn the millenary trade and dressmaking. At least one of her employees, a skilled seamstress or else a young woman hoping to learn the millinery business, came to her from Philadelphia under contract for twenty months.[21] Dowell's sister, Ruth, worked in Lydia's stores and appears to have managed them when Lydia was away on buying trips or tending to her Vicksburg business. Other females served as her agents and store managers over the years, one of whom received thirty dollars per month to supervise the Vicksburg store.[22] Except for Ruth McClure, Dowell's employees and slaves lived and worked together as single women in a uniquely female environment servicing female customers, and none appear to have married while working for her.

Available sources do not reveal fully the character of this community of females, but Dowell undoubtedly ran a tight ship as the boss lady rather than being a companion or friend to her workers. The free-black barber William Johnson describes Dowell as a "foul-mouthed" woman who alienated several young black apprentices, causing them to flee her establishment after less than two weeks working for her.[23] In another case, one of Dowell's store managers, her lead saleswoman, angrily sued her for back wages. In still another employee incident, a young woman brought from Philadelphia to Natchez by Dowell ran off, possibly to join her lover or else to work for a new employer. Dowell refused to surrender the woman's trunk and possessions until she reimbursed Dowell for travel costs, boarding, and the food and supplies she had consumed.[24]

Although Dowell grounded her entrepreneurial energy in her stores, she actively acquired downtown properties in Vicksburg and Natchez during the late 1830s and throughout the 1840s. Along with her two stores and residences in Natchez, she purchased eight downtown lots in Vicksburg, upon which she built houses as rental investments, expending an estimated $37,000 in acquiring and improving the property.[25] She then bought adjoining land in a tax sale, probably with an eye to duplicating her rental housing investments someday. Four years before her death, Dowell exchanged a dozen adult slaves, men and women under the age of twenty-five, for two other Vicksburg properties, none of which she apparently developed or rented out.[26]

Dowell's enterprise also included various dealings for rural lands, although she never actively pursued cotton farming or shifted from commerce to agriculture. In most cases, she held title to country lands in trust as collateral for loans or security for debts owed to her on store accounts. For example, in 1845 she loaned Ann Mix $5,000, secured by a mortgage on Mix's twelve slaves and 207 acres located twelve miles north of Natchez on the road to Port Gibson and Vicksburg. Mix used the money to settle a creditor's suit against her (most likely by Dowell), and she appears to have paid fully the mortgage to Dowell in due course.[27] In a more complicated land acquisition, Dowell exchanged a large Vicksburg lot and residence for seventeen or eighteen acres of land within the so-called Devil's Punch Bowl section of land just upriver from Natchez. To clear the title, she negotiated debtor's claims on three different parcels within the acreage, including a mortgage held by the Natchez Insurance Company. The available records do not reveal how this business deal turned out, but there is no evidence that she occupied, rented out, or farmed the land.[28]

From the moment she arrived in Natchez, Dowell had acquired slaves, and she continued throughout her life to value owning slaves as an accommodation to her commercial enterprise rather than as a speculative investment or with an eye to becoming a planter. Early on, for example, she purchased from her future brother-in-law a young woman who most likely worked as Dowell's domestic servant and in her stores in one capacity or another. By 1840 she owned a young male, who probably did the heavy work around the store, and four females who most likely worked as laundresses and cooks for her white employees and possibly as seamstresses and saleswomen in her stores. Dowell also acquired slaves in settlement of debts for store purchases via court-ordered attachments, and she may have bought one or two slaves from slave traders in Natchez. Toward the end of her life, seven slaves acquired in a debt settlement may have been part of the dozen that she exchanged for parcels of land in Vicksburg on which she erected rental housing.[29]

Lydia Dowell exploited every legal angle available to her as a *feme sole* to protect and expand her enterprise. In matters of law and commerce, nothing seemed to hold her back. She filed twenty-six known court cases as a plaintiff and faced fifteen contests, if not more, as a defendant. The cash value in dispute in these legal battles totaled approximately $66,000. Juries reached verdicts on

TABLE 2. Lydia Dowell's court cases

Range of value	No. of cases	Average value	Total value
Dowell as plaintiff*			
$1–$500	17	$189	$3,217
$501–$1,500	4	$844	$3,377
$1,501–$10,000	5	$6,627	$33,135
Total Value			$39,729
Dowell as defendant†			
$1–$500	4	$242	$968
$501–$1,500	7	$818	$5,724
$1,501–$10,000	4	$4,897	$19,587
Total Value			$26,279

Sources: CCAC; HNF; HCEA; and Supreme Court of Mississippi, MDAH.
*Total cases as plaintiff, 26: won 23, lost 2, unknown 1.
†Total cases as defendant, 15: won 3, lost 7, unknown 5.

many of her suits, and most of the cases in which she was a plaintiff involved unpaid promissory notes for merchandise purchased in her Natchez stores. The all-male juries almost always found for her in these cases, typically based on her detailed accounts and the eyewitness testimony of her store managers and employees. (See table 2.)

When she resorted to legal remedies, Dowell faced a court system that had been reformed and revitalized by changes made to the state constitution in 1832. Briefly told, circuit courts handled suits of less than $500 in value or involving breaches of contract for any amount, along with criminal cases, while chancery courts heard questions of equity and justice not involving a statute or a monetary settlement on a contract. These chancery courts, or courts of equity, which administered justice rather than statute law, handled divorces, probate matters, and pleas for court-ordered injunctions requiring fulfillment of a contract as equitable relief rather than monetary damages; monetary damages could be awarded only in a circuit court. The High Court of Errors and Appeals, sitting in Jackson, the state capital, heard cases appealed to it from both circuit and chancery courts. The circuit and chancery courts for Adams County met in the Natchez courthouse, and Warren County courts convened in the county courthouse in Vicksburg.[30]

As a shrewd and careful litigant, Dowell principally relied on the legal skills of her brother-in-law, Christopher McClure, and the respected John T. McMurran, an attorney and slaveholding planter, to protect and pursue her business interests. McClure represented Dowell in 40 percent of the twenty-five court cases in which her attorneys can be identified. McMurran carried 20 percent of such cases, and the lawyers Armat and Rawlings handled another 15 percent. Dowell shrewdly hooked up with McMurran, the most successful lawyer in the state during the 1830s, and she continued to rely on him, though not exclusively, for cases that involved sums of $1,000 or more. McMurran and his partner, John A. Quitman, specialized in debt cases, and their firm flourished, especially with the economic depression of the late 1830s. Both men had married into the family of the Superior Court judge Edward Turner, who later became the chief justice of the Mississippi High Court of Errors and Appeals. Although there is no evidence of a family connection between Dowell and McMurran, both hailed from Pennsylvania, and he may have known her or her family.[31]

Among the cases she undertook as a plaintiff, Dowell sued for the return of monies she had paid in purchasing an allegedly defective slave, for defaults on warrants issued to her by a railroad company, and on numerous promissory notes for purchased merchandise. She also sued the insolvent Planters' Bank of Mississippi to redeem a bill of exchange drawn upon the bank. In yet another case she sued her neighbor for $5,390 allegedly stolen by the neighbor's slave. She prevailed in almost 90 percent of these cases. As a defendant, however, Dowell did not always fare so well. Juries found against her in favor of a New Orleans merchant for unpaid goods, on monies due carpenters and former employees, and on her debt to a local lumber merchant for materials used in constructing her residence on Canal Street. Of these fifteen cases, she apparently won less than half.[32]

Four of Dowell's cases were appealed from the lower courts to the Mississippi High Court of Errors and Appeals, and no other woman in antebellum Mississippi, according to the legal historian Cai Hamilton, had so many cases heard before the High Court. She stood as the plaintiff in two cases and as defendant in the other two, and the High Court ruled for Dowell in each of the four, giving her a complete victory in the appellant hearings. The High Court overturned verdicts against her in two debt cases because the lower courts had disallowed essential evidence, and it affirmed lower-court rulings in her favor against the Planters' Bank of Mississippi and in support of a demurer writ filed by Dowell, which allowed her to avoid answering questions deemed irrelevant to the case.[33] According to Hamilton, Dowell's suits heard in both the lower and higher courts exceeded in number those of any woman in antebellum Mississippi. What is more, most civil cases involving women dealt with estate settlements, divorce, or joint litigation with husbands related to commerce or debt.[34]

A case lodged against Dowell by a Philadelphia supplier in 1846 reveals the character of her enterprise and her combative willingness to make a stand in an open court trial heard by jurors. One of her Philadelphia wholesalers took her to court for an unpaid bill of $12,454.25. The issue involved Dowell's refusal to pay for allegedly inferior goods. Dowell claimed that she had not selected the goods in question, describing them as "unseasonable" fashions, "old and damaged" goods, and inferior "job lots" unsuitable for her stores. The Philadelphia merchant countered that Dowell often and purposefully selected inferior goods for Natchez while sending superior goods to her other stores. Perhaps aware of Dowell's cranky disposition, and perhaps somewhat offended by the idea that she would allocate inferior goods to Natchez, the all-male jury found for the plaintiff, although the final verdict did not come until after Dowell's death.[35]

In a much more complicated contest, Dowell was accused of a conspiracy to commit fraud.[36] As the case played out in court, it revealed Dowell's willingness to use male agents in aspects of her enterprise that went beyond her commercial interests, as well as her entrepreneurial drive and keen eye for investment opportunities. In this case, Dowell had entered into a verbal agreement with a Natchez man, Cornelius Harring, to purchase seven Vicksburg lots in her name at a public auction. After Harring submitted the winning bid, Dowell transferred the necessary funds to Harring, but he (according to Dowell) failed to forward the funds to the seller, for unknown reasons. Dowell, assuming that she held legal title to the land, paid off a second lien and built rental houses on the property. Supposedly unbeknownst to Dowell, several Natchez creditors held unpaid promissory notes against Harring, and they sued to attach the Vicksburg land he had purchased for Dowell, claiming that Harring held legal title to the property. Dowell countersued in the Superior Court of Chancery, arguing that she had acquired part of the disputed property in a tax sale, paid off creditor liens against some of it, and transferred the purchase price of the land to Harring as her agent based on their verbal agreement. Harring's creditors argued that his claim to having bought the property for Dowell amounted to a surreptitious maneuver to defraud his creditors in conspiracy with Dowell. After years of litigation, the court ruled in Dowell's favor.[37]

Dowell's legal contests exposed her life and business to considerable public scrutiny. Lower-court jurors were selected from among white men in the county between the ages of twenty-one and sixty who qualified as householders, meaning those who owned property or had paid a poll tax. A prospective juror could not have been convicted of felonies or other crimes.[38] Court cases like Dowell's involved considerable give-and-take in the courtroom prior to a jury's deliberations, which contributed to the public spectacle that almost

Record of the trial in Adams County Circuit Court of *Mary Ann Stanton v. Lydia Dowell*, May term, 1844. Historic Natchez Foundation.

always occurred on court days. Both parties to a suit were allowed four peremptory challenges, and attorneys could offer instructions to the jurors, if accepted by the presiding judge. Once a trial began, the contesting attorneys typically presented witnesses, written interrogations, verbal testimonies, and evidence. Although it is unclear if Dowell ever appeared in person during these court hearings, it is likely that she did, standing before the court as a well-known public character whose business dealings were easily and perhaps eagerly observed by casual court watchers, her commercial competitors and customers, and other interested parties.[39]

Lydia Dowell died in 1850 from an inflammation of the stomach and bowels, perhaps stemming from an ulcerous condition aggravated by her complicated and tumultuous life as an ambitious and even ruthlessly competitive woman. Despite her rather notorious public record, almost nothing is known about her personal life. She does not appear to have been a member of any Natchez church or a participant in any of the city's female associations, such as the Protestant Orphans Society or various literary clubs. How she felt about men or what motivated her not to marry (or motivated men not to marry her) is a complete blank in the extant public and private records. All we know about her personality and character is what comes through in the court cases and what the observant William Johnson passed on to his readers when he candidly proclaimed in his journal that "the old lady was too Foul mouthed Intirely" to garner his respect as a woman.[40]

Johnson's depiction appears to be the only surviving epitaph for Dowell, but it was one with which almost everyone in Natchez who had run across her in court or had worked for her as an employee probably would have agreed. Had she been a man, Hamilton suggests, she might have been remembered with more flattering words, but perhaps not. She was, after all, a tenacious businesswoman living in a world that often judged merchants (male and female) as coldhearted connivers ready to profit from someone's troubles or take advantage of their customers if they could.[41] Nevertheless, of this there can be no doubt: the litigious Lydia Dowell stepped lively, and on more than a few toes, throughout her Natchez life as she sued, was sued, and pursued nearly every legal and entrepreneurial maneuver available to her as a not-married and quite extraordinary *feme sole*.

To better understand Dowell's life as a never-married woman, we now examine in contrast the genteel southern spinster Rebecca Mandeville. Unlike Dowell, Mandeville lived her life as a dignified and guardedly nonpublic spinster who almost certainly knew about the formidable Lydia Dowell, though the two women would most likely never have been friends. Their lived experiences as spinsters reveal what both women shared as never-married women and the ways in which they differed, providing thereby some perspective on what all the city's white spinsters might possibly have known as women living nondependent on husbands.

The Dignified Rebecca Mandeville

The Pulitzer Prize–winning journalist and amateur historian Hodding Carter writes about the spinster Rebecca Mandeville in *Lower Mississippi*, published in 1942. Carter had come across Mandeville's diary, which she kept for six months as a young, not-married woman, along with the lengthy journal written by the free-black barber William Johnson. For Carter, the Mandeville diary revealed, albeit briefly, the life of a single white woman "who might have been scissored from a *Godey's Lady Book*," a national publication offering advice to women that circulated widely in the antebellum South. Mandeville's diary depicts, in Carter's opinion, a genteel and fashionable lady living in the "insipidly placid Natchez," in contrast to Johnson's "turbulent, callous, and frontier-spirited" Natchez, "whose men were not yet as civilized as the homes they built."[42] Carter's proper and refined Rebecca Mandeville stands in stark contrast to the crude-talking and obstreperous Lydia Dowell.

Had Carter probed beyond Mandeville's diary, which he located in the archives of Louisiana State University at Baton Rouge, he might have found the cache of personal letters exchanged between members of the extended Mandeville family as well as an array of public records in Natchez and elsewhere that cover almost a century of Mandeville family life.[43] Most of the extant private and public records support Carter's view of Rebecca Mandeville as a genteel lady of impeccable manners caught up in an elite social order that existed quite apart from the "earthy" town depicted in William Johnson's journal.[44] These records also reveal and illuminate the factors that may well have influenced her to choose, or accept, her life as a spinster, namely, the character of her family, the urban scene in which she lived, and the ways that the people of antebellum Natchez responded to her as a never-married woman.

Henry Mandeville Sr. moved from Philadelphia to Natchez in 1835 to work as cashier of the Planters' Bank of Mississippi. He brought with him not only his considerable experience as a banker in New York and Philadelphia but also his wife, Charlotte, and their nine children: four girls and five boys. As the fifth child in the family, Rebecca became the family matriarch in the mid-1840s, following the deaths of her mother (1835) and two older sisters (Cornelia in 1841 and Charlotte in 1844). Rebecca's sister Cornelia had given birth to a daughter prior to her death, and her husband, James D. Oakley, who lived out of state, entrusted the child, Charlotte (known as Carlie, Sissie, or Sissy), to Rebecca (Bec or Beppie) and Josephine (Jose or Jo), Rebecca's younger sister, to be raised in the Mandeville household. Rebecca's management of her father's Natchez home initially included educating and mothering her young niece as well as her two younger brothers, Theodore (Theo) and Ellwyn (El). All her brothers and sisters had either died or else moved away from Natchez by the late 1850s, leaving Rebecca at home in Natchez on the eve of the Civil War with her father and the nineteen-year-old Carlie.[45]

The Mandeville family resided in a comfortable but not especially notable house in downtown Natchez, and its members enjoyed all the privileges stemming from the several plantations they owned in Louisiana as well as the senior Mandeville's position as cashier of the Planters' Bank of Mississippi. As the principal operating officer of the largest bank in the state, Mandeville oversaw several million dollars in assets and obligations, including federal monies deposited with it as one of Andrew Jackson's "pet banks." After the bank failed in the aftermath of the economic depression that ravaged the state and nation in the late 1830s, Mandeville continued to handle the bank's affairs as one of three trustees empowered to liquidate its holdings and pursue the numerous obligations owed to it. He remained in this salaried capacity for the rest of his life, traveling often throughout Mississippi and Louisiana collecting monies, foreclosing on properties, and handling litigation related to the bank's accountability to its creditors, stockholders, and depositors.[46]

As one of the city's most prominent men, the senior Mandeville counted among his friends and business associates eminent members of the community's mercantile and slaveholding elite. Many of the city's leading merchants, lawyers, and slaveholding planters had invested in the Planters' Bank; obtained loans from the bank secured by cotton receipts, land, and slaves; and deposited personal funds in the bank. When the bank failed, Mandeville retained, and battled in court, prominent Natchez lawyers as part of the process of its liquidation. More than a few of these prominent men and their families regularly visited Mandeville and his family in their Main Street home, known during the 1840s as "the Bank" because of the financial activity conducted therein.

Slave ownership was the litmus test for acceptance into the city's upper class, and the Mandeville family easily met that test. The senior Mandeville owned several enslaved women in Natchez, at least one enslaved carriage driver, and dozens of enslaved workers on the Mandeville family plantations in Louisiana. The oldest Mandeville son, Henry Jr., who worked as a Princeton-educated lawyer in Natchez until the mid-1840s, invested heavily in Natchez real estate before liquidating his properties and acquiring slaves and a plantation, Westwood, in Louisiana, in partnership with his father, which he thereafter managed.[47] The second son, George, married into a wealthy mercantile and slaveholding Natchez family, the Postlethwaites, and acquired at least one plantation located near Westwood in the 1840s.[48] Additionally, as the Planters' Bank's trustee, Henry Sr. controlled numerous slaves and thousands of acres owned by the bank or pledged to it as collateral for unpaid loans and mortgages.[49]

The Mandeville women, because of their father's prominence, shared fully in the upper-class ethos and sense of racial superiority that emanated from their status as members of the city's slave-holding elite. And because they lived in a remarkably sophisticated urban place, they took full advantage of the amenities and variety of life it offered to its wealthiest residents. Both their upper-class, slaveholding status and the urban scene in which they lived shaped and influenced their lifestyles and outlook on life. As privileged, slaveholding white women, Rebecca and Josephine daily walked around the city, either alone or together, depending on the weather. They frequently ventured on foot to the bluffs to observe the Mississippi River and spectacular sunsets, traversed the few blocks to their brother George's house (Myrtle Banks), took carriage rides to call on wealthy neighbors who lived on suburban estates just outside town, shopped in downtown stores, and tasted various treats in the upstairs "ladies only" room of a popular ice cream parlor.[50] They enjoyed attending festive circuses, traveling shows, the theater, concerts, seminars, and church services, sometimes going twice on Sunday when the Reverend Joseph B. Stratton preached at the First Presbyterian Church. For Rebecca Mandeville, Natchez was a wonderfully alive and vibrant urban scene that contrasted favorably, in her mind, with its wealthiest hinterland plantations.

Although always ready for a day's outing, Rebecca Mandeville also attended to domestic duties and chores as matron of the family household throughout the late 1840s and 1850s. Her daily routine revolved around supervising the household's enslaved domestics and teaching (assisted by tutors) her niece and younger brothers; overseeing meal preparation and food processing; napping and bathing; reading newspapers, magazines, and books; and the never-ending sewing of new clothes or repair of worn ones, which she frequently distributed to the family's enslaved workers. At any moment her daily ritual might be interrupted by visitors and guests, who often showed up unannounced and eager for gossip, a bite of tea and biscuits or orange sponge cake, and companionship. Rebecca occasionally complained about the monotony of her daily chores and the banality of entertaining those visitors whom she found uninteresting, but she prided herself on the efficiency with which she managed the household and attended to even the most unwelcome or last-minute visitors. Rebecca Mandeville mentions in her personal writings the names of twenty-five members of the most elite families of Natchez as among her friends and associates, and many of them were among the guests who visited her house or with whom she and her sister socialized. On one occasion, at least seven of the town's wealthiest women visited her and Josephine for a meeting of the Natchez Musical Club.[51]

Rebecca certainly understood that her domestic servants greatly freed her from household drudgery and the physical toil that such drudgery involved. Because of them, she and her sister could devour novels and newspapers, entertain guests, enjoy afternoon teas, indulge in leisurely baths, sleep late when they wanted to, take the time to "talk nonsense" with each other and with friends, and venture about town at their whim and whimsy. As was typical of the city's elite, slaveholding women, Rebecca tended to enforce boundaries carefully between her and the family's enslaved servants without demonstrating harshness or a mean-spirited attitude toward them, insofar as is known. She cheerfully extended greetings from traveling relatives to the family's enslaved domestic workers, hesitated to replace or transfer the most independent and undisciplined among them, sometimes assumed tasks that could have been done by them, nursed them when they were sick, and exercised a fairly lax authority over household servants without commenting much about them as fellow human beings.[52] Only once in her diary, for example, did she reflect on a personal relationship with her enslaved servants, and it was a connection that she found curiously puzzling. "Poor Emmeline died on the ninth, all of us around her doing our best to keep her from going—it being Sunday a great many of her colored friends came here and followed her remains to their last resting place—many bitter tears did we all shed over the poor creature—it is strange how we become attached to our servants and they to us."[53]

Besides liberating Rebecca Mandeville from life's most mundane chores, her enslaved workers freed Rebecca and Josephine to craft personal letters to family and friends as part of the routine and ritual that consumed their daily lives. Letter writing for women in elite southern families, according to historian Steven Stowe and others, was a revelatory act that enlightened and personalized relationships through innuendos and coded expressions meant to intimately engage authors and readers in ways not always possible through the spoken word alone. As personal commentary on what mattered most in their relationships, letters helped bond friends and kinfolk together and defined and shaped how they lived with, and among, one another as well as their acquaintances in the world beyond their families.[54]

Rebecca's correspondence (written and received) reveals not only the character of her relationship with her family but also her perspective on men and the special urban environment in which she lived. For her, letter writing amounted to a burden as well as a joy that she willingly performed, keenly aware that the heartfelt feelings expressed in the written words exchanged with her family members served as a cohesive force that largely defined the contours of her life. Her older sister Charlotte, who had moved for a brief time to a Louisiana plantation after her marriage, expected Rebecca to write two or three letters each week, filled with details about everything and anything going on in Natchez and the Mandeville household. Whenever Josephine traveled, she and Rebecca exchanged detailed letters about the weather, neighbors, family affairs, and their social and cultural life, including pithy gossip and comments on plays, concerts, books, and fashions. Once her two older brothers had married, Rebecca corresponded affectionately with their wives, who became like loving sisters to her.[55]

Obviously concerned about marriage and spinsterhood, in their letters to each other Josephine and Rebecca often allude, albeit obliquely rather than directly, to the men in their lives—or the absence of them. But the two sisters did not always share the same perspective about men or those social affairs that might result in courtship and marriage. For Josephine, always the flirt and eager for fun, marriage seemed the natural culmination of a youth spent playing the coquette and dabbling in love. Rebecca, although clearly interested in men, would not give her heart easily. Josephine frequently scolded Rebecca for her high-minded taste and unwillingness to join the social whirl of Natchez with quite the same abandonment that Josephine herself so easily exhibited. The more introverted Rebecca once copied into her diary a favorite poem that speaks volumes about her willingness to be above and apart from the social fray so enjoyed by her sister. The poem views life from the perspective of fresh flowers that grace the tresses of a beautiful young woman attending a festive ball. The flowers, giving off perfume and beauty for the special humans who cherish them not as diamonds but as fragile gifts of nature, beg to be left home where they are secure and happy in their virginal vases. Rebecca undoubtedly saw herself as a virgin blossom living safely and happily in her home but fearful of being taken to the ball and then discarded like a wilted weed.

> O! Take us not, young lady, to the ball. Alas, she heed not. We are twined in a fresh garland for her hair; we are blooming upon her bosom.
>
> Come, then, we must needs go. We are the flowers of the ballroom—the unhappy victims of the gay festivities.
>
> One by one, our petals will be pulled out, and will be trodden underfoot.
>
> Ere the ball is over, we shall lose our place in these tresses—this cincture will hold us no longer.
>
> Tomorrow some course servant will pick us up, and throw us into the street.
>
> Once more, young maiden, we entreat: leave us here, in thy virgin chambers, where we are happy.[56]

Rebecca's personal writings also reveal that the socializing that so enthralled Josephine did not always sit well with Rebecca. In one diary entry, for example, Rebecca tells how she avoided having to kiss a notorious theatrical visitor, the midget Tom Thumb, which was a public spectacle that delighted most of her female friends: "Strange fancy some women have of lavishing kisses in public, my face burnt at the very idea."[57] At another time, Rebecca stubbornly refused to join her sister in visiting neighbors and friends, which forced them to come to her house if they wanted to see her. As she grew older, Rebecca appears to have become more socially reticent while still partaking in the rich variety of the passing urban scene through her increasingly solitary walks around town, often with a book in hand.[58]

Although their different temperaments seem never to have caused friction between the two, the sisters well understood how others perceived them. In one letter, Josephine writes about a conversation with her niece that both angered and hurt her. The young niece had told Josephine that Robert Oakley (Carlie's uncle) had called Josephine a "regular flirt" and had admonished the young Carlie to model her life on Rebecca, claiming that she is more "both in person and mind like her dear mother." Josephine quoted Oakley's description of the "perfect woman," obviously meant to be a close approximation to Rebecca's character: "With all my admiration for an accomplished, thoroughly bred, self-possessed lady of the fashionable world, give me for a lifelong companion, a woman with more of the domestic virtues of constancy, sincerity, and a love of the fashionable accomplishments over the brilliant manners and splendid conversational powers of those who shine only or chiefly for gaslight companions."[59]

Incensed at this attack on her character, Josephine confided in coded words to Rebecca how much she resented Oakley's view of Rebecca as the more intelligent, sincere, and refined of the two sisters. Unable to deny perhaps what everyone knew, Josephine nevertheless hinted with some satisfaction at what must have been an equally obvious counterbalance in her mind, namely, that she considered herself the prettier sister: "Now if that is not impudent, I don't know what is. You see he thinks because I can talk, make myself fascinating and admired, that I must necessarily be thoroughly worldly and heartless. I wish I could talk to him half an hour and I'd make him think I was still more worldly and heartless than he now gives me credit for being. Perhaps if I had only one eye, half a nose, a crooked mouth, I'd be a good bargain in his eyes."[60]

In another letter, Josephine put her finger on the differences between her and Rebecca in words that seem to have been given as a compliment rather than a condemnation. On a warm August day in 1852, having just left Natchez on a steamboat, Josephine shot off a quick note of appreciation to Rebecca couched in words that suggest that Rebecca would make the perfect humdrum wife to men interested only in servants and caretakers: "What would I do when preparing to travel without your assistance? You think of things that never would enter my head. Oh! You are truly an inestimable creature. What a wife you would make. If I was a man I'd marry you tomorrow."[61] A year earlier, the younger sister had expressed her frustration in doing housework by saying that when the two of them one day married they would have to live together so that Rebecca could do the housekeeping.[62]

Few letters to Rebecca over the years mention much about her physical attributes, whereas her siblings frequently comment favorably on the beauty of both Josephine and Carlie, especially as the young niece grew into her teens. Rebecca was most likely taller than her younger sister, of darker complexion and hair, and less voluptuous. In a letter written from New Orleans, Augustus Mandeville describes an attractive woman who was almost as tall as Rebecca but "something of the same beauty as our oldest sister was," meaning the dead Cornelia. One gets the sense in reading these family letters that Rebecca was a tall, slender, charmingly attractive brunette but not an exceptionally beautiful or outgoing woman. Yet there is nothing in Rebecca's diary or in the many letters she authored and received to suggest that she considered herself, or was in fact, unappealing to men because of her physical looks.[63]

Similar to Josephine, the brothers Augustus, Theodore, and Ellwyn, who had left home to take jobs in New Orleans, often wrote to Rebecca the most detailed and intimate notes. They talked about the "amusements" of New Orleans and their prospects in life, and sometimes they asked her and Josephine to help them obtain loans and the good wishes of their father, who viewed his youngest sons less favorably than their older brothers. The brothers also confided to both sisters about their personal dealings with young women.[64] Even her older brother, Henry, felt comfortable in writing to Rebecca about his search for romance after the death of his wife. In one such letter he verbally paints a picture for Rebecca of a young woman who had aroused his passion: "[She is] of tall height, slender, erect, betraying the peaceful outlines and miniature developments of future glorious womanhood, so self-poised and confident in the responsive play of every muscle that her narrow footing betrays into one restrained or embarrassed movement, a movement that strikes the eyes as the very embodiment of perfected girlhood, as the rosy-kindred promise of approaching womanhood."[65]

Henry's letter is very personal and remarkably candid. His use of such words as "miniature developments of future glorious womanhood," a rather intimate description of the young woman's physical attributes, is typical of other letters he wrote to Rebecca over the years about his lack of success with women after the death of his wife. Although strongly attracted to the mysterious lady, Henry found himself unable to act, saying that he felt "as if I had nothing to say to her" and that she was simply "too pretty to be talked common place to." Rebecca, somewhat coldly and sternly judgmental, expressed doubt that her brother had been truly "smitten with Miss Lyons" or else he would have followed his heart.[66] Her remark suggests, perhaps, that she surely would act if ever she were truly attracted to a suitable gentleman.

Although the voluminous correspondence among the Mandeville clan reveals their devotion to each other and to their loving and often judgmental father, it is obvious that the senior Mandeville was especially connected to Rebecca. Perhaps she reminded him of his dead wife. Rebecca's willingness to assume the duties of the perfect matron and household governess even at an early age allowed her father to attend to his banking and plantation affairs and undoubtedly engendered within him profound gratitude for her service. It is unclear, however, if Henry Mandeville had pressured Rebecca to avoid marriage in favor of managing his household following the death of his wife and oldest daughters. Although there is nothing in the family's personal writings to indicate that Rebecca resented either her duties or her father, the senior Mandeville had tried to prevent both his older daughters from marrying, suggesting that he might have tried to control his daughters through his all-loving (perhaps suffocating) devotion to them. Cornelia Oakley wrote to her father while on her honeymoon, assuring him of her love for him but also chastising him for his apparent opposition to her marriage: "I know full well that solicitude for my welfare has induced your previous conduct in that you will throw aside all your former prejudices against him, when you know how happy I am."[67]

But there was something more involved in the relationship between Rebecca and her father than daughterly duty and parental affection. Rebecca viewed her father as the most romantic and chivalrous of men, a man who treated his daughter with great respect and loving reverence even as he relied on her for counsel and constant affirmation. With her father, Rebecca knew a perfect gentleman, someone whom she could trust and love completely because of the love, respect, and trust he bestowed on her.

As an example of the romantic ambiance that filled their letters, in 1854 Rebecca wrote to her brother Henry of the "joyful feelings" with which she always received and "devoured" her father's letters, describing them as "touchingly beautiful, containing in a few lines, so much to satisfy the loving heart."[68] Henry Jr., who frequently traveled with the senior Mandeville after his wife's death, knowing how much more eloquent and poetic were his father's missives home to Rebecca, generally refrained from writing detailed accounts of their trips. "Never mind, dear Bec," he once wrote, "when Father takes the pen all the romance of our journey will flow from it, for you, as freely as the ink."[69] A few days later the elder Henry apologized for not writing: "I have nothing of chivalry and romance to amuse you with as yet, nor do I think I have the spirit of either in my composition. But if dear and undying love will be received as a substitute you may revel in it with full confidence of the unfailing focus and aim in the heart of your ever affectionate Father."[70]

Although Rebecca Mandeville's spinsterhood appears not to have reflected an aversion to men, she found most eligible males in her circle lacking dignity and possessed of too much self-satisfaction for her taste, especially when compared to her father. Her journal entry for May 11, 1848, noting the young men seated next to her at a concert, is to the point and typical: "Mr. F. was one of them. He is not really handsome, as most think. There is something, *Je ne sai quoi,* wanting—perhaps it is dignity. His hair is perfect, so curly, and the Raven's wing is not more glossy, but still—.”[71]

For Rebecca, the qualities of a gentleman mattered greatly in her evaluation of men both as potential suitors and acquaintances. Several entries in her diary describe her reactions to being confronted by men who personified what she found disgusting and unappealing in males. During one morning walk, for example, a stranger tried to engage Josephine and Rebecca in conversation, calling their names and extending his hand in greeting. Astonished, Josephine icily replied, “I do not have the honor of your acquaintance!” He answered with an “impudent leer . . . not acquaintance—hey,” and then “marched off fast enough to soon be out of sight.” For the Mandeville sisters, the stranger had violated a fundamental principle of the Natchez social order by daring to engage two young women of significant social standing without having been properly introduced. His impudence was all “the more gross” because he had known their names without them knowing his. Not only did Rebecca feel personally violated, she believed that the Mandeville family name had been demeaned: “To dare insult a Mandeville! How my blood boils at the thought.” Rebecca's father exploded in rage when Rebecca told him about the incident, saying that the man “ought to have his head broke.” For the next few days, the doting father accompanied his daughters on their walks around town, armed with a heavy walking stick. Several days later, the family happened to find themselves seated near the stranger in church, which “kept Father's blood boiling all the time.” Afraid that her father might strike the stranger if he confronted him on the streets of Natchez, Rebecca curtailed her walks, although she confided in her diary that “the fellow deserves a good thrashing, but I prefer he should go unpunished to the risk of Father getting hurt.” Willfully determined, however, not to lose her claim to the public spaces that she valued so dearly, she soon nervously ventured out again to the bluffs unaccompanied by her father or anyone else.[72]

In contrast, another diary entry describes her encounter with yet another stranger whom she took to be a perfect gentleman.

> [I was] carrying some lunch up to Joe when I heard a man's step on the porch—a stranger—but I saw that he was a gentleman who wanted to see father about banking—Gibberish to me—as I was directing him to Mr. Walworth's house . . . when all of a sudden I became aware that his eyes were fastened upon my face and then thought how carelessly I had twisted up my hair and put on my clothes—I can only congratulate myself though, on my good fortune for one minute later and I would have met him with my hands full of toast—rather an embarrassing predicament for a young lady and gentleman, strangers to each other.[73]

Rebecca had immediately sized up this stranger to be a gentleman. It probably had to do with his manner. The context suggests that he had apologized profusely for his intrusion, begged forgiveness, and immediately identified himself as her father's business associate. At ease with the gentleman, Rebecca could feel flirtatious, even coy, and perhaps mildly titillated that he had found her in a state of unpreparedness and thus some intimacy. It thrilled her to think that this gentleman stranger might have seen her in an unguarded moment doing something that no lady of standing with enslaved servants should ever be caught doing by strangers, gentlemen notwithstanding: scurrying about like a common servant girl.

For Rebecca Mandeville, the trust and affection she held for her father and siblings, and the love that they extended to her, fortified her strong sense of self as a woman relatively satisfied with life in a city she cherished among family members who looked to her for emotional and psychological support. One incident in particular drives this point home. It began with a letter sent by her older and much respected brother upon the death of his wife. He appealed forcefully to Rebecca's sense of duty as a woman "to come and live with me, and take charge of my household and my children." He implored her to move from Natchez to rural Louisiana in consideration of his now-motherless children, demanding that she consider what would become of them should she not act responsibly: "Remember what it is to be motherless—to have none to care for their daily wants—none to draw forth their bitter feelings—none to make a home for them—none to shield them from the demoralizing intimacies of evil servants—none to instill into their young minds moral and religious principles, and to train them up to all excellence and love of virtue."[74]

Henry's letter touched on all the key points of maternal duty that he could evoke, including the image of his children being raised by "evil" slaves and Rebecca's spiritual responsibility for their souls; he promised that if she would accept his offer the "Savior Himself" would one day greet her with the welcome "well done, good and faithful servant." He further asserted that she would achieve "great moral discipline" along with a "full employment congenial" to her nature. Most importantly, his offer, should she accept it, would bring out her "best moral qualities, and educate [her] into a more perfect womanhood." His words questioned his sister's spiritual fervor and clearly expressed his belief that she seemed destined for a selfish spinsterhood, a fate that she could avoid only by becoming a surrogate mother and wife.[75]

In her older brother's mind, marriage called out the best moral qualities in women and thus enabled them to obtain "a more perfect womanhood" by servicing their husbands and their children as mothers. The opportunity for Rebecca to rear Henry's children and manage the domestic affairs of his rural household was the next best thing, in his mind, to being a wife and a mother for a woman who almost certainly would never marry. Thus Henry Jr. offered his sister a most self-serving, masculine argument backed by all the cultural and social rhetoric he could muster. Understanding that his sister would find it difficult to leave Natchez, what with its variety of life and worldly enticements, which he most likely frowned upon as frivolous, he offered her money and ample opportunity for travel. Aware that his sister felt a deep sense of responsibility to her family, especially to her father and her niece, as well as a strong attachment to Natchez, he urged her "to choose the path of duty" over a misguided affection for a mere place and for family members capable of taking care of themselves. With this appeal to Rebecca's sense of duty as a woman and surrogate mother, Henry closed his letter by telling her that he knew that she would do what was "right."[76]

Although the extant documents do not reveal Rebecca's response, it was most likely prompt and to the point. She apparently refused his request, undoubtedly encouraged him to find a suitable woman to marry, and probably assured him that her father's house remained always open to his children. Rebecca had clearly accepted the call to duty but not as dictated by her elder brother on his terms. Rather, she refused to abandon her father or her beloved Natchez no matter how urgently her brother pleaded with her to become the surrogate mother of his children. The assumption, moreover, that Rebecca would never take a husband may have infuriated her. The brother's plea rested on a call to duty and service that understood fully neither Rebecca's commitment to her father's well-being nor her deeply rooted connection to a special urban scene that offered her the security of a known but vibrant place of refuge. Shortly after Rebecca's emphatically (most likely) worded refusal, her brother profusely apologized for how he had presented his offer to her, clearly indicating just how much he had misjudged her as a woman secure in who she was and what she wanted out of life.[77]

Rebecca's rejection of her brother's offer, along with her reluctance to become as active a socialite as her younger sister, reflected a strong-willed personality with which she cultivated a spinsterhood that worked for her. There is little in her personal writings to suggest that she embraced spinsterhood as an act of resignation; rather, she valued living as a single woman in a vibrant urban setting where she was free to walk and shop and live openly as a solitary woman when she desired solitude while surrounded at other times by loving family members and friends. She obviously valued the freedom that spinsterhood allowed in preference to accepting a suitor lacking in dignity and the more gentlemanly qualities personified in her loving father. She may have feared marriage because of the early death of her sisters and mother, the burdens of children and the dangers of childbirth, and the monotony of living perhaps on a rural plantation, but nothing in the family correspondence confirms such speculation. What does come across is that it mattered very much to Rebecca that the world in which she lived accepted and valued her because of her willingness to assume matronly responsibilities for the welfare and well-being of her father, niece, and younger brothers, which she found personally fulfilling. She refused to be uprooted from her home and the vibrant urban scene she loved by marriage, surrogate or real, and not even the call of God or duty would deter her from remaining in the securely emotional "garden" of family and place where she had enclosed herself as a single woman.[78]

Religion seems to have played a relatively small part in Rebecca Mandeville's life (although it became more important to her after the Civil War) when compared to the importance she attached to kinship relations and her participation on her terms in the Natchez urban scene. She enjoyed going to church principally because she admired its preachers, especially the Reverend Joseph B. Stratton, as dignified gentlemen much like her beloved father; if a less refined or less articulate preacher orated from the pulpit, she simply attended services at one of the city's competing Protestant churches. Although a regular participant at Stratton's First Presbyterian Church, she avoided official induction as a church member until her mid- to late thirties. She appears to have joined principally at the urging of Reverend Stratton as well as her father and her older brother George, both long-standing church members.

In 1859, Rebecca Mandeville had no way of knowing that a great war would disrupt her life forever and that the "single blessedness" of her antebellum spinsterhood would become a tortured and relatively impoverished realm unlike anything she had ever experienced. Three of her brothers (Augustus, Ellwyn, and Theodore) would serve as Confederate soldiers, and her beloved sibling Theodore would perish in battle. Augustus died shortly after the war, probably weakened by his wartime experiences, and Rebecca's oldest and youngest brothers (Henry Jr. and Ellwyn) died on the same day in 1872, followed shortly after by her brother George, leaving his widow to carry on for a few years before she too passed away. Perhaps most tragically, Rebecca's beloved niece, who was like a daughter to her, scandalized the family during the war when she was impregnated by a northern stranger whom she would secretly marry (and who later divorced her), a blot upon the family name never to be forgiven by an angry grandfather, who banished his granddaughter from his household for the rest of Carlie's life. In the meantime, Rebecca's sister, Josephine, would leave Natchez for New Orleans right after her marriage in 1858 and then would leave the South for Chicago with her husband shortly after the New Orleans occupation by Union forces in 1863. Subsequently, Rebecca's father and older brothers (Henry Jr. and George) would lose almost all their money during the war's aftermath.[79]

After the Civil War ended, Rebecca lived on with her father as his principal caretaker in a rented house in Natchez until his death in 1878, at age ninety-one, and then on her own until she died in 1911. Her father appointed Rebecca the sole executrix in his will and bequeathed to her his remaining property, "real, personal, and mixed." She appears to have subsisted on monies sent by Josephine and her husband, George (until their deaths in 1900) and by leasing out her plantation, Westwood, and land in the Bayou Louis Tract near Harrisonburg, Louisiana. A Louisiana lawyer and judge, H. B. Taliaferro, probably a friend of her father, assisted Rebecca in these Louisiana transactions as her agent.[80] But how Rebecca persevered and coped emotionally and practically with life as a single woman in the aftermath of the Civil War is, as they say, another story. When it is told, there is a good chance that it will reveal a reserved but sure-stepping woman for whom family, dignity, and one's character mattered more than marriage.

Conclusion

In 1857, an article appeared in the *Southern Literary Messenger*, one of the South's most influential journals devoted to ideas and culture, urging its readers not to ridicule spinsters as redundant and ridiculous "old Maids." Its author, identified only by the letter "H," offered an alternative view that idealized "old maids" as "silent and active doers of good." He or she found that "old maids," as a class of women, "exceed even the goodness of preachers." They taught in and patronized Sunday Schools, promoted missions—including the American Colonization Society—subscribed to "Moral-Reform newspapers," served as busy secretaries to some "anti-Tobacco-chewing or Anti-young Men's-standing-in-the Church-door society," visited and cared for the sick, provided for poor children, stood vigilant when needed in times of plague, and affirmed the highest moral values when men deviated from them. For "H," public service rendered the "old maid" acceptable and even valued as a "good and faithful" servant to the community and enabled her to fulfill her female role in life without being married or becoming a mother.[81]

Some Natchez spinsters may have fit "H's" idealized image of the "old maid" as a dutiful community servant, but very few come to mind or turn up in the available public records. Certainly, neither Dowell nor Mandeville was a community-oriented or reform-minded woman who guarded community values, advocated high standards of public morality, or cared for the sick and needy (unless family called, as in Rebecca's case). Both were simply too busy with their personal and private affairs to contribute much assistance to the larger Natchez community, although Rebecca Mandeville had helped organize a local musical group and she worked as a home-front volunteer helping to sew clothes for the Confederacy prior to the city's fall to Union forces. She certainly had tried her best to uphold proper manners and decorum among her younger brothers, but she avoided service in the two most important female reform associations in town, the Natchez Protestant Orphanage and the Mississippi Colonization Society.[82] It is doubtful, too, that the spinsters Biggs, Dupuy, or Mayes resembled "H's" useful "old maid." Few of the city's working-class spinsters enjoyed the resources (money, education, or protective families) to do charity work, uphold decorum and standards, or pursue high-minded causes beneficial to the larger community.

If not useful "old maids," what can be said about Dowell and Mandeville as spinsters? Because of her extraordinary public persona as a merchant and litigant in the legal records, Dowell maneuvered through life as a public person. We know almost nothing about her private life (shrouded in secrecy or simply lost to history), except for what can be gleaned from her legal cases, which reveal quite a bit. Nearly everyone in town probably knew her, or about her. As public venues, her stores welcomed white female customers and shoppers (related to or married to some of the most prominent men in the city). Her court battles attracted interested spectators of the sort that followed jury trials, gossiped on court days about issues and personalities, and rendered judgmental opinions. It is not far-fetched to surmise that at least some of her business rivals closely watched her legal affairs with suspicious eyes, eager to spot an occasional shady business deal or two that might work to their advantage.

Rebecca Mandeville, on the other hand, while an avid voyeur throughout and within the city's public space, revealed little of herself to the public eye while traversing in and about the city, often alone with a book in hand. She shared intimate feelings with her family in personal writings that protected her privacy and guarded her honor, and when something occasionally happened that breached her privacy, such as the time a stranger dared to treat her as a public woman, or when her niece Carlie exposed the Mandeville family to community-wide scandal, Rebecca and her father walled themselves off as much as possible from prying eyes. Unlike Dowell, Rebecca Mandeville loved to explore the city's public spaces but resolutely avoided direct contact with the male-dominated legal arena. Public spectacles, avenues, and social affairs amused her as a genteel, urban voyeur, but the public scene never enticed her, insofar as we know, to exploit or even explore opportunities legally available to her as a *feme sole*, at least until well after the Civil War, and even then only in limited ways.

The spinsters Dowell and Mandeville, as well as Biggs, Dupuy, and Mayes, shared a common ability to step lively through life without challenging fundamentally the cultural norms of a place rooted in slavery and male mastery. Although they deviated from the useful "old maid" image, they did nothing to challenge slavery as the fundamental basis of southern society. As women fully ensconced within slavery as slaveholders or members of slaveholding families, their decisions and behavior, no matter how obstinate or unladylike, were tolerated by the males all around them. These women avoided stepping beyond the accepted, gendered boundaries of Natchez life to intrude on male prerogatives or challenge male mastery over women or the enslaved. Not only did they avoid politics, they made no attempt, so far as we know, to demand gender equality as women, and they relied on men (fathers, brothers, brothers-in-law, business retainers and agents, lawyers, judges, clients, patrons, and juries) to promote and protect their interests both within their family and in the public arenas in which they operated. No Natchez male's masculinity or sense of paternalism or male domination was challenged by Rebecca's decision not to marry or Lydia's court activities, even when their actions defied men, as was the case when Rebecca refused her older brother's request to live with him, or when Lydia regularly challenged men in court battles, which she usually won.

In fact, their life stories indicate a significant degree of community tolerance for both women as strong-willed spinsters. Dowell's legal victories in court, as well as her incredible enterprise, demonstrate the willingness of adjudicators to view her causes strictly in terms of evidence, law, and logic as well as the openness of Natchez society to a *feme sole* of seemingly inexhaustible entrepreneurial energy. Indeed, a careful reading of Dowell's legal proceedings finds little evidence to suggest that her gender worked against her in the eyes of a legal system administered, argued, and adjudicated by white men. When Dowell demonstrated that she had played by the rules governing contracts, debts, property, and slavery, she enjoyed substantial success in her litigation. As long as one's business activity accommodated and respected a culture that privileged men over women and whites over enslaved blacks, one's gender (if a *feme sole*) apparently could be ignored, especially when settling debts and conducting business. Lydia Dowell understood the rules of the dance, knew how to choose partners for the moment, and perfectly comprehended what legal rights she enjoyed as a single woman, even if she did not always know exactly how to act like a lady.

Each of the five women profiled in this chapter (and probably most Natchez spinsters of the time) very likely could have married had they really needed or wanted to. Certainly, enough men exhibited an interest in Rebecca along the way, and her sisters obviously tried to encourage her to seek a husband without demanding that she find a marriage partner suitable (or not) to her personality. This lack of pressure, especially by her father, made all the difference in the world. That she never married probably reflected her decision to remain within the cocoon of home, place, and family that she found nourishing, peaceful, and secure. Rebecca's existence as a somewhat solitary, introspective, and contemplative person, living in downtown Natchez (where she was free to explore its streets and public places, partake of its varied urban life, and then retreat home to her secluded nest), may have been too tempting a life to give up no matter how attractive she might have found even the most refined gentleman suitor. Being a prim and proper lady, free to venture out and about in the world as a voyeur without being drawn into it, appears to have fit her personality and needs abundantly.

Not every free Natchez woman was meant to marry, however, nor did they necessarily want to. It would have taken a special kind of man to wed Lydia Dowell, one different perhaps from those gentlemen who might have stood a chance with Rebecca, although affairs of the heart are always unpredictable. We have no idea about the type of man Dowell would have found acceptable or if she would have tolerated a man in her life, but she probably looked on most men, given her money and enterprise, with a suspicious eye. Lots of rough-edged women, far less prosperous than she, took up with husbands whom they found suitable, for whatever reasons. Perhaps the man to whom she entrusted money in buying Vicksburg town lots might have been a secret love interest. We simply don't know. It is a good guess, on the other hand, that few males would have found Lydia suitable as a marriage partner. Her aggressive nature, competitive personality, and combative character might have appealed to some men looking to be ordered about and dominated by strong women, but how many of them crossed her path or even wanted to? Unfortunately, there remains no extant evidence concerning Dowell's feelings about men or what else (or who else) might have mattered in her personal life.

The single white women of antebellum Natchez, collectively and individually, offered alternatives to the mother/wife ideal by their mere existence and the various ways in which they lived out their lives. We can never know for sure the degree to which their spinsterhood, especially for those who lived in female-only households, enabled them to challenge privately and among themselves the authority of males in their everyday living. Nor do we have access to information about their sexual preferences and inner thoughts. But two points now seem obvious: Natchez spinsters lived lives that amounted to a spectrum of individual experiences rather than any one, universal stereotype; and spinsterhood, in and of itself, did not necessarily threaten a male-privileged society rooted in white male dominance and mastery over women and slaves. Understanding both points helps to explain how women as different as Margaret Biggs, Jane Mayes, Eliza Dupuy, Lydia Dowell, and Rebecca Mandeville could maneuver or step lively as women without husbands in defiance of the wife/mother ideal and why antebellum Natchez society tolerated them not as deviant or aberrant women but as pragmatically adaptable members of a vibrant, urban community in which all its people lived as masters or servants of one sort or another.

CHAPTER THREE

Stepping Out on Their Own
The Divorcing Women of Antebellum Natchez

Sometime during the mid-1790s, Wilhelmina Aubaye sought refuge with friends in Natchez from her husband's beatings, fleeing from him "with all the clothes ripped from her body." According to witnesses, Joseph Aubaye had pursued his wife with a drawn sword and cocked pistol, and he surely would have killed her but for the intervention of friends. They also reported that Joseph planned to liquidate his property (so his wife could not "touch it") and carry Wilhelmina by force to his native France, where she would be imprisoned, if he did not kill her; at least, that was his boast. After leaving her husband, Wilhelmina hid out with her Natchez friends and eventually earned a living selling whiskey and supplies as a petty merchant; she knew, however, that Joseph could confiscate her earnings at any time and physically dominate her body through his common-law right of coverture. With this reality in mind, Wilhelmina petitioned the territorial legislature to permanently dissolve her marriage. After investigating her case and interviewing witnesses, the legislative body by a two-thirds vote granted Wilhelmina a permanent divorce in 1805, which restored her *feme sole* status and thereby prevented Joseph from legally claiming (then and forever) her assets or her body. In the eyes of the law, the divorce allowed Wilhelmina to live thereafter as though she had never married.[1]

Permanent divorces and separations from bed and board in territorial Mississippi required a two-thirds approval vote by members of the legislature upon the recommendation of a committee assigned to investigate the petition. It is surprising that the all-male legislature granted permanent divorce in this case rather than separation from bed and board, which was the statute remedy for extreme cruelty. Only adultery and impotence were grounds at the time for permanent dissolution of a marriage, suggesting that other factors had come into play, such as a criminal conviction or Joseph's departure from the territory or possibly the influence of important friends. Separations from bed and board did not permanently dissolve a marriage nor return a wife to her *feme sole* status.[2]

Fifty years later, in 1856, a similar divorce played out in Natchez when sixteen-year-old Laura McGill charged her forty-six-year-old husband, John McGill, a slaveholding, widowed father of two children whom she had married a year earlier, with extreme cruelty. Once married, the couple and his children (along with several enslaved servants) occupied a two-story house on the northeastern edge of town at High and Rankin Streets. To some observers, the match seemed questionable from the start because of the age difference between Laura and John, but neither family members nor friends suspected that the well-mannered and prosperous groom would brutally assault his young wife, nearly breaking her ribs in one attack and motivating her to flee, much as Wilhelmina Aubaye had fled her husband, to the home of a nearby relative. Unlike Joseph Aubaye, a seemingly repentant John McGill beseeched Laura to return home and drop the divorce suit, saying that they might "live in harmony" if she would acknowledge that she held "some small responsibility to his larger responsibility, and try to be a little bit more submissive." Although John McGill admitted striking Laura, he downplayed the viciousness of his attack, claiming that she had hit him first and that her injuries had happened as she hysterically assaulted him.[3]

The Chancery Court of the Southern District of Mississippi, meeting in Natchez, dissolved the couple's marriage because of John's extreme cruelty against his wife, a cause recently added by Mississippi lawmakers to the legal grounds for permanent divorce; the court also ordered John to pay Laura $800 per year in alimony based on what local merchants estimated it would cost to dress a lady of Laura's social standing. Mississippi transferred divorce jurisdiction from the legislature to the courts in 1822, although court-granted divorces continued to require legislative approval until 1842; it also established extreme cruelty as grounds for permanent divorce in 1850. In prior years, extreme cruelty might have won a divorce from bed and board, which did not restore the plaintiff to her *feme sole* standing nor allow either partner to remarry, but such cruelty was not grounds for absolute or permanent divorce.[4]

In between the Aubaye and McGill divorces, dozens of Natchez-area women petitioned the legislature or sued their husbands in chancery and circuit courts for dissolution of their marriages, and many of these women charged their spouses with extreme physical abuse. In 1849, for example, Margaret O'Conner documented in her divorce suit acts of violence by her husband Luke similar to those of Joseph Aubaye and John McGill, although Luke O'Conner's physical assaults were only a portion of his wife's complaint, which included his habitual inebriation and ongoing adultery with an enslaved woman and various "lewd" white women. She told the court that Luke had infected her with the venereal disease he had caught during his whoring escapades, regularly beat her with his fists, dragged her around the house by her hair, and might have killed her but for the intervention of unnamed family members and several lodgers in her Under-the-Hill boardinghouse. She also charged her husband with having squandered resources she owned as a separate estate or had acquired from her own earnings while married. The court granted Margaret's appeal for permanent divorce based on Luke's adultery rather than his violent actions, which Margaret presented as evidence of her husband's monstrous character and the scant likelihood that he would mend his ways in the future. The court could have considered Luke's physical abuse as extreme cruelty, which would have allowed for divorce from bed and board but not for a total or permanent divorce in which both parties could remarry and conduct their affairs as not-married persons.[5]

William Holmes, to give another example, faced the formidable legal team of John T. McMurran and John A. Quitman, the most successful lawyers in Natchez at the time, when Holmes's wife charged him with adultery and extreme cruelty. Louisa Holmes claimed that no matter how she had tried to placate her adulterous husband and ignore his sexual escapades, John continually and mercilessly had brutalized her in random acts of terror. He allegedly beat her with his fists, whips, switches, and canes. Her scarred body evinced the hundred lashes she had received at his hand, and she claimed that he even had beaten her while she lay in bed the day before birthing their child. A number of witnesses corroborated her story, testifying that they had seen the scars on her body from the whippings. The court granted her a separation of bed and board rather than a permanent divorce, most likely because extreme cruelty met the legal test allowed by the state in 1837 for separation but not for a permanent divorce. Importantly, Mississippi lawmakers essentially abandoned the bed-and-board separation aspect of divorce by 1840, when the state allowed any previously granted bed-and-board decree to become a permanent divorce after five years if the plaintiff wished for a permanent dissolution of the marriage.[6]

The Divorcing (and Divorced) Women of Antebellum Natchez

The cases mentioned above are taken from 110 investigated divorces filed by plaintiffs (wives and husbands) claiming actual residency in Natchez or Adams County during the years 1798 to 1860, which is a large sample of the total cases during these years.[7] Among these divorces, women petitioned or sued as plaintiffs in seventy-six cases, compared to thirty-four suits against wives by husbands.[8] At least two or three dozen divorced women lived in Natchez and Adams County on the eve of the Civil War, suggesting that many of the divorcing and divorced women in this sample remained in the Natchez District

TABLE 3. Divorces, Natchez and Adams County, 1798–1860

	Female plaintiff	*Male plaintiff*
1798–1810	5	6
1811–1820	10	4
1821–1830	10	2
1831–1840	9	11
1841–1850	26	6
1851–1860	16	5
Total	76	34

Sources: Docket Books, Records of Judgment, CHCAC, HNF and ORAC;
Territorial Petitions, Legislative Papers of the Mississippi Territory,
Legislative Records, and Supreme Court of Mississippi Records, and
HCEA MDAH.

rather than moving out of the area. This pattern probably held true for the years prior to 1850 as well.

Examining how and why the divorcing women of antebellum Natchez sought to have their marriages dissolved, or were divorced by their husbands, reveals what it meant to be a woman in an unhappy marital union in the wealthy, slave-based southern community that was antebellum Natchez. It also sheds light on the various coping strategies that Natchez married women used, or were allowed to use, in freeing themselves from the debilitating constraints of coverture, how they fared before the courts, and the range of experiences they shared, or did not, as divorcing women. Their stories illuminate as well the unwritten rules that dictated how divorcing women handled their husbands, the courts, and the larger public in their quests to regain their *feme sole* status as not-married women. Unlike spinsters, widows, and many women divorced by their husbands, the divorcing women of antebellum Natchez and Adams County rejected marriage, or at least a specific marriage, after having fully embraced it, at least for a time. How and why they did so is the story that follows.

Breaking the Bonds of Matrimony in Antebellum Mississippi

During the territorial years, Mississippi residents seeking absolute divorce (*a vinculo matrimonii*) or separation from bed and board (divorce *a mensa et thoro*), which allowed the parties to live separately but not to remarry, had to petition the Mississippi legislature. Either action required a two-thirds vote following upon the recommendation of an investigative committee to permanently dissolve a marriage or grant a separation of bed and board. In 1822, Mississippi lawmakers moved the power of granting divorce from the legislature to newly created chancery courts of equity; from *that* date until after the Civil War divorces were heard in circuit courts sitting in equity for divorces and in a series of shifting geographical chancery and vice chancery courts with jurisdiction broader than the one-county circuit courts. In 1857, the chancery court system was abolished and divorces and other equity matters were adjudicated thereafter by county circuit courts. Chancery divorces could be appealed to the Superior Court of Chancery and also to the Mississippi Supreme Court, which became the Mississippi High Court of Errors and Appeals in 1833.[9]

The state legislature steadily expanded the grounds for divorce over the years in steps similar to liberalization efforts in other states. By 1860, extreme cruelty, habitual drunkenness, penitentiary imprisonment for two years or more, insanity (or idiocy at the time of marriage), and incest had been added to bigamy, impotence, adultery, and desertion (an absence of three years) as legal grounds for permanently dissolving a marriage. Throughout the antebellum years, couples could informally separate and live apart by mutual agreement, but the separation had no legal standing and did not restore the wife's autonomous *feme sole* status. In cases where judges suspected subterfuge or collusion between the married partners, the court might uphold the marriage bond or grant legal separation from bed and board. This distinction between absolute divorce and divorce from bed and board fell aside somewhat when the legislature empowered the courts to grant permanent divorce for cause after three to five years of bed-and-board separation beginning in the mid-1830s.[10]

Divorce procedures in Mississippi by the mid-1850s incorporated a well-known ritual of sorts based on specific guidelines and strictures spelled out in state law, which in turn was based on practices found in other states and the equity and ecclesiastical courts of England.[11] Procedurally, a complainant in a divorce suit secured legal counsel to file the required plea with the clerk of the chancery court (or circuit court when sitting in chancery), and female plaintiffs typically filed under the authority of a best friend (often a family member) because of their nonlegal standing as married women. A court-appointed commissioner (usually a local justice of the peace or the county sheriff) served legal notice to the defendant and those witnesses listed by the conflicting parties. Defendants were informed of the pending divorce by a printed notice in a local newspaper that ran weekly for up to two months as well as by a hand-delivered subpoena whenever possible. The notifying officer also summoned witnesses by publishing in a local newspaper the place, date, and time when depositions would be heard as well as personally serving notice, if possible, on the des-

ignated witnesses. Neither defendants nor witnesses, unlike the plaintiff, answered interrogations or presented depositions under oath (unless of course the
defendant in the case countersued), and witnesses typically answered lawyer
interrogations in depositions given either at the Adams County courthouse in
Natchez or else in some designated place, such as the county sheriff's office, a
centrally located country store or inn, a lawyer's office, or a private residence.
Both parties to the divorce could attend the deposition meetings along with
counsel and cross-examine and interrogate witnesses. Courts typically deposed
female witnesses in their residences if convenient, in a lawyer's office, or at the
homes of female acquaintances and relatives; female participants could avoid
appearing in court unless specifically requested by the defendant or plaintiff
for reasons deemed essential to the case. A justice of the peace, for example,
notified John Mitchell of his intention to depose various witnesses in a typical
notice printed in the *Mississippi Free Trader* on July 27, 1842, which ran every
week for two months: "To Mr. John Mitchell: I will attend at the residence
of Mrs. Mary Mahan, in Natchez, on August 20, to take depositions of Mrs.
Mahan, Mrs. Ann Lambert, and John O'Ferrell—and you may attend if you
think proper."[12]

The hearing officer or commissioner recorded in writing the oral depositions
and responses to lawyer interrogations for submission to the presiding judge
as a matter of public record. Both parties could appeal a lower court's decision
to the Mississippi Superior Court of Chancery and then to the Mississippi
Supreme Court, which (as noted earlier) became the Mississippi High Court
of Errors and Appeals after 1833. The appellant court typically consulted the
written witness depositions, the lower court's written decision, and lawyers
representing the opposing parties, without recalling witnesses unless circumstances required it. Of the Natchez and Adams County divorces surveyed in
this study, only three advanced to the High Court, all of which involved alimony and marital property issues.[13]

Violence and Extreme Cruelty

Violence against wives by their husbands figured in more than 60 percent of
the Natchez-area divorces surveyed for the period from 1798 to 1860. According
to their divorcing wives, husbands attacked them with fists, canes, chains, cow-
hide whips, swords and knives, hatchets, dirks, pistols, and loaded firearms of
all sorts.[14] Husbands allegedly choked and strangled their wives, locked them
in rooms behind nailed-up doors, threw them from roofs and out windows,
and ripped the clothes from their bodies.[15] They allegedly chased their wives
through town and countryside, forcefully kidnapped their children, and threat-

ened to torture or to kill their wives if they did not submit, conform, or suffer disagreements in silence.[16] Some divorcing wives were beaten when they tried to interfere with husbands who molested and physically abused their children, complained too often and too loudly about a husband's adultery with enslaved women, or disrespected a husband's enslaved lovers.[17] Some husbands reportedly allowed their enslaved mistresses to dominate their households and even to physically harm their wives.[18]

It is important to note that abusive but less than extremely violent behavior toward wives by husbands did not meet the measure of extreme cruelty for chancery judges. In 1838, a Mississippi court ruled that in order to grant a divorce on the basis of extreme cruelty, actual bodily harm must have occurred: "Mere austerity of temper, petulance of manner, rudeness of intercourse, want of civil attention, and even occasional sallies of passion, if they do not threaten bodily harm, do not amount to that cruelty against which the law relieves." In 1856, another court ruled in similar fashion: "Mere intemperance in the husband's habits, connected with harshness of manner, threats of violence, and indecency of conduct, is no cause for a divorce *a mensa et thoro*."[19]

The physical and often violent altercations documented in divorce complaints were not always one-sided attacks on women by their husbands. In some cases women gave as good as they got, although they almost always ended up on the losing side of the physical encounters. Fighting women allegedly struck their husbands in defense of themselves or their children or when their mere words fell on deaf ears. Some women allegedly tried to poison or shoot their husbands.[20] Divorcing women lashed out at husbands with their fists, hit them with rods and sticks, and hurled at them anything handy, such as furniture, iron weights and flatirons, pots and pans, pokers, glasses, pottery, jars, farming tools, and kitchen utensils. They sometimes enlisted family members and friends to beat up their husbands or to intervene in a couple's physical conflicts.[21] Defiant, aggressive, and fed-up wives resorted to violence when they caught their husbands with prostitutes or having sex with enslaved women. Husbands' idleness, dissipation, drunkenness, and gambling addictions also provoked physical conflict between married couples.[22] Some women allegedly hit and threw objects at their mates for no apparent reason, especially when intoxicated or when they themselves were caught in, or charged with, adultery. And some wives even took out their anger at their husbands on his children, as was the case with Jane Carson, who allegedly tried to burn her stepchild with scalding water.[23] In most cases, women physically attacked their husbands in retaliation for spousal abuse or in self-defense, as in the case of Laura McGill mentioned above, who may have been hurt in warding off her attacking husband.[24]

Looking again at the O'Conner divorce, it is difficult to know who was the more abusive and violent of the two, Margaret or Luke. Witnesses speaking on Margaret O'Conner's behalf pictured her to have been an incredibly hard-working, entrepreneurial woman who operated the Boatmen's Exchange boardinghouse in Under-the-Hill Natchez as well as another such establishment in New Orleans. She allegedly furnished her boardinghouses with the finest materials in accommodating transient but respectable males who typically lodged one or two nights with her as boarders. She purchased all the supplies for the houses, kept well-stocked bars, and negotiated with her merchant suppliers, including slave traders at the Forks-of-the-Road market, as an independent woman relatively unconstrained by her marital status. Luke allegedly stayed out of sight or assisted her only infrequently, when sober. Although a strong-willed woman and the equal of any man when it came to business, she purportedly avoided, according to her friends, vulgarities and immodest behavior.[25]

Luke and his witnesses, on the other hand, depicted his wife as a mean-spirited, foul-mouthed, and immoral shrew who raged against her husband in irrational fits of jealousy. Margaret allegedly attacked Luke, according to him and his witnesses, with an iron weight, broke mirrors in her boardinghouse bar in violent outbursts, and tried to shoot him and his alleged mistress (the slave girl Jane). Luke testified that he sometimes had summoned the night watch to control Margaret, and he physically restrained her more than once, he claimed, to keep her from brutally whipping if not killing the enslaved Jane. Luke's witnesses characterized Margaret as a woman of enormous physical strength who drank to excess and sometimes cavorted at night with men other than her husband in the public streets of Natchez. One witness asserted that if he had to choose whom to fight, he would prefer Luke over Margaret because of her incredible strength. Several claimed that Margaret's New Orleans boardinghouse rented rooms to whores who serviced rough-edged male lodgers. Luke comes across in their depositions as a hardworking and industrious husband who helped manage the Boatmen's Exchange and its riverfront wharf while tending bar in its boardinghouse tavern; he earned money to supplement the family income, it was claimed, by catching runaway slaves for the rewards offered by their owners, working on lumber boats, and serving as a paid night watchman for the town.[26]

Faced with such conflicting evidence, the court issued an injunction temporarily forbidding Luke from leaving the state with the couple's movable property and slaves. When he failed to post bond equal to the value of the disputed property, the court jailed him for a few days until his friends came up with the bail money and sureties to guarantee the court-imposed bond. In its final decree, the court granted Margaret her divorce, allocating one-third of the couple's assets to Margaret and two-thirds to Luke, favoring the male combatant for reasons that are not obvious. Margaret then left for New Orleans, reportedly with a traveling trunk filled with gold; Luke also disappears from the public record at about the same time. Although it is impossible to know who had told the truth in this case, it seems obvious that Margaret O'Conner had stood her ground in whatever physical conflict occurred between the two. No one easily pushed her around, and it is doubtful that anyone who knew her would think her a woman terrified or intimidated by her husband or any man.[27]

Abandonment

Among the wives surveyed who filed for divorce in Natchez and Adams County, 48 percent charged their husbands with desertion, a number remarkably greater than the 28 percent cited by historian Loren Schweninger in his study of divorce in the antebellum South.[28] Mississippi required divorcing spouses to prove that their legal mates had abandoned them for a period exceeding five years prior to 1840 or three years thereafter. Deserting men often, but not always, left their wives without leaving the immediate environs, and most deserting husbands refused to answer the charges against them, which the courts took as tantamount to a confession of guilt.[29] Sometimes husbands confessed to their desertion rather than bother to contest the allegations, especially if they were insolvent and unlikely to face court-imposed alimony.[30] In the few cases where husbands challenged the abandonment charges, money and slaves figured into the picture.

Male plaintiffs charged wives with abandonment in 51 percent of their complaints, and in almost every case, women who had abandoned their husbands allegedly ran away to parts unknown, often with their lovers, reflecting perhaps the frontier character of the Natchez community throughout the antebellum years. Only one wife answered her husband's accusation of abandonment, claiming that she had been driven involuntarily from her home.[31] Unlike male defendants, most deserting wives left with no assets or property in hand. For poor and penniless women trapped in an unhappy or debilitating marriage, fleeing probably seemed the only way out, especially if the deserting woman loved another man and could run away with him, had little property or assets, or had children to protect. In the cases examined for this study the court granted divorces almost routinely when evidence demonstrated that a deserting spouse voluntarily had left the family household and had been away for the requisite number of years.

It is not surprising that the defendant James Russell failed to answer the charges of abandonment filed against him by his wife, Mary. He had moved to Natchez from New York supposedly as a grieving widower, wooed the "young and inexperienced" Mary, and married her in 1847. Within the year, James allegedly began treating Mary with extreme cruelty and physical abuse. Reflecting on their marriage, Mary recalled that James had exhibited on the very day of their wedding "an indelicate anxiety to see and get hold of her property," which would come to her from her dead father's estate upon her mother's death. When James deserted Mary after his indictment for stealing cotton and took up with a woman in Texas, Mary discovered that she had married a fugitive from New York and Massachusetts charged with murdering his wife and raping his dead wife's twelve-year-old half sister. The court granted Mary separation from bed and board, custody of her child, and an injunction forbidding James access to her property, person, and child. The next year, once the three-year waiting period required for permanent divorce based on abandonment had passed, Mary filed a petition for permanent divorce, which the court granted, along with the reinstatement of her maiden name.[32]

The suit Lydia Flynn filed against her husband, Alexander, in 1850 for adultery and abandonment was somewhat typical in cases where no assets were involved. Arriving in Natchez with her husband in 1843 from Indiana, after having married him in 1827, Lydia Flynn spent the next seven years raising their six children largely on her own and dealing with her husband's allegedly adulterous ways. Although she neither saw nor heard from her husband in the four years prior to filing her divorce suit, she knew from friends that he survived by selling to steamboats wood that he cut in the Louisiana swamps across the Mississippi River from Natchez, where he continued to indulge in his adulterous affairs. Alone with her children, Lydia had managed over the years "to pay her rent and to labor industriously" in the care of her family. She produced two character witnesses who signed their names with an *X*, as did she, indicative of their class standing as illiterate, working people. Alexander Flynn, having no estate of his own and with no property held between the two, admitted his adultery and abandonment in a deposition taken in Louisiana by a Mississippi justice of the peace. His admission, which constituted evidence of guilt, enabled the court to grant a divorce outright without further investigation of his adultery and abandonment. Had he contested the divorce, the outcome might have been different.[33]

Adultery with Black and White Women

Nearly half the women seeking divorces in the antebellum Natchez and Adams County cases examined charged their husbands with adultery as the primary cause of their grief, although most included other issues as well, such as drunkenness, gambling, cruelty, and desertion. Husbands consorting with prostitutes and enslaved women dominated charges leveled at adulterous husbands by their wives (73 percent). For male plaintiffs, all but two accused their wives of infidelity, and they usually coupled the adultery allegation with abandonment.[34]

Natchez-area wives rarely accused their adulterous husbands of having carnal relations with neighbors, friends, relatives, or otherwise respectable white women, probably because such charges were difficult to prove or substantiate. Only 22 percent of Natchez-area wives accused adulterous husbands of having affairs with white women not identified as prostitutes or lewd women.[35] Such affairs with relatives and acquaintances may have been too embarrassing for wives to openly admit, or perhaps they were brief encounters rather than habitual sexual adventures. Wives and husbands, moreover, undoubtedly understood, or were advised by counsel, that adulterous affairs with respectable white women might win separation from bed and board but did not meet the standard required by judges to permanently dissolve a marriage beyond the hope of repair, especially if the husband vowed to mend his ways. The case of Sarah and John Dye did involve, however, a somewhat respectable white woman. Sarah Dye accused her husband of adultery with his white paramour Mary Black, a young woman whom he had brought into the house as an orphan. She claimed that her husband fathered a child with Mary and that he had forced her to make the bed in which he slept with Mary and to perform other menial services for the younger woman. John Dye denied all charges, but the court granted the divorce and gave Sarah one-third of her husband's estate as well as their residence.[36]

As discussed in chapter 1, Natchez literally overflowed with dance hall girls, black and white prostitutes, and "women of easy virtue" who serviced riverboat men, travelers from the Ohio River Valley coming to town via the Natchez Trace, and scores of migrants passing through on their way west, not to mention the city's resident male inhabitants.[37] In other words, while access to enslaved women was always easy and available to slaveholding husbands and overseers, prostitutes and "wanton women" may have been even more available in Natchez, and relations with them possibly involved less risk or less community disapprobation than having sex with slaves. Husbands living farther from Natchez, on the other hand, probably victimized or had affairs with enslaved women working on rural farms and plantations rather than with Natchez prostitutes, although some rural husbands raped their slaves and also cavorted with prostitutes in town whenever they had the opportunity.[38]

Divorcing wives identified enslaved black women in 43 percent of the adultery cases, and in many of these cases the female plaintiffs accused their husbands of having had carnal relations with free black and white prostitutes, wanton and lewd women, "or women of easy virtue."[39] Divorcing husbands, on the other hand, typically accused their wives of having affairs with neighbors, overseers and workers, acquaintances, former boyfriends and previous lovers, or diverse wicked men, and only occasionally with paying customers.[40] In only one case surveyed did a divorcing husband accuse his wife of having sex with a black man, the proof of which was a mixed-race child allegedly born to her while married to her accusing husband. The story of divorce in Natchez differs from the pattern found by historian Loren Schweninger in the larger South, where 68 percent of divorcing husbands charged their wives with having sex with black men.[41] Both divorcing wives and husbands knew that the more precise they could be in their charges, including specific dates, names, and places for the alleged adultery, the better were their chances for court approval. As a result, many divorcing women named the women with whom their husbands were consorting, identified the places and times of the observed sexual affairs, and offered detailed descriptions of how they had caught their husbands committing the alleged acts of fornication.[42]

The divorce complaint filed by Susannah Sessions against her husband, William, in 1839 for his alleged adultery and abandonment followed a common format. Married as a young woman in 1830, Susannah came to the union as a member of the wealthy, slaveholding Bisland and Rucker families.[43] After nine years of marriage and the birth of her infant son, Susannah charged William with desertion and with committing adultery while frequenting "at diverse times Houses of Ill fame and similar places of improper resort, in the companionship of women of lewd and infamous character." Susannah named one of the Natchez prostitutes (Elizabeth Lawrence) with whom her husband had committed adultery, which had been going on, she claimed, since the first day of their marriage, and she produced witnesses who testified to William's habitual and quite public fornication. She proclaimed in the deposition taken by a justice of the peace that William's actions had "completely and entirely destroyed the domestic peace and happiness" of her family and had "blasted" all possible hope she might have for any future happiness. William refused to answer the charges even though his wife's notice of divorce appeared in a local newspaper for several weeks, as required by law. Based on the evidence presented by her witnesses along with her husband's nonresponse, which the court considered tantamount (as in the Flynn divorce) to a confession of guilt, the court dissolved the couple's marriage on April 18, 1839.[44]

As a wealthy slaveholder, it is surprising that William Sessions had refused to answer the charges Susannah leveled at him for adultery and abandonment. Perhaps William wanted out of a marriage that brought him little happiness.

In August 1839, a special jury summoned by the Adams County Probate Court to evaluate Susannah's mental condition found her to be *non compos mentis*—a person not of a sound mind who had been "predisposed to insanity for several years" and was unable to care for herself. The probate judge, as a result of the jury findings, placed the $30,000 in land, slaves, and personal property bequeathed to Susannah from her father's estate in a trust administered by her mother and stepfather, and then by her brother, William Bisland, until her son, Peter, reached his maturity in 1858. Perhaps William Session's notorious and quite public whoring had so humiliated Susannah (and her family) as to drive her to insanity. Or perhaps he had turned to whores in response to her insanity. Nothing in the public or private records answers these questions, although everyone involved probably supported a divorce that brought Susannah and her infant child and inherited property back to the care and management of her maternal family. William's refusal to live with his wife for over three years, the evidence of his adultery, his silence about any claim to her inherited property as her husband, his lack of a request for custody of their child, and his refusal to respond to the charges against him may have been the easiest way out of the marriage for all concerned.

Alimony and Guardianship of Children

Plaintiffs could request alimony and the guardianship of any children born to the divorcing couple under territorial and state laws, but such requests depended on the solvency and assets of both parties as determined by the court. Complaining wives seldom if ever requested a specific alimony allotment; rather, they relied on the court's wisdom to uphold the husband's obligation (if he was financially able) to support his children and provide for his wife even after the dissolution of the marriage in ways that "shall seem equitable and just."[45] Among the Natchez-area divorces surveyed, courts specified alimony in 23 percent of the cases—a small number, principally due to a defendant's insolvency, the plaintiff's independent wealth, or a specific request to forego alimony by the complaining wife.

By the 1850s, chancery courts typically considered eight dollars per month as a reasonable temporary alimony allotment pending investigation of a defendant's assets; in those cases where the complaining wife held significant resources in a separate estate, the court usually denied spousal alimony, although child support normally was allowed.[46] In 1856, a judge decreed that in those cases where a divorce was granted on account of the husband's adultery, and when the plaintiff was deemed a woman of proper "demeanor and decorum" and the husband a solid businessman, with no legitimate children to support, an "allowance of one-third of his estate is proper." This one-third allocation to the divorcing wife appears to have been the governing rule of thumb when assets could be ascertained and no separate trusts or estates benefited the wife.[47] Chancery judges attempted to assess the ability of male spouses to pay alimony by ordering an investigation of assets, income, and actual as well as potential wealth. If no alimony was awarded, or if alimony was not included in the divorce appeal, wives could return to the issue in a separate suit but could not claim alimony on the basis of wealth acquired by a former husband after their divorce.[48] No provision for alimony for husbands was allowed under state law, although precedent generally supported divisions of assets that typically supported a husband's claim to income even as a losing defendant in divorce. But the issue of alimony was more complicated than simple questions about solvency and assets. Mississippi courts, for example, did not view alimony as a necessary or required part of a divorce decree. What is more, a divorcing wife deemed guilty of adultery who had charged her husband with offenses other than adultery was ineligible for alimony, no matter her husband's assets or income.[49]

When victorious females of means won custody of their children, as happened increasingly over the years, the court typically placed them in their mother's care but under the guardianship of a male trustee or trustees (often the mother's father, an older brother, or an uncle) authorized to oversee and protect the interests of the minors. In most cases, the court assumed that children, especially in families with few resources or with children under the age of two years, would remain with the mother unless the father countersued for custody, which happened in less than 3 percent of the cases reviewed. The state legislature clarified this issue in 1857 when it granted to chancery courts the power to annul in divorce cases the "paramount right of the father, as it exists in common law, to the custody of the children." Thereafter, courts viewed the "mere legal right of the father as at end" unless it could be shown that the mother was unfit or ill prepared to care for her children.[50] Even in common law, according to court interpretation, "proof of adultery, intemperance, gross vulgarity and obscenity in language and actions" were all deemed sufficient reasons to deprive a father of the custody of a female child three years of age and younger in favor of the mother.[51]

Child custody was never as easy as these dictums and decisions suggest, however, because of the complex circumstances surrounding many of the cases analyzed. Forty-four Natchez-area divorces among the 110 cases surveyed involved children, and courts often confronted the thorny issue of parental fitness when both parties questioned one another's morality and competence. Eliza Spenser, for example, sued her husband for divorce and asked the court to grant her custody of her daughter because of her husband's "disgusting and brutal conduct" toward the child. Anne Marie Ventress told the court that her adulterous and violent husband had threatened to kidnap their daughter when she finished weaning her. Jane Carson's adulterous husband drove her from their house and placed her children with the "respectable" Mrs. Calhoun. When Calvin Bradley refused to let her children go to school and brutalized them to drive them from her house, the widow Lydia asked the court to grant her separation from bed and board and requested the appointment of a guardian to protect her children. And when Melinda Brice's husband tried to kill her child in one of his drunken rages, she fled to relatives and sued for divorce, alleging that her husband had committed adultery with the prostitute Sarah Ziegler. Obviously, in attempting to achieve justice for the complainants while protecting the allegedly abused and threatened children, chancery court judges often rendered Solomon-like decisions. In 90 percent of the cases surveyed involving children, the court awarded custody to the mother or else established guardianships for the children, although infrequently they split up the children between the two parents, with girls and infants going to the mother and sons beyond the age of six going to the father.[52]

Marital Property

Although the common law of coverture empowered a married woman's husband to possess his wife's personal and real property, including slaves, earnings, profits, and wages, as soon as their marriage vows were spoken, wives from well-off families did not always fall completely under the husband's control, at least in terms of property and material possessions. Prior to the passage of the Married Women's Property Law in 1839, married women in the Natchez area retained significant independence from their husbands by means of prenuptial contracts and separate estates supervised by a designated trustee responsible under bond to manage the assigned property in the interests of the wife. Prenuptial contracts, which usually dealt with the husband's agreement to honor his wife's inherited or acquired property, typically detailed which assets belonged to the wife and established instructions as to her rights regarding such property after marriage. A divorcing wife who had entered marriage with a separate estate in trust or a marriage contract could win the dissolution of her marriage with her assets intact, unless challenged by the husband, which then required a court investigation to determine the validity of any counterclaims. Surprisingly few of the divorcing women examined in this study evoked marriage contracts in their appeals or claimed that husbands had abused properties owned by them in their separate estates (15 percent). The small number reflects the class standing of the women seeking divorces in antebellum Natchez and Adams County, as less than 35 percent hailed from moderately wealthy to very wealthy families based on ownership of slaves and property. As with all other matters in a divorce appeal, final determination of how properties should be distributed rested with a male judge based on his interpretation of the facts as compiled by an investigating committee composed entirely of men.[53]

With passage of the Married Women's Property Law in 1839, married wives were able to control property they had inherited or acquired without resorting to a marriage contract or a separate estate in trust. The new law required registration of the specified property, usually with the husband's agreement, and empowered property-owning married women to act independently of their husbands insofar as how their registered property was managed. In the first few years after its passage, husbands retained their patriarchal authority to manage separate-estate property (especially enslaved chattel), and any profits or income realized from the property accrued to the husband under the common law of coverture. But modifications to the separate-estate property law during the 1840s and 1850s greatly weakened a husband's hold over his wife's inherited, earned, and gifted estates. Thereafter, married women with separate properties could sign contracts and deeds related to these assets, manage their holdings independently, and retain any profits earned from their separate estates.[54]

Did the Married Women's Property Law affect the rate or character of divorce in Natchez and Adams County? On the one hand, husbands theoretically had less reason after 1839 to stay married to women they did not love or whom they had married solely for control of their inherited property, and unhappily married women with some property could more easily walk away from their marriages with their property intact.[55] Based on the large sample of cases studied, women filed more divorce suits in the Natchez area during the twenty years between 1840 and 1860 (forty-two female plaintiffs) than took place during the forty years prior to the law's enactment (thirty-four female plaintiffs), while the number of male plaintiffs dropped off significantly (eleven compared to twenty-three). Natchez-area women obviously stepped more aggressively in their efforts to end unhappy marriages in the two decades prior to the Civil War, possibly because they felt more secure in their separate estates so as to initiate divorce suits that they might have feared undertaking prior to passage of the new law. But women with separate estates made up only a small share of those seeking divorces, suggesting that other factors came more heavily into play, such as the expanded grounds for divorce and the decrease in the period required for proving spousal abandonment from five to three years after 1840. The fact, moreover, that only six divorcing women held property and identifiable separate estates during the latter two decades (1840–60), compared to nine during the earlier four decades (1800–1840), suggests a weak correlation between the separate-estate law and divorce, at least in Adams County. For women of property, marriage contracts and separate estates in trust established by parents prior to the marriages of their daughters appear to have been as important as the separate-estate law in protecting the assets of married women in marriage and divorce.[56]

Decorum, Propriety, and the Servant Ideal

Women seeking divorce in antebellum Natchez and Adams County typically approached the court as chaste and devoted wives, pure of heart and innocent of any wrongdoing; they typically approached judicial authorities as faithful handmaidens who had tried their best to obey their husbands, even in the worst of times. And often they presented themselves as romantically inclined women who had entered marriage hoping to be loved by honest, affectionate, and reliable husbands. Divorcing women sought a measure of equity and justice before the court after having tried (or so they claimed) every possible option to save their marriages, even at the risk of their lives, the safety of their children, and their own sanity. They artfully framed their sorrowful appeals in the language of their social commitment to the servant ideal, portraying themselves as dutiful and loving wives and nurturing mothers, faithfully devoted to the male heads of their households and expecting only the court's recognition for such unselfish actions. Through their words, divorcing women and their male attorneys hoped to convince judges and the larger public of their deference and subservient meekness and humility in dealing with tyrannical and unloving men whose actions violated the norms of an acceptable marriage. None, moreover, presented their appeals as women down on marriage or hateful of men.

Alzomuth Whitehead typified this pattern when she petitioned for divorce from her drunken and adulterous husband, saying that she had always "conducted herself with propriety, managed the household affairs with prudence and economy, and at all time treated her husband with kindness and forbearance." So too did Louisa Holmes, who told the court that she had always acted "towards him [husband William] as a faithful and affectionate wife until by his acts of extreme cruelty and brutal barbarity, in utter disregard of the solemnity of the marriage vow and of the kind treatment that should characterize the union of man and wife, she was compelled to leave home and seek refuge with a brother to preserve her life and person from further abuse and violence."[57]

Defending and complaining husbands, on the other hand, painted a far different picture of themselves and their wives. They professed almost always, at least when they answered charges, to have been honest, hardworking, and protective husbands and fathers, committed to their marriages and fully responsible for the well-being of their families. When the evidence of their own adultery and abuse seemed overwhelming, husbands typically blamed their wives for driving them to drink and gamble, seek sexual and emotional connection with other women, and resort to physical abuse in their frustration or in self-defense. In many cases, husbands portrayed their wives as immoral, hysterical, and coldhearted scolds who failed to fulfill the role of a loving, compliant, and obedient spouse. Except for those few husbands who failed to answer the charges brought against them, most contesting husbands, as plaintiffs and defendants, professed their willingness to reconcile in order to save their marriage.

By 1840, lawyers, plaintiffs, and witnesses knew exactly what they were expected to say in their statements before the courts. Women were always virtuous and faithful servants of their husbands and families; men were always sober, hardworking, loving, and protective husbands and fathers. We have no way of knowing to what extent such language and tone mattered to the courts, but it is likely that any deviation from the norm would affect a judge's search for justice and equity because of how closely everyone adhered to the ritual. The language of that legal ritual was codified and regularly revised in clerk's manuals across the nation as early as 1814.[58] When the facts were clearly established, as they were in almost all the cases reviewed, the language of divorce served principally to assure both of the contesting parties of their own self-worth and to influence public opinion. The unwritten, gendered demeanor expected of divorcing women greatly limited, however, the ability of divorcing wives to focus on the unadorned facts that had propelled them into the public scene. Resolute, confident, and independent women who were unhappy with their marriages, possibly because of their own defiant and even deviant character, did not fit the image society demanded, that of women committed to the servant ideal that underlay all aspects of their gendered, supposedly subservient position in nineteenth-century life.

Public Spectacle

Natchez divorces exposed the warring contestants to a penetrating public gaze that almost certainly revealed most aspects of their marital strife for the entire community to observe and judge. Notices announcing the taking of depositions and witness testimony appeared in newspapers for months at a time as required by state law, and each divorce required the participation of lawyers, best friends, friendly and hostile witnesses, clerks, and judges, all of whom lived together in a relatively small community of several thousand whites, free blacks, and the enslaved on the eve of the Civil War. In many cases, divorcing women were openly ridiculed as liars, tramps, and hysterical females by their defendant husbands, and male defendants and plaintiffs were similarly slandered in words that appeared in the public record and most certainly spilled over from the hearing rooms into the arena of public gossip. Although few of these cases involved open trials by juries, they might as well have taken place at the bluffs overlooking the river. It mattered not if the contesting parties hailed from wealthy families or were among the city's poorest citizens: when abused wives fled enraged husbands to find shelter with family and friends, when well-known prostitutes were identified as having carnal relations with adulterous husbands, and when accused mates vanished into the night rather than face the consequences of public ridicule, almost everyone in the community soon knew about the charges and the countercharges flung back and forth between the battling spouses, including the most intimate and salacious details. Names were disclosed, places of assignation were identified, and reputations were assassinated and demeaned as part of a public record that most divorcing partners carried with them for the remainder of their lives.

In the McGill divorce discussed earlier, the plaintiff, Laura McGill, faced the most intrusive and evasive probing of her public and private character. To counter her husband's portrait of her as a hysterical woman, Louisa's friends, relatives, neighbors, a family physician, and a former teacher at Oakley Academy, located a few miles north of Natchez in the small hamlet of Washington, offered rebuttal testimony affirming her emotional stability, the extent of her bruises, and their shock at her husband's brutality. Every aspect of Laura's physical and emotional character appeared in the written depositions and recorded cross-examinations by the defendant's counsel, including her physician's testimony about Laura's coughing spells, various uterine problems, and "a more than active menses flow." John McGill's supporting witnesses portrayed Laura McGill to be a woman of "cold and even tyrannical character." One witness reported that Laura had been "pressured" by her father to marry the middle-aged planter even though she had rejected his numerous proposals time and again. The witness further testified that Laura (in words spoken to him in confidence) had refused "to let John touch her" after becoming his legal wife, suggesting that the McGill marriage may have gone unconsummated. In further exposing her to the public eye, John McGill notified numerous town merchants that they should no longer honor her charges on his accounts, and he published a similar notice in a local newspaper. To make matters worse, rather than pay the court-ordered alimony, John settled her debts to several local merchants on accounts obligated to him. His actions generated Laura's appeal for remedy to the Mississippi High Court of Errors and Appeals (which she won) and the notoriety that followed from the appeal.[59]

The lives of two defiant, divorcing women profiled below (one from the town and one from the countryside) illuminate in some detail exactly how at least two Natchez women engaged the legal boundaries they faced in seeking divorces as well as the cultural and societal demands imposed on them when attempting to legally end their unhappy marriages. Both women navigated similar legal currents in their determination to regain their independence from husbands whom they despised. Although their stories cannot be said to exemplify the experience of every divorcing woman in the city during the several generations preceding the Civil War, they illustrate close up the options available to all divorcing women in a place and time that privileged marriage, motherhood, slavery, patriarchy, and the servant ideal for women.

Martha Tewkesbury

In 1835, Martha Newcomer, an illiterate widow living in Natchez with two adult children from her first marriage to Jacob Newcomer, married Timothy Tewkesbury, a local carpenter well-known in the construction trade; she gave birth within a year to their baby daughter. She filed for divorce in 1837, accusing her husband of adultery and the theft (and intended theft) of her property. Timothy vehemently denied Martha's allegations and accused her in turn of infidelity, if not prostitution.[60]

Between the time of Martha's first husband's death and her divorce suit, the Adams County Probate Court divided her first husband's estate among his heirs, giving two slaves to Martha and two each to her children, along with property located Under-the-Hill; the court also appointed Martha administrator of the Newcomer estate and guardian of her two children. During and prior to her first marriage, Martha had purchased a town lot in Above-the-Hill Natchez on Commerce and High Streets on which she constructed two houses and a paint shop, sold a valuable piece of Under-the-Hill property to the wealthy Natchez lumberman Andrew Brown, kept an Under-the-Hill boardinghouse where she sometimes lived, earned monies from sewing and doing needlework, and supervised six enslaved workers (four women and two men) as administrator of her first husband's estate in the interest of her daughter and son. Her daughter, Sarah, married a local painter who rented one of Martha's houses, and Martha's new son-in-law took possession of his wife's two inherited slaves from her dead father's estate as property due him under the law upon their marriage. Martha's young adult son lived in Martha's other Above-the-Hill house when not staying in her waterfront boardinghouse.[61]

In her petition for divorce, Martha charged her second husband, Timothy, with having committed adultery with a local black woman and several notorious white prostitutes as well as with a black woman in Vicksburg whom he had "taken up her skirts" one dark night. She further alleged that to settle his gambling debts her husband had sold, without her permission, a slave belonging to the Newcomer estate; she also declared that Timothy was planning to sell or else take out of state the remainder of her personal property and enslaved chattel under his "pretended" authority as her husband. She complained that Timothy had misled her into thinking he was a Christian man of sobriety and much industry only to find him a drunken, idle, and "worthless, trifling man inattentive alike to the comforts of his family, and his own respectability and character, of which he was wholly lacking in both." She further accused him of infecting her with venereal disease one month after their wedding, which he allegedly had contracted from numerous prostitutes, a condition that she allegedly had concealed in shame from her most intimate female friends and acquaintances. Martha asked the court to grant her a permanent divorce, alimony, the return of the slave Timothy had sold, and a restraining order to prevent her husband from possessing any more of her contested property.

Timothy replied by accusing Martha of (1) coming to the marriage already infected with venereal disease, with which she had then infected him; (2) committing adultery in the bedchambers of her boardinghouse and in the house they shared Above-the-Hill; (3) renting rooms to prostitutes; and (4) lying to the court about his alleged theft of her separate property and the mismanagement of their shared properties. Timothy further besmirched Martha's character by claiming that she had committed adultery while married to her first husband and that she had planned to sue Newcomer for divorce prior to his death on the same grounds that she was now using to defame him. In response to his wife's charges of indolence and lack of industry, Timothy claimed to have built the two houses on Martha's lot in Above-the-Hill Natchez, paying for most of the expenses himself and doing most of the actual labor. He admitted selling the slave girl Sally to a local slave trader, but he claimed that she fell under his legal authority as Martha's husband once the probate court awarded the slave to Martha in settlement of the Newcomer estate. But Timothy denied ever plotting to sell slaves or property controlled by Martha as administrator of her first husband's estate, gambling to excess, or leading a life of drunken dissipation or immoral habits.

The Adams County Circuit Court ordered Timothy to post bond as security and imposed an injunction restraining him from removing beyond state boundaries any contested property and from entering the two houses in Above-the-Hill Natchez. When he failed to meet bond, the court imprisoned Timothy in the Adams County jail in Natchez. The court also required the buyers of the enslaved Sally to deliver her to the sheriff or else post a bond as security payable to Martha pending the divorce's outcome. After considering the evidence presented in various depositions from witnesses, the court freed Timothy from jail, rescinded the injunction against him, denied Martha's divorce plea, and ordered her to pay all court costs incurred in the case. Martha immediately filed an appeal with the Mississippi High Court of Errors and Appeals, which, after considering the evidence and the lower court's reasoning, found for Martha, permanently dissolved the marriage, and ordered all contested property returned to her.[62]

The lower court's ruling rested on the judge's interpretation that no divorce could be granted under state law when the plaintiff and defendant were both guilty of adultery. It deemed credible, moreover, the medical opinion of Timothy's doctor, who had found no evidence of syphilis, gonorrhea, clap, or pox when he had treated him for yellow fever. The judge dismissed the testimony of Martha's personal physician as opinion rather than fact, judging that the doctor's deposition supported Timothy's claim that both he and Martha were infected with secondary syphilis rather than primary syphilis during their marriage, which meant that the infections had most likely occurred prior to their marriage. It also discounted most of the evidence presented by witnesses as unsupported and less-than-impartial hearsay except for the words of one of the city's most respected citizens, Andrew Brown, a lumber merchant and slaveholder, who testified that Martha was known to be a less than virtuous woman. The lower court stood silent on the marital property issue, but it accepted Timothy's common-law right of coverture as Martha's legal husband to sell the slave Sally.

The High Court of Errors and Appeals took several months to reach its decision, eventually overturning the lower court's ruling and granting Martha's divorce petition in December 1839. The higher court apparently accepted those depositions supporting Timothy's adultery, gambling, and drunkenness as well as Martha's claim that her husband possessed no legal right to dispose of her slave prior to the court's division of the Newcomer estate. Had the Newcomer property been set up in trust for Martha and her children, the property issue would not have arisen. Perhaps the High Court acted cognizant of the recent debate in the state legislature about the Married Women's Property Law, which allowed married women for the first time to own property in their names and under their own authority. This law, passed in 1839, was already on the books when the High Court ruled in Martha's favor, although the court made no mention of this in its ruling, possibly because a defendant's mismanagement of a plaintiff's properties was not grounds for divorce. Nor did the High Court consider alimony, probably because of Timothy's insolvency; it explained, moreover, that guardianship of the couple's child would be left to the "future disposition of the law" because neither party had presented the question in their divorce appeals.

The Tewkesbury divorce established a precedent that helped solidify later divorce decisions favoring female plaintiffs. With the higher court's rejection of the contention that no divorce could be granted when both parties were tainted by immoral behavior, the ability of male defenders to castigate a woman's character as a defense against evidence of their own adultery was greatly weakened if not eliminated. Although it is likely that Martha Tewkesbury stood somewhat condemned as a less than virtuous woman, her husband's adultery seemed firmly established and of paramount importance. In this case, a remarkably combative woman threw every resource she had into battling her second husband for her property rights and independence, and she eventually prevailed.

Lydia Jane Ireson Phipps

Lydia Jane Ireson filed suit to divorce her husband, Lansford, on December 13, 1853, in the Chancery Court of the Southern District meeting in Natchez, but it would take more than four years for the court's verdict to be rendered, on May 18, 1857, and then another two years before the High Court of Errors and Appeals affirmed the lower court's divorce decree (favoring Lydia), which had been appealed to the higher court by her husband. Several years after Lydia first filed for divorce, she amended her original complaint, which alleged extreme cruelty by her husband as well as the mismanagement of her separate properties; her amended suit charged Lansford with committing adultery with various enslaved women, some of whom she owned. She also sought a separate court order to prevent her husband from any further management of, and all access to, her lands, personal property, and slaves, and she requested that the court appoint a receiver to handle her affairs until the outcome of the divorce appeal was settled. The Adams County Circuit Court appointed Owen Metcalf, a respected member of a wealthy plantation family, as receiver of Lydia's estate. Metcalf thereafter assumed full but temporary control of Lydia's plantations, crops, slaves, and other assets inherited from her parents; he also charged her husband with having committed fraud against Lydia.[63]

The Ireson marriage had been a rocky one from the start, and it was one that Lydia's father, Matthew Lassley, had not supported. The seventeen-year-old Lydia had run away with the twenty-one-year-old Lansford, who worked as

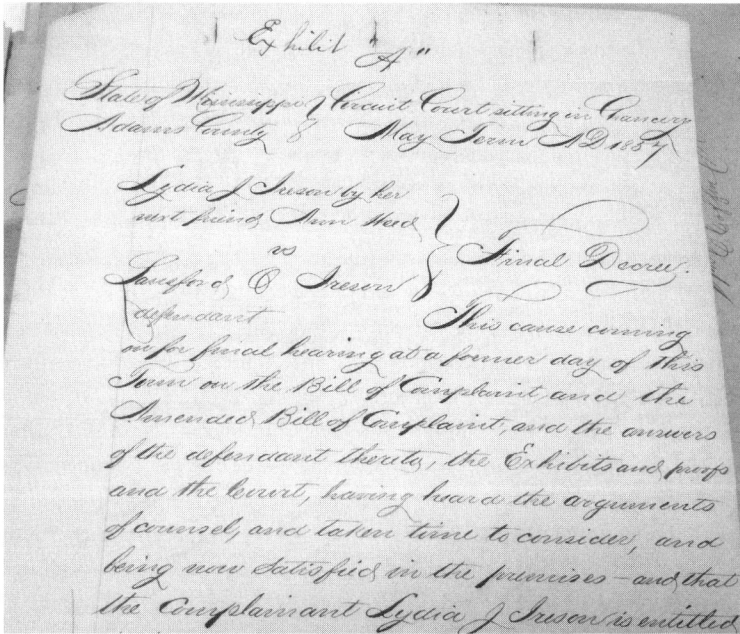

Final Divorce Decree, Adams County Circuit Court Sitting in Chancery, Adams County, Mississippi, *Lydia J. Ireson by her next friend . . . , v. Lansford O. Ireson*, May term, 1857. Adams County, Office of Records, Natchez, Mississippi.

the overseer on one of her father's plantations in the Kingston area south of Natchez, married him in Louisiana in 1846, and then returned to her home neighborhood, possibly to make amends with her parents. Her father reportedly never again spoke to his son-in-law, although he reconciled with his daughter and often welcomed her to his "Home Place" plantation prior to his death in 1853. Lansford worked after his marriage as an overseer for Lydia's uncle, Robert Lassley, who owned a nearby plantation on the Homochitto River in southern Adams County. Lydia and Lansford had at least four children, three boys and a girl, but only two of the boys (James, b. 1846, and Lansford Jr., b. 1849) survived to adulthood.[64]

The Ireson divorce played out as something of a family imbroglio involving cousins, siblings, uncles and aunts, parents, grandparents, and an array of friends connected to Lydia and Lansford by marriage, acquaintance, and blood. Lydia's mother, Euphemia, was the great-granddaughter of Richard Swayze, who along with his brother Samuel had acquired nearly twenty thousand acres of land south of Natchez in 1772 for less than twenty cents an acre on the condition that he sponsor and recruit settlers from New Jersey to inhabit the land. The two Swayze brothers brought to Mississippi their New Jersey families and friends to establish what became known as the Jersey Settlement, and after a few years of hard times the pioneers became prosperous planters and slaveholders. Lydia's husband was also her second cousin descended from her great-great-granduncle Samuel Swayze, as was Lydia's sister-in-law, Frances Swayze, who had married Lydia's older brother, James G. Lassley; the four had known each other all their lives.[65]

Neither public nor private records reveal the nature of the disagreement between Lassley and his son-in-law, whether personal or financial. It is likely, however, that it had something to do with the senior Lassley's properties and Lansford's character, given Lydia's accusations about her husband's mismanagement of her assets and his flagrant immorality. The senior Lassley owned, at his death in 1853, at least three plantations and eighty slaves in the Jersey Settlement neighborhood and several town lots and houses in Natchez, located near present-day Union and State Streets.

After his death, Mathew Lassley's widow, Euphemia, received the family's residential plantation, Home Place, along with twenty-six slaves as her dower in a life estate. Lydia and her brother inherited the remaining land, slaves, and livestock, valued at approximately $11,532. The siblings signed over their interest in Home Place to their mother along with a smaller tract of land nearby, all of which they would inherit upon their mother's death (which would come later that year, in August). Shortly after their father's death, James purchased his mother's and Lydia's claim to a twelve-hundred-acre plantation in Wilkinson County, south of Natchez, and a three-hundred-acre plantation in the Percy Creek neighborhood of the Jersey Settlement. Lydia also gained, perhaps as part of the swap with her brother, several Natchez lots and houses, which she quickly sold for around $2,300. Their mother's estate was eventually divided between the two siblings as well, with each sibling deeded one of the two tracts of land. Lydia received the Home Place plantation and held her share separate from her husband, as was allowed by the Married Women's Property Law of 1839, as amended in 1847. It was this property, willed to her by her parents, that Lydia accused her husband of mismanaging when she sued for a divorce at the end of 1853 and that the court eventually returned to Lydia to use as a *feme sole*, leaving Lansford practically penniless in the wake of his triumphant wife.[66]

As with the Tewkesbury divorce and most divorces in the area, lawyers representing the plaintiff and defendant examined carefully and vigilantly the numerous witnesses called to offer depositions. Both parties relied on the observations of relatives, close friends, and neighbors, most of whom offered circumstantial evidence, speculations, and local gossip about Lydia and Lansford; witnesses addressed, nevertheless, the three central issues in the case: Lansford's alleged physical abuse, his adultery with enslaved women, and his mismanagement of properties claimed by Lydia in a separate estate inherited from her parents. In her original suit, Lydia asserted that she had taken refuge from her husband's physical abuse at her mother's Home Place plantation and then, after her mother's death, with her brother in nearby Wilkinson County. She claimed that after her mother's death her husband had refused to leave her house on the Home Place tract, which rightfully belonged to her and her brother. Witnesses affirmed that the couple had lived separately since 1854, although they also reported that, from around 1852 to 1853, prior to the death of Lydia's father, the couple had lived in apparent harmony at her uncle's plantation, where Lansford worked as an overseer; none of the witnesses could offer direct evidence that Lansford had ever beaten his wife.[67] A neighbor and the family physician testified, however, that they once had witnessed Lydia beating and scratching Lansford, apparently angry with him for whipping one of her enslaved women. They also testified that Lydia had told them that she intended to leave Lansford because he had beaten her and squandered her property.[68]

Regarding Lansford's alleged adultery with Lydia's enslaved women, Lydia asserted that he had had repeated carnal relations with the enslaved Lucy and Caroline, whom she owned, as well as other enslaved women on her uncle's plantation; had fathered a child by one of them; and had caught venereal disease from them, which he had passed on to her. Lydia's uncle, Robert Lassley, explained that while he had no personal knowledge of such affairs, he had heard the rumors and knew that Lansford was considered something of "a rake by the neighborhood." Lansford's fellow overseer James Livesay testified that he had seen Lansford numerous times in the slave quarters, visiting women at night for the obvious purpose of having carnal relations with them. Livesay testified that Lansford had justified his adultery because Lydia had stopped sleeping with him and that Lansford had told him that he "had to get what he could however he could"; Lansford, according to Livesay, boasted of having had sex with fifteen or twenty of Robert Lassley's enslaved women.[69] Although the circumstantial evidence seemed overwhelming, no witnesses had observed Lansford's alleged fornications, and no enslaved woman (or man) could testify legally against a white man under any circumstances.

On the matter of Lansford's mismanagement of Lydia's property and slaves, not even her witnesses could verify this allegation other than to note Lydia's frequent complaints about her husband's malfeasance. On the contrary, several neighbors and the family's personal physician—who was also a neighboring planter—as well as the overseer and a ginwright on the Home Place plantation claimed that Lansford had been a sober and able manager who handled his duties "very well" and "took good care of the slaves."[70] When the chancery court granted Lydia's divorce petition, it returned her properties and appointed a receiver, who later charged Lansford with having tried to defraud Lydia of her property, thus implying that more evidence of Lansford's mismanagement came to the court's attention than the sources now reveal.[71]

Lansford tried to defend himself by attacking Lydia's character and denying that he had committed adultery with her enslaved women or with any other "women of color." He blamed Lydia's cold and taciturn character for the problems in their marriage, alleged that she had denied him his conjugal rights for more than four years, and asserted his devotion to his children despite Lydia's efforts to drive him from their lives. He also claimed that he had never given her any reason to divorce him and that he was willing to resume their former marital state; he speculated that Lydia was motivated to seek a divorce by "a capricious and vengeful desire of change." Lansford Ireson produced a number of witnesses that supported his depiction of Lydia as a "rather taciturn lady" whom they had observed being "unkind" and acting "very vulgar and unbecoming in her language" toward her husband. But even his favorable witnesses admitted that Lansford was known for his "sprightly and jovial character," suggesting grounds for assuming that he was the type of fun-loving man who might have committed adultery.[72]

When the High Court of Errors and Appeals upheld the lower court's divorce ruling and returned all contested properties to Lydia, it essentially acknowledged Lansford's adultery. Lansford's management of Lydia's properties had far less impact on the court decision than his adultery, because grounds for divorce in Mississippi did not include a husband's incompetence or malfeasance. This issue could be addressed in separate pleas, which is what Lydia did in asking the court to place her properties in receivership for the time being.

Two years after her divorce from Lansford Ireson, Lydia, now a divorced woman with substantial properties under her control and the mother of two surviving sons, married Henry "Max" Phipps.[73] As in her first marriage, Lydia wed a man closely connected to her family. Henry's sister, Susan Phipps, had married Lydia's brother, James, in 1857, after the death of his first wife. Henry Phipps was the nephew of Routh Henry Phipps, a member of another pioneer family of the Jersey Settlement. Routh Henry Phipps had married Caroline Mahala Ireson, the older sister of Lansford Ireson, Lydia's former husband. To complicate further the entangled Phipps, Lassley, and Ireson family ties, Routh Henry Phipps and Caroline Mahala (Ireson) Phipps's child, Lena Imogene Phipps, eventually married her second cousin Henry "Max" Phipps after his divorce from Lydia Jane Lassley Ireson Phipps.[74]

Lydia's second marriage was fraught with problems from the beginning, including mounting debts incurred in operating her inherited plantations, unpaid lawyer fees, and her tumultuous character. She filed for divorce in 1862, claiming that Henry had deserted her shortly after their marriage. Witnesses supported Lydia's claims and Henry responded with his confession, swearing that he had willfully abandoned Lydia and would never live with her again. Because the Civil War overtook Natchez within months of Lydia's suit for divorce, the Adams County Chancery Court did not render its verdict until 1867, when it granted Lydia's appeal and ordered Henry to pay all costs associated with the case.[75]

Conclusion

The divorcing women of antebellum Natchez reflected in their lives the full spectrum of Natchez and Adams County society. Individually and as a group, most were combative females, sometimes fully willing and sometimes forced reluctantly to do battle in the open marketplace of courts and public opinion in ways seldom experienced by most of their widowed and spinster contemporaries. They shared in common their participation in unhappy marriages as well as their willingness to publicly break the marriage contracts that had constrained them. Most sought divorces armed with enough support and resources to go toe-to-toe with their husbands in a male-dominated judicial surrounding not usually receptive to women. They brought to court family, friends, money, and sometimes the properties they had earned, inherited, or somehow acquired, and often these divorcing women exhibited confrontational personalities, which they tried to mask as best they could. Those Natchez women entrapped in abusive or unhappy marriages who lacked ample resources tended to remain married or else ran away, sometimes leaving with their children or lovers, never to be heard from again.

A common set of issues dominated the divorce appeals lodged by female plaintiffs in the Natchez area: extreme physical battery, adultery with enslaved or lewd women, abandonment, habitual inebriation, and addiction to gambling. Female plaintiffs couched their appeals in language supportive of the servant ideal for married women, swearing that they had been devoted and dutiful wives who turned to the courts only as a last resort in search of equity and justice. In most cases, divorcing women demonstrated a willingness to engage their husbands in public battle within the structured but limited arena open to them legally and culturally. Although divorce was no easy task to undertake personally or financially, most divorcing women achieved a measure of vindication as litigating women willing to use a male-dominated legal system to improve their lives. While no more than a handful of Natchez-area divorces happened in any one decade during the sixty years prior to the Civil War, they happened often enough, and with enough notoriety and public spectacle, to make divorce an accepted and common feature of antebellum Natchez.

Divorcing women moved resolutely but carefully within a prevailing culture that afforded them increasing legal rights and protections as long as they abided by certain unwritten, gendered norms of acceptable conduct and behavior as women. Although they entered court as the property of their husbands under the common law of coverture, they understood that certain abuses by their husbands placed them on equal footing with their spouses insofar as they were able to demonstrate, on the one hand, their willing subordination to the men they had married and, on the other hand, the failure of their husbands to protect, sustain, and care for them as honorable men married to dutiful and well-meaning wives. As long as they approached the court pleading for equity (rather than equality to males) at the hands of a paternalistic judge, they stood a good chance, if the evidence supported their claims, to have their marriages dissolved. In most cases, the outcome of their divorce suits was determined by how they approached the courts and on what grounds, largely because Mississippi, even from the earliest times, viewed divorce as a realistic solution to specific marital problems, a view that its lawmakers carefully codified in law. It was this codification that women living in unhappy and loveless marriages used to engage their husbands in public battle over their presumed equity rights as married women. Although court records do not yield verdicts in all cases, almost all known verdicts went to the plaintiffs, suggesting that most cases came to court carefully written, with compelling evidence.

Mid-nineteenth-century feminists such as Elizabeth Cady Stanton well understood the inequality of women in divorce contests with husbands. Stanton noted, for example, in a communication to Wendell Phillips, a fellow abolitionist and advocate for female suffrage, that divorcing women, if found guilty, left the marriage penniless in most cases, losing dower rights and often their children. If victorious, they were burdened with court costs, lost their claims to dower, and faced patriarchal male judges who most often looked askance at woman seeking to dissolve their marriages. The historian Hendrik Hartog offers insight into the "unwritten law" that continued to favor males in mid-nineteenth-century America in the face of advancing legal rights for women in marriage. He shows how husbands who killed or assaulted the lovers of their adulterous wives often escaped conviction when defended in trials as men protecting their claim to women as property, much like a man might kill a home invader or thief caught stealing his horse or money. On the other hand, although Hartog does not explore this aspect of marriage, divorcing women also were governed by an "unwritten law" that demanded they approach the court as obedient and faithful wives who had conducted themselves in marriage as the assumed property of their husbands.[76]

Divorcing women risked, on balance, more than what their defendant husbands or those husbands who sued their wives for divorce risked. Unless they had established prenuptial contracts or had registered properties as separate estates, which they could do after 1839, divorcing women might leave their marriages with little claim to a husband's assets, including their dower rights as married women, unless the judge or legislature awarded them alimony and child support. And of course, exposing themselves publicly as defiant women ran counter to the image of the passively subordinate woman as an ideal, a compliant woman subservient to her husband as his unequal companion, housekeeper, and the self-sacrificing mother of his children. What is more, divorcing women faced scathing counterattacks by their husbands that demeaned their character and exposed them to public ridicule; divorcing women became public women, similar to prostitutes and common criminal women, by the very public act of lodging a divorce appeal or suit.

Martha Tewkesbury and Lydia Ireson were two such public women once they filed their divorce papers, and their experience was a common one in certain respects. Both women ended up despising their husbands, won their divorces based on witness testimony confirming spousal adultery, sought help from family and friends, and argued in defense of their separate properties in language that upheld the servant ideal and the notion that honorable husbands would not have treated them as they had been treated. Each woman introduced race and sex into the story, condemning their husbands for their open and humiliating fornication with enslaved women. Both claimed that they, as members of the weaker sex, had been brutalized by their husbands without cause and to an extreme that exceeded the right of a husband, as the head of his household, to cautiously and moderately discipline his wife, children, workers, and slaves.

Both women were subjected to scathing attacks upon their character in which they were alleged to have been less than virtuous or sensible women, driven by unreasonable jealousy and by what amounted to female hysteria. They were ridiculed as conniving women intent on using the legal system to destroy the family unit, a bedrock pillar that supported the larger community in which they lived. And their husbands commonly attacked the women verbally for daring to suggest that they had mismanaged family properties when in fact they had labored (in their opinions) to protect and preserve their shared homesteads and property as dutiful heads of their respective households. These husbands also tried to convince the courts that they had worked to preserve their marriages and were willing to do whatever was necessary to affirm the matrimonial bond as long as their wives were willing to cooperate with them as dutifully subordinate mates.

Most importantly, nothing in the divorce procedures, laws, or actions of any of the divorcing women surveyed threatened fundamentally the gendered norms of the day or slavery as the bedrock institution upon which the social order rested. Rather, divorcing women, no matter how defiant or litigious they were as women, actually upheld the servant ideal in the manner by which they sued for divorce; they also upheld the society's fundamental commitment to slaves as property that all free people, including free women, could benefit from as slaveholders, which many of them were. To divorce one's husband in antebellum Natchez was no easy task for any woman, but it happened often enough when certain rules were followed, rules that sustained rather than threatened the prevailing male-centered social order.

CHAPTER FOUR

Stepping Beyond Their Husbands' Graves

The Widows of Antebellum Natchez

In late September 1857, the widow Catherine Moore walked into St. Mary's Orphanage to remove her infant daughter, Louisa, from the Catholic nuns with whom she had placed the child nine months earlier. Sister Mary Thomas, the mother superior of seventeen Daughters of Charity nuns, who cared for seventy or eighty young girls in their orphanage and a school, refused Moore's request. According to her testimony before Judge Stanhope Posey of the Adams County Circuit Court, Catherine Moore had pleaded with the sister to return her child, only to be thrown into the street and threatened "with imprisonment and severe punishment should she ever return with like purpose again." Not to be denied her child without a fight, the widow Moore hired a local attorney and obtained a writ of habeas corpus, which forced Sister Mary Thomas to defend in court her reasons for detaining the child.[1]

Established in 1847, St. Mary's cared for indigent and orphaned girls principally of the Catholic faith and Irish heritage, operating somewhat in competition with the Natchez Protestant Orphanage, an older organization founded in 1817. Much of the city's private and public benevolence during the 1840s and 1850s flowed toward these two institutions. Both institutions took in children orphaned by yellow fever and riverboat accidents or abandoned by their parents, and both garnered the lion's share of charitable work and beneficence offered by the middle- and upper-class white women of Natchez. Their Christmas parties and fund-raising social occasions competed for the public's eye and generosity in spectacles that featured tableaus and performances by children living in the orphanages.

For the nearly indigent Catherine Moore to confront the venerable Sister Mary Thomas in a court of law was no easy undertaking.[2] Moore admitted giving her infant daughter to St. Mary's in a moment of desperation following her husband's death, but she claimed that the sisters understood that it would be a temporary arrangement until she could get back on her feet. An unidentified male friend had advised Moore to entrust her daughter to the good sisters while she raised funds, with his help, for her and the child to move back east to live with her family. When the trusted friend abandoned her, Moore had no choice but to leave her daughter at St. Mary's for a few months longer than originally planned. According to Moore, the sisters had promised to return her daughter once the determined widow could provide for the child and herself. To not deliver the child to her natural mother, now that Moore was better positioned and able to care for her daughter, violated, in Moore's opinion, "religion, humanity, and the law." Sister Mary Thomas saw things differently. From her perspective, the child came to the orphanage when Moore was hauled off to serve a six-month prison term in the state penitentiary. To return the child to a convicted felon of dubious character, Sister Mary Thomas almost certainly had reasoned, would seriously harm the child.[3]

Most Natchez residents undoubtedly knew that Catherine Moore was no ordinary widowed mother. She stood out as one of a handful of female criminals who regularly appeared in the city's criminal courts throughout the mid-1850s. She had been arrested numerous times for illegal trading with slaves, selling liquor to slaves without a license, and allowing slaves in her shop (probably a tavern or grocery) on Sunday, incurring fines ranging from $25 to $200 and sometimes spending a few days in the county jail when unable to pay them. Her latest brush with the law sent her to the state penitentiary for attempting to take a slave out of state, an unusually severe punishment for a woman; it is unclear if she had tried to free the enslaved person or steal him or her or if she had conspired with the slave's owner in a nefarious scheme of one sort or another.[4]

Catherine Moore, although owning no real property, earned her living as a petty merchant whose assorted customers, including slaves, often dabbled in criminal enterprises, which should have ostracized her from the Natchez community. Yet despite Catherine's reputation and criminal record, Judge Posey ordered Sister Mary Thomas to return Louisa Moore to her natural mother. For all Sister Mary Thomas's influence and respect, the Natchez court found that justice stood with a penniless criminal woman who did an illegal business with enslaved people and possibly had been their confidant and accomplice in crime. The records unfortunately do not reveal Judge Posey's reasoning, but there can be no doubt that he ruled in favor of a known criminal against a woman highly respected in the community, thereby rendering a judgment that deemed Moore neither a threat to her child nor, by implication, to the community in which both women lived.

Moore remained in Natchez until her death in 1868, and she never again was arrested or faced charges of criminal activities. Her interment in the Catholic burial grounds of the Natchez cemetery suggests that the two women who faced off against each other in a Natchez court most likely shared the same confessor and certainly the same communion table. Because she came before

TABLE 4. White widows (aged thirty and older), Natchez and Adams County, 1860

	Natchez	*Adams County*	*Total*
As female head of household	77	37	114
Living in female-headed household	18	4	22
Living in male-headed household	30	13	43
Total	125	54	179

Sources: Death and Marriage Records, HNF and ORAC; U.S. Census, Manuscript Population Schedules (1830–80), Adams County, Miss., NARA.

the court as a widow, Moore stood equal legally, despite her criminal record, to Sister Mary Thomas as a *feme sole* rather than a *feme covert*, or a married woman with limited legal rights. Perhaps Moore's motherhood and once married state gave her a modicum of leverage against a respected opponent who never had wed or birthed a child. Exactly what explains Moore's victory in court may never be known, but her story suggests that a seemingly aberrant woman may have been viewed by those around her as a woman not so aberrant after all.[5]

The White Widows of Antebellum Natchez

On the eve of the American Civil War, Catherine Moore lived among approximately 125 white widows aged thirty years or older in Natchez. Most lived in female-only households (95 in number), and 77 (62 percent) are listed in the manuscript census as heads of the households in which they lived. Another 54 resided outside Natchez in Adams County, of which 37 (69 percent) headed their households, making for a total of 179 white widows in the county and city (see table 4). Of these, 48 owned at least 2 enslaved people each (18 in Natchez and 30 in the county). In Natchez, the number of slaves owned ranged from 2 to 17, but in the county, widows held from 5 to 174 slaves and the majority (usually the surviving wives of slaveholding planters) owned 50 or more.[6]

Only a few widows listed occupations in the census, principally working as dressmakers, teachers, milliners, and boardinghouse keepers. The majority lived off their widow's dower or resources bequeathed to them from their dead husbands and parents, which sometimes were protected in prenuptial contracts and inheritances independent of their husbands. Some, especially the elderly, lived with their adult children or other relatives, while the younger ones tended to live on their own. When the Civil War erupted, Natchez widows generally were better off financially than most other single women aged thirty and older living in the city and Adams County.[7]

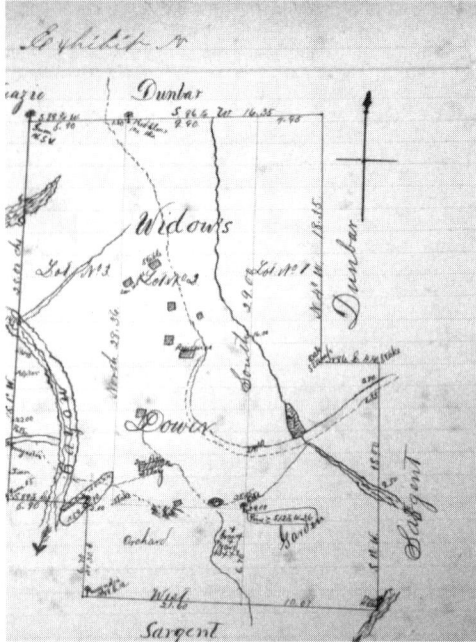

Widow's dower, Julia Nutt, Adams County, Mississippi. Estate of Haller Nutt, Probate Real Estate Record, book 3, 1873. Historic Natchez Foundation.

Natchez and Adams County widows also enjoyed, at least in theory, a certain level of societal respect that accompanied their wedding vows, as though their once married status allowed them to still be enveloped within the cloak of the good-and-faithful-servant ideal that privileged marriage over the single state for women. Motherhood, for those widows who had birthed or raised children, almost certainly enhanced their stature as dutiful servants of the marriage ideal in the eyes of most community members. Locals almost always addressed a Natchez widow as "Mrs." rather than "Miss," an indication that widows would remain "forever married" in public opinion, even though they were single women legally speaking.[8]

In addition to their continued fusion with a dead husband in language and in cultural images, many widows remained legally connected to their spouses by rights of dower and, in a few cases, as administrators of their husbands' estates. The widow's dower sheltered one-third of the dead husband's real and personal property from his creditors in a life estate to his surviving spouse. As a legal instrument, the widow's dower existed practically everywhere in the antebellum South to ensure that those widows whose husbands had died intestate, or who had excluded their wives from a legally created will, were not left completely destitute and thus a burden on the community. A widow could, however, relinquish her claim to dower in preference for a specific inheritance that she then would control solely as an independent woman legally defined as a *feme sole* upon her husband's death.[9]

In Mississippi, widows received a one-third share of the dead husband's real estate in a life bequest (meaning that the property would go to remaining heirs at her death); the right to live in the family domicile for one year or until the end of proceedings in probate; a year's supply of provisions; and personal paraphernalia, such as beds and clothing, suitable to her condition in life. A married woman's dower ostensibly protected her from the transfer or sale of property by a living husband without her express and written consent. Creditors could lay claims against a dead husband's estate that might be satisfied by sale or attachment of his personal property (including enslaved chattel) and real estate exclusive of the widow's dower. Creditors also could claim remaining dower assets after a widow's death and before they could be divided among her husband's heirs.[10]

Any free, white, adult female who was not married, a criminal, or insane could be named to administer estates, although a widow typically was required to post bonds unless her husband had provided the requisite bond as a part of his last will and testament, along with two good and sufficient sureties. Widowed executrixes were required, however, to post a bond equal to half the value of the administered estate unless explicitly exempted by a husband's written declaration. Executor/executrix duties and authority were all-embracing, including the power to settle debts, divide properties among heirs, and control the household's real and personal properties in settlement of the estate, which, if minor heirs were involved, entailed a legal process that could last for years. In intestate cases, the probate court judge decided who would administer the estate, and he could appoint a widow.

Among the 127 wills probated for males in Adams County during the 1850s, 19 identified a surviving wife as sole executrix. In these cases, husbands typically issued detailed instructions that left little or no independence for the surviving wife in handling the estate, whereas male executors generally enjoyed more leeway to settle issues and negotiate disputes. If a husband anticipated problems, he usually but not always named a male as administrator or coadministrator of his estate.[11] Twenty-seven Natchez and Adams County widows also filed wills during the 1850s, and nearly 50 percent deeded all or most of their properties to daughters rather than sons or sons-in-laws, but they appointed sons, male relatives, or sons-in-law as their executors in all cases but one. Few single women left wills (4 percent of total wills filed by women in the 1850s), most likely because they died relatively propertyless or had gifted assets to friends and relatives prior to their deaths. Of the eight who did leave wills, two bequeathed properties to male friends; another two named married couples as their heirs; one bequeathed her assets to a married female friend; and two women left estates to other women. In only one case did a single woman leave properties to a female friend, a woman also designated as the estate's sole executrix. Although two widows purposely excluded their daughters' husbands out of personal animosity toward them, they appear not to have been motivated by the desire to strike a blow for the independence of women as women.

Susan E. Conner, a prominent planter's widow whose husband died in 1852, named her spinster daughter, Louisa, as sole executrix but under the guardianship of Conner's brother-in-law, Dr. James Metcalf. Conner distributed the bulk of her monies and properties, including slaves, to Louisa, her two married daughters, and her deceased daughter's descendants. Two granddaughters, her brother, a sister, a cousin, assorted nephews and nieces, and two female friends also received small amounts of money, silver, and household furnishings. But Susan Conner made sure by the specific language she used in her will that most of her wealth would go to her not-married daughter and other women in the family and that the remainder of her estate would never be controlled by the men her daughters had married or their male heirs. The clause assigning estates to the offspring of her daughters read, "This provision is to guard against the heirs of my three sons-in-law becoming heirs to my property. They never assisted me, on the contrary they did all in their power to prevent my having any support from my noble husband's estate in Mississippi and Louisiana. Most especially, therefore, they should not have any of the results of my own gainings." Conner's anger with her sons-in-law stemmed from their alleged conspiratorial efforts to use their rights of coverture to claim, as the husbands of Susan's daughters, assets that Susan had inherited from her husband or had amassed on her own as a widow.[12]

Lavinia Ford took similar steps to isolate her assets from her son-in-law, William H. Thomas, by establishing a trust administered by her friend, George L. Guion, on behalf of her adopted daughter, Mary Thomas. The trust instructed Guion to hold and employ Ford's seven slaves and all of her household furniture, carriage, and horses for the benefit of her daughter, who would thereby, "notwithstanding her Coverture," enjoy their proceeds should she wish to sell them. Lavinia Ford explained her intent in creating this trust in no uncertain terms: "My object is to secure the income of said property to the said Mary [separate] from her husband." She further instructed in her will that all slaves and property remaining after her daughter's death should be given to the Methodist Episcopal Church. In other words, Ford established a life trust for her daughter with no possibility of any benefit ever accruing to Mary's husband.[13]

Susan Conner and Lavinia Ford were atypical in the lengths they went to to place their properties beyond the hands of specific male relatives. But any sense of sisterhood or female solidarity perceived or felt by these women did not extend to using their resources to undermine, consciously or unconsciously, the predominant view that men should manage affairs and control assets unless such an arrangement proved impractical or detrimental to the larger household, at least in the eyes of intervening judges or the wife's family. Natchez-area widows and men created separate estates in their wills for daughters and loved ones, as they had been doing since the 1820s, and most likely earlier, in order to perpetuate household independence and estate autonomy. The fact that husbands usually administered these separate estates suggests that convenience, concern for the perpetuity of estates, and parental desire to ensure their children's welfare drove inheritance decisions by both men and women testators to the exclusion of most other considerations. What is more, should a husband abuse his wife's separate estate, he could be held liable and subject to court review.

Historian Suzanne Lebsock's research on antebellum Petersburg, Virginia, indicates that white women in that city typically were kinder than men to their slaves and were more likely to manumit them in their wills. Petersburg women, married and not married, exerted thereby a subversive influence on slavery, not because they opposed slavery but because they related in a more personal way than men to the enslaved people, especially women, within their households.[14] The evidence for Natchez and Adams County is less conclusive in the case of widows and single women. Of the thirty-six wills filed by widows and single women during the 1850s, eighteen included slaves among the decedent's property. Only three of these women instructed executors to free the enslaved people they held and not one freed more than one or two personal servants, none of whom were females. Some women entrusted family servants and elderly enslaved women to relatives, usually daughters, whom they hoped would look after them in their old age and keep their families intact, but most slaveholding women treated even old family servants as mere chattel to be apportioned among their heirs, often dividing enslaved families in the process.

The widow Eliza C. Wood, for example, inherited thirty-nine enslaved people from her brother James Green, who instructed her to send them to Liberia after their manumission, but he left the timing and process up to her best judgment. Although the court probated Green's will in 1832, Eliza never manumitted any of his slaves. In her will, probated twenty years later, Wood explained that she had found only the enslaved Barnet deserving of emancipation; rather than freeing him, she deeded Barnet to her son-in-law, William G. Conner, with the stipulation that Conner pay her estate for Barnet's value should he decide to free

Barnet and his family. She left no instructions about keeping Barnet's family together and, as far as can be determined, he was never freed.[15]

Male testators tended to free slaves related to them as offspring or who had demonstrated their exceptional loyalty as "good and faithful servants." Widows and single women, on the other hand, usually freed slaves with few stipulations attached and did not identify blood ties or sexual connections between them and their chattel. Words, moreover, like "companion" and "dearly beloved" often appear in wills written by women, in contrast to terms like "faithful" and "trusted servants" typically used by males. These wordings possibly reflect differences in the character of the relationship between master and slave as well as the different ways, as suggested by Lebsock, that slaveholding men and women engaged life. Perhaps some female slaveholders viewed the manumission of enslaved women as a form of abandonment of female friends and companions who would best be served by remaining within a supportive and caring household; perhaps female slaveholders better understood, compared to men, what women faced living as free women without a supportive patriarchy to fall back upon; or perhaps none of that mattered. Slaveholding women may have refrained from manumitting their enslaved servants and workers simply because, after their deaths, they wanted their own families to enjoy the benefits provided by enslaved domestics subject to an owner's every beck and call.[16]

Although only a small percentage of widows drew up wills, they left more to their heirs, as a group, than married women or those women who had divorced or never married. For example, only two married women filed wills during the 1850s. A jingle published in a Natchez newspaper offered a satirical explanation for the discrepancy:

> Men dying, make their wills
> But wives Escape a work so sad;
> Why should they make what all their lives—
> The gentle dames have had?[17]

According to the jingle, few married women left wills because they were unaccustomed to taking care of themselves. There is more than a little truth to this explanation, but it fails to note the fundamental reason why married women left so few wills: the common law of coverture denied them the legal right to make a will while their husbands still lived unless they owned separate inherited estates, had acquired property in their own names, or held prenuptial marriage contracts. Widows, on the other hand, in being liberated from coverture, shared with single women the singular empowerment of being a *feme sole*, which meant that they could conduct their own affairs, including drafting wills, as though they had never married.

Legally, Natchez women who became widows exchanged (unwillingly in many cases) the protective but limiting status of the *feme covert* for that of the individualized *feme sole*, an exchange that enabled them to exercise all the legal rights of a male citizen except for suffrage, holding public office, jury duty, and serving in the militia. Widows could buy and sell property (including enslaved people) in their own names, sue and be sued in courts of law, and live as single women with no legal constraints on their actions based on their gender or marital state. The death of husbands freed married women to strike out on their own insofar as they were able, depending on their personalities and resources, even as their previous marital state continued to define them as women different from the married, divorced, and single women all around them.

The widows Mary Wattles and Felicite Gireaudeau shared much in common with the city's other free widows, and even with Catherine Moore, but their lives also differed from each other's and from those of other Natchez widows in remarkable ways. Their stories demonstrate the variety of life experiences open to Natchez widows, the boundaries within which they lived, and how they coped with life as ever-married women sans living husbands. It is to these similarities and differences that we now turn.

Mary A. Wattles

A sixty-year-old white widow, Mary A. Wattles may have struck some Natchez residents as a woman more witch than widow. She had all the earmarks of one: elderly, independent, combative, spiritual, and a consorter with uncommon companions. She lived, on the eve of the Civil War, with ten free people of color in a leased house in a notorious, mixed-race Above-the-Hill neighborhood that sat near the northern edge of the bluffs and was known for its whores and whoring customers. As the head of her household, Wattles shared living space with a fifty-year-old free-black woman (Eliza Smith). Also among the blacks living with Wattles were Smith's not-married spinster-aged daughter and two adult sons, a mixed-race teenage girl, and a young black woman who might have been married to Smith's oldest son. Four mixed-race children, probably Eliza Smith's grandchildren, also lived in the Wattles household. Everyone in the house lived as a free person, either born free or manumitted.[18] Mary had lived in Natchez since the early 1820s, having moved there from rural Mississippi to marry John Forsyth in 1825, and then as a widow following the death of her second husband, Alonzo Wattles, in 1843.[19]

When he died in 1829, Mary Wattles's first husband, John Forsyth, owned an Under-the-Hill wharf and substantial waterfront properties, two lots in the city's mercantile district, another eight elsewhere within the city or nearby, several dozen slaves, and a 150-acre farm (named Sheriff's Retreat). He lived with Mary and his children (none of which appeared to have been hers) on one of his lots outside the mercantile district. Forsyth served briefly as a county sheriff during the 1820s and operated a successful teamster business in connection with his wharf enterprise, blacksmith shop, wagon-making business, and a brick-making enterprise that handled orders for up to one million bricks at a time, among other ventures.[20] Mary inherited from Forsyth, as her widow's dower, one-third of her dead husband's waterfront, Above-the-Hill, and country properties in a life estate, which she held free of his creditors until her death, when the properties would pass to his children.[21] She brought these dower-based assets into her second marriage to Alonzo Wattles, the less-than-successful merchant she married in 1830 and with whom she lived until his death in 1843.[22]

After Alonzo Wattles's death, Mary maintained herself by leasing her dower properties on the waterfront and in uptown Natchez and selling her hold on a portion of her Under-the-Hill property in a temporary transfer of title to her life estate interest. Widows could sell their life estate claims to property they held in right of dower without selling perpetual rights to the property, which would have to be negotiated with the heirs of a dead husband at the time of a widow's death. Selling one's dower rights enabled the buyer to enjoy whatever profits might come from the property during a widow's lifetime.

In hanging on to her dower assets, Wattles faced stiff resistance from Dempsey P. Jackson, the husband of Forsyth's eldest daughter, Maria Jane, who wielded power of attorney over John Forsyth's affairs and served as one of the estate's two male administrators.[23] In that capacity, Jackson, a rough-talking, boisterously crude, and hard-drinking man destined to become a wealthy slave-holding planter and powerful state legislator, refused to pay numerous creditors' claims secured by Forsyth's properties or to finalize the Forsyth will in probate. His actions, which showed little affection or concern for his stepmother-in-law, pitted Mary Wattles against him in court battles to prevent him from selling her dower-based holdings and confiscating her rental income, a struggle in which she ultimately prevailed.

Over the years, Mary Wattles had signed away her dower's one-third claim to the rural Sheriff's Retreat, the Forsyth family's urban residence, and several Above-the-Hill properties in order to satisfy creditors or else obtain cash and loans to assist her second husband's mercantile business. Alonzo Wattles's shaky commercial ventures wiped out some of these dower-based assets pledged as collateral for loans, leaving Mary substantially in debt after Alonzo's death in 1843.[24] But after years of costly legal contests and numerous property transactions, Mary Wattles nevertheless had managed to retain her dower rights to the Forsyth wharf and its two adjacent stone houses, which secured for her an income of at least $300 per year in rents. This appears to have been enough for her to lease the house in which she lived with Eliza Smith and Smith's mixed-race offspring and their spouses and children.[25]

The exact nature of the relationship between Mary Wattles and Eliza Smith is unclear. Smith's twenty-year-old son carried the first name of Mary Wattles's second husband, Alonzo, perhaps for reasons of respect or blood (or both). Smith may have been the consort or wife or relative of a free man of color named George Smith, who lived next door to the Forsyth family during the 1820s, although there is no official record documenting this connection.[26] Perhaps Eliza Smith had worked as the enslaved nanny (or "Mammy") to the Forsyth children? Although no record of manumission exists for Eliza Smith or any member of her family, the Adams County Board of Police granted a petition to a woman named Eliza Smith in 1844 to remain in the state as a free person of color, along with her children, because of her "good moral character" and longtime residency.[27] It is unlikely that an enslaved Eliza Smith came to Mary Wattles as part of her dower inheritance because all Forsyth's personal property, including the enslaved people he had owned, was sold to satisfy his many creditors. In 1860, Eliza Smith's adult children each listed their occupation as servant, including the ten-year-old, suggesting that they may have worked in one of the city's mansions as hired staff while living with Wattles, possibly paying her rent for their quarters. Whatever their past connections, Mary Wattles and Eliza Smith shared a personal relationship manifested by their living together in what most likely was a close and cherished interdependence, perhaps both emotional and physical.

On her death from pneumonia in 1867, Mary Wattles bequeathed a $2,000 promissory note owed her to the four people whom she valued as "friends": the city's Catholic curate, Bishop William Elder; Sister Mary Thomas McSwiggan, the fifty-nine-year-old Catholic nun who headed St. Mary's orphanage; Eliza Smith, a free African-American woman and her longtime coresident; and Smith's not-married daughter Louisa. Each beneficiary would share equally in the interest and principal of the note's proceeds, which were owed to Wattles in payment for the recent sale of her dower rights to her waterfront holdings.[28] As the last remnant of her dower claim to Forsyth properties, Wattles's gift to the church and the mixed-race Smith women demonstrates what she had come to value in life, namely, her fictive mixed-race family and her membership in a spiritual community embodied by the Catholic Church. In view of this legacy gift to Smith and her daughter, there is little doubt but that the two women related to each other as close friends, two women afoot in the world without males in their lives as husbands. Whatever the actual circumstances, surely it was a relationship that bridged the racial differences envisioned by outsiders who saw them together on the city avenues and byways they traversed.

Little is known about Wattles's involvement with the Catholic Church, except to note that one of the Forsyth properties, which she held in dower, stood adjacent to properties later owned by the Catholic orphanage.[29] It is not far-fetched, however, to imagine Mary Wattles in church each Sunday, sitting in prayer (perhaps in segregated pews) with her black coresidents among the flock, partaking of liturgical services, and admiring with apparent pride the dozens of young children from the Catholic orphanages and school as they filed obediently into their designated pews. Nor is it difficult to envision her working closely with Sister Mary Thomas and Bishop William Elder as they struggled to minister to Natchez Catholics amid a sea of rising evangelical Protestantism that engulfed the town during the 1840s and 1850s.[30]

For widowed women like Mary Wattles, involvement with the Catholic Church associated them with a group of Catholic nuns who, like Wattles, lived out their lives in ways that were nonsubmissive to males as husbands while embracing the patriarchal but often less-controlling leadership (in comparison to husbands) of a male clergy. Mary Wattles most likely found fulfillment, community, and perhaps sisterhood with a group of religious women who faithfully served a father-like but unmarried clergyman, whom she also generally looked upon with devotion and respect—a man who, in most cases, intruded but little into her daily life while ministering to her spiritual needs. While we will never know the full extent, or even the character, of the personal and spiritual relationship between Wattles and her male confessor, or between her and the nun whom she called her friend, her acknowledgment of their friendship as symbolized by her willed legacy to them suggests that it was indeed a special one.

Wattles's final will also marked the empowerment and independence that the legal status of a not-married *feme sole*, in combination with a widow's dower, extended to those females who survived the death of a propertied husband, especially if they lived mindfully apart from white males in independent households. In a few words, her dower rights empowered Wattles to stand toe-to-toe with male heirs in court and to use her dower's income as she wished, free of male interference or companionship, while sustaining a mixed-race family with whom she shared her house. On the eve of the Civil War, Mary Wattles lived as a legally empowered individual able to function with full economic and legal authority regarding her own affairs, to litigate and challenge male mastery in matters of property and inheritance, and to head a household of her choosing even though she enjoyed no political rights to vote or formally participate in the body politic because of her gender. Perhaps most importantly, the character of her mixed-race household seems not to have defined her as an oddity among the women of Natchez. The Natchez community appears to have accepted her as a white woman who easily related to a black woman and her family as equals without challenging slavery as an institution or the male hierarchy it sustained. It was as though neither mattered much to Wattles in how she conducted her affairs; nor did anyone in Natchez seem terribly bothered that her mixed-race residency seemed immaterial to her or to how she maneuvered within a world rooted in slavery, whiteness, and the mastery of males over women, children, and the enslaved.

Felicite Gireaudeau

On a cold January day in 1862, Catholic parishioners and townspeople (possibly including Mary Wattles and the free-black Smith family) marched solemnly in a funeral procession from St. Mary's Cathedral to the Natchez cemetery on the northern outskirts of town. They walked in honor of the recently deceased but long-widowed Madame Felicite Gireaudeau, the "grandmother" of Natchez Catholicism, reportedly eighty years old at the time of her death. Referred to always as "Madame Gireaudeau" because of her French heritage, she was beloved in the community for her generosity and devotion to her church as well as for her refined stature and bearing. In the public memory of Catholic Natchez, Madame Gireaudeau embodied the servant ideal: a gracious and noble southern lady dedicated to serving her church and those less fortunate than herself.[31]

Ever since the 1820s, Madame Gireaudeau had worked tirelessly to sustain and support a parish that had suffered in its early years from want of a permanent clergy or a church building suitable for conducting mass and the various rites of Catholic worship. Gireaudeau's house on Rankin and State Streets, located in the middle of town near St. Mary's Cathedral and the town's original Catholic cemetery, had served in the city's formative years as a chapel and confessional. Pioneer Catholic priests lived there when visiting Natchez as a mission congregation. Among her other work on behalf of the church, Madame Gireaudeau had joined with the parish's most prominent Catholics, including some of the wealthiest slaveholders in the area, in raising funds to build St. Mary's Cathedral and support Catholic orphanages and schools. Over three score parishioners called her "godmother" in baptisms between the years 1836 and 1860, and she officially witnessed dozens of marriages, making no distinction based on the color or free or enslaved status of those baptized or married.[32] Her notes to Bishop William Henry Elder, which she penned as an old lady, became the basis for much of what was later known about the pioneer Catholic congregation in Natchez, which dates to the Spanish era.[33]

Felicite Gireaudeau had lived in Natchez as a widow since the death of her New Orleans–born goldsmith and merchant husband, Gabriel Gireaudeau, in 1827. The couple had married in New Orleans in 1817, signing a prenuptial contract in which they agreed to share equally their assets but no prior debts. The groom brought into the marriage few resources but for one enslaved man. She, on the other hand, owned nine enslaved people, consisting of a husband and wife and their four children as well as an eighteen-year-old woman and her two infants. Details about the exact location of Felicite's birth are murky; perhaps it took place during a sea passage from the West Indies to New Orleans or perhaps it occurred in Natchez around 1791. Her father, Leonard Pomet, a relatively prosperous merchant and planter driven out of Saint-Domingue in the Haitian Revolution, owned lands and slaves across the river from Natchez in Concordia Parish, Louisiana; he probably had gifted his daughter with the enslaved people she held as her dowry.[34]

The couple moved to Natchez after their marriage, where Gabriel worked hard to establish a mercantile and cotton factorage linked to a New Orleans commercial firm. In that endeavor, he bought and sold cotton, slaves, land, and animals; supplied groceries and agricultural tools and such to local farmers and planters; owned and operated a livery stable and tavern; and tried his hand at managing the Jefferson Hotel and boardinghouse. He, along with his brother, Antoine, and his father-in-law, Leonard Pomet, served as elected trustees of the town's Catholic parish throughout the 1820s.[35]

When malaria took her husband's life, Madame Gireaudeau was left as a thirty-six-year-old, childless widow with little prospect of continuing Gabriel's various mercantile ventures, most of which had failed or were failing. Named as the coexecutor in her husband's will along with Peter Lapice, a wealthy slaveholder, longtime friend of the family, and sometime business partner of her husband, the widow struggled to settle her husband's debts, which she appears to have accomplished by the mid-1830s. Because her husband left a will and named her as its coexecutrix, Madame Gireaudeau held no dower rights, which might otherwise have shielded some of her assets from her husband's creditors, although she legally could have forfeited her inheritance in favor of a claim to dower.[36]

Extant records do not reveal the full details of how the widow Gireaudeau persevered over the years, especially during the 1840s and 1850s, but she always maintained herself in a modest but relatively affluent style, owning the well-appointed house in which she lived with up to a dozen enslaved people at various times, principally young women and children. Probably she drew on family resources to sustain her household and its inhabitants. Her father, who moved to France in the 1830s, may have continued to provide her with funds, and her husband's brother, Antoine Gireaudeau, married to Felicite's younger sister, Delphine, lived in Natchez as a merchant well into the 1840s before relocating to New Orleans. He and her husband's coexecutor, Lapice, along with her paternal uncle, Joseph Pomet, were actively involved in various financial maneuvers that appear to have benefited the young widow, at least initially.[37] She also owned partial shares in her deceased mother's holdings in Louisiana, which had been protected in her marriage contract, some of which she eventually relinquished to her father in return for a small cash settlement. Her mother, Francoise Coco, had married Leonard Pomet in 1807, after bearing his children and having lived with him for years in a nonlegal relationship similar to concubinage.[38] However she had managed it, Madame Gireaudeau continued to live modestly but comfortably with a retinue of free-black women and enslaved servants in her Rankin Street house with no documented sign of economic deprivation or hardship.

There were, however, many facets to Felicite Gireaudeau's story, some of which she never revealed to anyone outside her immediate family and perhaps her priest confessor. Among the hundreds of baptisms listed in the church records over the years were those of fourteen enslaved women and children owned by Madame Gireaudeau; only one of these baptismal registrations indicates the name of a known male parent or spouse. Often, Gireaudeau and Pomet family members served as godparents to these enslaved and free household servants, who served in turn as co-godparents with whites related to Gireaudeau through marriage, blood, or friendship.[39] Time and time again (in church announcements and in open ceremonies of baptism) the old matriarch proudly proclaimed her commitment to the souls of her extended and racially mixed family. For her, perhaps being the "godmother" of Catholic Natchez was but a celebration of her faith in a public arena fully visible for all to see.

Perhaps more hidden from the public eye was her commitment to the temporal well-being of her enslaved entourage, many of whom she had manumitted over the years. Early in the 1830s, she sold the enslaved woman Nancy to a mixed-race, free-black man named George Smith, with the understanding that he then would allow Nancy's friends to purchase her freedom for $800. Nancy's new owner agreed to assist Nancy, who took the Gireaudeau family name as her own, in traveling to Ohio to be manumitted. Madame Gireaudeau had owned Nancy since before her marriage in 1817, and Nancy's two children grew from infancy into adult women in the Gireaudeau household. In 1833, Madame Gireaudeau sold another servant, Sally McFadden, to Nancy Gireaudeau, who now lived in her own household but still worked for her white benefactress.

Nancy, most likely following Gireaudeau's instructions, then carried the en-slaved Sally and Mary Jane, aged seventeen, along with Mary Jane's infant son, to Ohio, where the two women and child were manumitted. Gabriel Gireaudeau had purchased Mary Jane from Felicite's father in 1825, with the understanding that the young girl would be freed once she reached the age of eighteen. Sally and Mary Jane also returned to Natchez to live and work in the white Gireaudeau household as free women.[40]

It is doubtful that Gireaudeau's temporal and spiritual parenting went un-noticed by members of the city's Catholic community. Each baptism was duly recorded, and they always involved white witnesses; state statutes governed the manumission of enslaved chattel, and the process usually required complicated measures and the professional assistance of local and out-of-state lawyers.[41] Certainly everyone who knew the very public Madame Felicite Gireaudeau, especially the parish priests and church elders, understood that the free and enslaved, mixed-race and black women who most likely accompanied her to church each Sunday and for morning masses during the week were more than faithful servants within the Gireaudeau household.

Gireaudeau's manumission efforts during the 1830s were strikingly bold, especially for a widowed woman living without the protection of a husband, and they reflect the autonomy and empowerment of her *feme sole* status as well as the temper and culture of the time and place in which she lived. After 1822, manumissions in Mississippi were permitted only by special acts of the legisla-ture based on sworn evidence of good and exceptional service by the enslaved subjects. The difficulties of freeing slaves in Mississippi increased, moreover, after the Nat Turner rebellion in 1831, in which free blacks allegedly colluded with enslaved men and women to kill and overthrow white slaveholders in Virginia. The slave insurrection hysteria that broke out among whites living above Vicksburg, Mississippi, in 1835, moreover, greatly increased public anxiety throughout the state over the possibility of free blacks conspiring with the en-slaved to organize a Haitian-style uprising. In response, Mississippi legislators forbade free blacks from coming into the state and required all resident free people of color to leave the state unless they could be granted an exception to the law by petitioning local courts, posting bonds, and submitting signed endorsements from respected white citizens.[42]

In view of these legal obstacles, as well as mounting public opposition to the manumission of slaves, Gireaudeau moved carefully and adroitly in emanci-pating her remaining enslaved workers. She never freed them directly but sold them first to others who agreed to carry out her wishes. In all cases, moreover, she transferred title to the enslaved people she owned to free blacks in the community, rather than to whites. Perhaps she did this in order to distance herself from the manumitted people she freed so that she would be viewed as a respected white person and thus better able to endorse, as required by law, their good character when they returned to Natchez. But she also had another reason for wanting to avoid public scrutiny of her actions in liberating enslaved people. Madame Gireaudeau, along with her husband, mother, and his parents, had lived all their Natchez lives passing for white, and it was this secret that endured long after her death in the public memory of Catholic Natchez.[43] We will never know how many people in Natchez knew that this grand old matriarch was born the child of a mixed-race mother, but it is difficult to believe that her African heritage went undetected among her closest friends and certainly her enslaved and free-black servants, if not other segments of the city's white community.

Residents who had lived in the city for one or two generations certainly understood that New Orleans's vibrant Creole culture rested partly on the general acceptance of sexual intimacies between its white male residents and its enslaved and free-black women. They understood that Louisiana law and custom identified the offspring of these interracial couplings by such nuanced words as quadroon, octoroon, *pardo* (a light-skinned black), *moreno* (a dark-skinned black), *grifo* (offspring of a *pardo[a]* and a *morena[o]*), and *cuarteron* (offspring of a *pardo[a]* and a white). They knew, too, that these mixed-race sexual relationships in the multiethnic Crescent City gave rise to concubinage and *plaçage* (a long-standing sexual relationship based on consent between white males and enslaved or free-black women) as a deeply entrenched part of New Orleans society.[44]

It seems likely, therefore, that more than a few Natchez residents understood that at least some of those Creoles who had migrated from New Orleans to Natchez came with an African heritage mixed in with their French, Spanish, or Native American ancestry. Still, nothing in the city's public or private records, including church records, attests to Gireaudeau's mixed racial heritage or suggests that she was viewed as, or even rumored to be, a mixed-race Creole woman. Officially, she appears always to have been viewed as a white woman of French ancestry by city and church officials who kept public records. In her elderly years, and for the century after her death, local lore and church history celebrated her role as the community's most important lay woman in the formation of St. Mary's Parish, assuming if not asserting in doing so her whiteness as a European American.[45]

The truth about Madame Gireaudeau's passing for white emerged during the 1990s, when historian Charles E. Nolan, in researching the history of St. Mary's Church, discovered her marriage record in New Orleans. These documents, along with numerous others unearthed by Nolan, reveal that both she and her husband were of mixed-race heritage, stemming in her case from the African heritage of her mixed-race mother, Francoise Coco. The young Felicite Pomet most likely had been sent to New Orleans by her widowed father to marry a mixed-race but light-skinned Creole husband because of her own mixed-race heritage and the city's well-established acceptance of marriages and sexual relationships between whites and people of color, both enslaved and free. The marriage was mistakenly (or purposely) recorded in the white marriage registration book of the Catholic archdiocese of New Orleans but was changed sometime later to the registry for nonwhites when the cleric registrar discovered his error, thus attesting to the ease with which she and her husband had passed for white.[46] The couple then blended easily into the French mercantile families of Natchez because of their fair skin, undoubtedly superior airs, and the prominence of Felicite's white father and uncle, both of whom were prosperous merchants and landowners in Concordia Parish, across the Mississippi River from Natchez.

Had her secret racial identity been exposed, Gireaudeau, because of her elite Creole heritage, might have avoided expulsion from Mississippi by petitioning the local chancery court or the state legislature for permission to remain in the state, but she could not have been sure. And the mounting opposition to free blacks during the 1840s and 1850s would have left her fate uncertain. No person of known African heritage would have been allowed easily, if at all, to achieve the stature afforded her within the white community. Custom and law, depending on who was interpreting it, would have excluded her completely from Natchez society and from holding a position of power and influence in her white church. But with the secret of her African blood known to only a few close relatives and friends, and kept secret by all who knew or suspected it, Felicite Gireaudeau avoided the racial and caste stigma that separated whites from black and mixed-race people in antebellum Natchez. Her secret also enabled her to affect substantially the larger social order in which she lived, especially the Catholic community, in ways not possible for the majority of mixed-race, free women in antebellum Natchez.

Conclusion

These brief biographies of Wattles and Gireaudeau reveal a shared story that illuminates how some Natchez widows coped in a world rooted in a system of slavery that privileged white males, the perpetuation of the servant ideal, and the married state for white women. The widows Wattles and Gireaudeau participated fully, if guardedly, in the white and black communities of antebellum Natchez as sustaining supporters of an emerging Catholic Church, headed households that contained numerous black residents, lived as apparently childless and widowed members of the city's pioneer mercantile community, and shared for many long years in the bonds of widowhood and the legal status (and relative benefits) of not-married *feme sole* after the deaths of their husbands. The commonality of their lives probably outweighed the many differences stemming from their ethnic and racial lineages, especially because it is unlikely that Wattles knew that Madame Gireaudeau's fair complexion disguised her African heritage. It was, at least in part, these common traits that defined and empowered them as resolute though nonthreatening female participants in the male-dominated, slave-based social order in which they lived on the eve of the Civil War.

The support both women extended to the Catholic Church, and the support rendered to them by the church in return, happened in a social environment that valued and encouraged certain kinds of outside-the-home activities by married and not-married white women. Institutions ranging from the city's Protestant and Catholic orphanages to its churches, benevolent associations, free public school, and various private academies offered opportunities for the city's white women (both the prosperous and the less affluent) to work together as supporters of, and volunteers in, social endeavors that functioned largely independent of male involvement. The most notable of these was the Female Charitable Society, formed in 1816 by one hundred Protestant women to support and maintain a "Charity school for the city's poor orphans and widows."[47]

By 1860, the Natchez Orphan's Asylum, managed and controlled entirely by affluent women who were linked to some of the town's most eminent slaveholding families, oversaw one hundred or more orphans in a home-care system that placed orphaned children with local families to be cared for and taught a trade or else housed them in a large mansion where the children were nurtured, educated, and cared for over time. Because the Natchez orphanage offered asylum and religious instruction supported by the city's leading Protestant churches, Natchez Catholics may have feared (at least in part) that Catholic orphans would be evangelized and converted to the Protestant faith if they failed to provide a Catholic option for the city's orphaned and abandoned children. In 1847, the Catholic Church in Natchez established two gender-segregated asylums for Catholic orphans and poor and wayward children. Staffed by the Sisters of Charity, the Catholic orphanages offered opportunities for the town's white, Catholic women to work together in a feminized-benevolent culture that rivaled that of their Protestant counterparts but functioned under the direction of nuns and priests, as was the Catholic tradition.[48]

Female support for Natchez orphanages, schools, churches, and other benevolent societies contributed, in the words of historian Randy Sparks, "to the rise of a distinctive woman's culture nurtured through close friendships among women."[49] This culture allowed some white women, including the town's widows and spinsters, to find spiritual and personal involvement and perhaps fulfillment in activities that accepted the existing social order of slavery and male domination even as they avoided (whenever and wherever possible) the controlling involvement of men in their endeavors. In the case of the Catholic orphanages and schools, although under the ultimate control of male priests and bishops, female nuns essentially ran the establishments and worked with their lay female supporters in a community of women that functioned as a force unto itself. For the widows Gireaudeau and Wattles, association with religious and lay women almost certainly offered them companionship and emotional support as independent women. In addition, such associations offered them acceptable and nonintrusive (as well as presumably nonsexual) relationships with male authority figures such as the priests, whom they served and were in turn serviced by as their clergy.

The widows Wattles and Gireaudeau also shared in the unique character of their households, domiciles that they headed as *feme soles* and in which they lived with African American women and men who appear to have been much more than tenants or enslaved chattel. Because of Gireaudeau's early history of manumitting some of her enslaved women and children, as well as her role in caring for the spiritual health of the many enslaved and free blacks she embraced, it is tempting to assume that the enslaved women who lived with her in her later years were more than bonded property. The fact, however, that she never manumitted anyone after 1835 suggests caution.[50] Perhaps Gireaudeau failed to manumit any of her enslaved servants after 1835 because of the near impossibility of doing so without calling attention to herself as a free woman of color. Or perhaps she felt special affection for those women she manumitted during the 1830s because of possible family connections, an affection that never bonded her in the same way to the other enslaved women whom she later owned. The other possibility is that Madame Gireaudeau had freed the enslaved women during the 1830s in a rush, fearing that all chance of manumission might later be cut off due to growing public opposition to the presence of free blacks in the community. Nor do we know what verbal assurances she might have given to her enslaved servants prior to her death, nor how she actually treated them as their mistress and owner.[51] All we know is that she did not manumit any of the enslaved women she held as property during the last twenty-five years of her life.

Wattles's relationship with her black coresidents was no less complicated. It is likely that Wattles moved to the leased house where she lived with Eliza Smith and her family in 1860, in a less-than-respectable neighborhood near the bluff, as a cost-saving measure. After her marriage to Alonzo she appears to have lost to creditors the house where she had lived as her first husband's widow. The records do not reveal if Smith had lived with her then, nor do the two women appear to have been coresidents in 1850. Wattles and Smith seem to have lived apart and then together over the years for reasons that remain unclear. Recent scholarship dealing with the homoerotic relationships among not-married women in early modern Europe and the American South suggests that a sexual relationship between the two women cannot be ruled out.[52] What we do know is that their coresidency in 1860 reflected a bond of affection and shared regard that enabled both women to ignore social conventions and to stand firmly on their own as free and independent women, most likely unconcerned with their public image. Although it is impossible to know for sure, Wattles's friendship and association with the nuns and priests of her parish suggest that her coresidency with free blacks on a more-or-less equal footing appears not to have affected negatively her involvement with the city's Catholic community.

Wattles and Gireaudeau may have been linked together by yet another bond related to the black women in their lives. Felicite Gireaudeau freed the enslaved woman Nancy, who appears to have been her close companion and friend if not a blood relation, by selling her to a free-black man named George Smith, who then arranged to send Nancy to Ohio. This George Smith appears to have been the enslaved man freed by a white widow, Judith Kelleher, who had purchased him in 1826, shortly after her husband's death; Kelleher then had manumitted him in 1827 in Cincinnati, where she had relocated, as an act of defiance against a system of slavery that she "conscientiously opposed."[53] That George Smith may have been the George Smith who lived during the 1820s near the Forsyth property in Under-the-Hill Natchez, whom John Forsyth once referred to in correspondence as his neighbor.[54] In other words, there may have been a connection between the George Smith to whom Gireaudeau had sold the enslaved Nancy and the Eliza Smith who lived in the Wattles household in 1860. Or perhaps the connection between the three widows, Gireaudeau, Kelleher, and Wattles, the free-black George Smith, and the free and enslaved people in the Gireaudeau and Wattles households is but a coincidence of history.

Wattles and Gireaudeau also shared membership in the Natchez mercantile community within which their husbands had lived and labored. Although no record exists of their husbands having ever engaged in joint enterprise or business deals, their families had mutual business contacts. The wealthy slaveholder, planter, and merchant Peter Lapice, for example, who served as the coexecutor of Gabriel Gireaudeau's estate as well as his occasional business partner, provided financial backing for an aspect of John Forsyth's enterprise, loans secured by property that became one of the debts levied against Wattles's holdings during the 1830s.[55] Undoubtedly, too, the Forsyth/Wattles and Gireaudeau business activities functioned either in competition to each other or as parallel pursuits.[56] But by 1860 these business affairs were long-gone aspects of the two widows' lives and their husbands were long dead, as were many of the other men who had worked with or known them. Still, the memories of their common mercantile experiences, along with their shared identities as childless white widows living with black coresidents in Catholic households sans white males, certainly shaped, and perhaps determined, how the two widows coped with life as once married (or perhaps ever-married) women in the decades prior to the Civil War.

In the absence of letters, diaries, and other personal writings, more is unknown than known about the widows Wattles and Gireaudeau; nevertheless, based on a wealth of public records, the fabric of their lives seems clearly stitched. Looking first at the choices they made, the public record reveals them to have been women who chose, rather than being forced by circumstances, to live ultimately without white males in their lives. The record does not tell us if this was a decision rooted in desperation or in a quest for freedom. It seems likely that Madame Gireaudeau, a thirty-six-year-old woman with family connections and property when her husband died, could have taken a second husband. Although Wattles remarried after the death of her first husband, her decision not to wed a third time probably reflected the fewer options for marriage available due to her age and economic circumstances. That the widows Wattles and Gireaudeau chose to live without white men in their lives as husbands or resident authority figures appears to have caused them little economic stress, principally because of their inherited resources and a legal system that protected them as independent women. In Wattles's case, Natchez courts consistently upheld her dower rights in hard-fought conflicts with her son-in-law and stepchildren. Gireaudeau enjoyed similar advantages because of her inherited property and family resources, which she also controlled as a *feme sole*.

The most obvious difference between the widows Wattles and Gireaudeau and the other widows in their community, and perhaps all white women at the time, was in the racially mixed character of their households. Numerous other widows lived in households containing enslaved blacks, especially in the country, but Wattles and Gireaudeau coexisted with women of African heritage on what look to have been relatively equal terms. We simply don't know much, however, about the racial dynamics within their households or the intimacy that might have existed among these various women. The Smith family seems to have been an enterprising and self-sustaining group of free blacks. In the postwar era, the two Smith daughters worked as teachers, and the family's mixed-race matriarch acquired property not inherited from Wattles, suggesting that these free women of color may have been more than just cotenants in the Wattles household.[57] The enslaved and free women of color in the Gireaudeau household were also women of substance and determination, as exemplified by Nancy Gireaudeau, who owned property and assets at the time of her death in 1843, which she bequeathed to her three daughters. Although we can do little more than speculate about the relationships between the women in the Wattles and Gireaudeau households, it is clear that few if any other white Natchez widows lived in similar racially mixed domiciles on the eve of the Civil War.[58]

The widow Catherine Moore also should not be overlooked. Obviously, the criminal and impoverished Moore was a widow of a different sort than Wattles and Gireaudeau. But similar to Wattles and Gireaudeau, her *feme sole* status greatly empowered her as a woman living without a husband in her life. What is more, these three widows appear to have lived pretty much as they wished to live, and the larger community, although never fully endorsing their actions, appears to have been surprisingly tolerant of how they conducted their lives. All three stepped lively as women comfortable with the enslaved or free women of color with whom they lived and associated in business or in friendship, even to the point of embracing them on equal terms without directly challenging white male domination or slavery, although the verdict is still out on Moore. Certainly their actions challenged the racist assumptions that dictated in theory how whites and blacks were supposed to relate, but not to the point of subverting slavery or undermining the superiority of men over women. It was as though neither slavery nor the patriarchy mattered much to these widows in how they conducted their affairs, understanding as they did the limits and boundaries of what community standards, and the law, deemed acceptable behavior for not-married widows, even for those women, like Moore, who once had been arrested for stealing a slave.

CHAPTER FIVE

Stepping Lively in Place

The Free-Black, Not-Married Women of Antebellum Natchez

Margaret Dent, a light-skinned free woman of color living in Natchez in 1860, gave birth to her first child, a mixed-race son, in 1848, at the young age of sixteen. Over the years she bore four more mixed-race children and earned her living as a washerwoman. No apparent husband or other adult male lived with her when the census enumerator stopped by to tabulate the occupants of her residence, which she appears not to have owned.[1] But Margaret Dent was much more than a penniless washerwoman who fed and clothed her light-skinned children by doing the dirty laundry of the more fortunate. She also shared a personal relationship with a prosperous white planter and slaveholder, Allan Davis, who bequeathed to her four hundred acres of land and five enslaved people when he died suddenly in March 1861. He instructed the executors of his will to construct on the gifted land "comfortable houses for her and her servants and allow her full access to his cotton gin and mill," so that she could "supply her place with sufficient stock of all kinds." He wanted the gifted land to be carved from his fifteen-hundred-acre Magnolia plantation in Adams County, an allocation that amounted to almost 70 percent of its improved acreage.[2]

Although public records do not reveal much more information about Dent or her relationship to Davis, it is almost certain that he had fathered her children. It is unclear if she had once been his enslaved mistress and he had manumitted her, although he appears not to have had a white wife or children other than Dent's. A search of the manumission records turned up three manumitted women named Margaret, none with last names, all of whom were older than Dent would have been when they were freed during the 1830s.[3] Nor can the origins of her last name be ascertained for sure, although the surname Dent can be traced to the colonial days of the Natchez District. It is possible that she had had a relationship with someone named Dent at some time in her life, or perhaps Dent was her family name or that of a one-time owner; perhaps she had taken the name to protect her relationship with Davis. A free woman of color named Jane Dent (discussed briefly in chapter 7) lived with her husband in Washington, Mississippi, six miles east of Natchez, but there is nothing in the public record to confirm that Margaret was related to Jane by marriage or blood.[4] Nor do we know much about the enslaved people Davis deeded to Margaret, except their names and how they were related to each other: Lain Hark (or Fork), his wife, Caroline, and her mother, Betsey; and Miller Grover Hark and his wife, Violet. The two men possibly were brothers. Why these five were deeded to Dent is unknown. But this much is clear: the free-black washerwoman Margaret Dent had a special relationship with the white planter Allan Davis and he went to his death willing to let the world know about it.

The most fundamental unknown about Dent and Davis is the nature of their sexual relationship, if indeed Allan Davis fathered her children. Was it consensual? How did it happen? How did it play out over time? Whatever the facts, Dent's race, gender, and class position made it difficult for her or any free-black or enslaved woman to protest, resist, or challenge the sexual advances of white males if they demanded or offered sexual intimacy. No laws protected the enslaved against the sexual demands of the white men who held them in bondage; free women of color, although seemingly less vulnerable than the enslaved, desperately needed the support and goodwill of whites in order to survive in antebellum Natchez. In this reality, it makes little sense to speak of sexual relations between white men and black women as consensual, although some relationships certainly appear to have grown out of genuine affection between the involved parties.

For Margaret Dent, and most other free blacks in town, a white owner had to have manumitted her, or her parents or grandparents, in a carefully con-trolled legal process involving hefty bonds and testimonials confirming her, or their, good character. If freed after 1832, when state legislators strenuously began to limit manumissions, she probably was emancipated in Ohio or some other northern state, and her transportation expenses, legal fees, and court costs, as well as connections with appropriate people in Ohio or elsewhere, had to be covered, most likely by the slaveholder who manumitted her. Once freed, or even had she been born free, state and local ordinances demanded she file petitions to support her manumission and then be licensed to remain in the state, which required signed endorsements and the approval of white officials, especially during the anti-free-black purges that swept over the community with growing intensity throughout her antebellum life. Margaret Dent avoided enslavement, imprisonment, and forced removal from the state because local whites tolerated her freedom and supported her and her children, rendering her dependent on obliging whites.[5]

Although apparently a quiet and unobtrusive woman, Harriet Dowling, another free woman of color, faced the terrible prospect of being purged from the state or sold into slavery when two Natchez justices of the peace informed her in 1859 that she, as an unlicensed free woman of color, had to leave Mississippi, along with her children, within ten days. Rather than file a petition to remain, which required the endorsement of twenty prominent whites and a $5,000 bond, Dowling took her accusers to court, contending that not a drop of "Negro" blood flowed through her veins or the veins of her children.[6] Her somewhat dark complexion stemmed, she explained, from her Native American heritage, a common claim of Natchez residents suspected of African ancestry.[7] In her court suit, Dowling brought forth witnesses who testified that they always had known her to be a white woman and she always was treated as white by her white friends, neighbors, and spouses. After a quick jury trial, the widow Dowling walked from the courtroom as a white person, at least in the eyes of the court.[8]

Public records reveal, however, that Dowling had tricked the court or else the court had participated in a scheme that protected her alleged whiteness. According to these records, a white man named William Cullen had manumitted a nineteen-year-old "yellow girl" named Harriet Johnson and their mixed-race son in 1840. After her manumission, Harriet Johnson and William Cullen lived together as husband and wife, and she gave birth to three additional children prior to William's death. When William died, Harriet, who had taken Cullen's last name, inherited his house and a substantial sum of money. The widow Cullen then married another white man, Thomas Dowling, with whom she had two more children. Upon Dowling's death, Harriet became the executrix of her second husband's estate and is identified in the 1850 federal census as a white person, as are her six children.[9]

Obviously, the manumission records filed in the deed and mortgage books in the county courthouse, accessible and open to the public and certainly to lawyers and judges, were overlooked or ignored by court officials during the trial over Harriet's racial status. Had they been checked, Harriet Dowling's enslavement and manumission would easily have been verified, suggesting that some of Dowling's white contemporaries may have wanted her mixed racial origins and prior enslavement forgotten if not buried. The arresting justices of the peace had acted, most likely, at the behest of local residents who suspected or knew that Harriet Dowling and the former slave Harriet Johnson were the same person: a once enslaved woman who had lived thirty years among them while passing for white. Why the court ignored or refused to pursue the evidence is one of the many mysteries associated with the city's free-black community during the era of slavery. Perhaps the ruling came down on her side because Dowling's "whiteness" verdict safeguarded her family properties as well as the reputation of her dead husband and his white relatives. Or perhaps her favorable verdict expressed local opposition to the growing hysteria in the state against free blacks, which many Natchez slaveholders found personally repugnant because it threatened some of their own mixed-race children and many of the mixed-race people whom they deemed safe and valuable members of the community.[10]

In a well-known example, the enslaved Warner McCary, after escaping from Natchez, spent the rest of his life as a prominent entertainer and musician claiming that he was the son of a Native American woman and a white man and was falsely enslaved as a black child. In another notorious episode, the free-black Baylor Winn, who allegedly had murdered the free-black barber William Johnson, escaped conviction by convincing a jury in another county of his Native American heritage. The jury, by law, could not accept the testimony of the two black witnesses to the killing because blacks could not offer evidence against a white man, even one deemed to be part Native American.[11]

Unlike Dent or Dowling, the widow Ann (Battles) Johnson never hid in the shadows, attempted to pass for white, or faced expulsion from the state. She had been manumitted in 1826 as a young girl by her white owner (and probable father), the wealthy banker Gabriel Tichenor. He had sent her and her black mother, Harriet Battles (whom he had manumitted in Louisiana in 1822), twelve hundred miles up the Mississippi and Ohio Rivers to Cincinnati to be freed by petition to an Ohio court because it was a violation of Mississippi law during the 1820s to emancipate minors. Ann Battles then married the free-black William Johnson, who became a socially prominent and highly respected barber and small slaveholder prior to being murdered by another free-black man in 1851.

After her husband's death, Ann lived on in Natchez as the prosperous owner of seven or eight slaves and several downtown houses that she leased out or operated as barber shops. As with her husband, some of the most prominent slaveholders in the city and its surrounding county supported the widow Johnson as benefactors and even friends; she regularly channeled some of her surplus funds to them for investments and often sought their advice and counsel. Her four daughters and three sons, none of whom (although adults) were married in 1860, befriended the mixed-race children of several white elites in the community, especially the prominent Adam Bingaman Jr., a wealthy planter who moved his enslaved consort and their two daughters to New Orleans to escape the increasing opposition to free blacks in Mississippi. Bingaman eventually freed all three women, and he finally moved to New Orleans in the late 1850s to be with them; Johnson's not-married daughters frequently corresponded with and visited Bingaman's mixed-race daughters, whom they considered as close to them as sisters.[12]

The widow Johnson seems to have been largely unaffected by the animosity of Mississippi whites toward free people of color that swirled all around her.

She walked rather openly through the city's public streets, never submitted a petition to remain in the state, speculated in real estate, and hired prominent Natchez lawyers to defend her interests insofar as the law allowed. She educated her children privately, if not secretly, in a clandestine school operated by a family friend, the free-black barber Robert McCary, and she also sent them to schools for free people of color in New Orleans.

Although not actively persecuted or overtly threatened, the widow Johnson well understood the limitations imposed on her by a set of community standards that kept her from mingling socially with whites, forced her to seek out influential white patrons, forbade her travel in first-class accommodations on steamboats, and demanded that she faithfully uphold the legacy of a dead husband who wore as a badge of honor his service to a white community that consistently had demeaned and humiliated him as the price of his freedom and the safety of his family. William Johnson's memorable diary is filled with examples of the demeaning experiences he daily faced as a black man, constantly forced to demonstrate his inferiority to whites even as he manifested his superiority over enslaved blacks and poor free people of color. His widow's conformity to community standards and her submissive deportment, which elicited the support of various influential white patrons, freed her from persecutions as a free woman of color, just as her husband's conduct and demeanor had freed him. For those Natchez whites who protected and supported her, Ann Johnson's very existence demonstrated, at least in their eyes and in her particular case, how a free woman of color endowed with the proper temperament could fit into, prosper within, and accommodate a community that privileged whiteness and male mastery over black skin and women while keeping intact at least some of her own integrity as a free-black woman.[13]

Free-Black Women of Antebellum Natchez

In 1860, Dent, Dowling, and Johnson lived among 214 documented free people of color in Natchez, a number that had remained relatively stable since 1850. In Mississippi, free blacks numbered 773 in 1860, a dramatic decline from the 1,366 in 1830, and most of them lived in Natchez and Vicksburg or counties that bordered on the Mississippi River in the southwestern portion of the state. In Natchez, although the number had not declined, it grew only slightly from 202 in 1840 to 214 in 1860; the latter population lived in thirty-eight households, of which nine resembled a nuclear household, with a husband, wife, and children. The vast majority of free blacks in Adams County hailed from Mississippi, and most were of mixed-race ancestry (94 percent). Adult females outnumbered adult males (aged sixteen and older) sixty-four to fifty-one.

In 1860, the typical free person of color in Natchez lived in residences not clearly connected to whites: only 6 percent lived with whites in that year, compared to 74 percent in 1830 and 46 percent in 1840. This striking shift in residency patterns occurred partly because the city's free-black population consisted in 1860 of more free-born people than in earlier years, a circumstance that enabled second- and third-generation free blacks to live separate from the white men who had freed their black parents and grandparents. Not to be forgotten, some free blacks, like Margaret Dent, lived in households sustained by white men who did not want their black lovers and mixed-race children living in the same households as their white families. Some whites set up their mixed-race, adult children in independent households as the best means of helping them achieve a measure of self-sufficiency. Other free women and men of color lived apart from whites because they could, at least as long as they did not attempt, through their freedom, to challenge the prevailing social order.[14]

The decline in the number of free blacks in the state and in Natchez and Adams County over time occurred principally because Mississippi legislators made it increasingly difficult after 1832 to emancipate the enslaved or for free blacks to migrate into the state. The manumission restrictions came about as a reaction by Mississippi whites to northern abolitionists' increasing agitation against slavery as a moral evil, to the outbreak of slave rebellions—such as the Nat Turner rebellion in Virginia in 1831—and to several slave-conspiracy scares in Mississippi and Louisiana during the mid-1830s.

Beginning in the early 1830s, manumitting favored slaves required a costly process of submitting petitions to the state legislature rather than the simple filing of an act or deed of manumission with local authorities that had been the case in prior years. Mounting public opposition to the mere existence of free blacks also helped discourage all but a few slaveholders from filing manumission petitions. Beginning in 1822, free blacks in Mississippi had to register with a county court, and state law prohibited out-of-state free blacks from migrating into the state. In 1831, and again in 1842, the state legislature enacted laws requiring free blacks to leave the state unless they could provide the court with a written petition of support from local whites. For a manumitted slave, a properly executed manumission document, endorsed by a legal authority and recorded in the public record, served as proof of one's freedom. In the years prior to 1830, local authorities generally accepted manumission documents issued by other states.[15]

To counter the increased difficulty of manumission, a few determined slaveholders sent or carried enslaved people out of state to be manumitted. In most cases, the slave owner or owners then returned to Mississippi with the manumitted free person or persons, where they could be quietly licensed to remain in the state. Various local records for the years between 1830 and 1860 record 103 individual manumissions in Adams County, of which 66 were for adult men and women. Of these adults, 21 were manumitted by petitions to the legislature or in deeds of manumission processed in Mississippi, while all the others had traveled out of state to be freed. The overwhelming majority went to Ohio (70 percent), followed by Indiana, Tennessee, Pennsylvania, and Virginia. Of those freed in Mississippi, 9 were females, compared to 31 women freed out of state.

Among the 214 free people of color in Natchez in 1860 were 64 women aged sixteen or older.[16] The majority lived in households headed by their free-black husbands or fathers or some other male relative, but 23 women lived in sixteen households headed by free-black women, and eleven of these sixteen households included no adult males. In several houses a pair of sisters lived together, and one contained a mother and her spinster-aged daughters: the washerwoman Sarah Woods, aged fifty-five, who lived with her older sister Rachel, also a washerwoman; Elizabeth Cesson, aged thirty-eight, shared quarters with her younger sister Julia, both of whom were dressmakers; and Maria Winston, aged fifty-six, lived with her two daughters, Sarah and Elizabeth, twin girls aged twenty-six, and a young woman, Laura Cartwright, aged twenty-two (all of whom were mulattos and claimed to be dressmakers by occupation). Only Delilah Davis, aged forty, lived alone. The majority of households included children (69 percent), and all were single-family households except for Caroline Lawson's.[17] Lawson, a dressmaker, aged thirty-five, lived with two free-black washerwomen and their fourteen children. The building sat amid boardinghouses for white, working-class males and may have functioned as a lodging house for free-black women and their children.

Did the women in these female-only households have husbands living apart from them for various reasons? Perhaps they did, and their husbands may have been away from their homes when census enumerators made their household occupant counts; perhaps the absent males were enslaved men who could not live with these free women of color despite their conjugal ties. Were these sixteen free-black women heads of household divorced or abandoned women? Or were they women who had never married? It is not possible to know the answers to these questions because free-black marriages were neither recognized legally nor clearly documented except among a few prominent free-black families who occasionally show up in family and church records. Information about marital separation or divorce among free blacks in Natchez and Adams County is also limited. Divorces were not legally allowed for blacks (according to at least one newspaper account) until six years after the Civil War, although the military sanctioned separations from marriages for the formerly enslaved under certain conditions during the federal occupation of Natchez and in the early postwar years.[18]

If some free-black women chose to live without husbands, why did they? Historians Suzanne Lebsock, James Roark, and Michael Johnson hold conflicting views regarding why many urban, free women of color chose not to live with men in committed, long-term conjugal relationships. Lebsock speculates that some free-black women in Petersburg, Virginia, avoided marriage because they did not want to live under a husband's authority. Roark and Johnson see the scarcity of free-black men in Charleston to have affected a free-black woman's marital opportunities. In Natchez, seven of the sixteen free-black women who headed households were aged thirty-eight years and older, and the rest were between twenty-eight and thirty-seven years old. The youngest was twenty-eight. Among the thirteen documented, not-married free-black males in the city in 1860, six were younger than age twenty-nine while only one was older than thirty-eight. Under these circumstances, few eligible free-black males were available to marry and even fewer were older than many of the city's not-married free women of color. Unless these women found suitors from outside the city, a permanent conjugal tie similar to marriage with a black male was an unlikely prospect. Perhaps equally important, some free-black women may have loved men who dared not live openly with them, namely, enslaved men or white men who may have kept them as their unspoken lovers if not-always-hidden mistresses.[19]

The sixteen households headed by free-black women were scattered among the 815 households in Natchez. Six were located north of Main Street, seven to the south, and two at the eastern edge of the city. The wealthiest black woman in Natchez, Ann Johnson (discussed previously), lived in the very center of the city, sharing that prestigious location with other free-black families of equal prominence, headed by males: the Fitzhugh, Smith, and McCary households. The typical free-black household was located within four or five houses of another free-black household, and often free-black families lived next door to one another. Maria Winston, for example, lived next door to three other free-black families, and Cassandra Cesson lived in a house next to the free-black William Irvine and one house removed from Alonzo Nichols's family. Sarah Woods lived next door to Mathew West's family, and washerwoman Margaret Dent's house was located next to drayman Armstead Curtis's, a household that included a free-black barber, a steward, two women, and five mixed-race children, who probably intermingled with Dent's five children in ways that linked the two households into a mutually supportive unit.

Along with the free women of color who appear in the U.S. manuscript census schedules lived women who do not show up in the federal records, whose numbers amounted to several hundred over the years. Their names do appear, however, in legal documents, newspapers, criminal docket books, land records, and private correspondence. These women were like so many of the working-class whites who also passed through the town on their way to obscurity. Some died in yellow fever epidemics or were driven out of state if they had no family or white patrons to protect them; others avoided census enumerators, tax collectors, and the many local officials out of fear, especially those women who worked as prostitutes or had lost their freedom papers. But while lost to history in the federal records, they were there in Natchez and they undoubtedly shaped the larger community, although in ways difficult to ascertain.

The free-black women of Natchez (those living in male- and female-headed households) worked as seamstresses, dressmakers, washerwomen, and servants; a few held jobs as cooks and nurses. Some undoubtedly were prostitutes working in "bawdy houses," although none offered that profession as their source of income to the census enumerators. Most were poor but not desperately so, and a few had acquired property by 1860. Of the sixteen who headed households, nine owned at least one slave, and three women owned substantial real or personal property: Elizabeth Fitzgerald ($3,000 real, $7,000 personal), Ann Johnson ($10,000 real, $6,000 personal, including seven or eight slaves), and Nancy Kyle ($700 real, $1,000 personal, including one slave). These prosperous women, two of whom appear to have never married, were members of a small class of relatively elite free blacks who lived largely apart, separate and distinct from the city's less prosperous free people of color.[20]

In addition to laws affecting manumission, Mississippi established codes of conduct and behavioral expectations that all free blacks were required to follow. These strictures, firmly in place by 1855, prohibited free people of color from testifying against whites in criminal and civil cases, serving on juries and with the militia, voting and holding public office, owning guns without special permits, or operating a newspaper, grocery store, or tavern. Free blacks could not trade or conduct mercantile businesses outside town, engage in the sale of intoxicating liquor and spirits, or travel as first-class passengers on commercial steamboats or anywhere else without documented evidence of their freedom and employment. None could take lodging in hotels that serviced whites, work on commercial steamboats or river craft (although this legality was frequently ignored, according to historian Thomas C. Buchanan, by enterprising boat captains and risk-taking free blacks), use abusive language toward whites, or officially serve as a minister of the Gospel. Often these formal and informal codes of behavior were less than strictly enforced, especially when well-established free blacks committed offenses or broke minor laws, but violations could result in fines, imprisonment, whippings, and even enslavement or death.[21]

Many of these rules also applied to enslaved people, and the city's free people of color always tried to demonstrate by their actions and behavior how they differed from the enslaved fellow blacks all around them. For some free blacks, owning slaves and property, hobnobbing selectively but respectfully with wealthy white supporters and patrons, and traveling freely and openly in Natchez and its adjacent countryside demonstrated the reality of their freedom. Unlike the enslaved, the city's free blacks were legally permitted to learn to read and write, own licensed weapons, hunt and fish freely as long as they carried with them their freedom papers, conduct a service-oriented business (barbering, washing clothes, or driving hacks and carriages), and have recourse to the law and lawyers for the enforcement of contracts. Most importantly, they could demonstrate their freedom by their constant acknowledgment (through submissive and deferential behavior) that freedom was a gift from their previous owners (or the owners of their parents and grandparents) and patrons rather than an earned right or a privilege of birth.[22]

Because of their gender and race, free women of color in Natchez experienced life differently from free-black men, enslaved persons, and the white men and women with whom they interacted daily. As with free men of color, these women were black in a place and time when most people identified blackness with slavery and whiteness with freedom. As women, they lived in a world dominated by a male social order that deemed all women inferior to men because of their sex, but their race nevertheless undermined any possible sisterhood with white women in the community, regardless of their shared gender and lack of equality with males. No white woman in antebellum Natchez could be expelled from the state, whipped in public displays of punishment for crimes, or enslaved if she failed to carry her manumission documents with her. Neither did white women bear the social stigma of blackness, which presumed the sexual promiscuity of all black women, whether enslaved or free. On the other hand, as the objects, in many cases, of white male desire and even affection, free women of color occupied a position different and apart from that of the city's free men of color (none of whom, as men, appear to have been openly lusted after or sexually desired, insofar as we know).[23]

To better understand how the city's not-married free women of color coped without husbands at their sides in antebellum Natchez, this chapter now looks carefully at the lives of four such women who were living largely on their own when the Civil War swept over the land. Their biographies reveal what they held in common with each other and the ways in which they differed depending on their circumstances and personalities. Each of their stories, when compared to those of Dent, Dowling, and Johnson (profiled earlier) and of their free-black friends and neighbors, including those who lived with men as their wives and companions, illuminates the blurred boundaries and murky interstices of their lives. We begin with a free-black woman, Agnes Gordon Earhart, who maintained a long-term and relatively open relationship with a white man whose household included his white wife and his white and mixed-race children.

Agnes Gordon Earhart

In 1859, Agnes Gordon Earhart, aged fifty-six, petitioned the state legislature for permission to remain in Natchez, where she had lived for over thirty-five years, posting a hefty $5,000 bond "for the good behavior of herself & family." Agnes had had a long-term relationship with the prosperous Natchez merchant David Earhart, who most likely had fathered at least eight of her eleven children over the years. He also, at the time of Agnes's petition, was legally married to and still living with Louisa Therese Chambers Earhart, the white mother of his four white children. The legislature never acted on Agnes Earhart's petition, probably due to the outbreak of the Civil War.[24] The birthplace and manumission date for Agnes Earhart, if indeed she had been manumitted, are unknown. Evidently she remained in Natchez for the rest of her life, dying there on January 27, 1909, at age 106.

David Earhart, who died on January 5, 1860, was buried in the Earhart family plot near the grave of his father's wife, Cassandra Earhart, a well-known "free woman of color," who was recognized in the public record as David's mother and the mother of his many mixed-race brothers and sisters.[25] David's will lists his four children by his white wife as well as "several natural children," whom his wife and brother, William, are instructed to "support" and protect "as they may need until they shall be able to take care of themselves."[26] The federal manuscript census of 1850 shows David living with his twenty-nine-year-old white wife, Louisa, their infant daughter, and eight other children (all listed as free mulattos with the surname Earhart), ranging in age from one to fifteen.[27] Land records reveal that David Earhart had sold a small house and lot to Agnes Gordon, a "free woman of color," in 1841.[28]

David Earhart almost certainly had passed for white his entire life. He lived openly with a white wife while conducting an ongoing relationship with a free-black woman, although not necessarily in the same house. All four of David and Louisa Earhart's children appear in public records as white, as did David; only those children born to Agnes are designated mulattoes in the census. David Earhart's wife almost certainly knew about Agnes and her brood before she married David, and she surely knew later about their continuing relationship, but she never publicly protested, insofar as is known.

A long history of misinformation about Cassandra Earhart, the wife of

David's father, Jacob Earhart, runs through Natchez lore. The popular journalist and local historian Edith Wyatt Moore, whose work is filled with inaccuracies, writes about a runaway slave named Cassandra who fled from Tennessee in 1795 with a young Chickasaw slave.[29] Moore's story, based partly on the reminiscences of old-timers in 1930s Natchez, is romantic, intriguing, and dramatic, but not easily documented. According to legend (and a few documented facts in various public records), two runaways—Cassandra, a fifteen-year-old, light-skinned mulatto girl, and an enslaved Indian named "John Smith" (who was the "property of [a] General Colbert of the Chickasaw Nation" and allegedly had kidnapped Cassandra in Tennessee)—were arrested at the Natchez waterfront hiding in a flatboat. Soon thereafter, Cassandra's owner, James Bosley, sold her to the wealthy planter Anthony Hutchins, who then transferred her in turn to young Jacob Earhart, a "smarmy" Indian trader and merchant. In 1803, Earhart manumitted Cassandra, noting that as long as she remained unmarried she would "pass by the name of Cassandra Bosley."[30]

Sometime during the next five years Jacob Earhart's white wife, Elizabeth (according to terms agreed to in their legally granted articles of separation), left him and moved to New Orleans.[31] Natchez property records show Jacob, "along with his wife Cassandra," selling a house and lot in Natchez in 1809, thereby documenting their accepted marital status, even though he was still legally married to Elizabeth.[32] Cassandra bore five children to Jacob, and she also had a free-black daughter, Julia Ann Hutchins, apparently born while Anthony Hutchins held Cassandra in bondage, indicating that Hutchins may have been the child's father. Jacob Earhart apparently had freed Julia when he manumitted her mother. By 1824, Jacob and Cassandra had acquired about four hundred acres of plantation land and at least twenty-eight slaves, which they placed in trust for their six children, including Julia Hutchins.[33] All of their surviving children, including David Earhart, married whites, and none are identified as mulattos or free persons of color in any local records. After 1803, Cassandra is never again characterized as a black woman in Adams County legal records. Jacob Earhart died around 1824, and Cassandra lived the rest of her life just north of the city in a small house she had purchased at auction in 1835.[34]

Natchez apparently took the complex black and white Earhart family in stride. No evidence suggests that Jacob or his son David demonstrated much concern about living openly with black women or fathering their children; David likely had paid or pledged assets as the required security for the $5,000 bond to allow Agnes to remain in Mississippi. Although Jacob Earhart's first, white wife, Elizabeth, probably had left him because of Cassandra, David's white wife stayed with him and evidently accepted, or at least tolerated, Agnes's children. Neither father nor son seems to have suffered socially because of their open relations with black women, and David seems not to have been overtly stigmatized for his partially black ancestry. The full story, however, regarding his and Agnes's acceptability in the community is simply unknown.

Fanny Leiper

Fanny Leiper, a formerly enslaved free woman of color, filed suit in 1847 in the Southern District Chancery Court of Adams County against four defendants: Malvina Huffman (aka Hoffman, Matthews, and other aliases), a frequently arrested, locally notorious woman who may have been part black; Oliver L. Bemiss, Huffman's alleged paramour; James Walsh, Huffman's agent; and Joseph Winscot, a steamboat engineer in New Orleans who once had lived with Leiper in Natchez. Leiper, who took her surname from a free-black man she claimed to have married earlier in her life, charged the four with conspiracy and fraudulent possession of a city lot she allegedly had purchased in 1834 and the small house she claimed to have built on the property, living there until moving to Ohio in 1845. Although a local real estate agent named Samuel Hammett had kept the place rented for her, Leiper allegedly had learned while in Ohio, probably when the rental monies ceased coming, that her one-time friend and neighbor Malvina Huffman, having somehow acquired title to her house and lot, was renting out her Natchez property and keeping the money. Leiper hired a Natchez attorney, Lewis Sanders Jr., and took Huffman and her accomplices to court. The case eventually went to the state supreme court, where the entire story unfolded.[35]

The defendants argued that Leiper had never legally owned the house because she had bought it while still enslaved and she had no written evidence of her manumission. Fanny Leiper countered that she was free when she purchased the house, having been manumitted by her owner, Margaret Overaker, in 1831 or 1832. According to Gabriel Tichenor, a prominent white banker (noted earlier in this chapter in connection with Ann Johnson), Leiper's manumission papers had been filed locally but subsequently were lost, which is why Overaker then sent Leiper to Ohio to be liberated again. Overaker also testified that Leiper's white father, a wealthy planter named J. S. Miller, had paid her $300 to cover expenses for obtaining Fanny's freedom. Leiper, according to witnesses, then returned from Ohio a free woman, bought the lot in question, built her house, and made improvements to the grounds.

This seemingly straightforward transaction was complicated by several contested issues and questions grounded in the uncertainty surrounding the lives of all free women of color at the time. Leiper had not assumed sole ownership in clear title when she purchased the lot. Her attorney, Colonel Fleming Wood, had advised her to file for title jointly with Joseph Winscot, the white man with whom she had been living, because of "the temper of the times" (the public clamor for removing all free blacks from the state). For some reason Leiper never informed Winscot that his name was on the deed, but she did confide the full details to her friend and next-door neighbor Malvina Huffman.

Natchez constable Henry Dillon testified for Huffman and the other defendants. He claimed he had notified Leiper in 1843 that she would have to leave the state in twenty days or face arrest as an unlicensed free-black person, but he dropped the matter when she told him she was owned by a wealthy planter named Miller, who corroborated her story. Soon after Dillon's warning, Leiper moved to Cincinnati, where she worked as a washerwoman and lived with or married Gustavus Howard, who may have been white. After Leiper left for Ohio, Huffman and Bemiss allegedly told Winscot about the joint deed. The three allegedly obtained the house keys from the rental agent, Hammett, by telling him that Leiper would not be returning because of her questionable status as a free woman and that Winscot had sold the property to Huffman. Employing James Walsh as rental agent, the three defendants then rented out the house.

Malvina Huffman's criminal record suggests that she was a woman indeed capable of fraud, a notorious lawbreaker arrested eight times from 1841 to 1860, on charges ranging from keeping a bawdy house to assault and battery and selling liquor without a license. She is identified in the federal manuscript census for 1850 as heading a household that included four young white women and numerous beds, dressers, and cabinets: the typical furnishings of a bordello. During Reconstruction, Huffman (alias Matthews by 1860) shot to death a disgruntled Union soldier who had tried to break into the bordello she operated near the bluffs, probably the same bawdy house located next door to Leiper's house, which also may have serviced Natchez males as a house of ill repute.[36]

In 1854, the state supreme court found for Leiper, ruling that she had purchased the property with a white man who then held the property in trust for her. That she may have been a slave at the time was irrelevant to the court because in that case the property would have belonged to Leiper's owner, Margaret Overaker. Leiper's white partner, James Winscot, held the property in trust either for Leiper or for her owner, and he could not have sold the property to Huffman without Leiper's or the widow Overaker's consent. Leiper could bring suit, the court reasoned, because as a free woman of color she was allowed to use the law to protect her property and to enforce contracts. Her owner's expressed intention to free Leiper either in 1831 or in 1834, by sending her to Ohio, and the fact that Leiper had resided in a free state for several years, were all that mattered to the court, even though no written record of manumission existed.[37]

Almost every stratum of Natchez society was represented in Fanny Leiper's case, including eleven wealthy, prominent whites who spoke on her behalf, ranging from planters and lawyers to government officials and municipal employees. Their testimony confirmed for the court the story of Leiper's manumission in Natchez and again in Cincinnati. In addition, the witnesses helped establish Leiper's paternal kinship ties to the Millers. And no witness was more important than Gabriel Tichenor, a regionally prominent businessman and banker who had close familial and possibly sexual ties to black women. As noted earlier, in 1822 Tichenor had freed his own mulatto slave Harriet Battles, and he later sent Harriet and her young daughter Ann, who may have been Tichenor's daughter and who had remained Tichenor's slave under Louisiana law, to Cincinnati in 1826, where Harriet and Ann were formally and legally freed. After they returned to Adams County in 1829, Tichenor sold a lot on State Street in Natchez to Harriet, and she eventually built a house on the property with her free-black son-in-law, the barber William Johnson.[38] At some point during the 1830s Tichenor moved to Ohio, where he continued to assist enslaved Mississippians, including Leiper, in achieving their freedom.[39]

Nancy and Caroline Kyle

Nancy Kyle, a not-married free woman of color who was at least eighty years old in 1860, lived in a modest but stylish territorial-era townhouse on the northeast corner of High and Rankin Streets, a few city blocks from the Johnson household. Located in a part of Natchez that had been known in the 1830s as "Kyle Town," the house featured four entrance bays, a gabled roof, a central chimney, and a front gallery. In 1850 Nancy shared the home with her middle-aged daughter Caroline and six other free-black family members, including three males (Christopher, aged twenty; John, aged twenty-two; and Rufus, aged two) and three females (Frances, aged fourteen; Alzena, aged eight; and Sun, an infant). Most members of the household except for Nancy, Caroline, and Alzena Miller had moved away by 1860, but those remaining were joined by a seventeen-year-old free black named Angeline Morris and Nancy's infant great-grandson William. Nancy valued her residence at $700 and her personal property at $1,000, which probably included one or more slaves whom she reportedly owned.[40]

Situated north of Franklin Street, Kyle Town, known for its small residences and scattered free-black population, was by no means a segregated, strictly working-class enclave. Next door to the Kyles lived an unmarried, thirty-seven-year-old white woman, Emily Balance, her eighteen-year-old daughter, and the gin-right William Anderson and his wife and two children. The widow and dressmaker Margaret Link, also thirty-seven and white, lived with her five children, ages five to eighteen, on the other side of Nancy. Stanton Hall, Natchez's most impressive mansion, constructed in 1857 for Frederic Stanton, one of the wealthiest planters and merchants in the lower South, stood two short blocks north.[41]

Nancy's former owner, Christopher Kyle, a prosperous Natchez merchant, left his territorial-era house to Nancy in his will, a document that also freed Nancy and her three children (Caroline, John, and Christopher) in 1827 by authorizing that they be sent to Ohio with $1,000 in expense money to cover legal fees, even though he had freed Nancy by petition in Louisiana in 1819. Christopher and Nancy probably had lived together openly in the Kyle house, and Caroline and the other children were commonly recognized as their off-spring. The house remained in the hands of Nancy Kyle's descendants until the 1930s.[42]

Public records identify Nancy and Caroline as dressmakers and washer-women, but their property holdings made them equal to a handful of free-black barbers and hack drivers who socially dominated the free-black community.[43] The Kyle women were not above public scrutiny, though. In 1841, more than a decade after Christopher Kyle's death, a local white man, Dr. Woodson Wren, challenged the Kyles' lawfully filed petitions with the Board of Police to remain in Mississippi. He claimed that the two women kept "a House of ill fame, a House of asination [*sic*], a whore House, & c."[44] Similar charges had been leveled at the Kyle women previously. In the summer of 1838, "various . . . re-spected citizens of the City of Natchez" had petitioned the Adams County Board of Police to revoke the two women's licenses to remain in the city and state. The board ordered the women to leave the state within ninety days and labeled them "dangerous members of Society." After the Kyle women appealed its decision, the board suspended its removal order in January 1839 and then renewed their residency licenses in 1841.[45]

In commenting on the affair, William Johnson notes in his diary that the board's chairman, Henry Conner, shouted down the attacks on Caroline and Nancy Kyle made by "Old Dr. Wren" and threatened to jail him if he dared say "another word."[46] Wren, a local character, once had been the key witness against a white man brought up on charges of having sex with a black woman, testifying that he had watched the two through their window in an act of for-nication. The arrested man sued Wren for malicious prosecution, and the court eventually awarded the plaintiff fifty dollars in damages and court costs.[47]

Gravestone, Caroline Kyle, 1809–1899, Natchez City Cemetery, Adams County, Mississippi. Photo by author.

Support for the Kyle women came not only from Henry Conner but also from a "Great many [other leading members of the white community] that was very Glad of the old Fellows [Wren's] defeat." If the prostitution charges had any basis in fact, the two women probably would have counted among their customers some of the very citizens who had sponsored their petitions to stay in Mississippi. A more flattering entry in William Johnson's diary tells of Nancy Kyle's visit in 1843 to the nearby town of Rodney to minister to yellow fever victims. She was accompanied by "Lizor [Eliza] Cotton," another free black woman (discussed later), who appears more than once in the public record as a woman who most likely traded sex for money.[48]

That the Kyle women's residency licenses were renewed again and again, despite the clamor from some whites who wanted to expel them from the state, reveals much about how they had engaged life in Natchez as not-married free-black women. As well-known and even notorious free women of color, they enjoyed the patronage and support of white men who may have been their lovers, fathers, patients, or customers. The two women were tolerated, even accepted and welcomed, by some Natchez whites even as others resented them. In an honor bestowed on only a handful of the city's free-black residents, the notorious mother and daughter were buried side by side amid prominent white graves, and even today local tour guides comment favorably on the Kyle graves, as if to say that there was more to Natchez in slavery times than meets the eye.[49]

Eliza Cotton

A grand jury indictment charged Eliza Cotton (aka Eliza Holden or Eliza Bossack) on August 1, 1841, with keeping a disorderly house where, day and night, "evil" men and women engaged in "tippling" and general misbehavior, including nudity, to "the great damage and common nuisance of all the good citizens of the state." Eight months later Cotton was arrested for selling spirituous liquors "to diverse Negroes," a clientele that probably included enslaved customers. Eliza met a $1,500 bail, which allowed her to remain free while the case proceeded over the following six months, although the extant records do not reveal whether or not she was found guilty, served time in jail, or paid a fine for her alleged crime. The next year she was arrested again on identical charges.[50] Eliza's first documented run-in with the law occurred in 1832, when she was caught fornicating with a white man, John Holden. A few years later, in 1840, a local justice of the peace charged her with harboring slaves, a serious offense for a free-black person, but it is again unclear whether she paid fines, served jail time, or had the charges dismissed. In 1832, the Adams County Board of Police, despite the pending fornication charge, judged her to be a person of "good character and honest deportment" who should be allowed to remain in the state.[51]

Born around 1802 in Washington, D.C., Eliza Cotton/Bossack/Holden may have been brought to Natchez by slave traders and then manumitted, but no manumission papers have been located, which strongly suggests that she was freed prior to coming to Natchez or else had been born free and had moved to the river city on her own. She owned five slaves in 1840 as well as a lot and building on St. Catherine Street, which was a Franklin Street extension that terminated at the Forks-of-the-Road slave market east of town; she probably lived in the house with her slaves near a hospital for free and enslaved blacks that was located between the city's eastern edge and the slave market. During the 1840s, she and three other free-black women rented rooms in a downtown building across from the courthouse and next to the jail. According to the building's rental register, two of the women worked as washerwomen, but Eliza's occupation is not listed.[52] Nearly driven from the state when the Board of Police revoked her residency license on September 6, 1841, Cotton immediately appealed to the Adams County Circuit Court, and six months later, even as she was under grand jury indictment, the court granted her license to remain in response to a "bill of exceptions" filed by her attorneys, Alexander Montgomery and Samuel S. Boyd.[53]

Eliza had managed to remain in Natchez despite her numerous run-ins with the law thanks, in great part, to the many white men in her life, men who routinely had come to her aid by posting bonds (averaging about $200 each) or acting as security for her bonds while she fought various indictments. Some of the city's most respected lawyers represented her either as friends or as paid counsel; doing business from a rented room in a building on the courthouse square put Eliza in close proximity to the Natchez legal community. Perhaps she did laundry for the city jail or for the many lawyers who worked nearby, who may have known her as a woman who offered sex for money. And the three men (Holden, Cotton, and Bossack) whose names she claimed at one time or another may also help to explain her survival. Holden probably was the John Holden with whom she had been accused of fornication, but nothing is known of his background or occupation. Cotton may have been the prominent slave trader William Cotton, who died in 1843. His probate records list two bad loans to Eliza Bossack, for $280.00 and $666.50, which were endorsed by two of the city's most successful businessmen, Peter Gemmell and Samuel Wakefield. The origin of her surname Bossack is unknown.[54]

William Cotton's probate records also list a young enslaved woman named Eliza and her child Merial, whom he acknowledged as his mulatto daughter in his 1843 will. The probate record shows that Cotton had paid for the enslaved Eliza's steamboat passages, bought her calico dresses, provided her lodging, and instructed in his will that she be freed upon his death. When settling Cotton's estate, however, his executor and business associate, Rice C. Ballard, a notorious slave trader, sold four of Cotton's slaves to pay his debts, including the twenty-four-year-old Eliza, sold for $710 to the wealthy planter J. S. Gillespie. All traces of the girl Merial have disappeared, but she may have been William's child by the slave Eliza or his granddaughter by the Eliza Cotton/Bossack who owed him money at the time of his death, a debt that he apparently forgave or never sought to collect for unknown reasons. Perhaps the two Eliza Cottons were unrelated, but the favored treatment of the enslaved Eliza Cotton indicates a special link between her and William Cotton that quite possibly included Eliza Cotton/Bossack in the mix.[55]

The name Eliza Cotton appears in the municipal death records in 1854 and in the criminal court records for Adams County in 1867, when a black Eliza Cotton was arrested and jailed for petty theft, but no ages are given in either record. The Eliza Cotton arrested in 1867 was living in Under-the-Hill Natchez with an alleged co-conspirator, Eliza Smith (also black and possibly the same Eliza Smith discussed in chapter 4 of this study), at the time of her detainment, and it is a good bet that this Eliza Cotton was the mulatto daughter of Eliza Holden/Cotton/Bossack and William Cotton. But like so much else about the free women of color in antebellum Natchez, it is doubtful that we will ever know for sure.[56]

Conclusion

Each of the women profiled above was connected sexually or as family to white men, including some of the city's most prominent citizens. The merchant David Earhart, although apparently accepted as white by neighbors, friends, local document takers, and legal clerks despite his mixed-race ancestry, had embraced Agnes Gordon in a relationship that most likely produced at least eight of her recorded eleven children. Planter and slaveholder J. S. Miller, or someone in his family, apparently owned and may have fathered Fanny Leiper, who cohabited at one time or another with various white men. Merchant Christopher Kyle almost certainly lived with Nancy Kyle as his mistress and fathered their child Caroline. Eliza Cotton undoubtedly knew many white men as lovers or former owners, including John Holden, William Cotton, and the unknown Bossack. Margaret Dent, Harriet Dowling, and Ann Johnson also lived as the lovers or wives or daughters of white men. The two Kyle women and on occasion even Leiper shared rumored identities as prostitutes or bawdy house proprietors. Although none of the white men in these women's lives (except for Allan Davis and David Earhart) ever admitted (at least in writing) to loving them or fathering their mixed-race children, it is a good bet that most Natchez residents knew what was going on and the nature of their relationships.

Their sexual involvement with white men linked these women to the town's other free people of color. The free-black barber William Johnson probably had been sired by a prosperous but not especially wealthy white man who was also named William Johnson, and who had freed young William and his sister and mother, set up his mixed-race son in business, and provided William's mixed-race mother with a house and property. The free-black William Johnson's wife, Ann, was the mixed-race daughter of Harriet Battles, a former slave freed and given property by the white banker Gabriel Tichenor, who probably had fathered Ann. The most prominent free-black families in Natchez, the Barlands, Hoggatts, Fitzgeralds, Winstons, McCarys, and Smiths, were descended from prominent white men and enslaved but later freed women. William Johnson's best friend, the free-black barber Robert McCary, had been freed along with his sister by their white father, who set McCary up with property and even slaves, including one thought to have been his own half-brother.[57]

Adam Bingaman, one of the town's wealthiest planters, who traced his Mississippi ancestry to the Spanish colonial era, fathered several children with his beloved free-black consort, Mary Ellen Williams, one of his former slaves with whom he began a sexual relationship after losing his wife soon after they had married. When Bingaman's mother died in 1841, he took Mary Ellen and their children to New Orleans to live lavishly amid the city's multiracial social and cultural scene while he maintained his principal residence in Natchez. His mixed-race daughters, Charlotte and Eleanora, formed devoted friendships with William Johnson's daughters—young women who traveled frequently to New Orleans to visit relatives—relationships that lasted well after the Civil War. In 1859, as pressure mounted on state politicians to expel free blacks from Louisiana and Mississippi, Bingaman persuaded the state legislature to allow Mary Ellen and her children to remain within state boundaries as deserving free-black residents. At the end of the Civil War, Bingaman acknowledged both James A. Bingaman and Eleanora Lucille Bingaman as his "natural Children," and when he died in 1869, his entire estate passed to Eleanora, the sole surviving member of his black family.[58]

The sexual involvement of free-black women with prominent white men set their lives apart from those of the city's free men of color by eliminating, in some cases, black men as lovers and potential husbands. As free-black women, their sexuality also armed them with a gendered currency that permitted them to live in ways that would never have been tolerated for black men. No free man of color would have survived for long as the operator of a bawdy house or the seller of liquor to slaves. Except for those so light-skinned that they could pass for white (perhaps like David Earhart), none would have been allowed to walk the streets of Natchez as the consorts or husbands of white women, and none would have been allowed openly to father their children, and certainly not the children of elite white women. Such activities would have caused them to be arrested, whipped, exiled, enslaved, castrated, or killed.

Some historians contend that southern society exhibited more tolerance of white women's sexual involvement with black men than was once supposed, and there is evidence that a number of white women married or lived with mixed-race males who were so light skinned that they were able to pass for white.[59] The most notable example of white women involved openly with black and mixed-race men in antebellum Natchez was the Barland family. William Barland manumitted an enslaved woman named Elizabeth and her twelve children, whom he "acknowledged" as his children in a petition to the territorial legislature in 1815. Several of his light-skinned mulatto sons openly married white women with whom they lived out their lives in antebellum Natchez.[60]

The key to toleration and support for free-black males in antebellum Natchez lay in their deportment and deferential behavior, limited sexuality across the races, and the patronage of white protectors, who often were their fathers or grandfathers. As long as they did not threaten the system of slavery or cross the barriers that separated the races, those free-black males related to prominent whites could be accepted, albeit at a distance, and even valued for their services. Their proper deportment as faithful servants of the white social order mattered as much as if not more than the identities of their white fathers. The Natchez press, for example, applauded William Johnson after his death for being a "most inoffensive man," a former slave who had earned "a respected position on account of his character, intelligence, and deportment."[61] Similarly, the death in 1858 of Robert D. Smith, a free-black carriage business owner, led the Natchez *Courier* to write, "*All of our old citizens—indeed—we may say—all our citizens—will* regret to hear of the death of Robert D. Smith, a colored man of our city, but one who, by his industry, probity of life, correctness of demeanor and Christian-like character, had won the favor, and respect of the entire community. Every citizen knew him, and there are but few travelers, who frequented our city, who could not bear witness of his correct deportment and character."[62]

For Fanny Leiper, the Kyle women, Eliza Cotton, Cassandra and Agnes Earhart, and others like them, deportment was not the key to their survival. They almost always survived because of their sexual and familial links to white men, which enabled them to venture forth openly, even defiantly at times, as they "stepped lively in place" as free women of color. Even though free-black people in Natchez did not enjoy citizenship or equality before the law or in society, free-black women experienced life quite differently, as women, from free-black males. Despite the ban on interracial marriages, some of these women considered themselves married to the white men in their lives and often took their surnames. Society allowed them more latitude in their behavior than it did free-black men and even white women, who appear in police records charged with crimes that free-black women usually managed to escape.[63]

Amy Johnson, William Johnson's mother, provides a telling example of such relative freedom. Freed in 1819 by the white man who probably had fathered her two children, she lived as a Natchez character until her death in 1849. Licensed as a retailer during the early 1820s, she acquired a house and slaves with the help of William Johnson, the white father of her mixed-raced son. Just five feet tall, she was given to fighting real and imaginary enemies, and several of her battles wound up in court. In 1822, for example, she sued the free-black barber Arthur Mitchum for damages after a public fistfight with him, claiming that Mitchum had spit in her face, pulled her nose and hair, and ripped her dress and bonnet while beating her with brickbats. The court awarded her $27.50 in damages and costs instead of the $500 she originally had demanded. Back in court one month later, she testified against Mitchum on another assault-and-battery charge, lodged by a free-black woman named Delia Black. By 1837, Amy had become so uncontrollable that her son sometimes flicked his whip at her as "the quickest way to stop it." He estimated that his mother averaged three pubic quarrels a week and one nearly every day with her family.[64]

Despite her combative, irascible nature, Amy Johnson was never arrested. Her identity as the mother of the city's most prosperous free-black man probably had helped shield her, along with the fact that her wrath was mostly aimed at free blacks, slaves, and working-class whites. Such conduct would never have been tolerated from a free-black man, and no mention of similar disruptions by free-black men appears in William Johnson's extensive diary or in the city's voluminous public records. Occasionally enslaved women brawled in the street, but their owners or the slave patrol dealt with them quickly and severely.[65] Only free-black women with white male connections appeared able to get away with such behavior, or so the public record indicates.

Antebellum Natchez tolerated and embraced its free-black, single women as relatively free spirits who often lived in autonomous households because their sexual, emotional, and familial connections generally complemented, rather than threatened, a prevailing social order held together in large part by slavery, white male domination, and the servant ideal. These women, though often lively and demonstrative as compared to free-black males, ultimately mattered to the white men who loved them, regarded them as valued persons, and related to them as offspring or objects of affection for whom they felt responsible. Their partially European ancestry trumped their partially African ancestry to make them the cherished objects of white male affection or sexual desire. These women were always available to the white men who loved them as consorts or as daughters and granddaughters, and they typically obliged their white patrons, lovers, fathers, and grandfathers (uncles, brothers, cousins, and nephews) by remaining in the shadows. Such personal albeit often sexual connections with white men enabled many of the city's free-black women to step lively and often defiantly in ways that would not have been tolerated in free-black men. But it is important to understand that their behavior, and indeed their very existence, always left unchallenged the cohesive tissue that held antebellum Natchez together as a social order: slavery, white patriarchy, and the servant ideal.

CHAPTER SIX

Stepping Lively at the Edge

The Disorderly, Not-Married Women of Antebellum Natchez

In June 1823, a Natchez magistrate charged laborer Hiram Simmons and Sally Clarke, a spinster, with being "disorderly, evil disposed, irreligious and immoral persons" who "knowingly and willfully live together in a state of fornication in evil example to all others, offending, in contempt of morality, the peace and dignity of the state of Mississippi." Six witnesses testified to the couple's crime, and Hiram thereafter confessed "that he [had] had sexual intercourse with the said Sally Clarke many times both by day and night in private and in public." Deeming the couple guilty, the magistrate punished Clarke and Simmons with a fine and thirty days in the municipal jail, an unusually harsh verdict for sexual escapades in Natchez. Six months later the Natchez night patrol arrested Hiram for physically assaulting the spinster Sally; he subsequently appears for the last time in a public record upon the death of his infant son in 1826, from unknown causes, after which the couple vanish from sight and their names disappear from Natchez history. What happened to them, known fornicators in a city not unfriendly to illicit sex of all sorts, is anyone's guess, but no other resident or waterfront visitor ever again served jail time or paid fines for committing fornication, a misdemeanor offense that differed by definition in the minds of Mississippi lawmakers from prostitution in that fornication involved sex freely given rather than sold or purchased.[1]

A year earlier, in April 1821, Domingo Lemos accused the spinster Elizabeth Claravagal of living in open fornication with James Way. Lemos testified that "about two weeks ago he [had seen] the defendant in Elizabeth's bedroom, with her, in bed together. James was on top of Elizabeth in the act of sexual intercourse . . . [and] that the defendants live[d] together in the same house and that he [had] seen them in bed together numerous times." According to the transcript entered in the court ledger, Lemos had twice observed Way and Claravagal "in [the] act of carnal intercourse in public places outside of the house." In that same year, the spinster Susan Fry also faced a city magistrate who charged her with having sex with a man who was not her husband. State legislators in antebellum Mississippi considered fornication a misdemeanor punishable by up to six months in jail but not so severe a crime as to deserve time in the state penitentiary. Typically, women arrested for sex-related actions in antebellum Natchez were charged not with fornication or prostitution but with vagrancy or running brothels and servicing customers without the proper business licenses.[2]

The prostitute Lydia Pettits came to Natchez from Ohio as a married woman in 1834, only to be deserted by her husband, Alexander, after his failed divorce attempt. He had married Lydia in Cincinnati a few years earlier, believing her to be a "wholesome and untainted woman of high moral character," but he soon discovered that she and her mother had "lived in concubinage with various strangers" for weeks at a time. When he threatened divorce, Lydia begged for a second chance, which Alexander had agreed to give her in a moment of weakness, according to his testimony in the divorce suit that he eventually filed. Alexander then moved to Lexington, Kentucky, to complete his medical studies and sent his wife to live with her sister until he could establish himself as a doctor in Natchez. When he arrived in Natchez after completing his education, he found Lydia already there and working as a prostitute in several Under-the-Hill brothels. The chancery court dismissed his complaint because neither Lydia nor Alexander had lived in Mississippi long enough to satisfy its one-year residency requirement for divorce. Alexander thereafter disappears from the public record, but Lydia lived on for years in Natchez as a married but abandoned woman who pursued (most likely with her mother) one nefarious business or another, including selling liquor without a license and "entertaining Negroes." She never used her husband's abandonment as grounds for seeking a divorce, nor did she face jail as a convicted prostitute, most likely because no municipal, county, or state ordinance outlawed selling sex as an enterprise or money-making activity. Prostitutes could, however, be arrested as vagrants (as could gamblers), but only if they showed no visible means of employment other than trading sex for money.[3]

A few years later, on Christmas Eve 1840, an Adams County Circuit Court judge sentenced Elizabeth Payne to three years in the state penitentiary for stealing $100, which amounted to grand larceny (a charge applied for any value over $20). When asked if she had anything to say before being hauled off to prison, Payne offered no response. Two weeks later she petitioned the Mississippi House of Representatives for her release. She poured out her heart to the lawmakers in her request for clemency even as she admitted to the "degradation of [her] character and [the] fatal depth to which the most untoward circumstances had brought her." She explained that she had grown up in a "peaceful" and "virtuous" setting in rural New York, surrounded by loving parents and siblings, before being seduced "in an evil hour, [when] the villain came, one of your sex," and enticed her to run away with him by promising marriage.

The alleged seducer had abandoned Payne in Natchez, where she turned to thieving merely to survive. She promised that if the legislators would pass a resolution recommending her pardon to the governor of Mississippi she would return immediately to her father's protection and "the endearments of her childhood home" in New York. Sixty-two Mississippi residents, most of whom lived in Natchez, sent a signed appeal to the governor asking him to reconsider Payne's sentence because "the imprisonment of a Female for so long a term, for so small an offense, is repugnant to the spirit of the age, which extends to females in all cases the greatest levity." One week later, Governor Alexander G. McNutt, a Vicksburg attorney turned planter and slaveholder eyeing election to the U.S. Senate, pardoned Elizabeth Payne. She never returned to Natchez insofar as is known, despite the support manifested for her by many of its male residents. Perhaps leaving the state was an unwritten condition for her pardon. Why this penniless, thieving woman gained the support of so many Natchez males, including merchants, skilled workers, several planters, and a few prominent lawyers, remains a mystery.[4]

On the eve of the Civil War, the widow Catherine Johnson operated a boardinghouse that rented rooms with meals to nineteen men, principally Irish laborers, and two married couples. Johnson's thirty-two-year-old son, her teenage daughter, and an enslaved woman assisted her in running the business. As a devout Catholic, Johnson attended Mass each Sunday and undoubtedly offered small donations to the church, as was expected of the more pious and affluent women among its flock. But the widow Johnson was no saintly lady. Throughout the 1840s and 1850s, she faced numerous arrests for selling liquor without a license, stealing from her boarders, and running a bawdy house where disreputable men and women cavorted at all hours of the day and night in gambling, "tippling," and uncivil behavior.

Johnson's brother, John Tuomey, and his first wife, Elila, were among the city's most notorious criminals. He compiled fifteen arrests to Elila's nine for offenses ranging from assault and battery and receiving stolen goods to retailing liquor and other goods to slaves, whom they also allegedly had entertained. Surprisingly, neither Catherine nor Elila served jail time, and John spent only a few days behind bars; overall, less than a third of their alleged crimes brought guilty verdicts and fines. Elila Tuomey, the daughter of a notorious river pirate, divorced John after allegedly trying to kill him. John Tuomey then married a local prostitute, Bridget Noonan, who incurred fines and served jail time for illegally trading with slaves, but he divorced her in 1838, charging Bridget with adultery and pilfering goods from his store. Although it cannot be proven, the free-black daughters of William Johnson, Anna and Catherine, changed the family name to Johnston after the Civil War, quite likely to distance themselves and their family in the public record from the Johnson-Tuomey family of "bawdy ladies" and criminals.[5]

The Criminal Women of Antebellum Natchez

The Johnson, Pettits, and Tuomey women mentioned above were among the 4,620 people arrested in Natchez during the period 1835 through 1862 for whom records have been located: 182 white females, 13 free-black females, 1,230 white men, 38 free-black males, and 3,157 enslaved blacks, most of whom were male runaways (see table 5). Females made up around 16 percent of those arrested, including some repeat offenders. The widows Catherine Culhane and Jane Murry, for example, were arrested again and again for trading with slaves, selling liquor on Sunday, and marketing liquor without a license, as were Margaret Fulham (six arrests), Elizabeth Attaway (five arrests), and Sabrina Hitchins (five arrests), all of whom managed or owned boardinghouses, taverns, and hotels. The most frequently arrested woman in Natchez, the widow Elizabeth Wade, owned the White Horse Tavern in Under-the-Hill Natchez, traded with slaves, committed assault and battery, and dealt in stolen goods. All her run-ins with the law happened during the five years from 1835 to 1840, after which Wade disappears from the public record.[6]

Most arrested white and free-black women faced municipal and county magistrates for minor infractions of city and state laws, such as doing commerce without a license, on Sundays, or with blacks or assault and battery on other women (often alleged prostitutes), male acquaintances, and local police officers while resisting arrest. None of these females was alleged to have attacked or beaten anyone with intent to kill. Local authorities arrested twenty-seven white women (but no free-black women) for theft and receiving stolen goods, or less than one woman per year. These women, if found guilty or if they pleaded guilty, typically received small fines of $5 to $50 for petite larceny (stolen property or money valued at less than $20) or heavier fines, up to $500, for grand larceny (stolen property or money valued at more than $20). Some women, convicted of grand larceny, were required to post bonds (if repeat offenders) to ensure that they would not violate the law for at least a year following their convictions. A small handful committed felonies ("infamous crimes") that carried penitentiary sentences, such as Elizabeth Payne, mentioned earlier. White and free-black males in Natchez were arrested for numerous crimes not typically alleged of women: stealing horses or slaves, dueling, perjury, rape, embezzlement, passing counterfeit coins, fraud, and gaming. Except for harboring and stealing slaves, the city's criminal women participated in slave-related crimes more than males did, including offenses such as selling liquor to the enslaved, entertaining and

TABLE 5. Criminal arrests, all ages, Natchez and Adams County, 1835–62

	Whites		Slaves		Free blacks	
Crime	Male	Female	Male	Female	Male	Female
Assault & battery	614	27	79	6	6	2
Larceny	168	12	186	50	2	
Threats	153	8			4	
Receiving stolen goods	22	13			2	
Robbery	25	2	10	8		
Harboring slaves	18	6				3
Gaming	18					
Retailing	18	4			6	
Fraud	18					
Horse stealing	15					
Abusive language	15	2	67	6		1
Counterfeit	13					
Contempt	13					
Murder	13	2	19	1		
Slave stealing	12					
Selling to slaves	27	30				
Selling liquor to slaves	17	44				1
Tavern hours	3	6				1
Bawdy house	4	13				1
Forgery	8	7				
Dueling	7					
Perjury	7					
Breaking the peace	5			2		
Embezzlement	5					
Rape	3					
Arson	3		1			
Nuisance	2	5				
Bastardy	2	1				
Vagrancy	2					
Runaway slaves			2,216	475		
Without permit			25	6	18	4
Total arrests:	1,230	182	2,603	554	38	13

Source: Adams County Criminal Records, HNF.
Note: Total white arrests, 1,412; total slave arrests, 3,157; total free-black arrests, 51

housing them without permission from the men and women who owned them, and trading with the enslaved on Sundays or at any time without the permission of their owners.

If sexual activity happened between white women and enslaved men, it never showed up in the records for arrests in Natchez and Adams County for the years 1835 through 1862, the years for which the available record is most complete, although such activity sometimes came to light in divorce proceedings and slander suits. In one court case, the spinster Melissa Ayles sued Peter Southworth for slander after he accused her of having "carnal intercourse" one night in an open garden with one of his slaves. Ayles protested her innocence and brought forth a number of character witnesses to try to rescue her reputation. In asking for monetary damages, Ayles claimed that due to the allegation of fornication most of her friends and neighbors refused to speak with her, "invite her into their homes," or "walk in her vicinity." The suit's outcome is unknown, but no magistrate charged Ayles with fornication. In fact, no white or free-black woman in antebellum Natchez can be found in the public record to have been arrested or incarcerated for sexual relations with an enslaved man; such affairs undoubtedly happened but were kept out of the public eye. A few white women did marry or live with free-black men (usually men passing for white), sometimes openly, with few obvious repercussions, at least legally speaking.[7]

Overall, magistrates in antebellum Natchez seldom charged married women with committing crimes (less than 10 percent of those charged were married women), and few appear in the records more than once. It is impossible, however, to be certain of the marital status of the city's arrested women at the time of their arrests. It is likely that some were married but abandoned women, such as Lydia Pettits, discussed above, or had husbands who lived outside Natchez. A clearer picture exists for the years 1808 to 1837, because record keepers marked the word "spinster" beside the names of not-married female criminals older than the age when most women would have married (63 percent of female criminals were so identified during this period). Whether the other women arrested in these years were married, divorced, or widowed is hard to say, except for the three women listed as widows, including Jane Andre, who murdered her husband and was thus a widow when arrested. The arrest ledgers also record nine spinsters as the victims of rape and assault and battery. When Frances Surget, one of the town's most prominent planter elites, allegedly kidnapped and raped Mary Ellis, the daughter of an equally prominent and wealthy planter, the arrest ledger listed her marital status as spinster. Although he was arrested for a crime that carried jail time if convicted, there is no evidence that Surget ever faced a judge for his alleged sexual assault.[8]

During the years 1835 through 1862, Natchez police arrested women on four-teen separate occasions for keeping bawdy or disorderly houses (in which pros-titution, drinking, and lewd entertainment allegedly took place), but never for prostitution, fornication, or adultery. For the most part, these arrested women operated taverns, boardinghouses, and hotels in Under-the-Hill Natchez or ran one of several bordellos located at the top of the bluffs where the "road from the landing" gave way to the city's uptown grid. Some were repeat of-fenders, including the free woman of color Eliza Bossack (aka Eliza Cotton and Eliza Holden) and the white woman Catherine Johnson, but none appear to have been married at the time of their arrests or to have received jail or prison sentences. Most were life-long Natchez residents who show up in var-ious public and private records as small-scale property owners, slaveholders, churchgoers, and active participants in the larger public scene. The last record of a white woman or a free woman of color being arrested and fined for "whor-ing" appears in the early 1820s. A Natchez sheriff arrested the sisters Polly and Matilda Smith for "whoring," along with their mother, Sarah, who allegedly kept a "common, ill governed, disorderly house." If the two sisters claimed to be working at something other than prostitution, such as being seamstresses, a common occupational cover used by prostitutes, they probably escaped convic-tion for vagrancy.[9]

Nine of the fourteen arrests for keeping bawdy or disorderly houses occurred during the years 1841 and 1842, during the so-called Inquisition years, when Natchez authorities especially attempted to drive free blacks from the state. Because these bawdy houses sometimes employed black prostitutes, often free-black women who hailed from elsewhere, their proprietors faced stepped-up police scrutiny in response to mounting public pressure. But when the moment passed and the clamor died down, local authorities resumed their previous policies of benign neglect regarding brothels, whorehouses, and dance halls.[10] Although empowered to enforce ordinances promulgated in 1829 and 1843 that aimed at suppressing disorderly houses, Natchez police seldom raided the city's many brothels, preferring instead to levy fines on sex workers as vagrants in order to generate municipal revenue or to better impose some semblance of social order in the community. Consequently, prostitution assumed the status of a public nuisance, much like appearing drunk in public, cross-dressing, being nude in public, or disorderly conduct, all of which generated income for the municipality from the fines levied.[11]

It should not be forgotten that, although the city's sexual commerce might have offended many top-of-the-bluffs residents as well as their churchly min-isters and priests, it remained throughout the years a principal attraction for men traveling the river as well as a thriving convenience for some of the city's

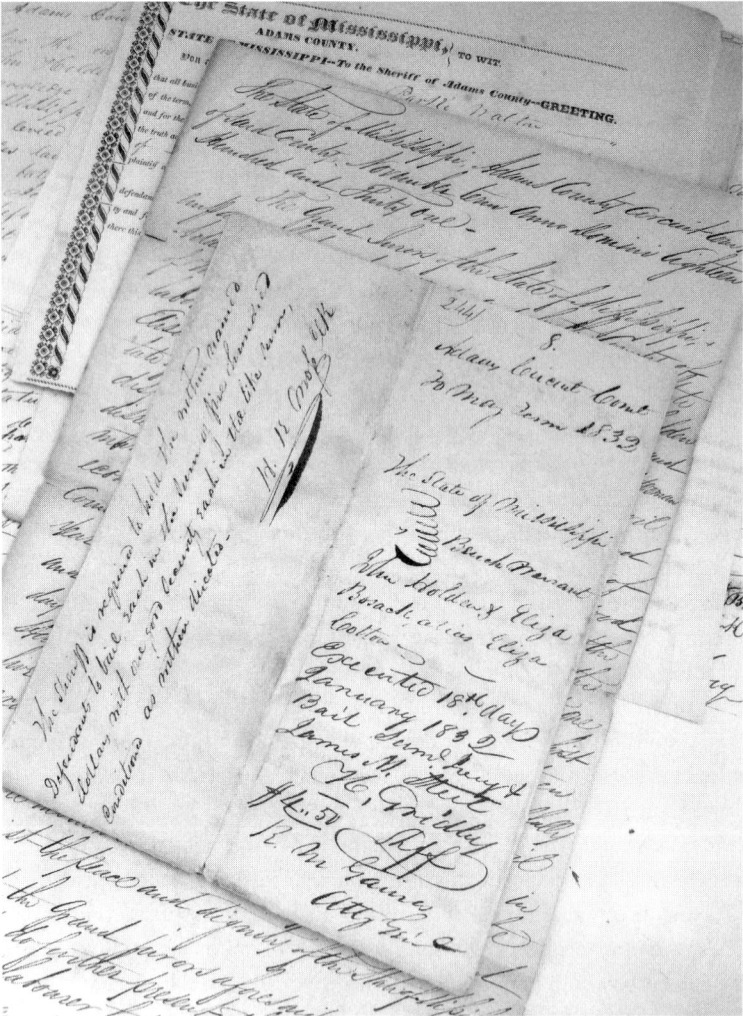

Bench Warrant, Adams County Circuit Court, *State of Mississippi v. John Holden &
Eliza Bossack, alias Eliza Cotton* (charge of "fornication"), May term, 1832. Historic
Natchez Foundation.

duplicitous white males of all classes, men who patronized the waterfront harlots and gaming houses in secrecy. An Under-the-Hill newspaper, the *Natchez Cutter*, captured this reality perfectly when it reported how respectable white men often "pretend to be fishing in Lake Concordia" across the Mississippi River in Louisiana only to never leave Under-the-Hill Natchez, asking them the rhetorical question, "Where do you fish, old boys?" Few Natchez whites holding influence during the 1850s wanted to shut down its bawdy houses or charge its customers, patrons, profiteers, and workers with crimes against morality, although probably everyone outside those directly involved considered them undesirable, to say the least.[12]

The few allegations of immoral activities leveled against Natchez women differ from what is known about women and sexual misbehavior in other parts of the antebellum South. Historian Victoria Bynum found 257 women charged with sexual misconduct in the lower courts of three Piedmont counties in North Carolina during the 1850s.[13] Why did so many acts of sexual misconduct by women occur in the North Carolina Piedmont in comparison to the handful in Natchez? It is unlikely that Natchez women prudishly avoided sexual misconduct and activities, in view of the notorious Under-the-Hill that overflowed with bars, bawdy houses, assorted prostitutes, and madams. Natchez residents most likely tolerated and perhaps condoned the ongoing illicit though not always illegal sexual activity that was obviously rampant both in Under-the-Hill and above the bluffs where the landing road met the city, as long as such goings-on did not spill over into Main Street commercial venues and residential neighborhoods, threaten the sexual purity of church-going and respectable white women and children, publicly implicate white customers, or promote illicit sex as normative rather than an accepted aberration in which some nonrespectable women serviced and privileged more than a few white males and some black men on the sly. Nearly every traveler to Natchez knew about its bawdy Under-the-Hill social life and the tatterdemalions of its waterfront, its numerous gambling and dance halls, and the moral laxity of its riverfront men and women. Despite several crusades that drove gamblers from the city during the 1830s, sexual escapades and commerce reflected a vibrantly urban milieu, and this sexual liberalism remained an integral part of the city's cognitive and physical reality throughout its antebellum history.[14]

Although a well-established police apparatus had emerged by the 1850s to deal with the city's more dangerous criminal activity and protect its warehouses from burglary and fires, it was not much concerned with policing morality or harassing the town's criminal women. Town and county militia organizations patrolled Natchez and the surrounding countryside to capture runaway slaves, break up slave gatherings, and keep a watchful eye out for any sign of slave insurrection. The mayor and city aldermen appointed seven squad leaders who selected five men from within each of the city's seven districts for this patrol duty, a civic duty that every able-bodied white male was obligated to perform if called upon. In addition, the city aldermen elected a city marshal, a constable, and a policeman to keep the peace in cooperation with a night guard and a city patrol. Each officer had duties beyond keeping the peace, such as collecting taxes, patrolling warehouses, supervising the removal of rotten garbage and dead animals, serving warrants, attending court, and taking depositions, but they also could make arrests whenever they observed laws being broken. The mayor served as the city's justice of the peace, empowered to make arrests, appoint lower-level police officers, and hold criminal court for minor crimes.[15]

Most policing fell, however, to the city patrol, which could arrest anyone observed breaking the law and hold him or her until the alleged criminal could be turned over to a local magistrate. In their vigilant efforts to arrest slaves and free blacks suspected of being runaways or violating city curfews applicable to both enslaved and free blacks, members of the patrol had little time for policing harlots or reining in the many dance halls and bars where prostitution undoubtedly happened every night throughout the years. Little attention was paid to arresting whores, stopping fights that involved only women, or curtailing the sexual trade and frivolity in waterfront taverns and hotels (as long as locals limited their activities to sex and drink) by either the vigilantes or the city's policing apparatus, partly because such activities did not much disturb the peace and because most "bawdy ladies" knew perfectly well just how far they could go before bringing down police surveillance. Perhaps most importantly, many in the city's watch and patrol were themselves working-class men who knew Natchez's whores, tavern keepers, and less than respectable working-class women as relatives, friends, customers, and providers of goods and services that included bribes, potential municipal revenues, and sex.[16]

Bawdy-house madams and other criminal women seldom went to jail when arrested in antebellum Natchez, and their businesses continued to operate, including those selling whiskey to slaves or dealing in stolen goods. These women, like Catherine Johnson, paid their fines and resumed doing business because their activities generally were accepted, supported, and tolerated by the larger community. The remarkable career of the city's most notorious madam and brothel proprietor, Malvina Matthews, is illustrative of how at least one not-married, often arrested free woman navigated life in Natchez in the years before the Civil War. Although her story cannot be said to typify the city's not-married criminal women, it does illuminate what such women faced as they skirted the legal strictures established by the larger Natchez community as well as the kind of resiliency demanded of them if they were to survive and sometimes prosper as women without husbands at their sides.

Malvina Matthews

On the night of May 26, 1868, Malvina Matthews, the notorious sixty-some-year-old proprietress of Natchez's most well-established brothel, allegedly shot to death Private John Moffatt, a U.S. soldier stationed at Fort McPherson in Union-occupied Natchez. According to eyewitnesses, an intoxicated Moffatt and a fellow soldier, Phillip Bilo, forced their way into Matthews's "house of ill fame" on the bluffs, where they confronted several prostitutes and their male customers. Private Bilo later testified that an intoxicated Moffatt, eager for a fight, boasted that he "could whip any man in the house." After exchanging rough words with the women and their patrons, the two soldiers departed the house only to find their way blocked by a locked gate. Moffatt, in a drunken rage, demanded loudly that someone had better come quick to let them out. Within minutes, if not seconds, a shot (or shots) struck Moffatt, killing him instantly. Private Bilo then leaped over the fence and ran several blocks to the Union encampment, Fort McPherson, where he awaited morning before informing his superior officer of the shooting. Once alerted, the command-ing officer of the Natchez Post rounded up the women living and working as prostitutes in the brothel (at least four blacks and one white), several black servant girls, and the four male patrons (white residents of Natchez) from the previous night. Two days later, a civilian coroner's jury of inquest determined that Moffatt "came to his death by a gunshot wound in the head and neck [inflicted] by Lavina J. Matthews," the not-married white woman who owned the racially mixed whorehouse where the shooting had occurred, along with the residence next door in which she lived. At her ensuing trial, a civilian jury acquitted Matthews, who was represented by the Confederate war hero and successful Natchez lawyer William T. Martin.[17]

The Malvina Matthews who allegedly killed a Yankee soldier in 1868 first appears in the public records of Natchez in 1833, as a woman somewhere be-tween the ages of twenty-one and thirty-six who had inherited what looks like the furnishings and accoutrements of a bordello. Eliza Perry, who died while visiting Natchez from New Orleans, bequeathed (in a nuncupative or "deathbed" will) to Malvina Jane Houghman, later known as Malvina Jane Matthews, six beds, card tables, dining-room tables, chairs, washbasins, and assorted bureaus.[18] Matthews had migrated as a single woman to Natchez from Virginia, possibly arriving with Perry to work as a prostitute or to operate a whorehouse. Matthews's exact age in 1832 is difficult to discern. She is reported to have been sixty-five to seventy years old in 1868, yet other records have her born in 1812. It is likely that she never revealed her true age in the public records. She appears in the legal records under a number of aliases: Melvina or Malvina Jane Houghman; Lavine or Lavina or Lavinia or Malvina or Melvina Jane Huffman (or Hoffman); Malvina or Melvina or Lavine or Lavinia Jane Mitchell; and Malvina or Malvina or Lavine or Lavinia J. Matthews. After she married Edward Matthews in 1852, she often appears in the records as Malvina (or Melvina) Jane Matthews. The various versions of Houghman (i.e., Huffman, Hoffman, etc.) probably reflect mistakes in spelling by clerks rather than attempts to mislead, although she may have been of Jewish ancestry. Ever capable of adapting, Matthews converted to Catholicism during her trial for the murder of Private Moffatt.

When she arrived in Natchez, the city's prostitutes principally worked in the bars, dance halls, gambling dens, and brothels at the Under-the-Hill waterfront, an area much wilder than what she and Perry had probably experienced in New Orleans, where some brothels were highly fashionable places of business. Antebellum New Orleans, operating according to the customs and laws of the Napoleonic Code, reigned as the libertine, multiracial, and cosmopolitan "Queen City" of the lower South. It sported a long history of concubinage and interracial sex, a thriving market for "fancy girls" (light-skinned female slaves marketed for sex), and the open acceptance of the interracial sexual institution known as *plaçage* (long-term, carefully committed, and often contractual relationships between white men and free women of color). Nothing as institutionalized or sophisticated existed in Natchez, although forms of concubinage or long-term sexual affairs between white men and their enslaved women often played out in well-known but never fully acknowledged relationships. Natchez residents generally tolerated prostitution, tending to view it as a somewhat nefarious, ubiquitous but not publicly acknowledged commerce engaged in by a diverse array of people: low-down black and white residents of the worst sorts, well-heeled visitors to the city, riverboat ruffians and their retainers, and various uptown dandies and otherwise respected white men who indulged themselves secretly in illicit sexual activity with fallen women.[19]

In 1845, Matthews purchased a lot and house located at the bluffs that overlooked the Mississippi River, near the city's abandoned lighthouse (which was completely destroyed by a tornado in 1840) and the landing road connecting Natchez Above-the-Hill to the waterfront. She lived in this house until her death in 1875, having acquired sometime during the 1840s or 1850s two adjoining lots, or portions of them, and at least two other domiciles from which she ran her business, along with other select properties in town. By the time of her trial for murder, Matthews owned three brick houses, all facing east along Broadway Street, two of which she rented to black prostitutes.[20]

Matthews's place sat on the bluffs fronting the city proper, near a road leading down to the waterfront and a long, rough-hewn, wooden staircase that climbed up from the landing to the top of the bluffs, which provided easy access to her business for riverboat men, dock workers, travelers coming to Natchez via the Natchez Trace and the Mississippi River, slave traders, and all types of men interested in prostitutes, including some of the city's respectable white males. While Malvina's place of business extended the Under-the-Hill waterfront to the uplands, it stood much removed and separate from the squalid bars, gambling parlors, saloons, and other dens of iniquity below while also remaining distinct from the rest of Above-the-Hill Natchez. Her holdings occupied the near center of a grassy promenade that ran along the bluffs, with spectacular views of the river and the Louisiana delta (more fully described in chapter 1). This commons separated the bluffs' edge from the lowlands below and from the city's commercial streets and residential neighborhoods that lay to the south and east. Matthews's property, situated amid several working-class houses (one owned by a riverboat captain and another by a former lighthouse keeper turned blacksmith), stood out during the 1850s as a rough-edged enclave most likely marked in the public imagination as the one-time "lighthouse district" that featured a thriving top-of-the-bluffs whorehouse.

According to city and county justice dockets, Matthews was arrested for "keeping a bawdy house" in only two years, 1841 and 1842, during the stepped-up but momentary campaign by reform-minded municipal authorities to drive out free blacks, gamblers, and vagrants, including prostitutes (discussed earlier in this chapter).[21] Among the 182 criminal actions allegedly committed by Natchez white women from 1835 through 1862, only thirteen females faced charges for keeping brothels (meaning disorderly houses), and Matthews's arrests account for four of the total; none were ever charged directly with prostitution by municipal or county authorities, even though selling sex was a thriving business in Natchez for all of its antebellum history.[22]

Other than her arrests for keeping a disorderly house, Matthews never shows up in municipal or county criminal records, except for one assault-and-battery case in 1846. Moreover, of the six or seven other women who were known to have owned or managed bordellos, none ever faced arrest for thieving, assault and battery, or trading with slaves. Some of these brothel madams, like Matthews, owned or rented houses in Above-the-Hill Natchez, namely, Elizabeth Lawrence, Jane Mayes, and Mary Simmons. Two other women, the free blacks Nancy and Caroline Kyle, lived as mother and daughter in a dwelling inherited from the white merchant Christopher Kyle, probably the father of Caroline, in an area east of Matthews's property. Although never arrested as prostitutes nor charged with other crimes, the Kyle women were nearly driven from town in 1841 by a local zealot who accused them at a meeting of the Adams County Board of Police of keeping "a House of ill fame, a house of asination [*sic*], a whore House, & c."[23]

Although never just a common criminal, Matthews was a notorious character in Natchez by the 1840s. A divorce suit in 1839 named her as a woman of "ill fame" with whom William Ducay had had "sexual connection," along with several "diverse other women of evil and dissolute habits."[24] A grand jury indictment against Matthews in 1841 for keeping "a certain ill-governed and disorderly house" accused her in no uncertain terms of being an "evil woman of evil name and fame" who ran an establishment wherein evil women and men engaged in "dishonest conversation," coming together at all hours of the day and night in "drinking, tippling, whoring, and misbehaving themselves." Matthews denied the allegations, possibly claiming that her business did not fit the ordinance definition of disorderly houses, which specifically referred to dance halls and gambling dens. In likely anticipation of trouble ahead, in 1841 she deeded in trust her residence, along with her slaves and personal property, to Alfred Bemiss, who may have been Matthews's sexual companion at the time. Although the evidence is uncertain, this transfer of title possibly enabled her to claim that she could not be held personally responsible for operating a disorderly house under any definition.[25] Although it is unclear from the extant records how the grand jury case ended, she probably paid a small fine; thereafter she never again faced similar charges by any municipal authority, despite continuing to operate a thriving prostitution business up through the time she was briefly jailed for killing the Yankee soldier in 1868.[26]

This legal maneuvering by Matthews reflected the workings of an astute mind (probably enhanced by information gleaned from her male patrons) and a determined business sense unusual in a day and place where women, enslaved and free, were severely constrained in both their private lives and public affairs. As a not-married woman until 1852, Matthews enjoyed the legal status of the *feme sole*, meaning that she could wheel and deal as an independent agent insofar as local custom would allow.[27] Matthews's name appears frequently in legal cases as well as in the county mortgage and deed books documenting loans, property transactions, foreclosure actions, and suits for debt collections and fraudulent activities in Natchez.[28] (See chapter 5 for Matthews and her alleged fraudulent actions against Fanny Leiper.)

Living as a spinster for all of the 1820s, 1830s, and 1840s, and operating under the legal status of a *feme sole* until her marriage to Edward J. Matthews in 1852, Malvina Matthews exhibited all the traits of an ambitious, entrepreneurial woman up to the point when the Civil War engulfed her life and the lives of all those around her. Her enterprise rested on operating a bordello of long standing as well as owning, buying, selling, and managing property. While running her brothel business, Matthews aggressively used her properties in the "lighthouse district" as security for loans; she held promissory notes for at least $3,500 by 1860, and she most likely had other investments not recorded in the public records.[29] She counted among her friends and business associates working-class women like herself, both free blacks and whites, as well as the enslaved women that she owned. Among the public records is an apprenticeship document indicating that Matthews had assumed responsibility for raising and educating a two-year-old child, the daughter of a neighbor who was a known prostitute.[30]

On November 5, 1852, Matthews married Edward (aka Edwin) J. Matthews, an Irishman from Louisiana, who thereafter appears to have worked with her as a business partner. Their marriage was not an easy one, however, and she sued for divorce on January 5, 1860, alleging that he had had numerous sexual encounters with various "lewd women" during the prior seven or eight years, including a prostitute, Mary Simmons, to whom Matthews had once sold some of her bluffs property and who had apprenticed her two-year-old daughter to Matthews in 1852. To make matters worse, Malvina charged her husband with having had "carnal and adulterous intercourse" with the enslaved Sabra, a mulatto whom Malvina had purchased as her separate property. The affair with the enslaved woman, according to Matthews, had been going on for years, but it recently had taken a new course when Edward ran off with Sabra, keeping "her as a concubine in a room attached to a stable in town."[31] As with all women seeking divorce in antebellum Mississippi, Matthews's suit, according to the state's legal code, could be granted only on grounds of adultery, impotence, or abandonment, a legal rigidity that required her to present herself as a "dutiful and faithful wife" who had fully abided by her marriage vows. Also, as a *feme covert*, or a married woman with few independent legal rights, Matthews was required by law and custom to file her petition for divorce by way of a "best friend" (because married women, like minors and "idiots," could not sue under their own name), so Joseph C. Russell acted in her behalf.[32]

There is no way of knowing whether or not Malvina had been a "faithful and dutiful" wife to Edward, as she claimed, but it probably seemed unlikely to most observers, given her profession and reputation. More was at stake for her, however, than ending an unhappy marriage. She had property to protect under the Married Women's Property Law, in force as Mississippi state law since 1839 (discussed in chapter 3), which enabled her to claim independent title to both personal and real property despite being married. Although the law protecting married women's property existed on the books, her claim to separate status in property ownership could be contested in a court of law, and she undoubtedly feared that her estranged husband would run off with her slaves, or at least one of them, and try to claim her other assets. With this in mind, Malvina obtained a writ of injunction forbidding Edward, under any claim of "marital control," from seizing her house, real estate, notes due her (which she held in her name for loans and mortgages given), and the eight enslaved people she owned at the time of the suit. She portrayed Edward Matthews as a no-account, impoverished scoundrel without assets of his own or even a job, saying that all that he "possessed and consumed" came from her.[33]

Two months later, Malvina abruptly withdrew her petition for divorce. What happened to persuade her to change her mind is unclear, but Edward left the state soon after to live in Louisiana, possibly taking the enslaved Sabra with him. Perhaps rather than fight with Edward over their properties in divorce litigation, Malvina had paid him to leave Natchez in order to satisfy the three-year-absence provision for claiming spousal abandonment. Whatever the reality, the war intervened. She filed a second petition for divorce on September 17, 1866, limiting her justification for divorce to her husband's abandonment in 1861. Edward never responded to the subpoenas issued by the court, and Malvina's witnesses affirmed that he had been living somewhere in Louisiana following her first divorce appeal. Because Edward failed to contest or challenge Malvina's divorce petition, the court finally granted her divorce on April 25, 1867, a year prior to her alleged shooting of Private Moffatt.[34]

When Yankee soldiers descended on Natchez in the summer of 1863, Matthews stood ready to greet them as customers. Little did they know that this much-experienced and resolute whorehouse madam would one day shoot one of them dead in her yard and be found innocent of her alleged crime by a jury of local men, which included blacks.[35] But anyone who knew her, or knew Natchez, would not have been surprised.

Conclusion

The female criminals of antebellum Natchez were no ordinary women. They engaged in petty and sometimes major criminal activities that ranged from prostitution to trading with slaves. Yet despite their defiance of the law in matters often small and hidden from the public eye, they appear to have been mostly tolerated in their lifestyles by much of the larger community in which they lived, especially its male police, magistrates, lawyers, and judges. Little effort was made by Natchez citizenry to control their sexual behavior, criminal activities (especially after the mid-1840s), entrepreneurial ventures, or general conduct either through the law or through social ostracism, except in rare cases. Surely no one considered these women to have been on equal footing with the city's elite slave-holding ladies, merchant wives, schoolteachers, governesses, and women of the better sort, whether married or not, and most white and free-black, middle- and upper-class women simply ignored them. But it would be misleading to think of them as women out of step with their time and place.

The city's criminal women, like many other Natchez women, were accepted, and behaved, as servants of the larger social order in which they lived. Some owned slaves, others traded with them on terms of near equality in various shady dealings, and most of them probably participated in an under-the-table illegal trade more often than their extant arrests and indictments suggest. But their criminality did not always marginalize them or cast them out of the community. No better proof of this can be found than the white Catherine Johnson's will. Although a member of the notorious Tuomey family—career lawbreakers—she bequeathed fifty dollars to the esteemed Catholic prelate of Natchez, Bishop William Elder, and consigned her affairs to her "good personal friend" John B. Nevitt, one of the most prominent plantation slaveholders in the state.[36] And some of them, like Catherine Culhane, lost sons and brothers in the Civil War, a cause that many local whites supported in allegiance to their state, their community, and slavery. Culhane's four sons, for example, perished as loyal Confederate volunteers during the war, a sacrifice unmatched by any other Natchez mother surveyed for this study.[37]

It is in this context of tolerance for the city's nefarious but never greatly troublesome nor especially unruly criminal women that a bold and semiliterate rogue who lived on a flatboat anchored at the landing penned a poetic marriage proposal to the widow Sally Junks, a longtime resident of a street named Rotten Row, located just off the waterfront. Its author wrote with tongue in cheek, but his verses ring true to the popular image of how the rough-hewn women of the city's waterfront engaged life on their own terms.

> *The Maid under the Hill*
> Oh sweet, she's sweet that rosey maid,
> 　The maid that dwells under the Hill,
> She wears her hair in witching braid,
> 　With ringlets twisted up to kill!
> And killed me quite that fair maid has,
> 　She lives somewhere in Rotton Row,
> I feel as if I'd swallowed gas,
> 　and found the gas itself "no go!"

That lovely killing female girl
   Tobacco chews and smokes a pipe,
She takes gin toddies with a whirl,
   then gives her reeking lips a wipe.
Oh, she's the girl for me, for me,
   If I can only catch the game,
And I will link my destiny,
   With one who never cries, "for shame!"
I'd tell her name, but I'm afraid,
   Some dandy in the Upper Town
With soapy locks to steal my maid,
   Would, like a fox, come stealthy down.
The maid that lives beneath the Hill!
   If I lose her I'm dished forever;
The thought of it gives me the chill—
   I can not lose her—never! never!
Last night I went to see my dear,
   I found her taking punch and smoking,
Says I, I want to linger here,
   Says she, get out you brute you're joking.
I wouldn't budge, but caught her hand,
   She drew her fist and knocked me over;
She laid me senseless to the land,
   Just when I thought I was in the clover.
Oh, that stout maid beneath the Hill,
   She'll whip her weight in wild cats sure,
her voice would make ten thousand still—
   She's mine—or life I'll not endure.
                —Jim Bowser
                Flat-Boat Nancy[38]

Although no trace can be found in public records of Jim Bowser or his love Sally Junks, it is no matter whether they were real people or not; their love affair struck a true chord for most observers of and participants in the city's Under-the-Hill antebellum life and times. Sally Junks, what is more, typified the Natchez woman valued for her rough-hewn physical beauty and for her ability to more than hold her own as an independently minded female, as a woman a lot like Malvina Matthews. One day after Bowser's marriage proposal, the unmoved Sally answered with a poem of her own:

To Jim Bowser

Sheep's head and pluck, Jim Bowser,
You ain't much of a real rouser,
And I can never take a fancy
To be your wife on flatboat Nancy.
You are a sneak, Jim Bowser, Jim,
You can't bamboozle me, my Jim,
You owl, you goose, you snaky brute,
You have a snout, pray can you toot?
You talk of toddy, sling, and such,
My toddies never cost you much,
For when I asked you once to treat,
You bolted off a quick retreat.
It tickles me, Jim Bowser, you,
To think of how sadly you will rue
The day you wrote that poetry
With aching heart and many a sigh.
You elephant, you coon, you pig,
Now don't you feel almighty big?
To let a gal like me get round you
And with my fist and verses pound you!
                              —Sally Junks[39]

These Under-the-Hill poetic expressions of unrequited and unreciprocated love expressed publicly the somewhat ambivalent but commonly accepted feelings about social class, gender identifications, and the importance of physical place in the everyday life of antebellum Natchez. Although Sally Junks could never have been mistaken for a lady, the likes of those who lived in Natchez Above-the-Hill, nor could Jim Bowser be mistaken for a smoothly groomed uptown dandy, both characters seemed to fit comfortably within the larger social fabric of Natchez life. Sally could easily have been the fornicator Sally Clark or the career criminal Elila Tuomey, a young Malvina Matthews, or any one of the dozen other women arrested for petty and larger crimes. The images of Jim Bowser and Sally Junks are whimsical portraits to be sure, but whimsy often masks acceptance as much as contempt. In these depictions, tough-dealing women and blunt-speaking confidence men enjoyed a level of acceptance and tolerance on the part of the larger community that enabled men and women of their stripes to move securely in place. Sally Junks apparently needed no man in her life to be happy and secure, and she was not a woman who suffered fools lightly. Most importantly, her tough talk and straight-dealing ways, and the honesty of her character as a woman who could not be shamed, threatened neither the dandies who lived in Natchez Above-the-Hill nor anyone else in antebellum Natchez so long as she stayed in her shanty on a street named Rotten Row in Under-the-Hill Natchez.

The entrepreneurial Catherine Johnson and Malvina Matthews were equally street savvy, but they, more than Sally, moved comfortably and even more adroitly between the two worlds above and below the bluffs. They did so largely because they accommodated, serviced, and supported slavery and a social order that privileged white, male domination over women and the enslaved, which they catered to as madams and criminal women even as they stepped in and out of the shadows. For all we know, Johnson, Junks, and Matthews could have been soul sisters (if not in blood then certainly in their common professions); they appear to have shared a relative invincibility toward any feelings of guilt or shame. They were women who could not be dishonored because honor for them was only among thieves, and they obviously had seen their share of hypocrisy from those honorable gentlemen from Above-the-Hill that frequented their establishments. The significant resiliency and adroitness these women exhibited as they maneuvered through their lives reflected their acceptance of a social order that privileged the servant ideal for women, slavery, and male domination in ways that worked for them as well as for the many men in their lives. Although they clearly stepped lively, in and out of the boundaries of the law, they seldom deviated from or challenged the prevailing givens of Natchez life, and their contemporaries seldom, if ever, viewed their actions as deviating much from community standards of acceptable behavior for free women, regardless of their marital circumstances.

CHAPTER SEVEN

Stepping Through the Tumult

Not-Married Women in Confederate and Yankee-Occupied Natchez

On May 23, 1867, Private James Carr, a musician in Company H of the Twenty-Fourth Regiment U.S. Infantry, sat drinking just before midnight with Mollie Matthews, a black prostitute, and her white coworker Mollie Williams in a bordello located near the top of the bluffs in Natchez. A fellow soldier, Private Charles Leonard, appeared at Matthews's back door demanding to see Lizzy, another one of the girls. Stepping outside, Lizzy quickly returned, telling Carr that a drunken Leonard had tried to shoot her. A third soldier, Private Samuel McCrudden, confronted Leonard, but Carr persuaded, or else forced, the inebriated McCrudden to return to their barracks at Fort McPherson, the Union fortress a few blocks from the brothel. Moments later, McCrudden broke away from Carr and headed back to Matthews's house, where Leonard shot him point-blank in the eye, killing him instantly. A few hours later a military guard arrested Leonard and hauled him off to jail; the young soldier then faced a civil indictment (rather than a court-martial commission) for murder and a jury trial that never reached a verdict because the army transferred Carr, the key witness in the case, to Tennessee.[1]

The three women involved in this murderous incident were among the numerous Natchez prostitutes who serviced the five thousand U.S. soldiers (around thirty-two hundred blacks and eighteen hundred whites) stationed in Natchez once it fell to federal forces in the summer of 1863.[2] Mollie Matthews possibly came to Natchez as one of the thousands of black refugees from slavery who poured into the city during the war, of which only one in six was a man.[3] She may have followed a man to Natchez after he joined one of the city's four black regiments set up as a home guard to protect Union-controlled plantations on which black women, children, and the elderly worked and lived as refugees from slavery. Perhaps her soldier had then died from disease or in battle, which many hundreds did, leaving her very much on her own.[4] She appears not to have lived in Natchez prior to the war as a free person of color, nor does she (or Mollie Williams or Lizzy) subsequently show up in the vicinity after Private McCrudden's death.[5] Exactly where these women came from, how they ended up in Natchez, and what happened to them after the war are questions not easily answered, but more than a few Natchez women, black and white, engaged a war that ultimately destroyed slavery, as well as the societal moorings and bonds that slavery had created, as women without husbands or other male relatives close at hand.

Martha Dunbar

Martha Willis Dunbar's Civil War experience differed markedly from what the prostitutes on the bluff underwent, but she too confronted uniformed and dangerous soldiers as a not-married woman. Martha, an eighty-one-year-old widow, was living on her three-thousand-acre plantation, Dunbarton, ten miles east of Natchez when the war began. She remained there for the war's duration with her forty-some-year-old spinster daughter, Emily, and her married, oldest daughter, Martha Dunbar Claiborne.[6] Her son-in-law, John F. H. Claiborne, a noted historian, large slaveholder, planter, and staunch Unionist, spent most of the war years on the Mississippi Gulf Coast protecting his plantation and slaves from marauding soldiers and collaborating with Union forces in New Orleans in exchange for federal protection and trading permits.[7] The matriarch Martha's longtime manager and overseer, a proclaimed opponent of secession, had fled to Union-controlled Natchez to avoid capture by Confederate "guerrillas," who had threatened to hang him.[8] Most of Martha's enslaved workers, numbering perhaps several hundred, also left Dunbarton when the Yankees came, and it is a good bet that some of them lived as refugees in Natchez, worked for the Union army in fatigue labor, or joined one of the black regiments stationed there as soldiers.[9]

Martha had sent Emily into Natchez to swear an oath of allegiance to the Union at the first opportunity in order to obtain federal permits granted to loyalists to sell their garden produce, firewood, and some cotton in Natchez, even as she negotiated with Confederate regular and "irregular" troops to protect her family and properties as longtime residents, defenseless women, and committed slaveholders.[10] With the Confederates, it probably helped that Martha's grandson had served and died as an officer in the rebel army, but neither allegiance to the Union nor the family's commitment to slavery as an institution stopped both Union and Confederate troopers from plundering Dunbarton and terrifying its occupants.[11] The Yankees stripped Dunbarton of its foodstuffs, livestock, saddles, and plantation tools as well as the clothing, shoes, poultry, and garden crops belonging to its few remaining enslaved people. Confederates were no better. They burned Dunbarton cotton and raided its crops and animals. Rebel "jayhawkers" allegedly murdered two enslaved workers caught returning to Dunbarton in Union bluecoats after having sold a wagonload of cotton in Natchez for Martha and her daughters.[12]

The spinster daughter Emily lived throughout the war years always terrified that Confederate soldiers or "jayhawkers" and "irregular" troops would "arrest [her] or burn out" her and her mother's house or sexually "molest" and "possibly injure" her and her sister as unprotected women and Union sympathizers. According to her sister and several former slaves, the terror Emily experienced during the war drove her insane and brought on her death in 1869.[13] The Dunbar women may have worried too about the loyalty of their once enslaved workers, some of whom most certainly knew about the rumored slave conspiracy to kill slave owners and ravish white women at the first sign of Union troops. A "vigilance committee" of local slaveholders, including some of Martha's neighbors, had executed in a largely unwarranted burst of hysteria dozens of neighborhood slaves in 1861, for allegedly plotting just such a slave uprising.[14]

Ellen Shields

Ellen Shields, who undoubtedly knew the Dunbar women, recalled in a memoir written years after the war how Yankee soldiers had terrorized her family and plundered her father's villa, Montebello, located on the outskirts of Natchez. According to Ellen, the incident happened in August 1864, when the Yankee provost marshal in Natchez tried to force her father, Gabriel Shields, to release for burial the body of his youngest child, who lay dead from malaria in the family residence. The old man refused to give up his son's corpse and vowed to defend Montebello to the death if necessary from any Yankee attempt to invade his house, claiming that Montebello was his "castle" and that every man had a fundamental right to defend hearth and home. Shields armed his two teenage sons, Surget and Wilmer, and prepared for the worst, while his two daughters, Kate and Ellen, unmarried women in their early twenties, huddled together upstairs with their mother, grandmother, and younger sister.[15]

Events then happened quickly: twenty Union soldiers "led by the country's terror—Earl himself" (Lieutenant Isaac N. Earl) assaulted the villa's heavy oak doors with axes while firing their weapons into its first-floor, glass windows. Shields and his older son fired back at the soldiers while the youngest son stood guard upstairs. Earl, who commanded a special unit of mounted scouts authorized to gather intelligence about Confederate sympathizers, suspected that Shields had been aiding rebel troops in the Natchez hinterland with money, supplies, and weapons.[16] The battle lasted for nearly two hours before Ellen's uncle, James Surget, and a wealthy slaveholding neighbor, Douglas Rivers, who had taken the oath of loyalty to the Union, convinced Shields to surrender.[17] According to Ellen, her father agreed to give up the house if the Union scouts stacked their weapons and entered the house unarmed. Earl accepted the terms and Shields left the house with his seventeen-year-old son and two oldest daughters walking proudly beside him while the rest of the family remained in the locked rooms upstairs. Once outside, the Yankees grabbed the young Surget Shields and prepared to execute him on the spot. A wounded soldier gallantly intervened because of the women present, thereby saving the boy's life. Gabriel Shields, again according to Ellen, had resisted the scouts under the advice of his old friend Adjutant General Lorenzo Thomas, who told him that he had a right to defend his home against "bushwhackers." The Yankee troops then transported Shields, his two sons, and Kate and Ellen to Natchez, turning them over to the Union provost marshal, who locked the men in jail and ordered the two sisters back to Montebello; if they refused, the provost marshal threatened to incarcerate them in the women's jail at the courthouse, which overflowed with white and black females arrested for petty theft, prostitution, public drunkenness, selling liquor, and smuggling.[18]

The sisters agreed to return to their family villa, but before going Kate sought out General Lorenzo Thomas, her father's old friend and the Union officer supervising refugee camps in the lower Mississippi River Valley, asking his help in freeing her father and brothers. When Thomas refused, Kate rejoined her sister, whom she found being harassed by a gang of Union soldiers on a downtown street corner. The whooping and cursing soldiers threatened to send the women across the river to Vidalia, Louisiana, "where the greatest number of negro troops was stationed." Fearing that they would be molested by black men in uniform, the two women raced in their carriage toward Montebello, but they were soon overtaken by "the rest of Earl's band, with Earl at their head."[19]

Earl accompanied the two sisters to Montebello and proceeded to ransack and search the house and grounds while Kate and Ellen pleaded with the Yankees to remember that they were gentlemen in the presence of defenseless ladies. Their admonitions somewhat calmed the soldiers, according to Ellen, and Earl then tried to explain, by way of an apology to the young women, that he had acted not as an uncivilized barbarian but as a dutiful Union officer operating under orders to gather contraband and intelligence in a time of war.[20] For whatever reason, the Yankees soon released Gabriel Shields and his sons, who made their way back to Montebello through woods and bayous to avoid Union pickets; Wilmer and Surget Shields thereafter snuck away to join their older brother in the Confederate army.

After the war ended, a demoralized and much less wealthy, though still afflu-ent, Gabriel Shields sent his family to live for a while with his wife's relatives in France. The family eventually returned to Natchez and their Montebello home, but neither their Montebello mansion nor their lives were ever again the same. Ellen Shields never married (Kate married in 1866) and Montebello, having been sold by the family during the 1880s to settle family debts, was reduced to ruins and burned to the ground sometime during the 1890s.[21]

Jane Dent

Jane Dent, aged fifty-eight in 1860, and her husband, Thomas Dent, both free persons of color, owned a few acres of land, five or six horses, and a blacksmith business adjacent to their modest but comfortable house in Washington, a small village located a few miles east of Natchez.[22] The Dent family, which included two sons, aged ten and twenty-one, had managed to survive during the war years prior to the arrival of Yankee troops by keeping a low profile. Aware that a vigilance committee of prominent slaveholders had tortured and murdered dozens of enslaved men for talking positively about the war, the Dents spoke about the war and their feelings most likely in whispers to their most trusted friends and never openly to any whites or the many Confederate soldiers stationed in and around Natchez during its Confederate occupation. A witness later testified before the Southern Claims Commission that both he and Jane Dent "were afraid to talk much [about their loyalty to the Union] —as there [were] some 25 or 30 people hung—for talking too much."[23]

When the Yankees came, the Dents' neighborhood became a no-man's-land swarming with rebel soldiers and marauders on the one hand and Yankee troopers on the other, similar to the situation faced by the Dunbar and Shields women. Thomas Dent, similar to Emily Dunbar, was so terrorized by the new circumstances that he fell mentally ill and may have killed himself, leaving Jane largely on her own to deal with the chaos and terror all around her.[24] Her old-est son joined, or was recruited into, a local Union regiment of black soldiers, which undoubtedly complicated her already precarious position.

With the family no longer able to earn a living from Thomas's blacksmith business, the Dents' eleven-year-old son sold eggs and chickens to the several thousand Union soldiers encamped in Natchez, traveling easily without a per-mit through Union pickets, most likely because of his older brother's status as a Federal soldier. Confederates in the area, observing her son's movements, allegedly pressured Jane to spy for them; when she refused, they took her household furniture, blacksmith tools, and four of her five horses. Fearing for her life, she ceased trading with Union soldiers and tried to persevere as best she could by keeping out of sight. When the rebels threatened to hang her and her boy as Yankee collaborators, Dent fled to Natchez. Soon thereafter, a Union foraging party of black soldiers dismantled her house and blacksmith shop for the lumber and took her one remaining horse.[25]

Jane Dent and her youngest son survived the war by nursing sick and wounded Yankee soldiers in Natchez, washing their dirty laundry, and cooking for them. Her status as a free person of color and the mother of a Union soldier probably had enabled her to avoid being warehoused in one of the disease-ridden refugee camps located at the waterfront or just outside town, evacuated to the "home farm" a few miles upriver, or sent to do manual labor growing cotton for subsistence wages on abandoned plantations leased to northern speculators under the protection of Yankee soldiers.[26] A few years later she filed a claim with the Southern Claims Commission for compensation as a Union loyalist (as had Martha Dunbar Claiborne) for the property taken by Union soldiers, asserting that she always had supported the Union, even when threatened with bodily harm and death by Confederate soldiers.[27] According to her estimate, she lost nearly $3,000 in confiscated lumber, but the claims commission allowed her only $300 because she personally had not witnessed Yankee soldiers taking her property. For Jane Dent, the Civil War brought misery, terror, and impoverishment, reducing her from a once prosperous free woman of color to an impoverished laundress and nurse without a home of her own. But life went on for her in the postwar years. She apparently prospered and became a respected member of the city's African American community as a devoutly religious woman; she remained affiliated with the city's white Presbyterian Church as an "excellent colored woman" until her death in 1900 at age ninety.[28]

The women profiled above endured the war largely without men in their lives. Husbands, fathers, and other male relatives were either dead or in hiding, mentally or physically incapacitated, away from Natchez serving in the army, or if still at home, rendered irrelevant by their diminished patriarchal authority. But how typical were their experiences compared to those of the city's other women, including the enslaved refugees who flocked to Natchez after it fell to the Yankees? Did the war diminish, strengthen, or affect but little the distinction between the married and not-married women, between the enslaved and the free? Were all Natchez women, married and not-married, black and white, forced by the circumstances of war to engage life as a new hybrid of their former selves, as women who behaved more like men or like single women had lived prior to the war, relatively independent of males as husbands and protectors? How, to put it simply, did the women of Natchez cope once the Civil War ripped slavery (and the peculiar type of white male mastery it supported) from their lives?

Confederate Natchez

The majority of white voters in Adams County and Natchez cast their ballots overwhelmingly against the secessionist candidate John C. Breckinridge in the presidential election of 1860, and they sent two so-called Unionist or "Cooperationist" delegates to the state's secession convention.[29] Once Mississippi joined the Confederacy, however, most Natchez whites supported the war with money, supplies, home-front aid, and their service as soldiers.[30] Until Vicksburg (located eighty miles north of Natchez) fell to Union troops in the summer of 1863, Confederate Natchez served as a rendezvous and staging ground for Confederate soldiers in the region, sending off to battle fifteen hundred white men in fifteen homegrown volunteer companies. Some of these companies were long-established militia groups, of which the most famous was the Natchez Fencibles, but most were newly formed, including the Adams Troop, Southrons, Tom Weldon Rebels, and the English Battery.[31] A few wealthy Natchez men, such as the former Unionist William T. Martin and Alfred V. Davis, personally provided horses, arms, and uniforms for the militia units they organized or sponsored and even commanded as Confederate officers. Mary McMurran, mistress of Melrose mansion and wife of John T. McMurran, a prominent lawyer and planter, describes thusly the character of the Adams Troop, commanded by William T. Martin: "The Natchez Troop left yesterday week—cavalry composed as an old negro said of the 'bloom of the county,' which means all our young aristocrats proud rich & lazy, unaccustomed to any hardships in fact nothing but luxury—yet with a spirit to do & sacrifice anything rather than submit."[32]

The multitude of able-bodied males from miles around descending on the city, eager to join the fight for the Confederacy, created a public spectacle unlike anything previously experienced in the community. Hundreds of young Confederate warriors proudly marched, strutted, and showed off in the public spaces in and around the municipality. Every open woodland, public grounds, park, and esplanade became a reviewing field where Natchez women, young and old, married or single, flocked to see these bold young men maneuver and drill.[33] Many of the city's young, single women pampered, praised, and, in some cases, promised their hands and hearts to the young soldiers. They baked pies and cookies for their favorites, bundled up gift packages, danced with them, toured visiting gunboats, kept company with them in the campgrounds and various public and private gardens, participated as observers and actresses in the many tableaus conducted for various war-related fund-raising efforts, partook of military concerts put on for their pleasure, and enjoyed fantastic times with their valiant soldiers in the first year or so of the war.[34]

The Natchez courthouse during the Civil War era. Thomas H. Gandy and Joan W. Gandy Photo Collection, Louisiana and Lower Mississippi Valley Collections, LSU Libraries, Baton Rouge, Louisiana.

The willingness of young Natchez women to flirt and enjoy the company of uniformed strangers disturbed more than a few Natchez males already serving in the Confederate army miles from Natchez. They expressed their displeasure in letters home to their wives, sweethearts, sisters, and female friends and relatives, and some Natchez women took umbrage over such criticism. The unmarried Kate Foster's brother, a soldier with the Adams Troop in Virginia, sternly admonished his sister for performing in a tableau to raise money for the war effort, saying that he did not favor "the appearance of young ladies on the public stage for any purpose."[35] Another woman responded to critics by asking in a letter to a Natchez newspaper if it would be better for Natchez ladies to "shut ourselves up at home as if our town was garrisoned by the hated Yankees."[36] When Lizzy Brown's future husband, Rufus Learned, a Confederate soldier on the Virginia front, complained about her writing so many letters to soldiers whom she hardly knew, she politely but firmly told him that it was "none of his business who I write to."[37]

Never in their lives had Natchez women experienced such concentrated male attention from so many different men, day in and day out, and sometimes unforeseen consequences followed. The young Charlotte "Carlie" Mandeville, impregnated by a uniformed stranger from St. Louis, arranged a secret wedding across the river in Vidalia, Louisiana, to avoid having her family's reputation ruined by her sexual adventures. Although her female relatives rose to her defense and helped care for the child, the episode turned her grandfather and uncles against her for years. Everyone in town seemed to know that the young Carlie had lost her heart and virginity to a smooth-talking uniformed stranger from out of town.[38]

The young Lizzy Brown wrote in her diary about the unease she felt toward unknown men who watched her "ankles" when she walked among them; their stares and attention did not stop her, however, from venturing to town at a moment's notice, usually with female companions but sometimes alone, to experience the abundant offerings of prime manhood everywhere on display. Nor did they stop her from actively flirting with the more attractive soldiers at every opportunity. She once teased a group of Confederate conscript hunters, telling them that several eligible men were hiding out in her father's mansion. When the men visited the estate and found that she had tricked them, they teasingly told her and her friend that they would be arrested for their tall tales. Brown's diary is filled with similar entries, including those that show her entertaining numerous young Confederates in her father's parlor until dawn. On one occasion she even confesses to falling in love with three different soldiers at the same time.[39]

By the spring of 1862, several hundred Natchez women had formed a Ladies Military Aid Society in response to the needs of the increasing number of sick and wounded soldiers sheltered in the city, displaced whites moving to Natchez from the countryside, and the hard-pressed families of soldiers away at war. The group, which included participants from all strata of Natchez society, turned the county courthouse into a sewing center where the women sewed, knitted, darned, patched, and repaired shirts and pants, drawers and underclothes, blankets, socks, scarves, and hats for distribution to needy troops in the area; sponsored sewing bees in the city's public school building and several prominent private residences; and held fairs and festivals to raise money for the war effort.[40] One young woman recalled that "the Society formed in Natchez sent bundles of work to the country [probably to women like those at Montebello and Dunbarton] so that all had an opportunity for helping others."[41] Another remembered the "vast quantities of clothing [that] were made in an astonishingly short time. All the negro seamstresses [were] being set to work also."[42] Natchez women organized food drives for the Natchez free market; collected fresh produce, dairy products, and meat for distribution to the city's increasingly hungry residents among its once thriving working class; and lobbied the city council to purchase corn for baking breads and "Confederate cakes," made of finely sifted cornmeal instead of flour, which they distributed to rebel soldiers and the needy with much affected ceremony.[43] Few Natchez women dared spend time in idle chitchat, unless they had a soldier's sock and knitting needle in hand.[44]

Natchez women did more than sewing and baking: a squad of twelve Natchez women, including some who were not married, began nursing young soldiers in the city's two hospitals, working thereby in an environment unprecedented for its intimacy between men and women not related to each other as family members. In April 1862, Natchez women known as the "Nightingale Brigade" traveled to Corinth, Mississippi, to nurse the sick and dying casualties in the aftermath of the battle of Shiloh between the armies of generals Ulysses S. Grant and Earl Van Dorn. Led by Natchez resident Mrs. E. L. Glassburn, who became chief matron at the Corinth military hospital, the group included both married and single women.[45] When word spread that the Natchez women might be transferred to another battlefield, the medical director at Corinth threatened to post a guard to prevent them from leaving and confided to an emissary from the Catholic bishop of Mississippi that he simply could not "spare the ladies."[46]

The large number of Confederate soldiers in Natchez offered employment for many of the city's working-class women as washerwomen, cooks for the army, boardinghouse and hotel staff, nurses, teachers, and prostitutes. Numerous women prepared and sold food to rebel soldiers in restaurants and open-air markets while others peddled groceries and garden crops to the military and local consumers. Natchez women, for example, replaced the entire teaching staff of the city's free public school when its male instructors joined the army. And some women rented (or donated) rooms to uniformed strangers who often appeared out of nowhere, sometimes in the middle of the night, in need of a bed and food.[47]

As the war progressed, more and more displaced women streamed into Natchez from the countryside, some of whom were the wives, mothers, and daughters of Confederate soldiers too poor to care for them or who had died or were wounded in service. Many of these women, who looked to Natchez's free markets for food and necessities, formed a new urban population of near-pauperized women, some of whom undoubtedly turned to prostitution and petty crime to survive; some were forced by their impoverishment to place their children in one of the town's three orphanages. Bishop William Elder appealed to his Catholic parishioners for donations to help support the growing number of orphans under his care, "children or near relations of soldiers now engaged in fighting our battles and some of these have already fallen in the cause."[48] But because of Natchez's relative wealth, its poor and destitute women managed to hang on for the most part without rioting for food, as had happened in other southern towns, or by pleading with their soldier husbands to rescue them from starvation by deserting from the army.[49]

The days of celebration and public spectacle peaked in the summer of 1862, at which point the war's death and destruction began to touch nearly every Natchez family. "How we idolized our boys in gray, with their glittering guns and swords," recalled Annie Harper. She, along with most of her friends, had thought their young soldiers "invincible," but they soon learned that the brave lads who left Natchez for the battlefields of Virginia "were marching to their graves."[50] Lizzy Brown captured the new sentiment best in a journal entry dated May 1, 1863, two days after receiving news that a Yankee cavalry was headed for Natchez.

> How very different this May day has been from that of three years ago, the flow-ers were allowed to wither on the Parent stem, and maidens fair brow was not decked with Flora's crown. What has caused the omission of the usual festive scene at the Hall today? Listen to that noise like distant thunder, and look on the blood stained turf, and your question is answered. The women and children of the South have hearts, and how could they enter into the May-day frolic, when all they hold dear may be bleeding on the Battle field, with no one to give assistance, or hear their last wishes, and messages to the loved ones at home, I hope on _____ another first of May the War will have ceased, and our Country be at rest. Where will we be a year from this night? Will our home be taken from us, or laid waste beneath the iron heel of war? I trust in our Heavenly Father that will not . . . but that we shall live under his protecting care.[51]

Occupied Natchez

Natchez fell to the Yankees in the summer of 1863, with few shots fired in its capture. After the fall of New Orleans, Confederate forces concentrated their defense of the Mississippi River at Vicksburg, eighty miles upriver, and at Port Hudson, located the same distance below Natchez. When both fortresses surrendered to Federal forces, few or no significant Confederate obstacles pre-vented a rapid Union advance on Natchez, and the city soon became a fortified Yankee encampment occupied by up to five thousand Federal soldiers at its peak strength in 1864, including around thirty-two hundred black troopers. Union soldiers pitched tents and set up their messes and latrines in nearly every open space, filling up the city's two racetracks, courthouse square, the bluffs esplanade, Forks-of-the-Road slave market, private and public gardens, and the spacious grounds of suburban villa estates with strange men similar to but quite unlike the gray-coated soldiers who had come before them. The Yankee occupiers quickly established a contraband camp known as the "corral" to warehouse refugee blacks in a swampy, mosquito-infested area Under-the-Hill just north of the landing, built Fort McPherson at the northern edge of the bluffs overlooking the Mississippi River, stationed troops across the river in the Louisiana town of Vidalia, laid out picket lines to police and secure the city's boundaries, and dispersed scouting patrols and foraging parties that ranged widely through the countryside. The Union army also promulgated martial law, which replaced the city's municipal and county governments with one stroke of a sharp-edged pen.[52]

Union officers jailed and roughly handled Confederate sympathizers among the planter elite, and they expected, though did not require, the city's self-declared Unionists to swear oaths of loyalty to the Union (especially "Unionist" women with sons, brothers, grandsons, and husbands in Confederate ranks) to better avoid having their real and personal property confiscated.[53] Official prayers offered for the protection of President Lincoln and the Union replaced prayers for Jefferson Davis and the Confederacy in church services.[54] All Natchez residents, moreover, regardless of their class standing, needed permits to travel within various sections of the city or into and out of the surrounding countryside, making supplicants of even the city's most prominent white men and women.[55] Perhaps most importantly, the military encouraged enslaved blacks to abandon their owners and join the army if they were able-bodied males or, for those who remained on their home plantations, to spy for the Union and support in any way possible rebel defeat.[56] As a result, those white men still living in Natchez found themselves stripped of their traditional authority as masterful slaveholders, household protectors, and family providers even as the city's women were forced to deal with an army of male strangers as conquered females.

Some of the city's class- and race-privileged women attempted to engage Yankee officers as they once had any respectable white male: with grace, reserve, and a sense of certitude about themselves as women whom no gentleman would dare harm.[57] When the elite head of the Protestant Orphans Home, for example, approached General Walter Gresham, the Union commander at Natchez, to request supplies for the orphan children under her charge, she stood before him cloaked in all the matronly dignity she could muster. She respectfully but firmly refused to meet Gresham inside the Rosalie mansion near the bluffs, which served as Gresham's residence and headquarters, because she could not bring herself to cross under the U.S. flag draped above its door, a step she would not take even for her own children or the orphans who de-

Map of the defenses of Natchez and vicinity, Adams County, Mississippi, 1863–64. Historic Natchez Foundation.

pended on her for support. Gresham, impressed by her dignity and poise and the selflessness of her mission, responded as she had hoped a true gentleman would respond to a "lady" of good intentions: with respect and compassion. He stepped outside to meet her and then granted her wishes fully.[58]

Other women exhibited a sense of proud detachment and superiority when dealing with the Yankees, which sometimes worked but often did not. After visiting Union headquarters to request supplies for her family and slaves, Elizabeth Conway Shields, an aristocratic Virginian and ardent Confederate, was not as fortunate as the head of the orphans' home had been. When Shields refused, in puffed-up arrogance, to exit the same Union headquarters through its front door because of the Union flag unfurled overhead, another post commandant, General Thomas Ransom, banned her and her husband, Joseph, from Natchez, confiscating their family villa, "Birds Nest, for the benefit of the government."[59]

Some Natchez women, especially those among the educated and more affluent, tried to "southernize" the Yankee conquerors by charming them into
behaving like southern gentlemen, whom they would honor in return for their
good conduct with conversation, spirited interaction, and even romance. So
obvious were these efforts by the city's young Confederate belles to manipulate
their conquerors that General Gresham warned his staff, half-jokingly, "that
they would be surprised and captured some evening when calling on the ladies."[60] Historian Drew Gilpin Faust finds that fraternization between southern women and Yankees, although not uncommon elsewhere in the occupied
South, "reached its apogee in Natchez."[61] She credits its extent and cause to the
sophisticated character of the place, citing Annie Harper, the twenty-two-year-
old daughter of a Natchez clothing merchant who recorded her experiences in
her journal, to prove her point. Harper justified returning Yankee generosity
with sociability, and kindness with hospitality, as a practical way of dealing with
the potentially belligerent uniformed males to whom Natchez women were
forced to look for protection. But she also cautioned that only the better classes
and those "people of the highest culture and dignity can sustain themselves honorably in such an anomalous position, and Natchez was the place to find such
people." According to Harper, elite females socialized with their Yankee conquerors principally to protect their households and families, procure passes and
permits that allowed them to travel to and from the countryside to sell pies
and vegetables in Yankee camps, obtain reimbursement for confiscated animals
and supplies, trade and sell cotton, and escape detention for actions not always
legal. For Annie Harper, Natchez women "lavished Natchez hospitality upon
the Yankees" because they knew "that no weapon was ever so disarming, so
irresistible, [or] so undefeatable as kindness."[62]

Such "irresistible" acts of feminine "kindness" might well have "disarmed"
the Yankee conquerors, but they also provided the opportunity for sexual
transgression, marital infidelity, and broken promises. Absent Natchez males
undoubtedly shared Robert E. Lee's concern that clever Yankee soldiers might
use the inexperienced southern belles to gather information harmful to the
Confederacy.[63] Lee's perceptions were not far from wrong: at least one Yankee
commandant in Natchez encouraged Union officers and soldiers to cultivate
in military balls and parades open to the public "a social feeling between"
Natchez women and Union officers. Such mingling at a social level between
rebel women and their Yankee conquerors, if done with respect and constraint,
facilitated military control of the community and provided intelligence about
male relatives and friends in gray uniforms, many of whom maneuvered freely
in the countryside surrounding Natchez.[64]

Sometimes fraternization between not-married Natchez women and Union soldiers blossomed into romance. The young, single Mary Ker, with a brother in the Confederate militia, entertained a Yankee officer, Colonel Loren Kent, in her home so frequently that it must have seemed that he was courting her. He spoke of her as his "very particular friend" in their correspondence.[65] Another adventuresome Natchez belle sent a bouquet of flowers every few days to her "Wild American Boy," a Yankee officer in town.[66] Two rather matronly women used their friendship with the Yankee wife of the post commandant to make sure that a young solider served guard duty at their mansion home instead of a "stupid" older one. They got their way, and the lad remained on hand, often playing cards, listening to music, and chatting away for hours with Miss Thornhill, the teenaged granddaughter in their charge, whom he returned to marry after the war.[67]

More than a few and perhaps scores of Natchez women used their feminine wiles to aid the Confederacy as spies and smugglers.[68] Yankee soldiers often imagined that every southern woman they met while on patrol or on picket duty on the city's outskirts carried information or contraband to the enemy.[69] Annie Harper remembered the frequency with which large numbers of Natchez women from all classes engaged in smuggling and eavesdropping, always ready to pass on whatever they could to their Confederate brothers, sweethearts, sons, and fathers in uniform. Everything from desperately needed woolen cloth, boots, belts, and flannel for shirts to pistols, money, and ammunition could be hidden under the long, full skirts Natchez women favored, and those women who came into the city from the immediate countryside with authorized passes to peddle pies, cakes, vegetables, firewood, and cotton were especially suspect.[70] What these women found and heard while in Natchez easily could be handed over or surreptitiously passed on to rebel soldiers visiting relatives in the Natchez countryside or finding momentary shelter in the estate mansions of loved ones and female friends located just beyond the Union picket lines.[71] The unannounced visits of Confederate soldiers, or scouts, to "solitary young women left at home" in outlying estates were "the joy of their hearts and lives," according to Harper.[72]

One "charming lady" allegedly secreted nearly $10,000 in U.S. currency beneath the wagon seat on which she sat with her skirt unfurled about her as she passed into Natchez from her brother's country estate. In this episode the young woman flirtatiously dared a shy Yankee lieutenant to search under her skirts, knowing full well that no gentleman would ever force a lady to undergo such an indignity. The officer, surprised by her audacity, "charming" femininity, sense of expected propriety, and confidence in his inability to do the unthinkable, let her pass unmolested. The whole episode played itself out like a grace-fully conducted yet sexually laden minuet that the audacious lady's family and friends revisited again and again over the years.[73]

Even those Natchez women who refused to accept the Yankees, engage in smuggling, or condone the actions of those who did emphasized in their personal writings how they had used their femininity to manipulate and con-trol their male occupiers. The not-married Kate Foster, who would lose both brothers to Yankee bullets, had nothing good to say about fraternization. "I think it shows so little character," she wrote about those Natchez women who socialized with the Yankees, "not to resist love of admiration more." She ad-mitted that some Yankees acted like gentlemen and that their military con-certs offered well-played and entertaining music, "but we ought to remember that we all have relatives, friends or lovers in our army and if they hear these things it might weaken a strong arm in time of battle and sicken a stout and loving heart." Kate Foster understood, too, that gentlemanly Yankees sorely tempted young women like herself, women whose maiden years might never be redeemed if the war lasted much longer.[74]

Kate struggled more than most with the ordeal of having Yankees in her presence, men whom she found attractive but who were still, at the end of the day, the hated enemy. Her journal is filled with remorse about her lonely state in life, not having a beau or lover, and the dilemma she faced as a single woman (whom a suitor once called a "heartless flirt") surrounded by so many available males whom she dared not love nor even respect.

> I had a visit from a Yankee officer . . . , and he stayed nearly three hours. I think his sympathies are with us and his opinion of the Lincoln government is not better than mine. I did not ask him to take a seat but if he was on our side I should have a very good opinion of him, all but his flattery and I dislike that even in a friend, coming from one of our enemies it is an insult. But enough of this Yankee Lieut. Furlong. I could write a great deal about my opinion of him.[75]

No matter how much Lieutenant Furlong tried to please her, Kate Foster found his attempted friendship demeaning, as though he thought that she cared so little for herself and her cause as to be charmed by Yankee flirtation and soliciting conduct. The humiliation of having him present in her house, a residence that had, in her mind, sheltered true southern gentlemen, was too much for her to tolerate. Yet she did not turn him away, nor did she treat him rudely or let him know what she thought directly; to keep him standing in her presence for three hours suggests that she relished his interest in her as a woman even as she understood that she dared not antagonize him as a conquering male. On another occasion, she almost gave in, writing regretfully about not being able to accept the advances of two Federal officers whom she found attractive and true gentlemen: "If only they wore our uniform how happy I should be to entertain them."[76]

By the summer of 1864, the success of Natchez women in winning favors and benefits from obliging Yankee officers and soldiers had effectively undermined Union picket lines and fortification security. The army relieved Brigadier General James M. Tuttle of his command at Natchez in May 1864, partly because he allowed suspect women to cross Union picket lines without having taken oaths of loyalty or being searched for contraband. In a scathing report to his superiors, Major General D. N. A. Dana accused Tuttle of falling victim "to the influence of female charms" to the point where he allowed "certain supplies in large amounts [to have been] carried into the enemy's country beyond our lines." According to Dana, the provost marshal at Vicksburg also regularly permitted a number of Natchez women to procure supplies from his city without having taken the oath of loyalty to the Union. Specifically named were four single women (Mary Buckner, Alice Jenkins, Mary Ker, and Ophelia Meyers) and the prominent widows "Mrs. Dunbar" and "Mrs. Hampton Elliott."[77]

On July 12, 1864, General Mason Brayman replaced Colonel Bernard Farrar, who had replaced Tuttle, to become the new Natchez commandant. Brayman was a zealot reformer who cracked down severely on the city's manipulating women and men of questionable loyalty and honesty.[78] He arrested and jailed Natchez women for smuggling and making rude remarks to his officers and he refused to accept loyalty oaths from the wives and mothers of Confederate soldiers because they, in his opinion, could not be trusted.[79] In doing this, Brayman denied scores of Natchez women permits that would allow them to travel easily in and out of Union lines to sell or barter their garden products, even denying those avowed Unionists whose families had taken loyalty oaths, such as Martha Dunbar.[80] Ironically, the military removed Brayman as post commander after a few months for allegedly consorting with known prostitutes and granting trading permits to women in exchange for sex.[81] His replacement, General J. W. Davidson, moved quickly in early 1865 to reform what had become, in his opinion, a corrupt and ineffective picket system easily infiltrated by females sympathetic to the Confederacy and those opportunistic women and men who blatantly defied Yankee rules and procedures for conducting commerce and doing business. He tried to do this by requesting two regiments commanded by officers whom he trusted would resist even the most artful female temptresses. Because the war was winding down and would soon be over, Davidson never implemented his plan.[82]

Besides having to develop strategies for dealing with their male conquerors, the former slaveholding women of Natchez were forced to cope without the workers on whom their privileged status had once rested. Former slaveholding Natchez women tended to castigate those slaves who left their households as ingrates and traitors while praising those who remained as loyal, faithful servants. Regardless of what they thought about their formerly enslaved retainers, once their workers stopped acting like slaves, many Natchez women had to put aside their privileged status as nonlaborers to work at tasks few had experienced prior to the war.[83] Ruth Britton said as much in a letter to her sister in New York: "You need not be surprised if in a few weeks you should hear that I am nurse, cook, chambermaid, wash and ironer, seamstress and everything else."[84]

Kate Foster also captured this new anxiety in her diary when her household slaves walked away from the enslaved residence where they had long lived and worked once Federal soldiers liberated Natchez: "Rose [the one remaining slave in the household] is sick so the last two mornings we [meaning Kate and her sisters] have been obliged to do a greater part of the house work. It is not hard to do. Taking out the slops is the only part that I do not like." But Kate soon reconsidered her opinion about not minding most of the work: "I did the washing for six weeks, came near ruining myself for life as I was too delicately raised for such hard work."[85]

Six years later, Kate mourned for her old life, writing that she wished she "had more time to devote to study but I might grow selfish if I were to have more time for myself—I hope I may work more willingly but [it] is so hard to come down to a level with a servant."[86] And Kate's friend Annie Harper pointed an accusing finger at the institution of slavery itself for not preparing slaveholding women for the practical necessities of life: "It is hard to realize how helpless the mass of Southern women were—never a day in their lives had they ever had to work with their hands, and thro' most bitter experience did they learn."[87]

It was one thing to lose the war for southern independence and quite another to lose the services of the enslaved men and women upon whom one's very identity and economic status rested as a human being. Without their slaves, women who had once owned their workers were simply cut adrift. Although they could tackle the tasks once done by males, they found it increasingly difficult to function as successful male substitutes in their handling of life and its wartime exigencies because there was no one left to execute their commands faithfully. This new impotence, or loss of class power, was the essential crisis that the elite women of Natchez faced in the new order that emerged when the Yankees came. To put it simply, such "ladies," married and single, were reduced to the status of menial servants, sometimes even forced by the new circumstances to take out their own "slop." These formerly elite women faced the hard truth that they would have to work like the subordinate men and women who had once served them.

In this new work situation, these women sometimes came to understand that even as slavery had enabled them to live as ladies it also had enabled their one-time slaveholding males to live as gentlemen, especially in their relationship to the women in their lives. This gentlemanly ideal for slaveholding men may have undermined, at least one Natchez lady surmised, the ability of slaveholding men to successfully fight and kill the less chivalrous Yankees. Kate Foster said it best when she noted in her journal the key distinction between southern men and Yankees: "We ought not to speak of a Yankee and one of our soldiers in the same breath. The meanest of our men are ten times better and more a gentleman than the best of the Yankees."[88]

Kate's words meant that southern men might not be quite manly enough to defeat the Yankee barbarians and that it might be better to suffer loss than imitate the unrefined warriors of the North simply for the sake of victory. With these words, Kate Foster began to lay the groundwork for pulling honor and laurels from the coming loss of the Civil War, for eulogizing the Confederate effort as a noble but hopeless cause.[89] No matter the absurdity of this perspective, it enabled some Natchez women to view, perhaps for the first time, their defeated men as innocents to be loved because of their newfound vulnerability in defeat. Louisa Conner noted as much when she wrote about never being able to forget the sight of her once proud and masterly brother-in-law leaving his wife and children behind as he set off with a long train of wagons, mules, horses, carriages, and slaves in deadly fear of being captured by the Yankees.[90] Something similar comes through in Ellen Shields's memoir (discussed earlier in this chapter), in which she credits herself and her sister, but not her father, with saving their family home from the destructive Yankees.[91]

From this perspective, some of the city's white women possibly began to view their defeated southern males as honorable men too decent and too delicate to conquer a barbarous enemy, as men who became disempowered males, unable even to protect or sustain their own households. Although it is impossible to know for sure, it is likely that some Natchez white women began to nurture and care for their newly emasculated males as a continuation of the antebellum servant ideal even as they assumed new burdens and roles in their vanquished households, even as they engaged the conquering Yankees as less than honorable men on whom they would work every manipulative, feminine trick available to them. It mattered little, moreover, whether they were married, single, or divorced women, slaveholding or nonslaveholding women. They all shared in the burden of losing sons, brothers, and fathers on the one hand and, on the other hand, having to engage as women on their own a conquering army of white and black males, regardless of their marital state. As a result, the distinction between being married, single, divorced, or widowed seemed largely irrelevant for the white women of Civil War Natchez.

The City's Single and Married Black Women during Occupation

With the outbreak of the Civil War, Adams County and Natchez slaveholders, fearful of a slave uprising and hoping to stem the increasing number of run-aways, began exerting greater vigilance over their enslaved workers. No longer could the enslaved market their garden produce in Natchez on Sundays, and their visits to neighboring plantations or midnight fishing and hunting trips quickly became a thing of the past. Armed patrols visited slave cabins after sundown with a stepped-up diligence to enforce discipline or administer whip-pings, compared to their supervision before the war.[92] This concern with incipi-ent slave rebellion peaked in September 1861, when armed slaveholders rounded up hundreds of Adams County blacks suspected of plotting to overthrow white rule and summarily executed at least forty enslaved men and boys (and perhaps as many as two hundred) by hanging at the China Grove plantation southeast of the city and at a Natchez racetrack, as their mates, mothers, and children looked on helplessly. Historians debate whether this "tumult at Second Creek" was an authentic slave conspiracy or but a figment of the paranoid mind-set raging among Adams County and Natchez whites, who magnified hopeful talk and chatter among the enslaved about a Yankee victory into a plot to murder slaveholders, ravish white women, and set Natchez ablaze. Whatever the real-ity, few Natchez blacks doubted the will and ability of area slaveholders to meet any hint of insubordination or rebellion among the enslaved with absolute and murderous violence.[93]

All of this changed, however, when Yankee soldiers arrived in Natchez nine days after Vicksburg fell to Union forces on Independence Day, July 4, 1863.[94] Almost immediately the surge of black refugees descending on Natchez became a tidal wave of humanity, in which only one in six was a man.[95] Annie Harper captures the exuberance of this flight from slavery to freedom with a woman's eye for the female-dominated character of the exo-dus: "On every road they came in crowds, mothers carrying their babies, with every size and age streaming along behind. . . . The day of jubilee had come."[96] The local newspaper also noted the exhilaration with which an elderly black lady danced with joy at the sight of Union soldiers entering Natchez, grab-bing "passing soldiers, hugging them, and making a tremendous ado over them."[97] One black woman arrived in Natchez, in a continuing cavalcade of female refugees, carrying her dead baby, killed as they escaped amid a "shower of bullets" from a pursuing slaveholder, so that her "child could be buried free."[98] These determined women arrived with just the clothes on their backs, blankets for their children, and whatever they had managed to carry with them in hand-pulled carts or in baskets; because they came to Natchez in midsummer they were able to pitch camps and erect temporary open-air shelters almost anywhere they could find a bit of clearing, but especially on the Natchez bluffs at the western edge of town.[99] Yankee soldiers doled out rations to the nearly starving refugees, whose unkempt and impoverished presence had turned Natchez, in the opinion of one local white woman, into a veritable "hog pen." But for the formerly enslaved, Natchez, which they had known principally for its jails, executions, and Forks-of-the-Road slave sales, shined brightly as freedom city.[100]

To deal with the mounting refugee population that followed in the wake of Union troops as they engaged the Confederacy from Memphis to New Orleans, President Lincoln instructed Adjutant General Lorenzo Thomas to create a system of Union-controlled plantations (abandoned by their Confederate owners or confiscated by the Union military) where the once enslaved women, elderly, and children could be worked for wages while their able-bodied mates, fathers, and other male relatives and friends could join newly organized "colored" army units or be employed by the army corps of engineers on defensive fortifications. Thomas also put in place a number of black refugee camps and "home farms," including several in and around Natchez, especially the infamous "corral" in Under-the-Hill Natchez. These camps would serve as temporary refugee depots from which those healthy enough to work could be transported to plantations protected by the U.S. military in the countryside adjacent to the Mississippi River.[101]

Of those refugees warehoused in the Natchez "corral" in July 1863, some two thousand had died by September, as many as seventy-five in a single day. Although the death rate subsided somewhat over the next year, hundreds continued to die in the Natchez camp and in the one across the Mississippi River from Natchez in Vidalia, Louisiana; usually between fifteen and twenty perished each day. Women, children, and the elderly made up the majority of the corral's occupants, and most of its dead perished from a myriad of diseases and ailments, such as dysentery, malaria, measles, smallpox, pneumonia, and typhoid, as well as from untreated infections, especially among the elderly and the very young.[102]

Understanding just how deadly the refugee depots were, black women and their children increasingly tried to avoid them, seeking instead to live in town near their enlisted mates, the fathers of their children, and other male relatives and friends encamped in or around Fort McPherson, or else they fled into the nearby countryside to survive as best they could in squatter villages populated by women, children, and the elderly. In response to the growing urban congestion of black women and children, the military unsuccessfully moved in the early winter of 1863 to arrest any "negro woman within [army] camps without a pass, employed or unemployed."[103] But this initial attempt to remove refugee women from the municipality was halfheartedly enforced, and in the early winter of 1864 Natchez continued to overflow with thousands of black women and children, living in crudely built shanties and huts thrown up just about everywhere in the city.[104]

In April 1864, the military health officer in Natchez, A. W. Kelly, convinced the post commandant, Brigadier General J. M. Tuttle, to order every black person "not employed by some responsible white person" or living somewhere other than with his or her employer to be sent to the contraband depot at the waterfront. This order supposedly excluded the legally married wives of black soldiers, but its initial enforcement failed to discriminate between actual vagrants and soldiers' wives living in rented rooms paid for by their husbands, entrepreneurial blacks not employed by whites or living with whites (such as hack drivers, washerwomen, marketers, and cooks), and the many domestic workers who no longer lived in the houses of their former owners but continued to work for them as wage servants and housekeepers. In enforcing the order, white soldiers removed black children from newly established schools, wives married in slavery but not legally married in the eyes of the army, hucksters and washerwomen not employed by whites or living with them, and just about any black woman or child who looked to be a vagrant, confining them in a corral Under-the-Hill or across the river in a large refugee depot in Vidalia, Louisiana. During one military sweep, some 250 refugees, mostly women and children, were marched under armed military escort from the town to the corral as whites mocked them for having left slavery for this so-called freedom.[105]

In response, black refugee women evaded the arresting soldiers (almost always white troopers) as much as possible, and their soldier husbands threatened to desert unless their wives, mothers, and daughters were allowed to live outside the camps.[106] A number of prominent Natchez whites (men and women who had hired blacks without boarding them in their homes), the local superintendent of freedmen, representatives of the American Missionary Association, and other Freedmen Aid groups petitioned the post commandant Brigadier General Tuttle and his superiors to rescind the order.[107] The military responded to the public outcry by removing Kelly and Tuttle (who also was under criticism from superior officers for fraternization with Natchez belles who allegedly supported rebel soldiers in the area) and appointing Colonel Bernard Farrar in Tuttle's place as post commander. Farrar, who had commanded a black regiment stationed in the area, believed that the city's disorderly scene stemmed less from the vagrancy of its refugee blacks than from the undisciplined, drunken, thieving, and brawling Union soldiers, white and black, who roamed its streets when not on maneuvers or kept busy working on its fortifications. Without addressing the housing issue for the city's seething black population, Farrar cancelled all soldier passes and banned Yankee troopers from the city unless they were carrying out specific orders.[108]

Many of the black women who had fled to Natchez came searching for mates or loved ones who had joined, or were coerced into joining, the newly formed "colored" units authorized by President Lincoln following his Emancipation Proclamation issued in early 1863. Many others undoubtedly arrived as widows, abandoned women (or women who had abandoned their spouses), young single women, and older women who had never married. Although most refugee women probably had lived in a nuclear family environment in slavery, many arrived unattached to men as husbands and mates. Historian Ronald L. F. Davis estimates that 60 percent of the slaves in Concordia Parish (located directly across the Mississippi River from Natchez) lived in two-parent family households on the eve of the Civil War. If these figures are correct, it is likely that numerous female refugees arrived in Natchez as women unattached to husbands for whatever reason.[109]

Once in Natchez, black women survived by accepting army-issued rations, were supported by their soldier husbands, and earned money working at jobs of all sorts. Each company of Union soldiers was authorized to employ female cooks and washerwomen for wages, one cook for each fifteen men; numerous other black women offered their services to soldiers in jobs that ranged from preparing and selling meals to doing extra laundry work, nursing, and hawking fruits and vegetables (usually without permits) brought in from the countryside. Some also earned money through prostitution and thievery; some elderly women worked as babysitters for soldiers' wives who were employed by the army.[110] It is unknown how many of the city's formerly enslaved continued to work as house servants for wages, even though many had little choice but to do so. Numerous black women nevertheless earned enough money to rent housing on their own, pay modest tuition fees to support the newly established private and government-sponsored freedmen schools, and sustain several newly formed black churches that sprang up within days of the city's liberation from Confederate rule.[111]

Some of the more prosperous black women who had been free during slavery, like the spinsters Anna and Catherine Johnson, daughters of William Johnson, used their education and connections to become schoolteachers for the newly freed slaves. Educated at the hands of their parents, in New Orleans schools, and at a local school for free blacks operated by the free-black barber William McCary, these women, perhaps a dozen in number and principally single women, joined with newly arrived Yankee "schoolmarms" under the auspices of the American Missionary Association to create makeshift schools for blacks in Natchez and on the safer plantations out in the country. Some had operated their own fee-based schools, principally for the children of the city's antebellum free blacks, prior to the arrival of any American Missionary Association teachers. By the end of the war, eleven hundred black children filled eleven schools for blacks in Natchez and Adams County, staffed by twenty-two teachers, mostly white women brought in from the North. The schools employed literate black women as assistants, trained them to take over teaching duties as soon as possible, and thereby created a group of educated and skilled black women, most of whom were single, and ready to engage the postwar world as professional women not dependent on males for their livelihood. Many of the white teachers eventually abandoned their efforts amid the chaos of Reconstruction, but the city's black female instructors more often than not remained steadfast within the postbellum, segregated Natchez public schools in teaching careers that spanned over the next forty years.[112]

One formerly enslaved widow, Lilly Ann Granderson, had operated a clandestine school for enslaved children in Natchez for seven years or more when the American Missionary Association teachers discovered her upon their arrival in fall 1863. Granderson had educated twelve students at a time, secretly and at night, teaching them to read and write before taking on a new group. In this way she educated perhaps hundreds of enslaved children (some of whom allegedly wrote their own passes to travel out of slavery). Some of her students later found work as teaching assistants and teachers in the city's black schools. Her school probably had been tolerated by the white community because it may have educated some of the enslaved children of white fathers. She later claimed, although it is difficult to believe, that a local white man had given her permission to teach because no state law prohibited enslaved women or men from teaching enslaved children. The American Missionary Association immediately hired her as a missionary teacher, paying her ten dollars per month. Granderson remained employed as a Natchez teacher for the next twenty years and lived as a widow for the remainder of her life in a small house on St. Catherine Street until her death in 1889. Her three children, born into slavery, also became teachers.[113]

Conclusion

Many white women of Confederate Natchez, married and single, responded to the war by building upon and greatly expanding their traditional commitment to a servant ideal in support of Confederate soldiers and the war effort on the home front. For those among the city's white women who had worked in support of its churches, orphanages, and other charitable causes prior to 1861, the war only continued, at a greater scale and faster pace, the service efforts they had practiced and honed in antebellum Natchez. Those who, for whatever reasons, had not participated in community service prior to the war similarly became caught up in the war's demand for their support and contributions as women. If anything, their experiences during the Confederate occupation of Natchez often enhanced and deepened their commitment as dutifully subordinate women to a hierarchical order of a life firmly rooted in slavery and a male mastery that was more and more personified in the southern soldiers all around them. The intensity of their service often united them, regardless of their marital status and class, as southern women working side by side in sewing clothes, nursing, and raising money and supplies to support their Confederate relatives and friends as they fought and died for a cause deemed noble even in defeat.

The experiences of Natchez white women changed fundamentally, however, when Yankee soldiers overran their city in July 1863, holding it tightly as an occupied city for the Civil War's remaining two years. White women dutifully serving their families and their community became a conquered population left to fend for themselves in terrifying and unprecedented circumstances. Most everything that had made sense to them as women committed to a servant ideal and a way of life that embraced male dominance and mastery rooted in slavery seemed suddenly questionable, impractical, and perhaps irrelevant once the enslaved among them became free people. With the Yankee occupation, the white women of Natchez faced (many for the first time in their lives) white males whom they feared if not hated; the servant ideal had to be modified and reshaped to better accommodate the strangers among them and to protect themselves and their families. Masterful appearances (sometimes necessary for southern women in daily negotiations with their own men before the war) now took on a new and perhaps more cunning dimension, accommodating the new circumstances that occupation by the Union enemy demanded.

For the formerly enslaved and free women of color in the city and countryside, the Yankee arrival had just the opposite effect in most cases, at least initially. They looked at the occupying Yankee soldiers and officers with both a sense of jubilation and a cautious uncertainty, seeing them as white strangers fomenting a war of liberation on their behalf (or at least so they often naïvely believed), with unknown consequences for them as women largely on their own amid the collapse of slavery. Freedom clearly posed undeniable risks for the black women who fled from slavery to Natchez: disease-ridden refugee depots; forced separation from their mates and male relatives to work on poorly protected rural plantations; re-enslavement by Confederate guerrillas if they remained on their home plantations outside Union lines; possible brutalization and rape by their new liberators; and the forced regimentation that reminded them of slavery. Still, these dangers did not stop thousands of enslaved and formerly enslaved women from taking a chance with the conquering Yankees. What they found in Natchez were the new circumstances associated with being free women: job opportunities as wage workers for the military; new labor conditions for those working as employees for whites who previously had related to them as enslaved property; professional opportunities in teaching; a new social order in which they could live pretty much on their own (even if as squatters and vagrants) for the remaining years of the war; and a modicum of protection offered at times by black soldiers in uniform, sympathetic northern schoolteachers and seemingly benevolent missionaries, and government agencies not totally controlled by white planters and slaveholders. For the black female refugees living in Natchez under Union occupation, the new circumstances amounted to a revolutionary change that opened new possibilities for them to affect their own destinies as women, both married and single, not necessarily subordinate to men, white or black.

Perhaps the most dramatic, and most serious, impact of the Civil War on the white and black women of Natchez had to do with their shared experiences as women forced to navigate life relatively independent of males as husbands, mates, brothers, and fathers, even for those who were married women. This commonality of independence also sometimes obliterated, at least for the moment, prior differences rooted in their marital status even as it rendered largely irrelevant what had passed for a servant ideal (largely a superimposed white ideal), which few black women had internalized as enslaved workers, even though they were expected by their owners to behave as though they had. It is what the Dunbar women shared with Mollie Matthews and Mollie Williams, Ellen and Katherine Shields, Jane Dent, and thousands of other women, including the formerly enslaved, free blacks, and middle- and working-class white women, as well as the city's once elite slaveholding women. Neither white male mastery nor the servant ideal seemed especially relevant in the crisis Natchez women faced when a Yankee conqueror ripped the city from its antebellum, slave-encrusted moorings. Nearly all of the city's women were compelled to cope alone in a world rapidly devoid of slavery and, at least for the moment, devoid of an entrenched, white patriarchy. The Civil War indeed opened avenues over which the city's women were compelled to step quickly and adroitly to survive in circumstances in which most were less protected and less constrained compared to anything they had experienced in their previous lives. How the city's growing number of not-married women coped in the aftermath of slavery's demise and a destructive Civil War is the story that follows.

CHAPTER EIGHT

Stepping into the Breach

The Women of Postbellum Natchez— Single and Married, Black and White

In 1865, Kate Foster, a Confederate belle in her midtwenties, lived with her widowed father, Dr. James Foster, and her older, not-married sisters Elizabeth and Sinah at the Hermitage, their 111-acre plantation just outside Natchez. The Civil War had taken her two brothers, John and Isaac, and many of her one-time beaus and male friends, and for the next decade she spent much of her time caring for her elderly father, helping to manage the family's plantations (the Hermitage in Adams County and Spring Bayou in Madison Parish, Louisiana), and living in Natchez with her spinster sisters, one of whom taught school. In the immediate postwar years, the women, their family finances diminished, survived by pooling their resources and leasing their plantations, prior to selling them in the mid-1870s. Following their father's death in 1880, the sisters opened a small downtown hotel called the Foster House and thereafter began their long and active participation in the Confederate Memorial Association of Natchez and Adams County.

Although not as wealthy as members of some of the larger planter families in her neighborhood, Kate Foster was related, on her mother's side (the Gaillards), to many who were. Prior to the war, she and her sisters frequently spent days at a time visiting and living with these relatives and assorted family friends. In her father's will, Kate and her sister Sinah inherited the Spring Bayou plantation in Louisiana, while her sisters Lizzy and Sinah inherited the Hermitage residence and lands in Adams County. The family no longer owned the Hermitage by 1869, however, and appears to have lost Spring Bayou sometime during the 1870s. Because Natchez hotels had closed during the Civil War, the Foster House on Canal and Main, although small in size, served as the city's sole hotel until the grand Natchez Hotel opened in 1892; several boardinghouses also offered accommodations during the postwar years, and many private citizens rented rooms to travelers and local residents. Kate's older sister Elizabeth (Lizzy) Foster, while still living at the Foster House with Kate and Sinah, also worked at the Natchez Hotel in some capacity or other when it opened, probably as one of its managers.[1]

Life for the Foster sisters became increasingly difficult over the ensuing years, especially as their father's health deteriorated.[2] As single women, they struggled to ward off creditors, borrowed money from friends, and eventually gave up their hotel business just prior to or following Sinah's death in 1894.[3] Elizabeth Foster died in 1899, six years prior to Kate's demise in 1905. At her death, Kate, who had handled most of the family's business affairs after her father's passing, owned little beyond two suburban lots the sisters had somehow acquired, household furniture, and eighty dollars in cash, all of which she willed to her longtime lawyer and friend, Lemuel P. Conner Jr., who had married Kate's childhood friend Mary Britton. Conner settled Kate's few remaining debts and funeral expenses without charging her estate as a final expression of his affection for the old spinster lady he had known all his life.

Lemuel Conner Jr. hailed from a once prominent slaveholding family headed by his planter-turned-lawyer father, Lemuel Conner Sr. The senior Conner, a colonel during the Civil War and a key player in rounding up and executing dozens of enslaved people or more in 1861 for plotting an alleged insurrection, lost his plantation lands when he was forced into bankruptcy in 1869 and thereafter barely eked out a living for his family by working as a lawyer (in partnership with his son), hired plantation manager, and agent for a distilling business until his death in 1891. He lived with his wife, Fanny, and his widowed sister-in-law Mary McMurran at Woodlands, the home of his widowed mother-in-law, Elizabeth Turner, on the outskirts of Natchez. Although the junior Conner married Mary Britton, the daughter of the prominent local banker Audley Britton, he struggled financially most of his life. His legal practice in Natchez was somewhat profitable until the middle of the 1890s, after which he supplemented his legal income by trading in commodity futures contracts, selling real estate, and working as a regional census commissioner before landing something of a sinecure position during the 1920s as clerk of the Adams County Circuit Court.[4]

When the Civil War ended, Kate desperately hoped to find a husband with whom she could create "soul music." She apparently was engaged and on the verge of being married in 1886 to an unknown man, but something happened and the marriage never occurred. At one point in her diary, Kate expressed her belief that a woman's happiness could best be achieved as a faithful and obedient wife living under the care and protection of a loving husband: "I know I would make a faithful, obedient wife, loving with all my heart, yielding entire trust in my husband and his acts." In her mind, she was raised to find her happiness in being "secure in the love of *some chosen* one to whom I shall look for protection and guidance in the vicissitudes of this life." That Kate underlined the words "some chosen" emphasized that although she desperately wanted to be loved and to love in return as an obedient servant to an honorable husband, she would not marry just anyone simply to be married. Still, spinsterhood, in Kate's mind, meant an incomplete life for any woman but especially for a romantic like herself. As the years passed and no worthy suitor appeared on the scene, she eventually accepted "her cup of bitterness," no longer asking forlornly, "Love and Happiness, where are they?"[5] When it became clear to her that she might never marry, she began thinking of herself as playing a role in a "drama of Bygones."[6]

Perhaps to help fill the void she undoubtedly felt as a spinster who had hoped to marry, Kate, along with her sisters, embraced the city's newly formed Confederate Memorial Association, which they helped establish with like-minded women during the late 1880s. Thereafter the Foster sisters devoted significant energy to promoting a memorial park in the city featuring a statue of a Confederate soldier and a romanticized view of the Civil War that came to be known as the "Lost Cause," which in proponents' minds mythically commemorated the undying courage of the South's rebel soldiers, whom they believed had tenaciously fought a superior foe despite little chance of victory in order to protect the southern white household and its women. Thanks largely to the work done by the Foster women and their "lady" companions, during the 1890s the city began celebrating an annual Confederate Memorial Day, a day set aside for the city's white women to decorate Confederate graves in the Natchez cemetery and to participate with its white citizenry in speeches and parades honoring dead soldiers and any surviving Confederate veterans. These memorial activities, unlike any voluntary effort previously undertaken by Natchez women, propelled the Fosters and their fellow female volunteers in the memorial effort into the city's public arena as ideological players, although they labored principally as an auxiliary force under various males who headed the memorial efforts. When the Daughters of the Confederacy emerged as a national organization in the 1890s, Kate became a charter member and president of its Natchez chapter. Kate and her women friends thereafter carried out their memorial efforts independent of men through fund-raising activities and organizational work.[7]

By embracing the Lost Cause, Kate Foster worked to create, in her words, a mythic "drama of Bygones," a nostalgic, romanticized vision of an antebellum social order wherein elite white women once had lived happily as faithful subordinates to venerable, slaveholding white men who headed households filled with loving family members and dutiful servants. Subsequently, their work honoring the young men who had fought and died during the Civil War may well have enabled Kate and her spinster sisters to play suffering mothers to all the children they had never birthed, grieving wives to gallant Confederate husbands they had never married, and faithful servants to a patriarchal ideal they had experienced only as young women and girls. Foster's Lost Cause memorial work rejuvenated in memory rather than reality the servant ideal on which she had been raised and the hierarchical social order that slavery had created and the Civil War had so fundamentally destroyed.[8]

Although the Lost Cause movement gave meaning and purpose to the lives of the Foster women as spinsters, it was but a fictional artifice that had little to do with the day-to-day maneuvering the sisters were forced to undertake as once prosperous women cut adrift from all that had sustained them prior to the Civil War. As not-married and relatively penniless women, the Fosters were largely on their own. The once relevant servant ideal mattered little in a world where male mastery and female dependency stood diminished in value by the necessity of striking out on one's own with few guideposts along the way. Without a husband or father to sustain her, Kate Foster relied on her own sense of self in her struggles to persevere, because she had little choice. Fortunately, perhaps, for her and her sisters, Kate's close friendship with the young lawyer Lemuel Conner Jr. and his father, Lemuel Conner Sr., a much decorated Confederate officer, offered stand-ins for the lost brothers and non-existent husband that she, in her youth, had desperately hoped to love and serve as a devoted sister and wife. But the relationship with the Conner men also did something more: it enabled Kate and her sisters to navigate legally, and perhaps socially, the tumult of the postwar years with informed male friends at their side. Still, she and her sisters, and possibly hundreds of the city's widows and spinsters, had little choice but to make the most of what they could retain from the past as they tried to shape the future.

Postbellum Natchez

The Natchez where Kate Foster lived, toiled, and grew old following the Civil War was almost completely transformed from the antebellum community it had been when she and her sisters were growing up. Scores of its wealthiest white families were reduced to near poverty with the death of slavery, even as thousands of the formerly enslaved filled the city as freed but impoverished people determined to secure their freedom politically and socially. Although Natchez escaped the worst physical ravages of war, thanks largely to its early fall to Union troops and the relatively few Confederate operations in its rural environs, the city housed some one hundred white Yankee soldiers well into the 1870s, and several hundred African American soldiers remained posted in and around the city until 1867.[9]

During the decade after the fighting ended, Natchez witnessed the rise of a powerful Republican political operation that, working in partnership with northern-born white Republicans, propelled several of the city's black politicos into municipal, county, state, and national offices. This political insurgency and quest for civil rights and social equality among blacks enraged large sections of the state's white population, men and women still clinging to the South's antebellum social and racial order. In their anger, furious whites unleashed waves of terror against black and white Republicans, culminating in bloody conflicts, the rise of paramilitary white supremacist groups like the Ku Klux Klan, the eventual downfall of Reconstruction, and the return of white rule to Natchez and Mississippi. After 1876, the "Mississippi Plan" effectively limited the black vote in Natchez and throughout the state, drove white Republicans (including the state's northern-born governor, Adelbert Ames) from power, and set Mississippi on the road to a draconian system of near-total racial segregation in public spaces and state institutions, accompanied by the Jim Crow disfranchisement of black voters upon enactment of the state constitution of 1890.[10]

Amid such social and political turmoil, the city's economy only slowly recovered, dominated by a new class of merchants, including several Jewish entrepreneurs who had arrived during and after the war to service the growing supply and furnishing business associated with the changed agricultural system. Almost overnight a new system of farming known as sharecropping or share-tenancy replaced slavery as the dominant form of cotton production and employment for black farmworkers throughout the Natchez hinterland and nearly everywhere in the cotton South. Under this system, black and white farmers negotiated contracts with local supply merchants for advances to produce a crop on lands leased from white landlords—typically but not always former slaveholders. In time, Natchez merchants began buying or leasing lands outright (often replacing or displacing antebellum landowners) and contracting with the formerly enslaved. The sharecroppers generally farmed the rented plots in family units, paying a share of their crops as rent, with any remaining shares allotted to their merchant landlords (or other furnishing merchants) in exchange for supply advances, in a contractual obligation enforced by crop lien laws. As cotton prices declined, these laws created an economic box from which few indebted farmers could escape. By the 1880s, a small group of Natchez merchants had become the area's dominant landholders and controlled the lion's share of the crop supply business with black sharecroppers in the city's cotton hinterland. These merchants also invested in local banks and several cotton mills, promoted railroad-building schemes, speculated in and developed new residential tracts, and, except for the Jewish merchants, intermarried with many of the city's antebellum elite families.[11]

These merchants, many of whom were northern born, embraced and generally supported the Jim Crow disfranchisement strictures imposed on the city's black men after Reconstruction ended as well as the creation of a racially driven caste system that relegated all blacks in the city and state to the status of a people deemed biologically inferior to whites. As elsewhere in the state and the former Confederacy, Natchez blacks became in law and custom a subordinate people who posed, many whites believed, a potential threat to the purity of white women and the authority and prestige of white men as masters of their households. This racially driven political economy did not take hold fully in Natchez or Mississippi until the late 1880s, but contests over its creation and implementation dominated local and state politics and shaped social relations during the several decades following the Civil War.[12]

Historians well understand that the Civil War and its tumultuous aftermath presented southern women, both black and white, with unprecedented challenges and opportunities as they coped with the death and evisceration of male authority figures (husbands, fathers, and brothers), the collapse of slavery, and the transition to a new economic and social order in which little that once was considered a "given" of life could easily be taken for granted. Among these changes were significant modifications of the power that white males traditionally held over their wives, daughters, and female siblings as well as changes that broached the question of black (and white) male authority over African American women. This new era, historians agree, seldom found southern white women actively participating in organized reform efforts aimed at their political and social liberation as women, especially compared to what was going on among many reform-minded white women in the North. But historians also generally agree that southern women clearly engaged life in ways few had experienced before the war. In many cases, the South's white women were forced to function as heads of their households while their husbands were away at war and even after their husbands came home, often as impoverished men broken in body and spirit. Under these new circumstances, many women, even those who were married, were forced to sustain themselves and their families independent of, or "non-dependent" on, once dominant husbands, fathers, and brothers.[13]

Historian Jane Turner Censer argues that the Civil War ushered in a new, feminine ideal for many of the South's elite white women that privileged "non-dependence" on men. For Censer, the Civil War forced elite planter women, married and not married, to reconfigure what it meant to be a "southern lady" as they struggled to deal with the social and economic crises of lost fortunes or greatly diminished affluence. There emerged, according to Censer, a new image of the white southern belle that was articulated in literature and the public arena and that emphasized "non-dependence" on men (rather than independence from men) in women's domestic and other roles. This new ideal privileged "self-reliance" and "female capability" as white southern females were forced after the Civil War to manage social and economic matters traditionally handled by fathers and husbands during the antebellum era. Censer also explains that younger, unmarried women more often and more easily embraced this new attitude, in contrast to those who were older and married.[14]

Many African American women in Natchez and Mississippi faced somewhat similar circumstances, namely, physically and psychologically impaired men vitiated by war as well as slavery, with few resources available to sustain themselves or their families. But there were important differences. Some African American women in Natchez and elsewhere in the former Confederacy began to see themselves as role models for the less educated members of their race or those just emerging from slavery, assuming leadership in the community as teachers, in newly formed churches, and in philanthropic and club activities.[15] What is more, some of these women, especially among the formerly enslaved, confronted efforts by black males to mimic the privileged position of the white husband as the dominant and masterful partner in legalized marriages and household cohabitations. Although it is impossible to know the extent, many of the city's black women probably accepted this male dominance as a necessary bulwark of black manliness, while others most likely refused to tolerate or enter into domestic arrangements in which they would be treated as inferior dependents.[16]

White males in the state met this growing non-dependency on men among southern women—black and white, single and married—with an organized and often violent backlash that grew in force and passion in the decade following the Civil War. This white male–led counterrevolution against black political and social equality vigorously reasserted male mastery over the southern household and southern women as protectors of the white race against sexually aggressive black men and promiscuous black women. For many southern white men and white women, any efforts toward political or social equality between the races amounted to a direct threat to white masculinity and the purity of white women, a threat that all white men of whatever class were culturally bound to reject and suppress. Historian Nancy Bercaw argues that after Reconstruction ended this effort to restore white male power over blacks and women in Mississippi played out in the courts and the Mississippi legislature through conservative attacks on integrated public schools, worker rights, household autonomy of blacks, "alternative households" occupied by couples not legally married, and interracial marriage as threats to white males' mastery over their households. By the 1890s, this conservative effort to present white males, regardless of their actual household status, as the protectors of white women effectively curbed and displaced any political gains that might have accrued to Mississippi women under a weakened male authority in the immediate postwar years. Although the South's white men succeeded in once again privileging white males as masters of their households and over the women and children in their lives, the patriarchal household as a bastion of white mastery never fully regained the unquestionable hold on southern life that it had maintained in the antebellum era.[17]

The Single Women of Postbellum Natchez

The Foster sisters numbered among postbellum Natchez's 355 single white women aged thirty and above in 1880, a significant increase compared to 1860 (199); among these single women, widows (257) far outnumbered spinsters (98), and 173 not-married women headed households as relatively independent women. Although the number of single white women living in Natchez in 1880 had nearly doubled compared to 1860, a slightly smaller percentage headed households (49 percent) compared to before the war (54 percent). In the county, 316 single black women and 30 single white women (out of a total population of 723 single black women and 63 single white women) headed households (or 44 percent for blacks and 48 percent for whites), indicative of the greater difficulty women faced in trying to live on their own as sharecroppers and tenant or landowning farmers and planters.[18]

Many of the city's white spinsters in 1880 had been young women or girls in 1860 who most likely would later have married but for the war's impact. Also, the number of white women who legally married fell off dramatically during the twenty years following the war compared to before the war. During the years from 1835 to 1855, white marriages in Adams County totaled 1,480, or around 74 per year, compared to 643 marriages in the postwar years (around 32 marriages per year from 1866 to 1885). Marriage rates throughout the South soared after the Civil War, principally among white men too young to have served in the military who quickly married young women like themselves during the 1870s and 1880s. But this phenomenon did not happen in Natchez and Adams County, probably because the white population had declined substantially and fewer young white men were financially able to marry after the war compared to before the war.[19]

The increase in the number of the city's single white women partly stemmed from their movement to Natchez, seeking protection from the military invaders and refuge from the relative lawlessness of the countryside during the war. It was a migration that continued during the immediate postbellum years, often as a result of the wartime deaths of husbands and sweethearts and the dwindling supply of desirable marriage partners for both men and women. Historian Ronald L. F. Davis and others estimate that 1,444 Natchez-area men fought in the Civil War, of which 144 perished in battle or from diseases. The city's white population decreased from 4,272 in 1860 to 3,421 in 1880.[20] After the war, few among the city's formerly elite, single white women, for example, could offer dowries or debt-free assets to potential husbands, what with their family wealth having been severely reduced because of the war.[21] Additionally, the deaths of overbearing fathers and brothers during the war and the diminished influence of surviving white males over their households in the wake of slavery's end undoubtedly freed some white women from unwelcome marriages to undesirable men, or to any man, for that matter. Historian Anya Jabour argues that the Civil War may have liberated scores of elite white women from marriage, enabling them to embrace the "single blessedness" that many young women had seriously considered and even desired in the antebellum era.[22]

The once wealthy Alice Jenkins, for example, perhaps mindful of her sister Kate's marriage to an incompetent if not totally incapable husband (whom her once prosperous sister now supported by working as a seamstress), rejected five marriage proposals over the years, proposals that she might have been hard-pressed to turn down had her parents not perished in a yellow fever epidemic that had ravaged the lower Mississippi River Valley during the mid-1850s. After Alice, born in 1841, lost her parents in 1855, a local attorney, Josiah Winchester, assumed guardianship responsibilities over her and her brothers. The Jenkins family owned Elgin plantation in Adams County as well as two plantations in neighboring Wilkinson County, Mississippi. Alice, a strong-willed young woman, moved to New York after the war for a few years before returning to Natchez, where she battled furiously with the Southern Claims Commission for reparation to compensate her loyal Unionist family for properties confiscated or destroyed by Yankee soldiers. Men literally threw themselves at her and Alice played the field with a flirtatious glee that complemented her beauty and spunk, often to the dismay of other single women in Natchez. Alice Jenkins liked men, enjoyed flirting with them, and loved being courted by them, but she set high standards when it came to marriage.[23]

Alice Jenkins's girlhood friend, the once wealthy Mary Susan Ker, to give another example, turned down several marriage proposals prior to and following the war from men she considered unworthy because of their personal habits and demeanor or less-than-prosperous standing in the community; according to family legend, she once called off a planned wedding practically at the chapel's door when she smelled alcohol on her betrothed's breath.[24] Some of Natchez's single women, like Rebecca Mandeville and the Foster sisters, avoided marriage or remarriage to men who paled in comparison to their dead but idealized fathers, husbands, sweethearts, or brothers—men whom they mourned all their lives. For others, caretaking responsibilities for aging parents and younger siblings orphaned by the war left little time or desire for courtship and marriage, especially if their family's financial circumstances had deteriorated in the economic collapse following the war or if no prosperous and capable males appeared on the scene.[25]

In 1880, the city's 552 single African American women (aged thirty and older) far outnumbered its 355 single white women, and a large number of these black women (251) headed their own households. As with the city's not-married white women, many if not most of its single black women also had moved there from the country and for many of the same reasons. Some of the city's African American spinsters and widows had moved to Natchez from the country during and after the war to seek protection and job opportunities, to escape unhappy slave-based marriage-like arrangements, to cope with being abandoned by their slave-era mates, or to better enable them to remain single (or not to remarry) if they could find work to sustain themselves and their children.

Although numerous black women in Adams County and Natchez were legally married during and after the war (1866–82)—with an average of around 149 legally recorded marriages among African Americans each year—others lived with men as fictive or common-law husbands, because legalized marriage seemed unimportant in their relationships despite ongoing pressure from federal officials and northern-born missionaries and teachers, as well as black and white church officials. Additionally, federal pension policies motivated some African American widows whose husbands had served in the Civil War to remain single or "take up" with men informally rather than enter into legalized marriages in order to avoid losing their pension payments. County marriage records indicate that 2,536 African American couples in Natchez and Adams County were married in civil and religious ceremonies during the years 1866 to 1882, joining thereby the many hundreds whose slave-based marriages the state deemed legal with a blanket legislative decree in 1871.[26]

The Not-Married Working Women of Postbellum Natchez

Approximately 68 percent of the city's single white women aged thirty and older (264 out of 387) appear in the manuscript census without jobs or occupations, reflecting the scant work opportunities available for single women and the reluctance of some women to reveal illegal or less respected work, such as prostitution or, if white, work as a servant. In most cases, these "at-home" and "keeping house" women lived, as they had before the war, in households sustained by sons, parents, brothers, and other relatives, and more than a few, especially among the antebellum elite, sewed clothes and made dresses for money without reporting this work to census enumerators.[27] They resemble in many ways the "poor African-American women and common whites" detailed by historian Laura Edwards in her study of postbellum North Carolina, although the similarities are stronger for country women in Adams County than its urban residents.[28]

A few single white women provided rooms and meals to respectable boarders and visitors to the city. Because no large commercial hotel reemerged in Natchez until 1892, many of its short-term visitors and long-term renters stayed in a few licensed boardinghouses, most of which generally accommodated rough-edged, working-class lodgers; no lady or gentleman would stay in such an establishment. The widow Catherine Culhane's boardinghouse, for example, provided bed, meals, and clandestine services such as gaming tables, alcohol, and various nefarious options to lodgers before and after the Civil War, which sometimes got her in trouble with the law. Rooms rented out in private homes, on the other hand, accommodated the more respectable male and female travelers in Natchez attending court or visiting families as well as boarders needing longer stays; keeping house in their private homes for one or two lodgers enabled some women to earn money without paying a boardinghouse license fee.[29]

The city's not-married, working white women earned their living as seamstresses, dressmakers, teachers, governesses, nurses, servants, and factory workers as well as boardinghouse proprietors and managers—occupations generally available to women everywhere in the United States at the time. Three of the Miller sisters, for example, toiled for years alongside their mother as much-valued dressmakers, one of the few skilled trades (along with millinery work, midwifery, nursing, prostitution, and teaching) open to postbellum white women in the city, married or single.

Some single white women and widows (sixteen in total) staffed the reopened Natchez public school (the Natchez Institute) as well as several rural schools that serviced white children in the county, but most white public schoolteachers were married or else younger women who eventually married, a pattern that conforms somewhat to the norm in other postbellum southern cities and towns.[30] Mary Susan Ker, for example, due to her family's impoverishment after the war, worked first as a governess and traveling companion to women once her social equals and then as a dressmaker before finding steady employment in teaching, although she moved around frequently from rural to city schools, including a brief stint in New Orleans.[31]

Several other white women appear sporadically in public records as merchants and dressmakers, but none endured for more than a few years at a time, and only one black woman appears to have operated a legally licensed store in postbellum Natchez, which lasted for only a few years.[32] Few female retailers could compete with the emerging mercantile stores that throve by furnishing supplies on credit to thousands of African American sharecropping families in the countryside and to urban customers. These new postbellum merchants offered credit and installment payment terms as well as lower prices and a greater variety of female attire and sewing supplies than were available in specialty shops operated by women. A few more female-oriented stores began to appear in Natchez toward the end of the century, however.[33]

Most single black women in the city older than age thirty worked outside their homes after the war (310 out of 569, or about 55 percent, compared to around 32 percent for whites in 1880), principally as domestic servants (cooks and housekeepers) and washerwomen. Some of these domestic servants and laundresses lived within their employers' houses, but most did not, and this marked a significant change from before the war, when enslaved domestics almost always lived in the houses in which they worked or in attached quarters.[34] Some single black women who owned or rented houses but reported no occupation to the census takers likely earned a living by renting rooms to boarders, doing laundry, hawking vegetables, dealing in contraband and spirits, sewing, or selling sex. Such work—which was carried on by both married and single as well as black and white women—composed an underground economy of sorts not always subject to municipal licenses or taxes. No black women, moreover, married or single, child or adult, worked in the city's two cotton mills.[35]

A number of single black women (18) taught in the city and county's public schools for black children, funded initially by municipal revenues and then by county taxes and state allocations. Most of these African American teachers, unlike their white counterparts, seldom married or remarried, and many remained teachers for their entire working lives. The age and marital status of the black women who taught in the forty-four schools for African American children in the county is information not easily discerned from the public record, but most appear to have been single women.[36]

Divorce in Postbellum Natchez

Although the total number of whites who filed for divorce in Natchez and Adams County between 1865 and 1890 remains unknown, relatively complete legal records can be found for a total of fifty-one individuals—twenty-nine female plaintiffs and twenty-two male plaintiffs. Most white women in this sample were younger than thirty when their marriages ended (68 percent), and they seldom remarried (as far as can be determined from Adams County marriage records). Divorcing white women and men charged their spouses with adultery, desertion, and extreme cruelty before and after the war. Interestingly, allegations of spousal adultery dominated those postbellum divorces filed by the city's white men through the 1880s. Whether this pattern indicates a greater willingness among postbellum white women to indulge in affairs outside marriage as compared to before the Civil War or whether it demonstrates the greater willingness of husbands to go public in their adultery allegations amid the social chaos that characterized postwar Natchez is difficult to know. In one postbellum case, but only one, a white woman landed in jail for adultery following her husband's divorce suit and the accusatory witness testimony that it entailed.[37]

State law shifted divorce jurisdiction after the war from circuit courts to a new system of chancery courts, but filing procedures and the authority of precedent used by courts in divorce, child custody, and alimony decisions remained essentially the same between 1857 and 1890. Several modifications in Mississippi's postbellum marriage laws nevertheless affected divorce in important ways. First, in 1871, the state legislature reduced the requirement for desertion or abandonment as grounds for divorce from a period of three years to two, which may explain the increased number of divorce complaints based on abandonment in postbellum Natchez. In cases where adultery and extreme cruelty accompanied abandonment charges, divorcing spouses could focus on the more easily demonstrated abandonment allegations in their pleas. Charges of extreme cruelty and adultery required witnesses to substantiate or contest the allegations, and their testimony usually included character assassination and embarrassing details about bruises, broken bones, and internal injuries. Abandonment allegations, on the other hand, typically relied on little more than credible testimony, often by uninvolved observers, verifying a spouse's prolonged absence.[38]

Second, more precise language regarding extreme cruelty as a basis for divorce allowed courts to consider mental and emotional abuse along with extreme physical violence in rendering their verdicts. Unlike before the Civil War, during the 1870s Mississippi granted permanent divorce (rather than bed-and-board separation) for extreme cruelty, defined as "habitual, cruel and inhuman treatment, marked by personal violence." Several postbellum plaintiffs emphasized nonphysical abuse as the principal reason for requesting a divorce. It was not until the 1890s, however, that Mississippi legislators began fully to recognize nonphysical abuse and emotional cruelty as grounds for divorce, which Mississippi courts also acknowledged by ruling that "personal violence was not required in order to constitute cruel and inhumane treatment."[39]

Third, although the provision was nullified by the U.S. Congress in 1867 and excluded from the Mississippi constitution of 1871, marriage and cohabitation between whites and blacks was included as grounds for divorce in Mississippi beginning in 1866, foretelling what was to come when Reconstruction ended in 1877. With the return of white rule, Mississippi banned black-white marriages and cohabitation, making it a crime punishable as incest (if married) and adultery (if living together but not legally married), providing that "the marriage of a white person and a negro or mulatto or person who shall have one-fourth or more of negro blood, shall be unlawful, and such marriage shall be incestuous and void." If convicted, each individual faced up to $500 in fines and penitentiary imprisonment for up to ten years. Similar laws banning black-white sexual activity swept across the post-Reconstruction South. Among the cases examined for this study, only one Natchez plaintiff, a white male, divorced his mixed-race wife because their marriage violated state law, although that probably was a cover for other issues; only a few mixed-race couples faced arrest for "unlawful cohabitation," although more than a few individuals, white and black, paid fines or were incarcerated for committing adultery or for cohabitating with racially different sexual partners outside a legal marriage. In one case, Samuel Pickering accused his wife, Delia, both white, of having abandoned him and taken up with a black man who treated her as his mistress.[40]

Despite state bans on black-white marriages and so-called unlawful cohabitation across the color line, relatively few white women (no more than five or six among the cases reviewed) accused their husbands in court of committing adultery with black women. This is explained partly by the declining empowerment of white males over black women with the end of slavery and partly by the stepped-up public opposition to black-white marriages and cohabitation with the return of white rule to Mississippi in 1877. At a time when rampaging white men whipped, tortured, and murdered other white men for living with black women, and when Mississippi courts jailed white men for adulterous or unlawful cohabitation with black women, fewer white males in the city dared live openly or even guardedly with black women than had before the Civil War. This is not to say that sex across the color line did not occur or that it occurred less frequently, especially in view of the many black and white prostitutes who continued to operate in the city during and after Reconstruction as well as the occasional example of black-white cohabitation in living arrangements similar to marriage, but seldom did white males openly acknowledge their black mistresses and wives, or their mixed-race children, in the ways that they had before the war.[41] And as the years advanced toward century's end, matters worsened. Some cohabitation among well-established white men and black women was quietly accepted in Natchez in the first half of the twentieth century, but it was not as readily condoned as it had been before the war. A pioneering study on Natchez's racial character and social order in the 1930s found that sexual relationships between cohabiting whites and blacks were considered dangerous violations of the city's carefully enforced caste boundaries and were kept hidden as much as possible, a practice that began in earnest after the Civil War.[42]

Also, growing racial solidarity among Natchez blacks may have stigmatized black women who consorted with white men, whereas before the war enslaved and free blacks were unable to oppose publicly or actively resist interracial sexual liaisons based on force or contrived consent. By the 1880s, an elite aristocracy had emerged among the city's African Americans, consisting of the educated descendants of free-born antebellum blacks and former slaves, many of whom were the light-skinned offspring of white fathers. These elite African Americans most likely viewed interracial affairs as ignoble behavior that undermined (especially among African American teachers) their relations with individual whites on whom they depended for patronage and personal safety. Nevertheless, as committed as they often were to uplifting African Americans through education and an emphasis on middle-class (albeit Victorian) behavior—attitudes that many of the city's white elite applauded—the city's black elite most likely viewed sex across the color line as weakening the racial solidarity, consciousness, and pride that they tried to encourage, especially in African American churches and schools and at political rallies. In other words, by the 1880s, opposition to interracial sexual activity, long- or short-term, had emerged in all segments of the Natchez community, which may have reduced the number of prolonged and even brief interracial affairs, at least among the city's more affluent and educated African Americans, and thus might have reduced the number of divorces based on interracial adultery.[43]

Relatively few affluent white men and women sued for divorce during and after Reconstruction compared to before the war. Among the divorces surveyed from 1865 to 1890, less than 10 percent involved individuals with substantial wealth or family ties to prosperous relatives, compared to nearly 40 percent during the years 1835 to 1860; female plaintiffs in the postwar years principally alleged spousal cruelty and adultery rather than abandonment in their divorce pleas.[44] Perhaps this decline in divorce among affluent white men and women reflected changes in separate estate laws (or the Married Women's Property Law) enacted by the Mississippi legislature during the 1870s and 1880s. With these changes, Mississippi greatly strengthened a married woman's control over her property and income during and after Reconstruction by including her earned wages and investments (rather than just her real estate and personal possessions) as property beyond her husband's control, thus empowering her to function more fully in law as though she were a man (acting as a *feme sole*) in matters pertaining to her income and assets. Prosperous or income-producing women no longer needed to pursue divorce to safeguard their wages, earned income, and propertied assets from abusive husbands. What is more, an abandoned woman could, through a court order and without divorce, seek full control of a husband's assets and property when the offending spouse had vacated a family domicile for at least two years.[45]

The *Natchez Weekly Democrat* publicized what it claimed was the first black divorce in Natchez on September 27, 1871, predicting that it foretold the imminent destruction of the black family because irresponsible blacks would opt out of marriage for the slightest reasons once the courts allowed blacks to divorce on grounds similar to those available to whites.[46] But while the exact number of divorces filed by African Americans in Natchez and Adams County remains unknown, extant court records suggest that far fewer blacks (25) than whites (51) sued for divorce in the twenty-five years after the Civil War, even though black residents age twenty-one and older exceeded whites in the city by nearly two to one: 3,948 blacks to 2,210 whites in 1886. In the cases located, combating spouses cited adultery, desertion, and extreme cruelty as their principal complaints, but desertion was the main reason listed by both black women and men for wanting to dissolve their marriages. For black women, a husband's cruelty figured high among complaints, compared to the few white women alleging spousal abuse as grounds for divorce. Because of the costs, publicity, and lengthy process involved in filing a legal divorce, it is a good bet that more than a few working-class blacks (as well as working-class whites) simply abandoned their spouses, or just separated from them without leaving the area, rather than pursuing a legal divorce.[47]

Conclusion

Much was changed for the single women of Natchez in the aftermath of the Civil War. Their numbers had increased substantially in the years between 1865 and 1880 while their occupational opportunities diminished. For the city's single white women, employment opportunities had narrowed even as many who had never worked outside the home were forced to find employment. Some were able to work as teachers, servants, and governesses, while others earned their living by letting out rooms. Fewer white women, single or married, operated as merchants compared to before the war. Of course, for the city's formerly enslaved women, working as free women offered unprecedented opportunities for controlling their own lives insofar as choosing where they lived, how they behaved, and what they consumed, although they continued to labor much as they had during slavery, as domestics, agricultural laborers, and washerwomen. For a few, employment as teachers enabled them to play a public role unlike anything they, or any black person in Natchez, had ever known.

Important changes in divorce and dower laws made it easier for men and women to seek divorce, but fewer whites appear to have sought to end their marriages through divorce compared to before the war (although, based on the sample studied, more white men did seek divorce). In suing for divorce, white males cited adultery over all other issues by a large margin compared to before the war, and female plaintiffs more often listed extreme cruelty along with adultery as their reasons for seeking divorce compared to earlier times. Relatively few blacks, however, appear to have sought legal divorces in the postwar years, and those who did typically cited spousal abandonment in their suits. Among the city's divorcing African Americans, both spouses tended to rank abandonment rather than cruelty or even adultery as the principal reason for ending unhappy marriages.

For the city's free single women, the Civil War greatly disrupted the once relatively cohesive community in which they lived. The ways in which these single women worked and used the law to sustain themselves as women without husbands amid the turmoil, challenges, and opportunities they confronted were always personal choices, with no one woman acting exactly the same as any other. Just as before the war, a woman's class, color, kinship relations, and marital status mattered. How Kate Foster and her sisters coped with their not-married state differed markedly from how the city's not-married African American women, whether born free before the war or only recently freed from slavery, navigated their postbellum lives. What they all shared in common, however, was an altered physical and social environment in which prewar expectations (based on slavery, the servant ideal for women, and patriarchy) were no longer as relevant in the decisions they made as not-married women.

CHAPTER NINE

Stepping Through the Ruins

Personal Sketches

Malvina Matthews

Kate Foster undoubtedly knew about Malvina Matthews, the divorced long-time Natchez madam who faced a much publicized trial in 1868 for the alleged murder of a Union solider, even if the two did not know each other personally, and both women certainly shared a common ambivalence, if not animosity, toward the Yankee troopers still in the city when Matthews went to trial. As first noted in chapter 6, Matthews allegedly killed Private John Moffatt after a scuffle of some sort in the bordello she owned and operated adjacent to her downtown residence, which faced east along Broadway Street, near the Natchez bluffs.[1]

The Union commander of the Natchez Post, Brevet Colonel Nathan A. M. Dudley, consented to a civilian trial for Matthews rather than a military commission, largely as a gesture of reconciliation with the community.[2] Although empowered to prosecute civilians in military commission trials, the U.S. Army was directed by the Military Reconstruction Act of 1867 to support "competent civil officers" whenever possible. As it happened, only a few cases involving civilians and soldiers in Mississippi were tried by the military, but the determination of which cases would be so handled was left to the discretion of local commanders, subject to review by superior officers. In 1868, two other commission trials originating at the Natchez Post were in process, thus possibly explaining, in part, Matthews's case being tried by a civilian court.[3]

Dudley soon regretted his decision, however, once it became clear that few Natchez whites would hold the divorced and notorious but very southern, hometown Malvina Matthews accountable for killing a drunken Yankee soldier. It took Dudley only a few months in service as commander of the Natchez Post to mistrust the "sincerity and integrity" of the city's civilian officials, no matter, in his opinion, what actions he took to appease them. In a letter to his superior officer, Dudley asserted that "the people here are just as bad rebels as ever they were, and would say so, and glory in it if they dared; and I want more troops to protect the loyal citizens and the Negroes, and prevent riots and insurrections."[4]

Matthews's trial occurred amid a virulent and often bloody struggle by the city's formerly enslaved blacks, aided by Yankee soldiers and outsider white and black Republicans, to exercise their citizenship by demanding male suffrage, rejecting slave-like working conditions, establishing separate churches under black control, calling for free public schools, and insisting on full social equality with whites on the city's streets and in its public buildings, marketplaces, and parks. These efforts aroused furious and sometimes violent opposition from many of the city's whites, who quickly attempted to create and enforce a series of racial laws and practices that relegated the formerly enslaved to an inferior citizenship status socially, economically, and politically. This struggle peaked in 1867, when the federal government imposed military rule on Mississippi and the former Confederacy, a period known as Radical Reconstruction; thereafter Natchez became one of five military posts in the Fourth Military District, which included Mississippi, and Private Moffatt was among the one hundred white soldiers still stationed there when he died.[5]

Matthews hired the city's most prominent attorney, William T. Martin, a former Confederate general, as her defense lawyer. Because it was a capital case, Matthews's jury consisted of a special panel of jurors separate from the regular jury panel, as required by state law. Her jury included six whites, several of whom hailed from wealthy antebellum planter families, and six blacks, and it may have been the first Adams County trial including black jurors. Much of the evidence against Matthews came from two prostitutes, a black one named Francis Harrison and a white one named Louisa Guido, who claimed they had heard Matthews admit to shooting Moffatt, although neither had been present at the time of the murder. Martin effectively undermined their testimony by depicting them as untrustworthy strangers angling as nonresident whores to take over the aging madam's well-known and more trusted business.[6] Martin's defense emphasized that no one actually saw Matthews fire the gun or guns that killed Moffatt. He argued that even if Matthews had fired the fatal shots, there was no way of knowing, considering the darkness of the night and the lack of eyewitnesses, if she had shot to kill or just to scare off the drunken soldier in defense of her property and life. Martin won a not guilty verdict for his aging and obese client.

By the time of the trial in 1868, the lawyer Martin had moved from outright opposition to black civil rights to embrace "fusion politics" after the infamous Black Codes were overturned by Military Reconstruction in 1867, but he remained steadfastly opposed to full equality for the formerly enslaved, even as he befriended, represented as a lawyer, and worked closely with many of the city's most active black politicians, including some from its leading antebellum free-black families. Although he had been a Whig and had voted against secession as a delegate to the state secession convention in 1860, Martin subsequently raised a Confederate cavalry troop of the wealthiest men in the area and led them to war on the Virginia front. Serving with Jeb Stuart in the east and then in the Western Theater under Generals Braxton Bragg, James Longstreet, Earl Van Dorn, and Joseph Wheeler, Martin advanced quickly to the rank of major general and garnered much honor and recognition for his "invincible cavalry." No Natchez Confederate soldier or officer returned home from war to greater acclaim.

Back in Natchez after the war, Martin assumed leadership of the city's conservative elements, won election as president of the Adams County Board of Police (which later became the Board of Supervisors), organized a white militia group to confiscate guns from blacks throughout the county, served as a delegate to the state's constitutional convention in 1865 and again in 1890, became a Democratic candidate for Congress in 1868 (but was rejected by the U.S. Congress after he was elected), was involved in numerous business ventures (including holding the presidency of the Natchez, Jackson, & Columbus Railroad), and practiced law at a feverish pace. During Reconstruction (1865–77) Martin and his firm handled over seventeen hundred legal cases in a whirlwind of activity that restored a measure of his family's antebellum wealth. His fusionist political agenda accepted a token role for educated blacks in appointed and elected government positions, and he had hoped to induce propertied blacks to join a new political party that he called the Conservative Union Party (later named the National Republican Union Party) as an alternative to the Republican Party.[7]

Besides Martin's prestige, Matthews benefited from several factors that almost certainly frustrated Colonel Dudley as he watched the case go to trial. Matthews's white jurors included two men, Melvin Gibson and George Sargent Jr., whose relatives allegedly were murdered by Yankee soldiers during the botched robberies of their villas.[8] Gibson's family, moreover, owned a Louisiana plantation where the white fugitive William Hewett, a firebrand Natchez lawyer convicted of torturing a white northerner who had taught black students and married a black woman, hid out, with Colonel Dudley in hot pursuit, after escaping from a Vicksburg jail.[9]

The fact, moreover, that Matthews, a slaveholder prior to the war, most likely had favored local white customers over drunken Yankee soldiers in her whorehouse business almost certainly helped her case. Matthews, who had owned eight enslaved people during the 1850s, including four women who apparently worked for her as prostitutes, was entertaining several local male customers on the night she allegedly shot the Union soldier. Her preference for local whites may have angered the murdered soldier, who may have been refused service at the bordello. One of her whorehouse customers present that night testified that Matthews had directed Jane Duncan, the black prostitute who ran the bordello in which the soldier had died, to turn away any and all Union soldiers, explaining that rowdy Yankee soldiers would be coming "in droves with whiskey," having "been paid off the day before." When a local newspaper reported Moffatt's death, it speculated that the dead soldier had broken into Matthews's house, enraged by "whiskey, bestial lust, or a revengeful spirit for attempted outrages by the roommates of the establishment."[10]

Matthews also may have benefited from her ownership of a house situated on lands coveted by Martin for a terminal for a railroad company he hoped to control and build, lands that he eventually acquired. High among Martin's many entrepreneurial ambitions stood his hope to develop a rail line from Natchez to Jackson, Mississippi, with a train station or rail terminal located on the bluffs near the old lighthouse site and adjacent to, or directly on, Matthews's whorehouse property. There is no way of knowing if his railroad schemes influenced Martin to defend Matthews, but it seems likely in view of the fact that she mortgaged a portion of her bluff property to him in 1872 and then sold a twenty-foot strip of it to the Natchez, Jackson, & Columbus Railroad on the same day. Martin's wife, moreover, acquired the remainder of Matthews's prime bluffs property in a tax sale in 1881, six years after the notorious madam's death. By 1882, Martin, as president of that same railroad, erected his envisioned railroad station, rails, and yards on lands once owned by the notorious madam he had defended in the killing of Private Moffatt.[11]

After the jury reached its unanimous verdict in her favor, Matthews walked from the courtroom undoubtedly aware that six black jurors had cooperated with six white former slaveholders on her behalf in what may have been, as noted earlier, the first Adams County jury including black men. The black jurors perhaps had voted to acquit Matthews because they saw her as a businesswoman who, although a former slaveholder, had employed black and white women as fellow workers, possibly on somewhat similar terms. Although there is no clear evidence that she or her employees had serviced enslaved or free blacks before the war or black soldiers during the Union occupation of Natchez, Matthews's prostitutes almost certainly had offered sex to black men in uniform, given the numerous complaints from Union officers about lewd women fraternizing with their soldiers. Moreover, in supporting her innocence, Matthews's black jurors, none of whom had been Union soldiers and many of whom owned property—exactly the type of men Martin was attempting to entice into joining his class-conscious fusion Conservative Union

Party—perhaps saw little reason to alienate powerful white men over an issue that affected them but little. For them, the murder of a drunken white soldier most likely was of little if any consequence to them as black men.[12]

Given these facts, a southern, white divorcee of great notoriety appears to have gotten away with murder. Matthews lived another half-dozen years, and she passed into old age as a newly participating member of St. Mary's Catholic Church, even as she continued to operate her bordello in an entrepreneurial role that resembled in some ways Kate Foster's work as a hotel keeper servicing traveling males. It is likely that Matthews lived on as a local heroine of sorts among Natchez whites (although no discovered evidence supports this conjecture), a lone women who had confronted Yankee soldiers physically, just as Kate Foster confronted them emotionally in memorializing the city's Confederate and antebellum past. But the similarities between the two women go even further when it is remembered that prominent Natchez lawyers (Lemuel P. Conner Jr. for Foster and William T. Martin for Matthews), men distinguished by their connection to the Civil War, served and represented the two women as dutiful legal counsels and surrogates for husbands, fathers, and brothers. Of the two women, Matthews was probably better equipped to deal with the uncertain circumstances they faced, principally because of her prewar entrepreneurial experiences, the street-savvy character of her profession, and a lifetime of having to negotiate largely on her own.

What it meant to be female and not married after the demise of slavery, the onset of Radical Reconstruction, and the violent reassertion of white rule in Natchez and Adams County, Mississippi, differed for each not-married woman who lived during those years, and no one woman can be seen as a universal model whose experiences were applicable to all others. Few were like Matthews or Foster, but almost all of the city's single women, black and white, faced unprecedented circumstances in the war's aftermath and in the context of the emancipation of a once enslaved people.[13] What follows are several personal sketches that illuminate how a select group of not-married Natchez women (three widows, a divorcee, and two spinsters, one of whom was black) navigated their individual lives during the aftermath of the American Civil War. The difficulties these women faced and the ways they coped reveal the challenges and maneuverings many of the city's single women experienced in postbellum Natchez as they tried to negotiate a world turned upside down, one that they faced free of, or unsupported by, men as husbands. In providing these sketches, this study will have come full circle, illuminating how the impact of slavery's demise and a weakened patriarchy greatly altered the stage on which the city's single women stepped.

Mary McMurran

On January 28, 1868, the elite Natchez matron Mary McMurran, aged fifty-three, answered a heartfelt letter from a distant cousin who offered to "do anything in his power" to assist her in coping with life as a newly widowed woman, left on her own in what her correspondent considered overwhelming circumstances.[14] Her husband, John, a once wealthy slaveholder and one of the most successful lawyers in the state, had died on December 30, 1866, in a tragic accident aboard a steamboat bound from Natchez for New Orleans.[15] Mary McMurran thanked her cousin kindly, leaving open the possibility that she might accept his offer at some later date. She mentioned as well in the letter, almost as a given, that although her family now lived poorly and in want because of the Civil War, they would persevere somehow.[16]

John McMurran's death seemed like the last blow to the McMurran family, and especially to Mary McMurran, who confided to her cousin how she felt about her marriage: "You know ours was no ordinary love: in each other we found everything married life could expect. We were all in all to each other."[17] Although John McMurran held on to his five plantations during the Civil War, he died nearly bankrupt, leaving his wife with over $33,000 in debts.[18] The family even had to sell its manorial house Melrose, located on the outskirts of Natchez, which John had built in 1845.[19] In January 1866, eleven months prior to John's death, the family moved to Woodlands, the suburban villa owned by Mary's widowed mother, Elizabeth Turner, whose husband, the esteemed judge Edward Turner, had died in 1860.[20] A few months after John McMurran's tragic death, Mary's sister, Fanny Conner, and her financially devastated husband, Lemuel P. Conner Sr., a once affluent antebellum planter and an esteemed Confederate officer, joined the Turner-McMurran family at Woodlands, undoubtedly to save on expenses.[21]

Mary McMurran's only daughter, Mary Elizabeth McMurran Conner, had suffered a painful and prolonged death in 1864, leaving her three small children in their grandmother's care. A few months after their mother's death, Mary Elizabeth's young daughter and youngest son perished from "camp dysentery," a common enough malady that sometimes spread from the Yankee army camps and refugee corrals located in and around the city. Their father, Farrar Conner, Mary's son-in-law and the younger brother of Lemuel P. Conner Sr., had served as an officer in the Confederate army and spent the last thirteen months of the war in a prisoner-of-war camp in Tennessee. Walking on foot the nearly four hundred miles home, he arrived in Natchez broken in spirit and health by the war only to learn of the loss of his wife, daughter, and youngest son.[22]

Almost all aspects of Mary's life worsened during the war's aftermath.

Her only son, John Jr., wounded during the war, struggled to find work in Washington, D.C., and then spent years unsuccessfully trying his hand at dairy farming in Maryland on marginal lands owned by his father-in-law, an endeavor that most likely undermined his marriage, which eventually failed. For the rest of his life, John Jr. eked out a living by borrowing money and jumping from one job to another, and he seldom returned to Natchez until late in the century, after his mother's death. Mary's son-in-law, Farrar Conner, shattered by his wartime experiences, left his surviving son, Benjamin, lovingly called Fazee by the family, with his mother-in-law to be educated and nurtured while he searched for work as an overseer in Louisiana and Texas for much of the next decade. He finally returned to Natchez during the mid-1880s to marry one of the three not-married Chotard sisters, the spinster daughter of a once prominent family that also had fallen on hard times.[23] The young Fazee grew to manhood in Adams County and lived his entire life in Natchez as a "single man"—preferring, like a character from a Faulkner novel, the company of "cats, horses, and Negroes" to that of white people.[24]

During the twenty-five years following her husband's death, Mary McMurran struggled to keep her extended household together, pay off her husband's debts, and retain as many of her landed properties as possible, especially the beloved Woodlands estate house and its surrounding lands, which had belonged to her widowed mother. Of the once extensive Turner-Conner-McMurran landholdings, only hers survived relatively intact after the Civil War. To cope with the household's dire economic circumstances, McMurran borrowed often against her plantation properties, signing short-term promissory notes secured by liens, which typically she renegotiated when they fell due. The basic income to meet interest payments on these notes came from renting her lands to white tenants, including former overseers, who contracted with black sharecroppers. As the price of cotton declined to ruinous levels, and once it became clear that her son would never return to manage the family properties, McMurran sold three of her five plantations. She thereafter borrowed against her remaining plantations from anyone willing to offer her funding, including local furnishing merchants who loaned her cash secured by liens on those portions of the crops due as rent from her tenants and sharecroppers. This pattern continued for two decades, up to the time of her death.[25]

Remarkably, Mary McMurran carried on with little or no financial help from her family or from the numerous friends and associates who had filled her antebellum life, principally because most of them were in equally difficult or worse financial straits. Her immediate and extended family proved more of a burden than a resource, and her son's creditors pestered her throughout these years as they tried to collect money owed them by a debtor whom none could

Woodlands, the estate of Edward Turner and Elizabeth Turner, Adams County, Mississippi, and the postbellum residence of Mary McMurran, ca. 1870s. Historic Natchez Foundation.

locate. But Mary McMurran possessed an indomitable will to persevere, and she appears to have been a clear-thinking realist who fully understood both the temperamental unsuitability and the striking incompetence of her lawyer brother-in-law, her son, and her grandson when compared to her dead husband and her illustrious father. In the case of her brother-in-law, Lemuel Conner Sr., his seeming inability to handle her legal affairs may have stemmed from the constant stress of his own financial problems as well as his frequent absence from Natchez as he pursued business in Louisiana and elsewhere. Whatever the reasons, Mary McMurran seldom turned to her male family members for assistance in her legal and plantation affairs.

Left on her own with no competent male relative to intervene on her behalf or to protect her interests, McMurran turned to her dead husband's law partner, James Carson, perhaps out of loyalty to her husband's memory or perhaps because she liked and trusted him given their long-standing relationship via her husband's legal business and plantation affairs, which included their joint ownership for a time of an Arkansas plantation. Over the course of her remaining life, McMurran relied almost exclusively on this lawyer and friend as her most trusted confidant until his death in 1889.[26] McMurran allowed Carson a free hand in leasing and operating her plantations, and he in turn reported in detail his actions on her behalf and the reasons for his decisions. No

Mary McMurran, ca. 1870s. Edward Turner Collection, Louisiana and Lower Mississippi Valley Collections, LSU Libraries, Baton Rouge, Louisiana.

matter was too small for him to handle nor too contentious for him to engage, whether disputes with troublesome overseers and renters, crop failures (which happened frequently during the early 1870s), or loan negotiations. In these business dealings, McMurran seldom disagreed with Carson's advice, although she frequently requested additional information.[27]

The correspondence between James Carson and Mary McMurran principally relates to business affairs, but many of their letters talk freely about family matters, health, politics, gossip, friends, and one another's emotional well-being. The Carson family exchanged Christmas gifts with Mary McMurran, and James and Mary commiserated over lost relatives and lost fortunes and shared numerous personal thoughts about the small things of life that bespeak an intimacy based on mutual respect and affection. Understanding their similar financial straits, Carson seldom billed McMurran for his services until he was sure that she had the cash available to pay him. He helped raise funds to pay her son's debts, and she sometimes cosigned his loans by pledging her property as collateral. Most importantly, Carson never overstepped his authority or patronized McMurran as an uninformed female in need of his manly advice, authority, and experience. She trusted him as her confidant but not as a surrogate husband or authoritarian father figure to whom she deferred. It was almost as though she set the policy and then relied on him to carry out her wishes, mindful that it would take a male hand to deal with her creditors, her tenants, and the messy business affairs of her son and other family members. Carson in turn always related to McMurran as more than a client; he clearly felt responsible for her financial security and he behaved toward her in ways that made him much more than a mere agent or retainer, reflecting his friendship with her husband but also, certainly, with her. He acted very much like the quintessential southern gentleman, in a manner befitting his profession and his antebellum sense of duty, but he also knew his place. Based on their letters, he understood that McMurran was his benefactress and employer and she certainly understood the practical basis of their personal relationship.

After Carson's death in 1889, McMurran's financial situation worsened. She continued as best she could to manage her plantations by renting them out and piling new loans on top of old ones, including mortgaging her beloved Woodlands, but her debts only increased and she fell behind in her accounts more often than before. In the last years of her life, Lemuel P. Conner Jr., her lawyer nephew and her most competent family member, tried to help, but her precarious financial situation, stemming from low cotton prices and a generally depressed economy, left little that could be done. Her economic problems were compounded by the increasing number of family quarrels among her absent son and her present but largely out-of-touch grandson Fazee, whom Mary truly loved and doted on. At the time of her death she was deeply in debt, and the Adams County probate court had little choice but to sell her personal and real property, including Woodlands, to pay her creditors. Her son John returned briefly to Natchez just prior to his mother's funeral, principally to contest her will, which left her few remaining assets to her beloved Fazee, whom she had named executor of her estate.[28]

Mary McMurran probably never fully understood the extent of her impoverishment in the last few years of her life, nor would she have imagined in 1860, when she lived grandly at Melrose, how precarious her life would become in the ensuing years. In the aftermath of the Civil War, Mary McMurran persevered as a widowed woman by borrowing against and leasing her plantation properties, producing barely enough income to sustain her financially strapped extended family, who lived with her (and "off" her) at Woodlands as they struggled to share expenses and resources. With this one viable asset—her remaining plantation lands—she managed to live respectably, if not comfortably, in her father's Woodland estate house, surrounded by loving but largely dependent kin, until the end of her days. It is clear that Mary McMurran endured and persevered largely because of the relationship that existed between her and a trusted, nonfamily male advisor who assisted her as a friend and confidant in the absence of any other competent or suitable family member, male or female, on whom she could rely. Mary McMurran's strategy for coping as a woman without a husband and with the loss of the antebellum fortune she had once enjoyed was not an uncommon experience among her once elite peers. She, and other Natchez women like her, commonly turned to trusted males, men like James Carson, who helped to fill the void left by dead, absent, or emasculated husbands, fathers, sons, and brothers—if they were lucky enough, that is, to know such men.

Julia Nutt

Just outside Natchez lived the resolute widow Julia Nutt, an Adams County neighbor to Mary McMurran and her social equal, a strongly resolute woman who confronted the war's aftermath with few male confidants to help her navigate the debacle left behind by her dead husband and the ruination of her family's fortune due to the Civil War and slavery's demise. From the end of the war until her death in 1897, she continued to reside with her eight surviving children, who ranged from a toddler to a twenty-year-old in 1865, in the unfinished Moorish-style mansion, Longwood, that her husband began constructing in 1860.[29] She and her deceased husband, Haller Nutt, an avowed Unionist and second-generation nabob, owned five plantations and nearly eight hundred slaves on the eve of the Civil War, and her family tree included two prominent Natchez branches (the Rouths and the Williamses) that dated to the early colonial era. Although Julia Nutt embodied the outward manifestations of the faithful plantation mistress and child-breeding wife and mother, she was known to have been a "high-tempered" and "spicy" woman when young who became more than a little "petulant" and independent-minded in later life. She once stormed off from her husband to live with her family for several days in what he thought was an immature but typical display of anger because he had sided with her enslaved household workers when they complained about her mistreatment of them.[30]

Haller Nutt began constructing his magnificent, octagonal, and multistoried villa, which many of his wealthy neighbors considered outlandish, just a short carriage ride from Natchez in 1859. Using a Philadelphia architect and imported Philadelphia craftsmen assisted by enslaved workers, work on the house progressed rapidly until 1861, when, with the outer structure and roof completed, the northern carpenters and brick masons abruptly departed for home, fearful that the war might leave them stranded in Natchez. Using his slaves and local artisans to finish the first, or basement, floor of the house, Nutt moved in with his wife, children, and household slaves to wait out the war.[31] Confederate and Union soldiers thereafter plundered Nutt's country plantations and his

Longwood. Cooper Postcard
Collection, Archives and
Records Services Division,
Mississippi Department of
Archives and History, Jackson.

Longwood property for supplies, crops, stock, and farming implements. Most of his enslaved workers abandoned his rural plantations at the first sign of Union troops or else, if they stayed in place, were cut off completely from his authority by the Yankee soldiers that patrolled much of the Natchez hinterland and prevented him from visiting his country properties.

Devastated by the collapse of the world he had once dominated as a wealthy slaveholder, Haller died suddenly from pneumonia on July 15, 1864, at the age of forty-eight. He left behind plantations that were heavily mortgaged for monies advanced to him prior to the war at high interest rates and in ruin from marauding soldiers, as well as large debts incurred for household furnishings and construction costs.[32] Julia Nutt summed up the situation in sworn testimony before the Southern Claims Commission in her appeal for reparations as a loyal Unionist: "It was not pneumonia that killed him. It was his troubles.

Three million dollars of property swept away, the labor of a lifetime gone, large debts incurred by the War; pressing on him, and his helpless wife with eight children and two other families looking to him for support. All were reared in the lap of luxury and now utter poverty stood before them. This crushed him and he died."[33] For the next thirty years, Julia struggled to keep Longwood from foreclosure, ward off creditors, retain the family plantations, pay interest on her debts, hold the family intact, and educate her children, three of whom she managed to send to private, eastern schools.[34]

Truly a powerful figure, Julia Nutt reigned over the Longwood household and her family until she died, intestate, in 1897. Her spinster daughters Mary Ella and Julia, as well as her sons Sargeant Prentiss and Calvin, along with her married daughter Lillie and Lillie's husband, James Ward, and their five children, frequently lived with her at Longwood, cramped together with little personal space or privacy to keep them from arguing with one another.[35] Julia bickered constantly with her live-at-home daughters, thinking Mary Ella too strange to be good company and her namesake daughter Julia too full of herself for her own good. She mistrusted Lillie's husband, whom she believed connived to obtain what little money she still retained as the family matriarch or what she might someday acquire if government reparations for Nutt properties destroyed or confiscated by Union soldiers during the Civil War ever materialized. She thought her son Calvin a foolish gambler whose good-hearted wife had squandered her family money on his harebrained business schemes before divorcing him. Although she usually fawned over Prentiss, her well-educated (University of Virginia) lawyer son, she considered him too much of a social butterfly and reckless spendthrift to ever amount to much. Only her oldest son, John Ker Nutt, who lived as a modest and largely self-sufficient planter-farmer with his childless wife two counties removed from Longwood, enjoyed a somewhat tranquil relationship with the iron-willed matriarch.[36]

Julia faced the aftermath of the Civil War with a steely determination to carry on. At her death she still held Longwood and her rural Cloverdale plantation, which she had mortgaged again and again over the years. To survive as a cash-strapped but land-rich widow, she tried every experiment imaginable to wring income from the five plantations scattered around Mississippi and Louisiana that were left in her charge as her husband's executrix: she hired her sons to manage them (unsuccessfully) from time to time; leased them to white tenants who worked the land with black sharecroppers, many of whom her husband had once owned as enslaved chattel; borrowed against them to pay off loans for supplies and taxes; temporarily transferred title in trust to her daughters to avoid foreclosure; and eventually sold parcels surrounding her precious Longwood as well as three of her plantations, including the one that had been the family home prior to Longwood, known as Winter Quarters, in Louisiana.[37]

While executing these financial maneuvers, Julia denied herself food, or so she claimed in testimony before the Southern Claims Commission, so that her children would not go hungry, battled creditors in court, dismissed household servants rather than pay their wages, prevailed upon lenders to extend her notes or accept interest-only payments, turned down social engagements rather than attend underdressed or in threadbare attire, and badgered her family to scrimp, save, and stick together no matter what difficulties they faced. Through it all, Julia felt terribly impoverished by the fate that had befallen her, complaining constantly about the shabbiness of her beloved Longwood and the sad fact that she and her remaining kin "all look like a broken down southern family," with little left but "family pride keeping us up."[38]

It was more than pride, however, that kept her going. Her appeal for federal compensation as an allegedly loyal Unionist for Nutt properties destroyed or confiscated during the war by Union soldiers—claims that she estimated at upward of $800,000—greatly fortified her and offered hope to her many creditors that she might someday pay their accounts. She waged this appeal using Washington, D.C., lawyers as well as her son Prentiss to represent her. Although the Southern Claims Commission granted her over $56,000 in damages in the mid-1870s, which enabled her to pay something on her numerous debts and tuition for her sons' private school education in Washington, D.C., and Richmond, Virginia, it barely enabled her to sustain her large and exhaustively dependent family. Battling onward, she appealed this initial award, after accepting and spending the awarded cash, and fought vigorously for her full claim until her very death.[39]

Tired of paying legal fees to Washington, D.C., lawyers, she eventually sent her son Prentiss to practice law in the nation's capital and to handle her reparation claims. In the process, Prentiss Nutt developed a marginal practice that specialized in reparation cases for other Natchez families. Unfortunately, the less-than-resolute son proved to be more of a socialite and dandy than a competent lawyer. At his best in attending parties and lobbying prominent Washington politicos, Prentiss showed few results for his work. Over the years, Julia urged, cajoled, lectured, and pleaded with her son to pursue the claims at every opportunity, demanding detailed reports from him weekly if not daily at times. He usually complied, sending letters home year after year, noting his social meetings with key congressional leaders and influential D.C. political operatives and personalities whom he believed might help advance his cause. Always, however, just beneath the surface in these letters lay Julia's irritation at her son's lack of success, profligate habits, and spendthrift lifestyle. Finally, achieving little success through Prentiss, she once again hired a prominent D.C. law firm, instructing her son to swallow his pride and work with the new legal team. The Nutt family eventually received several hundred thousand dollars in reparation payments: $18,000 in 1866, $56,000 in 1873, $35,000 in 1884, and a final $159,884 award that came shortly after Julia Nutt's death, most of which was consumed by legal fees and payments to the twenty-nine creditors who held claims against her estate.[40]

The voluminous Nutt letters illuminate how Julia had used her claim for reparations to avoid complete financial ruin. She frequently carried Prentiss's letters to her creditors, citing their optimistic predictions about the likelihood of payment to buy more time or secure needed advances. The letters also reveal how close to the edge the family lived. Cash, bank notes, and petitions for help passed among and between its members in these letters on a weekly basis, sometimes including sums as small as ten dollars to help one or another of the family members to persevere. Almost every letter expressed dismay over the potential loss of lands and even Longwood to hungry creditors. What remained constant in Julia's life, as revealed in the family correspondence, was her often desperate battle to hold the family together despite its weakness as a family unit and to retain, at all costs, her beloved Longwood estate house as the symbol of what the family had once been and might someday, she hoped, become again. She did this, moreover, with little effective assistance from her immediate family or from the many neighbors and friends whom she once had enjoyed as social companions during the days of slavery.

In the end, it was the promise of government payments at some future date, Julia Nutt's formidable ability to use her plantation properties as sources of credit and loans, and her determination to persevere against all odds that carried her through. Her immediate family proved more burdensome than not to Julia's survival during the aftermath of the Civil War. Although no reliable male confidant stood by her side to offer advice and assistance, her son Prentiss, whom she directed to a career in law (mistakenly hopeful that his legal training would perhaps revive the family's fortune or at least succeed in securing her claim for reparations soon enough to matter), always provided her with a measure of moral support as only a son could offer. Also, Julia used her lands as collateral for loans and rental income that enabled her to eke out a living for herself and her family within the potentially grand but stillborn Longwood mansion house. She had only herself to look to for reliable counsel and support as she engaged a postwar life wherein the subservience of females to a male hierarchy as well as the servant/marriage ideal for women no longer necessarily afforded an especially viable strategy on which to base female behavior or to reap rewards for any such deferential posturing.

Katherine Minor

Unlike Mary McMurran and Julia Nutt, the widow Katherine Minor, member of perhaps the most elite family in antebellum Natchez, navigated the aftermath of the Civil War from a relatively prosperous position. Though never again as wealthy as she had been before the war, her substantial assets continued to set her apart in ways that highlight both the differences and the similarities among and between her and Kate Foster, Mary McMurran, and Julia Nutt in how they coped as once wealthy white women in the Civil War's chaotic aftermath.

Kate Minor's husband, John, traced his family's origins to the earliest British settlers in the Natchez District. His ancestors had acquired large tracts of land from the Spanish when Natchez was part of Spain's global empire. Kate Minor's family, the French-born Surgets of Natchez, also dated to the Spanish era as a landed elite, and her father, James, and uncles, Jacob and Eustace, were among the wealthiest planter slaveholders in the entire South on the eve of the Civil War. What is more, Kate was connected through marriage to a prominent New York and New Orleans banking, mercantile, and cotton factorage firm operated by the husbands (Charles and Henry Leverich) of John Minor's maternal aunts, Margaret and Matilda, née Gustine. The combined wealth of the Surget and Minor households included hundreds of slaves and at least a dozen plantations in Mississippi and Louisiana.[41]

The war severely affected Kate's family fortune, but not to the extent felt by most of her once wealthy neighbors. During the immediate postwar years Kate and John lived with their three children at Oakland (two other children having died just before or during the war), the grand Natchez estate house they had purchased jointly with inherited monies, and they managed their remaining plantations by contracting with many of the enslaved workers they had once owned, first as wage hands and then as sharecroppers. In Kate Minor's own words, the family faced the postwar era with "nothing in the world," clearly an exaggeration spoken in support of her claim for federal reparations as a Union loyalist for properties confiscated or destroyed by Union troops during the Civil War.[42]

The Minors had been reluctant Confederates when the Civil War broke out, and they cooperated openly with the city's Yankee occupiers once Natchez fell to Union forces in the summer of 1863. John and Kate Minor were among those wealthy planter families that tried to have it both ways: opposed to secession prior to the war, guardedly cooperating with the Confederacy until Natchez fell to Union forces, and then vocally and openly supportive of the Union, hosting sumptuous parties and dinners for their Yankee conquerors while using family connections in the North to protect their plantation interests in Mississippi and Louisiana. Unlike many of his pro-Union neighbors who joined up as Confederate soldiers once the war broke out, John hired a substitute to take his place when he was drafted and candidly cautioned his fellow nabobs to prepare for the worst. The Minor family's pro-Union actions and open socializing with the enemy once the city fell to Federal forces, not surprisingly, enraged those among their neighbors who had lost kin, friends, and sweethearts fighting for the Confederacy, and some local whites refused to speak to John or Kate for years, if ever again.[43]

John's duplicity and fraternization with the enemy took a heavy toll on his mental and physical health, and he often could be seen after the war walking drunk and despondent through the city's streets, complaining bitterly that the "treatment from his old friends had been such that he didn't care if or whether he lived or died."[44] In 1869, during a hasty visit to New York City, John, perhaps in a drunken stupor, suffered massive head injuries from a fall in his hotel quarters; he died a few days later far from family and home, leaving the thirty-four-year-old Katherine to cope with life as his widow.[45] Barely two months after his son's death, William Minor, the family patriarch, succumbed to a stroke while at home on his plantation in Louisiana.[46] Katherine Minor's father, James Surget Sr., had died in 1855, and her uncle Eustace Surget, a confirmed rebel, left Mississippi for France during the Civil War and later resided in New York City, where he was joined by Kate's uncle Jacob Surget, who lived there until his death in 1869.[47]

Unlike Haller Nutt and John McMurran, John Minor had been something of a playboy all his life, one of those wealthy Natchez Nabobs who wasted time and inherited money in gambling, horse racing, and drinking. Despite his alcoholism and spendthrift gambling habits, Katherine Minor always had leaned on her husband for emotional support and lovingly accepted his suggestions regarding investments and their plantations. Her friends and family knew, however, that she rather than John had managed their extensive enslaved and landed properties, assisted by her wealthy brother James, her uncle Eustace, and her father-in-law, William Minor. After his death, Katherine missed her husband terribly, but his loss did not leave her totally unprepared to operate on her own, given the role she always had played in family affairs. She lived the rest of her days as a widow at Oakland, dying at age ninety-one in 1926.[48]

John Minor's death freed Katherine from having to sustain his costly lifestyle but did not greatly alleviate her financial difficulties. In the years from 1865 to 1869, she relied heavily on her brother James's assistance to manage her plantations and on financing from her uncles (by marriage), the Leverich brothers, to provision her plantations with supplies and capital for working them with sharecroppers, thereby freeing her from depending on local merchants, who sometimes charged usurious interest rates for advances.[49] The first few years after the war were by far the worst. Before John's death, Katherine and John Minor mortgaged three plantations (Carthage, Palo Alto, and Poverty Hill) and sold another (Wannacutt) to raise enough capital to operate their other plantations and to pay off debts acquired during the war.[50] At one point John deeded their home place, Oakland, which he held in a separate estate, to Katherine's brother, James Surget Jr., to be held in trust for Katherine, supposedly to compensate her for the many thousands of dollars she had provided him over the years from her inherited assets, which she controlled independently or jointly with her brother, thanks to the Married Women's Property Laws in Mississippi and Louisiana.[51] From all indications, the transfer, which masqueraded as payment for his debts to her, prevented John's creditors from seizing his property.[52] To make matters even worse, the years 1865 through 1869 witnessed crop failures brought on by flooding and infestations of the so-called army worm, a precipitous drop in cotton prices, and problems with less easily disciplined laborers, who often refused to contract as sharecroppers or wage workers unless allowed considerable independence in their daily lives and release from the old gang-labor plantation system.[53]

Unlike Mary McMurran and Julia Nutt, Katherine Minor weathered the bad times through infusions of capital (in 1869 and 1870) that enabled her to regain her footing and to establish a basis for her future prosperity. Two things happened almost simultaneously. First, the debts owed to her father's estate from the formerly wealthy but now bankrupt planter Adam L. Bingaman fell into default, which brought Katherine and her brother two additional plantations in settlement, thereby increasing her joint and independent ownership to eight plantations. Second, she inherited $26,000 and a life interest with her brother in three additional plantations upon her uncle Jacob Surget's death in 1869, which linked her even more than before the war into a working partnership with her brother. With this infusion of capital and lands, she and her brother operated both their jointly inherited plantations as well as those she owned independently in a successful business partnership that lasted for the duration of her life.[54]

Although never again the fabulously wealthy woman she had been in the antebellum era, Katherine Minor nonetheless regained a mode and manner of living that set her apart from, if not above, all but a few of the formerly elite white women of Natchez. Unlike her contemporaries the widows Mary McMurran and Julia Nutt, she never borrowed heavily against her properties or from nonfamily members after her husband's death, and she enjoyed the distinct advantage of having an astute and wealthy brother to help manage her plantations. Her family connections to the Leverich brothers—owners of one of the most prominent and prosperous factorage commission houses in the nation, which, unlike so many antebellum factorage houses, survived and prospered after the Civil War because of its extensive banking operations in the North and South—provided her with operational capital and credit that separated her from most of her formerly elite neighbors. By the mid-1880s, Katherine Minor exhibited all the trappings of the truly wealthy, patronizing the best shops in New Orleans, ordering fancy goods on account via her family connections in New York, and staging a wedding for her daughter in 1882 that the local press proclaimed the "most brilliant wedding which has ever transpired in Natchez."[55]

Katherine Minor's wealth and family connections were not shared by her friend and fellow Unionist Julia Nutt, but her determined pursuit of reparations for crops, animals, and supplies confiscated or destroyed by Union soldiers during the Civil War linked the widows together as mutually supportive petitioners. As with Julia Nutt, Minor's case dragged on for years, requiring several visits to the nation's capital by Minor and by numerous witnesses, for whom she paid travel expenses, all of whom verified her and her husband's loyalty to the Union during the Civil War. Partly because other witnesses disputed her loyalty claims to the Union and the quantity of crops and stores taken by federal forces, Katherine received less than a fifth of what she originally had sought from the U.S. government ($13,000 instead of the $65,000 originally declared). Her victory, moreover, was double edged. The money barely covered her expenses, and her reputation as a turncoat to the Confederacy followed her to her grave, with many of her former friends referring to her among themselves as "Yankee Kate" or the "little Yankee."[56]

Clearly Katherine Minor's postwar experience differed from those of the widows McMurran and Nutt, but there were some striking similarities. The important role played by Katherine's brother was never matched within the Nutt household, and Katherine Minor's son, Duncan, aged twenty-eight in 1890, unlike Julia Nutt's sons, eventually assumed, with Katherine's brother's assistance, the overall management of her numerous plantations, especially as her brother aged and around the time of his death in 1920.[57] Still, a close look at the family's history shows a tumultuous household that found Katherine's son and two daughters and the daughter of James Surget Jr., who had married late in life, in bitter conflict over control of the Minor-Surget properties in the new century. And there is more than a little evidence to suggest that Duncan Minor had always been somewhat unbalanced emotionally, living in angry contest

Katherine Surget Minor.
Thomas H. Gandy and Joan W.
Gandy Photo Collection,
Louisiana and Lower Mississippi
Valley Collections, LSU Libraries,
Baton Rouge, Louisiana.

as a lifelong bachelor at Oakland with his mother and aging, childless sister
Jeanne Marie McDowell (a spinster-like lady whose husband seems to have
disappeared from the historical record), carrying on a distinctly bizarre love
affair for three decades with an equally odd spinster cousin, and ending his days
as little more than a recluse.[58]

Natchez lawyers also figured importantly in Katherine Minor's postwar
history, including the venerable Confederate veteran Major General William
T. Martin, who handled most of Katherine Minor's legal affairs, although she
continued to supervise carefully and closely the management of her plantations.
Martin proved to be her most credible witness before the Southern Claims
Commission. In a remarkable example of continuity, Martin's son served as
the Surget and Minor counsel well into the 1930s.[59] The lawyer Martin used
his professional skills to pursue numerous business opportunities and counted
Kate's brother and uncles, the other men in her life, as close friends and busi-

ness associates. This male coterie of kin and counsel never replaced Kate's dead husband as her chief counsel, but they were there on the few occasions when she needed them.

It is doubtful that the married Kate Minor ever had thought of herself as a woman who took second seat to her husband, principally because she understood from an early age that she held assets and responsibilities independent of him, largely due to her family's wealth. But she also may have viewed John Minor as less competent than her uncles, brother, and father-in-law when it came to making wise choices about finances and plantation management. With John Minor's death, unlike with Mary McMurran and Julia Nutt, Katherine appears to have stepped easily into a take-charge role. For Kate, female subservience and the servant ideal were never truly relevant either before or after the Civil War, largely due to her wealth and family position. This is not to say that she ever had doubted what it meant to be a married woman in a world where only males could practice law, easily own property, or make a binding contract outside certain circumstances specified in court declarations or marriage contracts. Rather, it is to acknowledge that her status as a wealthy slaveholder married to a weak but loving husband, despite her claims of having been a Union loyalist, found her fully committed to slavery and the facade of male dominance even as she knew how to step gracefully in and around the cultural constraints for married women. When left on her own after the war, Kate turned to her brother as an equal partner in navigating the financial circumstances that she previously had experience in managing, at least in part, even while married.

Annie M. Sessions

A fourteen-year-old girl when the Civil War began, Anna M. Sessions (always called Annie) lived her entire life as a Natchez spinster until her death in 1931, at age eighty-four.[60] Her life as a never-married woman played out somewhat differently from Kate Foster's, although they shared a class-privileged social standing. Her father, the antebellum planter and slaveholder Joseph Sessions, died mysteriously while on a steamship traveling to New York in 1870, leaving his wife, Maria P. Sessions, to cope on her own as a financially strapped widow with four children to educate and sustain. Except for a few years in Washington, D.C., where she worked as a secretary, Annie spent the next thirty-seven years living in Natchez with her widowed mother (who passed away at age seventy-nine in 1904) in a stately though not ostentatious house acquired in 1870, when the widow moved to town from her rural plantation, Woodstock.[61]

When federal efforts to reconstruct Mississippi ended in 1877, Annie and her mother, aged twenty-five and fifty-one, respectively, were both young enough to marry, but they never did.

In the decade after Joseph Sessions's demise, Maria and her two daughters, Annie and Susan, lived together largely off the rents obtained from leasing the family's two remaining plantations, Woodstock in Mississippi, which Maria owned as a separate estate inherited from her father in 1855, and Palmetto, located across the river from Natchez in Concordia Parish, Louisiana.[62] Maria worked her plantations with black sharecroppers supervised by her sons, Jonathan and Richard, who advanced supplies and tools to the workers through local furnishing merchants. Although income from the properties enabled the family to cover expenses, they lived in a state of genteel poverty unlike anything the family had experienced prior to the war.[63] In the early 1880s, Maria, angry with her spendthrift sons and suspicious of her son-in-law's honesty, appointed Annie as the sole executor and manager-in-trust of her properties. The distraught Maria believed that her children were conspiring to gain control of her property and money in violation of the terms of a trust she had established between herself and her daughters. She accused her daughter Susan G. McConnell of conspiring with Susan's husband and brother to divide and sell Maria's properties and to defraud her of income from the crops and rents due her. Maria trusted only her spinster daughter Annie.[64]

Annie Sessions, a confirmed spinster in her thirties, returned from Washington, D.C., to Natchez sometime in the 1880s to live with her mother as her caretaker under the assumption that she would inherit her mother's estate upon Maria's death, a situation that put her at odds with her sisters and brothers as well as her mother. Although Maria eventually resumed a working relationship with her sons and son-in-law, paying them to manage her plantations, she continued to exclude them from her will in favor of Annie, except for a few family heirlooms willed to Annie's sister. But in a codicil to her will filed in 1898, Maria changed some of its provisions to give these family keepsakes to Annie. Six months later, in another codicil, she provided an allowance to Annie of "38 dollars per month for her maintenance and support," until the Woodstock plantation was delivered to her after Maria's death. In her final word, Maria instructed Annie to be sure to pay all debts due her brothers and sister for managing Woodstock as well as all taxes due at the time of Maria's death or else the property would revert, surprisingly, to Annie's sister. Although it is unclear what happened to the family's Louisiana plantation, it appears that Palmetto was deeded to Annie Sessions's siblings, suggesting that Maria considered Woodstock as payment to Annie for having taken care of her in her old age.[65]

This internal family turmoil over who was actually in charge of family assets and land left Annie Sessions forever suspicious of her sister and brothers. Upon her mother's death in August 1904, Annie was shocked to discover that her mother's will limited her inheritance to a lifetime legacy in the property that she had always thought would be hers alone. According to the life estate provisions of the will, Annie could neither sell nor mortgage any of her inherited properties without the consent of her siblings, although all income would accrue to her alone as long as she lived; upon her death, were Annie to remain childless, the holdings would be divided among her siblings and their heirs. Furious with her sister and brothers for going along with her mother's plans, she seldom thereafter spoke to them.[66]

Although disheartened and even embittered that her family, in her opinion, had duped her into wasting her life as her mother's spinster caretaker, Annie Sessions never lacked resources of her own. Two men appear always to have been at her side as faithful advisors and supporters: her bachelor cousin, Dr. John M. Gillespie, and her lawyer friend, Lemuel P. Conner Jr. A medical doctor and the son of Maria Sessions's wealthy brother, Gillespie had been friends with Annie since childhood. Conner's father, Lemuel P. Sr. (discussed earlier in this chapter), a once wealthy slaveholder left bankrupt by the war, lived in his mother-in-law's villa estate, Woodlands, just outside Natchez with his wife, Fanny, and his widowed sister-in-law, Mary McMurran.[67] Annie Sessions had known the Conner family all her life, and she easily followed her cousin's advice when he told her "to trust Lemuel P. Conner, Jr., above all others."[68] Conner's father had served as Maria Sessions's lawyer in the initial postwar years, and Conner Jr. continued this service for Annie, handling especially the leasing and operation of the family plantations and conflicting at times with Annie's sister and brothers. When Gillespie learned of Annie's financial plight upon Maria's death, he contracted with the Sessions siblings for a long-term lease of Woodstock, which provided his cousin with a steady source of income independent of her sister and brothers.[69]

Annie Sessions knew that Lemuel Conner Jr. "had always been there for her, no matter the need," and that his "unfailing courtesy" and "patient attention" to her every concern went far beyond the duties of a mere lawyer.[70] It was because of his devoted care for her that she bequeathed her entire fortune to him upon her death, almost $100,000, which she had inherited in 1908, quite to her surprise, from her devoted bachelor cousin John Gillespie.[71] When Annie disinherited her brothers and sister in favor of her lawyer (an action she kept secret from Conner Jr. by filing a codicil unbeknownst to him with another legal firm), she completed the process of stepping away from her relatives that she had begun years earlier in favor of a man who had embraced her not unlike

(Miss) Annie Sessions. Thomas H. Gandy and Joan W. Gandy Photo Collection, Louisiana and Lower Mississippi Valley Collections, LSU Libraries, Baton Rouge, Louisiana.

a loving husband, father, or brother, although there is no indication of a sexual or romantic character to their relationship; indeed, she considered his wife, Mary (née Britton) Conner, among her closest friends.

Just prior to her death, Annie Sessions purchased her siblings' shares of their mutually owned house in Natchez, in which she had lived with her mother for much of her adult life. She then immediately sold the house for $7,300 and used the money to buy property in Palm Beach, Florida. She had been careful over the years to expend only the interest from her windfall $100,000 inheritance as well as whatever rents she obtained from her inherited properties. Obviously, in giving up her house in Natchez, Annie Sessions was preparing to undertake a permanent move to Florida; at her death, that property too was bequeathed to Lemuel Conner Jr.[72]

Annie Sessions survived as a spinster lady of some social ranking who fulfilled much of the traditional caretaker role expected of not-married daughters and sisters by taking care of her widowed mother in her declining years. The family's reduced circumstances, however, found her pitted against her sister and brothers in heated conflicts that left her estranged from them but defiantly determined not to be managed or bullied. Fortunately for her, she could always count on advice and monetary support from several male friends who served almost as surrogate husbands or brothers in financial affairs as she moved through life, demonstrating an independent streak that must have caused talk among her friends and relatives. Once she came into her cousin's inheritance, she traveled extensively throughout Europe and the United States, enjoying to the utmost her freedom as a never-married woman of means.

Anna Johnson

Most postbellum Natchez widows and spinsters engaged their world with far fewer assets than the formerly elite white women profiled above. Among them was the remarkable Anna Johnson, one of the four spinster daughters of the free-black barber William Johnson. She survived the war and lived thereafter as a modestly paid public schoolteacher and leading role model for black youth, while stretching her paychecks to provide for an extended family of nieces and nephews from 1865 until her death in 1911. Upon her mother's death in 1866, Anna, aged twenty-four, the oldest daughter of William and Ann Johnson, assumed a matriarchal position in the Johnson household. Like her three sisters, Anna never married; instead, she devoted her life to taking care of them and her four brothers, running a household, and managing inherited properties that included town lots and several hundred farm acres located a few miles north of Natchez. In addition, Anna taught elementary school at the Natchez Union School, a free, public school serving the city's black children, from 1874 until her retirement in 1907.[73]

As one of the few educated black women in the city when slavery ended, schooled before the war in New Orleans and by private tutors, Anna Johnson occupied a unique position compared to the city's other African American women, set apart by her education, assets, and family heritage. She and her three younger sisters, Catherine, Alice, and Josephine, who also worked as teachers in Natchez, at various country schools in Mississippi, and across the river in Louisiana, composed the core if not the feminine foundation of the emerging "blue vein" elite among the city's black men and women, many of whom were the light-skinned descendants of mixed-race parents or grandparents. Anna lived throughout her life in her father's house above the family barber shop on State Street and commuted regularly to the not-too-productive but nearby Peachland plantation, which the family had purchased in 1874. She traced her life through the pages of Natchez history, quietly but firmly determined to sustain her identity as a black woman of substance, cultural refinement, and Victorian comportment—a "lady of color"—devoted to uplifting and educating slavery's children.[74]

(Miss) Anna L. Johnson, Natchez, Mississippi, ca. 1880. From Virginia M. Gould, ed. *Chained to the Rock of Adversity: To Be Free, Black, & Female in the Old South* (Athens: University of Georgia Press, 1998).

As discussed in chapter 5, Anna's father was murdered in 1852 by a free person of color; so too was his son Byron, shot to death twenty years later by an African American neighbor well known to the family. The oldest brother, William, suffered from mental illness and spent most of his postwar adult life in an insane asylum in New Orleans, prior to his death in 1873. The burden of educating and maintaining William's and Byron's children consequently fell to Anna and Catherine. The youngest Johnson son, Clarence, eventually married the sister of a leading black politician, John R. Lynch, and possibly moved for a time to New Orleans, leaving only Richard, who suffered from a heart condition, to help Anna and his sisters in managing their properties while dabbling in local politics during and shortly after Reconstruction.

Anna Johnson and her sisters managed to hold on to much of their widowed mother's urban properties, especially the house and shop on State Street, although the family lost their dozen or more slaves with the Civil War; Anna's mother had sold the family's farmlands shortly after William Johnson's death. The sisters also had somehow acquired a run-down plantation (Peachland) located in bottomlands north of Natchez shortly after the war, which they worked by contracting with blacks as sharecroppers, much as their parents had worked the family farm, Hard Scrabble, before the war with enslaved workers. Anna also rented out rooms in her house to fellow teachers and speculated in urban real estate, an enterprise principally undertaken by Richard Johnson prior to his death.[75]

Similar to the other women profiled in this chapter, several male friends helped the Johnson women cope during the Civil War's aftermath. None was more important during the war and shortly after than the wealthy former slaveholder and planter Adam L. Bingaman. To recap the story partially told in chapter 5, upon the death of his first wife, the white Bingaman lived openly with a free-black woman, Mary Williams, who bore him three mulatto daughters. Just prior to the war, Bingaman moved to New Orleans, where he married Mary and remained until his death. He exposed his mixed-race daughters to the best of New Orleans Creole/free-black society and culture while retaining a warm and lively friendship with Anna Johnson's aunt and cousins in New Orleans and with the Johnson family back in Natchez. Bingaman assumed responsibility, until his death in 1869, for looking after the mentally deranged William, advised the Johnson sisters about business prospects for the Johnson men, and generally delighted in their companionship whenever they visited his daughters in New Orleans or when he and his daughters traveled to Natchez. Bingaman related to the sisters much like a loving uncle, and although sources do not reveal the full extent of his support for the Johnson family after Ann Johnson died, there can be no doubt but that his influence as a member of one of the pioneer white slaveholding families in the original Natchez District mattered greatly to Anna and her sisters.[76]

Another white male who was supportive prior to the war and continued in this role throughout Anna's life was the venerable Confederate veteran, lawyer, and antebellum slaveholder Major General William T. Martin, who also served as Malvina Matthews's defense counsel in her murder trial and offered legal counsel to Katherine Minor. Perhaps the most respected of Natchez's Civil War soldiers, as noted earlier, Martin achieved military fame as an officer in the Confederate Army, including service as staff to General Robert E. Lee, after having vigorously opposed secession during the late 1850s. Once the war began, Martin organized a troop of elite planters' sons, providing weaponry and horses at his own expense, and then won distinction serving principally in the Virginia Theater.

With the war's end, Martin threw himself into his law practice, entrepreneurial activities, and politics, becoming perhaps the city's leading white Democrat and an outspoken advocate of a so-called fusionist strategy aimed at uniting moderate black and white Republicans with moderate Democrats during Reconstruction. He served as a delegate to both the 1866 and 1890 state constitutional conventions, the latter of which formally disfranchised Mississippi blacks. Known as a conservative on economic matters, Martin held moderate opinions on racial issues, and he accepted the political participation of the city's more educated and prosperous African Americans as well as public school education for all the city's African American children.

Martin served as the prosecuting attorney during the murder trials of William Johnson in 1852 and Byron Johnson in 1872. He apparently took on both cases because of his respect and affection for the Johnson family. Although not in the same capacity as Bingaman, Martin offered support for the Johnson women throughout much of the 1870s and 1880s, lending his name to note endorsements and financial arrangements that included other prominent Natchez residents close to Martin's family.[77]

Along with Bingaman and Martin, the black politician John R. Lynch, one of the most powerful political figures in the state from 1865 to 1890, stood behind the Johnson women, especially after his sister married Clarence Johnson in 1873 or 1874. Born a slave, Lynch was appointed justice of the peace in Natchez in 1869 by the radical military governor Adelbert Ames. Lynch parlayed that position to become a representative in and then speaker of the Mississippi House of Representatives (1870–72). He was elected representative to the U.S. House of Representatives at age twenty-four, making him the youngest member of that body at the time, and served for three terms. He headed the Mississippi Republican Party's state organization throughout the 1880s and served as interim chair of the Republican National Convention in June 1884, the first African American to serve in that capacity for a national political party. With the onset of Jim Crow and the disfranchisement of black voters, Lynch failed to again win elected office but was appointed auditor of the U.S. Treasury in 1892; he served as a major in the U.S. Army during the Spanish American War and then as paymaster of the army before moving to Chicago in 1912, where he practiced law and authored several important books and articles about Reconstruction in Mississippi.

John and his brother, William, also a prominent Natchez politician, never missed an opportunity to prosper even as they pursued politics, acquiring municipal lots in Natchez that they used as residences, rented, or speculated with as income properties, along with plantation lands in Adams County, using black sharecroppers to farm the land. The Lynch brothers appear to have had a special, protective relationship with the Johnson women. Their names frequently appear in the public record as note holders on Johnson properties for monies loaned to the sisters, and Anna's nieces and nephews affectionately referred to John over the years as Uncle Lynch. As late as 1932, the old politico, then living in retirement in Chicago, was still receiving warm, personal letters from Johnson family members. Although the details of the Johnson-Lynch relationship are unclear, there can be no doubt that having John R. Lynch, who had studied law and engaged in business with William T. Martin, among their friends, family, and creditors offered Anna and her sisters a financial and personal harbor that most likely helped sustain them as they navigated life as single free-black women in the postbellum South.[78]

Along with the Lynches, Bingaman, and Martin, the successful Natchez politician Louis W. Winston could also be counted among Anna Johnson's long-term associates. Born a free man, Winston served as the Adams County sheriff during the 1870s, county assessor in 1876, circuit clerk of Adams County for twenty terms from 1876 to 1896, trustee of the Union School, and collector of the Port of Natchez during the 1890s. He also published the *Natchez Reporter*, a local black newspaper. The son of a wealthy white planter and an enslaved or free-black mother, Winston ran a successful insurance company and a land office business that built and sold houses to African American families on installment credit; like Lynch, Winston purchased lots in town and substantial acreage in the county, including a one-thousand-acre plantation, making him one of the city's wealthiest African Americans. Winston associated, moreover, with both Lynch and Martin in business and politics, and when Jim Crow disfranchisement finally drove him from office, he studied law, obtaining his license in the late 1890s, and moved to the Mississippi Delta. Like Martin and Lynch, Winston loaned money to the Johnson sisters, endorsed their notes for loans, and served as a financial advisor to the women throughout their lives. And his wife, Hannah Winston, taught alongside Anna at the Union School and was one of her closest and dearest friends.[79]

Although Anna Johnson and her sisters coped as single women with the important help afforded them by significant males who assisted them as counsel, creditors, and friends, and though this reliance on various nonfamily males resembled how the other women profiled in this chapter had survived in postbellum Natchez, there were several important differences. Unlike the others, the Johnson women were gainfully employed as public school teachers throughout their lives, which provided them with a small, steady income. As noted earlier, Anna taught for over thirty-five years at the Union School, a free, municipally supported school for black children, earning pay that averaged around forty dollars per month. She had obtained a state teaching certificate based on her antebellum education and her experience during and immediately after the Civil War teaching African American children whose parents paid tuition in a private school that she operated (perhaps out of her home). Not only did her teaching provide her with a modest but steady income, it also enmeshed her

Miss Anna L. Johnson, Union School pay ledger, "Register of Teachers and Teachers Pay Certificates Issued for the Year, 1877." Historic Natchez Foundation.

within a network of fellow teachers and students that greatly sustained her over the years. Throughout her teaching life, in order to maintain herself and her family, Anna rented out rooms in her house to fellow teachers and associated with the dozen or more fellow female teachers who consistently staffed the Union School in a community of likeminded women, many of whom were single women for all or a large portion of their teaching lives. A number of her early students eventually joined her as teachers at Union, and some of her colleagues were married to, or eventually married, some of the most prominent African American men in the city.[80]

Anna Johnson's career as well as her community of friends, male supporters both black and white, fellow teachers, and nurturing family provided immeasurable resources for her in comparison to what many divorced, single, and widowed women faced during the postwar years. Compared to the other single women profiled in this chapter, including Kate Foster, the Johnson sisters lived out their postbellum lives as single, professional women enmeshed within a supportive web of family and community relationships that enabled them to prosper and improve their economic situation over the years. They lived among a handful of pragmatic black landowners who cultivated cotton with share-croppers or tenant farmers, rented rooms in the city to cash-paying tenants and shopkeepers, and strived to achieve a middle-class standard of living based on their salaries as public servants. The Johnson sisters also enjoyed amiable relationships among themselves and their kin as well as a coterie of loyal male supporters, black and white, who valued them because of their free-born status, mixed-race heritage, education, culture, and class standing. And when Adam Bingaman passed away, other members of the antebellum white slaveholding elite, such as Duncan Minor and James Surget Jr., sometimes loaned the sisters money and assisted them in their economic dealings.[81]

On the other hand, it is also clear that Anna Johnson, as a black woman, operated far less independently than the widows McMurran, Nutt, and Minor, the spinsters Annie Sessions and Kate Foster, or the notorious Malvina Matthews. Totally dependent, as had been her father, upon the goodwill of prominent whites in the community, Anna and her sisters were obliged to conduct themselves in accordance with the Victorian mores and deferential behavior that whites expected of black women in postwar Mississippi, or else lose their salaried positions and the other advantages they enjoyed. Although the leading members of the white community in Natchez supported, even into the early twentieth century, free public school education for the city's black children, they expected teachers to be locally raised and preferably mixed-race, middle-class women who would strive to inculcate into their students proper behavior and a deferential acceptance of the prevailing racial and class-based societal order.

Anna Johnson clearly embraced this newly refurbished image of the servant ideal, at least for African Americans, in her teaching and personal conduct, un-doubtedly understanding what was at stake. This is not to say that she and her teaching associates at the Union School feigned acceptance of such Victorian values; rather they undoubtedly embraced and even internalized such values in their teaching and in their lives. They did so in ways that privileged industry, honesty, hard work, and propriety among their students because of their own cultural upbringings, even as they understood the risks associated with any signs on their part of nonconformity to the existing and realigning social mi-lieu after the war. Although gendered expectations and notions of acceptable female behavior undoubtedly continued to influence how Kate Foster, Malvina Matthews, Mary McMurran, Julia Nutt, Kate Minor, and Annie Sessions con-ducted themselves during their postwar lives, none appeared as constrained to uphold a servant ideal as did Anna Johnson and most of her African American female friends and colleagues. Additionally, many educated African American women saw themselves as role models, women dedicated to elevating their race through education, which greatly affected their behavior in conformity to a servant ideal that did not offend whites.[82]

Conclusion

The not-married women profiled in this chapter had lived relatively privileged lives prior to the war, and their postwar experiences reflected these antebellum advantages. Each had owned slaves or had been members of slaveholding families, even Malvina Matthews and Anna Johnson, and each but for Julia Nutt called on prominent males in the community to assist them as they struggled to adjust and survive slavery's demise and the world it had created. They all owned property, which they vigorously defended and used adroitly and with surprising dexterity as a resource, although four of these women (Johnson, McMurran, Nutt, and Sessions) were burdened with relatives who greatly complicated and even undermined their efforts. None, not even Kate Minor and Annie Sessions, ended their lives better off than before the war.

Some might have wished nostalgically for a return to a way of life wherein marriage, the servant ideal, patriarchy, and slavery shaped the social and cultural expectations for women. But nothing in their postwar experiences suggests that any such prewar scripting governed their postwar behavior to any great degree. None of these six women, not even the wishful Kate Foster, appears to have pursued energetically the prospect of being attached to men as husbands after the war, and none but Kate Minor had the time or resources to pursue impractical cultural expectations for women once slavery and the world it supported had ended. The important exception in regard to the servant ideal, however, was Anna Johnson, who appears to have embraced this ideal as a means of placating whites and thereby uplifting her fellow African Americans through education.

But what can be said about the city's many other single women, whom those profiled above neither represent nor reflect? It is likely that many of these women faced difficulties similar to those confronted by Matthews, McMurran, Nutt, Minor, Sessions, and Johnson, but they met them with far fewer economic resources. A considerable number were abjectly poor and lived precariously, drawing on family, friends, and employers (for those lucky enough to find work) to survive in ways similar to how historian Laura Edwards indicates poor black and white women coped with life in North Carolina and elsewhere, namely, by doing what they could to empower themselves as much as possible.[83] The experiences of the women profiled here strongly suggest that some, if not many, of the city's single women had neither the time nor the inclination, opportunity, or energy, at least initially following the war, to embrace marriage and servitude to males as an ideal for women or male mastery as an ideal for men. And it is likely that few of the city's less privileged single women, black or white, had the time, opportunity, or desire to embrace those antebellum cultural norms that offered them little practical advantage or benefit given their circumstances as single women living on the margin. It was not that such traditional values and gendered precepts were rejected as much as that they simply did not apply in the new circumstances following slavery's death and a vitiated patriarchy during the Civil War's aftermath. This reality would demand a more innovative choreography on the part of its women as they continued to step lively in place.

EPILOGUE

May 25, 1849. Visited a poor young woman—a Miss Leroy—who sent for me to see her. She is a prostitute and near her end with consumption. I talked long and tried to talk faithfully; prayed and left her promising to follow my instructions. But what a forlorn case! Why do I not feel more for her soul? So near God and yet so guilty. Oh that I had more faith!

May 26, 1849. Went to see the poor girl whom I visited yesterday and found her dying. It was an awful scene. I would have shrunk from it, but the friends seemed to wish me to be with them and I stayed for their good and my own, to see the Prostitute die. She was speechless, but seemed to have some power of comprehension and I tried still to turn her mind to Jesus. But it was a death that gives no tangible ground for hope. O that I could realize more deeply what it is— thus to die! The guilty members of the family, all I believe of the same profession, seemed much affected and I tried to impress upon them the necessity of preparing to meet God. In the afternoon I went down to conduct the funeral services. My hearers were of the same family. I spoke solemnly and plainly to them.

—Rev. Joseph B. Stratton

When Joseph B. Stratton entered the above words in his diary, he was in his sixth year of ministry as the northern-born head pastor of the First Presbyterian Church of Natchez. He remained in that position for over fifty years, retiring in 1894. During those years of service, Stratton had done well for himself materially speaking, owning on the eve of the Civil War substantial real property in Natchez and several slaves. His annual salary in the 1840s totaled more than $4,000, a princely wage for a minister, which reflected the wealth of his flock; but it was his marriage to his second wife, Caroline M. Williams, the daughter of a wealthy slaveholder, in 1852, four years after the death of his first wife, that secured for him the bulk of his fortune.[1]

Born in New Jersey on Christmas Eve 1815 and educated in the law in New Jersey and Philadelphia with a divinity degree from Princeton University earned in 1840, Stratton began his Natchez ministry in 1843, probably already acquainted with other Philadelphia-born church members in the city. His congregation included wealthy slaveholders, families of much more modest means, a small number of free blacks, and the enslaved chattel of his more devout white congregants, whom he often ministered to on nearby plantations. Typically he, or in later years, his assistant, preached each Sunday to his white congregation in the morning (which also included free blacks and those enslaved domestics brought to church by their owners) and then to his enslaved congregation in the afternoon or on special visits to neighboring plantations. He almost never preached the same sermon in the afternoon as he preached in the mornings, when his chapel filled with wealthy slaveholders whose carriages lined up for blocks around as their black drivers amused themselves while waiting for their Christian masters and mistresses to be driven home when church services concluded.

Stratton recorded his ministry in a six-hundred-page diary, which he filled with brief but often pithy reports noting the sermons he preached, ministry exercised, and musings about his own behavior and the world in which he lived.[2] The diary documents, among other things, Stratton's dedicated efforts to bring into his church young, single women, whom he undoubtedly hoped would one day marry and raise their families as supportive church members, as well as his ministry to the least of the city's residents, including the enslaved and prostitutes the likes of Miss Louisa Leroy.[3] The vast majority of Stratton's work during the week involved holding special services for young women at the various private Natchez academies that instructed the daughters of its wealthier church members, officiating at graduation ceremonies and special events in these private schools as well as in the city's public school, working closely with the Natchez (Protestant) Orphanage and the Natchez Women's Benevolent Society whenever he was needed, conducting weddings and funerals for his congregants, and encouraging young, single women to become church members in frequent personal visits to their homes.[4]

But it was difficult work, and he was not always successful. After years of private meetings with the not-married Rebecca Mandeville, for example, he finally managed to have her inducted into his church, undoubtedly puzzled and perplexed that she had resisted his efforts for so long despite his close friendship with her father and an elder brother, both long-standing church members.[5] And when the dying Miss Leroy showed last-minute but less than enthusiastic interest in her own redemption, Stratton experienced something of an existential crisis as he tried to understand why she had lived her life as a sinner, seemingly unrepentant even as she faced her final judgment. Despite his own puzzlement about women like Rebecca Mandeville and Miss Leroy, Stratton nevertheless related to them as potential members of his churchly community rather than as aberrations out of step because of their not-married circumstances or life choices. Stratton even accepted Miss Leroy's "guilty" and

Gravestone, "Louise. The Unfortunate." Marker for prostitute Louisa Leroy, 1849, Natchez City Cemetery, Adam County, Mississippi. Photo by author.

probably not-married fellow workers as women fully capable of redemption, and church membership, regardless of their marital circumstances or how they had conducted themselves as less than respectable women.

Stratton's few words about Miss Leroy and an entry in the city's death records are all that we know about her. But with her story in mind, along with all the other stories told in the forgoing pages, we can reflect on what this book tells us about the not-married women of midcentury Natchez. Clearly, many of the city's free, not-married women lived incredibly engaged lives; they were women aware to a person of their rights as *feme soles* legally and socially. They sued in local and state courts; divorced, often successfully; and frequently headed households while living in shared residential circumstances with other not-married women and apart from adult males. Class and race mattered greatly in their lives, but few of them, especially among the middle and upper classes, lived lives greatly constrained by their not-married situations. Free from husbands as domineering or supportive mates, depending on their circumstances, they frequently drew upon their own resources and those of their families to sustain themselves in a society that privileged male hegemony over women, children, and the enslaved. These women engaged their not-married lives with surprising agility and incredible adroitness, often defying what the uninformed outsider might have taken for societal opprobrium against single women as unfulfilled women. But the women whose stories are depicted in this study were no mere aberrations.

So what explains their inclusion in the Natchez social order as insiders rather than outsiders, as legitimate participants rather than aberrations? The words written in 1852 by the Natchez widow Susan E. Conner justifying her claim to properties denied her in her husband's will speak volumes: "There is a great hue & cry raised against me as a womans rights woman, . . . but I am not one except where the U. S. and reason, give me a right to be a rights woman. I care not a copper to be a governor a Legislator, or any other 'or, but if I can protect my own rights, and those of others, I hold it my duty to resist the united world, with my *single Will*."[6] Similar sentiments could have been expressed by the resolute and litigious spinster Lydia Dowell, or the combative divorcées Malvina Matthews and Lydia Phipps, or the brickbat-hurling free-black widow Amy Johnson, and most of the other not-married women profiled in this study. They were aware of their legal rights as *feme soles*, knew what could be expected from the courts when they were deferentially approached by women seeking justice in equity or statute law, and understood (as did Conner) that mindfully exercising their rights threatened neither male hegemony nor the bedrock institutions on which that hegemony rested in antebellum Natchez: slavery, a white patriarchy, and the servant ideal. As long as the city's single women maneuvered mindfully, they knew few behavioral limitations despite living without husbands at their sides.

The degree of their inclusion within the Natchez community depended greatly, however, on how they approached the courts and the manner in which they related to the men in their lives. Divorcing women, for example, typically knew that they had to present themselves as virtuous women whose husbands had violated the servant ideal that underlay the concept of a patriarchal marriage, a cultural perspective in which husbands as all-powerful masters of their households (even those households sans slaves) were expected to conduct themselves as responsible (and hopefully loving) guardians of their women and children. They also understood that the city's rather cosmopolitan character, the prosperity of its slaveholding elite, and its bustling riverfront urban scene provided ample opportunity for them to exert a degree of individualism and freedom of movement as women unattached to men.

The close family and sexual ties between most of the city's married and not-married free-black women and the white men in their lives enabled them sometimes to step aggressively, although seldom defiantly, in their everyday dealings and affairs. Less than proper deportment among these free-black women did not always produce harsh consequences because of the white men who loved, desired, or protected them. Beyond this sexual and familial context, moreover, the most raucous free single women, black and white, including many of the city's criminal women, also enjoyed a level of societal tolerance (an acceptance of behavior that was not necessarily approved) among Natchez whites because their actions seldom challenged the gendered inequality of their society or the male hegemony that governed social relationships, no matter how far beyond the law or societal norms these women lived. In fact, these unruly women often serviced—as prostitutes, lovers, and tavern and boarding-house keepers—the white males who made and enforced the law.

The Civil War and Reconstruction dramatically affected what it meant to be a Natchez woman, married or single, black or white. The agility with which the city's single women had navigated life prior to the war continued during the war years and for a generation after the fighting had stopped as the city's women, married and not married, poor and rich, black and white, struggled to survive, often as women on their own. In these new circumstances, conformity to the servant ideal for women or to the supremacy of white males offered little practical benefit in helping the city's women cope with the tumultuous postwar world they faced; nor did these new circumstances afford them much time for honoring, except perhaps in memory, the old cultural order that had supported, nurtured, and privileged female servitude to a male master of the household. But their behavior as women less dependent on men than ever before did not foretell the emergence of a newly liberated woman demanding political rights as much as it set the stage for the development of a less cohesive community of women, a city wherein some white women tried to resurrect the past as a mythical era in which white males served as the paternalistic protectors and sustainers of their women, children, workers, and the enslaved.

For the city's single black women, the Civil War and Reconstruction brought death, repeated trauma, incredible hardships, and yet vibrant hopes for a new world free of slavery and the domination, at least for some, of any man, white or black. The number of single black women in Natchez increased substantially as the city filled up with the formerly enslaved, some of whom undoubtedly refrained from taking husbands in order to protect their federal pensions as soldiers' widows or to avoid becoming entangled legally with formerly en-slaved men who wanted to dominate them as patriarchal husbands. For others, formalized marriage seemed less important simply because no clear benefit accrued to them from embracing the institution. For most, it is likely that the abject poverty of their circumstances shaped their experiences much more than their marital situation.

A small number of not-married and married African American women emerged from the war to become career teachers in the city's segregated public schools. Some of these women, like Anna Johnson, were wedded to their jobs and took seriously their responsibilities as role models for the city's black students, committed to educating and uplifting them as best they could. Ironically, these women may have best approximated the traditional antebellum servant ideal, not in homage to the cultural and social dominance of white males but from a sense of duty to the larger African American community. In doing so, these women shouldered the burden of behaving in ways that leading whites, who employed them as public servants in the city's school system, expected, namely, teaching and conducting themselves with a measure of decorum and deference to the emerging Jim Crow racial dictums imposed on the city's African Americans in the post-Reconstruction era.

In telling a few of the stories of the not-married women who lived in nineteenth-century Natchez during slavery, the Civil War, Reconstruction, and its aftermath, this book does not speak for all its single women. And because even the tales told here are not the full picture, the profiles of women in this book are but shadows of their actual lives and experiences, images garnered from the traces left behind in an array of public and private records. Also, because Natchez was a unique place (as are most places when examined close up)—unlike any other in the South due to its history, culture, economy, and location—depictions of its single women cannot be said to represent fully the single women of other southern communities or the larger South. But they do fit a pattern that was most likely replicated in other southern towns and cities, one in which the city's not-married women, free black and white, both before and after the Civil War, seldom lived as aberrant women due to their marital circumstances. Rather, they often were lively stepping women who adroitly manipulated the male-dominated world in which they lived with amazing agility and a consciousness of how the game of life had to be played given their gendered and marital situations and the place in which they lived.

For these women, acceptance and survival prior to the Civil War depended on their adherence to a set of community standards that accommodated male hegemony, slavery as the bedrock institution of the Natchez social order, and a servant ideal that applied to the city's residents, male and female, enslaved or free. These "givens" underlay a relatively cohesive community, covering over the horrors of slavery and the gendered inequality of its females even as they allowed those able and willing to tolerate the culture's dictums to survive as functioning members of its societal order. Once war and its aftermath destroyed slavery and weakened the power of a slave-driven patriarchy, the city's single and married women continued to maneuver with amazing dexterity. But their lively movements no longer required adherence to slavery or those antebellum cultural imperatives that had limited what they as women could do, married or not, rich or poor, black or white.

The single women depicted in this study seemed always ready and able to seize the opportunity to step adroitly and with determination, and most members of the city's male-dominated antebellum community not only tolerated but often accepted, while not always condoning, their actions. At no time during the years before, during, or after the Civil War would it be accurate to paint the single women of Natchez (those free before the war and all its single women after the war) as aberrations, as women out of step with the times because of their marital status. But with this said, it is also clear that survival, both within the city's vibrantly cohesive antebellum milieu as well as during its wartime and postwar upheaval, for the city's not-married women required knowing just what was expected of them and how best to step. For the savvy among them, figuring out how to manipulate the men all around them was almost second nature—or so it seems—both during slavery and even more so after slavery ended.

NOTES

INTRODUCTION

1. See Mary M[artha] Gaillard to Sinah Foster, January 22, 1869, James Foster Papers, Louisiana and Lower Mississippi Valley Collections, Louisiana State University, Baton Rouge (LSU); and Kate Foster File, Genealogy, Alma Carpenter Papers, Historic Natchez Foundation, Natchez, Miss. (HNF).

2. Sources for Natchez divorces can be found in the divorce case files housed in the Office of Records for Adams County, Mississippi (ORAC). Historian Loren Schweninger's pathbreaking research has uncovered thousands of antebellum southern divorces for many of the same causes claimed by the divorcing men and women of antebellum Natchez. See Schweninger, *Families in Crisis in the Old South*.

3. U.S. Manuscript Census (1860), Natchez, Adams County, Miss., NARA.

4. *Caroline Jennings v. Edward Jennings*, 1843, Chancery Court Records for Adams County, Miss. (CHCAC), HNF.

5. *State v. Jane Andre*, 1832, Circuit Court Records for Adams County, Mississippi (CCAC), HNF.

6. See Fuller, "Great Lawsuit"; and Fuller, *Women in the Nineteenth Century*. For examples of newspaper coverage of marital disputes, see the *Mississippi Free Trader* (Natchez), July 2, 9; August 9; October 15, 25; November 15, 29; December 27, 1851; and April 3, 17; August 18, 1852.

7. Cox, *Young Lady's Companion*, 249–58.

8. For more on the Grimke sisters and the women's rights reform movement, see Lerner, *Grimke Sisters from South Carolina*; and G. Riley, *Divorce*, 34–62.

9. For examples of Natchez white women traveling in the North and abroad as well as their intermarriage to northern men, see Mary L. McMurran to F. E. Conner, June 18; July 7, 23, 30; August 26; and October 1, 1854, Lemuel P. Conner Family Papers, LSU; and Mary E. McMurran to Charlotte Calhoun, August 4 and October 15, 1854, John T. McMurran Family Papers, LSU. Other sources documenting the travels and intermarriage of Natchez women to northern men include DeVille, *Mississippi Land Papers*; and C. O. Johnson, *Order of the First Families of Mississippi*. See also Brazy, *An American Planter*; D. James, *Antebellum Natchez*, 14–24, 65–82, 101–82; May, *John A. Quitman*; Powell, *New Masters*; Rothstein, "Changing Social Networks"; and Broussard, "Profile: John T. McMurran."

10. Bercaw, *Gender and the Southern Body Politic*, xiii; J. Cashin, *Family Venture*, 32–51; Crowley, "Importance of Kinship"; and Genovese, "Our Family, White and Black."

11. Chestnut, *Diary from Dixie*, 122. For discussion of the double standards that applied to sexual impropriety vis-à-vis white women, white men, and slave women, see Alexander, *Ambiguous Lives*, 66–67; Bardaglio, "Rape and the Law"; and Getman, "Sexual Control in the Slaveholding South."

12. Broussard, "Naked before the Law."

13. For contemporary examples of southern males' typical beliefs about the benefits that society and women derived from marriage and motherhood, see "From a Discourse on Marriage"; J. A. M., "Thoughts on Married Life"; and "Married Life as a Theme." For the interconnection among and value of marriage, kinship, and religion for southern women, see Billingsley, *Communities of Kinship*; Burton, *In My Father's House*; J. Cashin, *Family Venture*; Friedman, *Enclosed Garden*; Glover, *All Our Relations;* and Stowe, *Intimacy and Power*. On how the marriage/mother ideal played out for free women in the antebellum South, see Bynum, *Unruly Women*, 34–37; C. Carter, *Southern Single Blessedness*, 1–4; Edwards, "Law, Domestic Violence"; Fox-Genovese, *Within the Plantation Household*, 256–57; C. Kennedy, *Braided Relations, Entwined Lives*, 77–110; and Stevenson, *Life in Black and White*, 37–158.

14. J. Thompson, "Woman's True Mission"; and Broussard, "Naked before the Law."

15. For theoretical insights on male dominance and the subordination of women, see especially Benjamin, *Bonds of Love*. According to Benjamin, domination and submission result from a breakdown of the necessary tension between self-assertion and mutual recognition that allows "the self" and "the other" to meet as "sovereign equals." Although highly theoretical, Benjamin's perspective helps to clarify why some southern women may well have found psychological and emotional fulfillment in their subordination as married women despite their loss of autonomy as individuals. This master/slave dialectic is expanded on and most fully articulated for the antebellum South in the writings of Eugene Genovese, especially his *Roll, Jordan, Roll* and the book he coauthored with Elizabeth-Fox Genovese, *The Mind of the Master Class*. For how the paternalistic ideal played out in southern cities, see E. Cashin, "Paternalism in Augusta." With regard to how this servant ideal applied to Natchez women, see Broussard "Naked before the Law"; and Broussard "Female Solitaires."

16. Fox-Genovese, *Within the Plantation Household*; Genovese, *Roll, Jordan, Roll*; and Genovese and Fox-Genovese, *Mind of the Master Class*. For examples of how the servant ideal was supported and affirmed in the popular print material read by elite planters, see "Plantation Life—Duties and Responsibilities"; and "Moral and Natural Law Contradistinguished." For contrasting views that raise questions about the extent to which an ideology of mastery actually governed antebellum southern life, see Censer, *North Carolina Planters and Their Children*; May, "Southern Elite Women"; Oakes, *Ruling Race*; and Scarborough, *Masters of the Big House*. For analysis of the conflicting interpretations of southern paternalism and the patriarchy, see Parish, *Slavery*, 50–61. For the operation of courts of equity and the dispensing of justice to married women unprotected by statutes and laws, see Broussard, "Naked before the Law."

17. Dow Jr., "Get Married," *Mississippi Free Trader*, March 20, 1852; Froide, *Never Married*, 1–14; and Ulrich, *Good Wives*. Froide refers to women who "never married" as

"single women" rather than by the term "spinsters," which she finds derogatory in English culture. Among scholars who have touched on the spinster's supposedly aberrant status in southern life, see Bynum, *Unruly Women*, 59–87; Carvill, "Stereotype of Spinsters"; Clinton, *Plantation Mistress*, 38–39, 56, 59, 85–86, 169; Fox-Genovese, *Within the Plantation Household*, 193–242; Lebsock, *Free Women of Petersburg*, 88–112; and O'Brien, *An Evening When Alone*, 226–53.

18. For Charleston and Savannah, see C. Carter, *Southern Single Blessedness*; and Pease and Pease, *Ladies, Women and Wenches*. For relevant scholarship on New Orleans and the customs of *plaçage*, see Clark, *Strange History of the American Quadroon*; Everett, "Free Persons of Color," 230–267; M. Johnson and Roark, "Middle Ground"; Long, *Great Southern Babylon*, 6–20; J. Martin, "*Plaçage* and the Louisiana *Gens de Couleur Libre*"; and Spear, *Race, Sex, and Social Order*. For interracial sexual behavior in antebellum Natchez, see Broussard, "Stepping Lively in Place."

19. C. Carter, *Southern Single Blessedness*; Chambers-Schiller, *Liberty, a Better Husband*; Simon, *Never Married Women*; Smith-Rosenberg, *Disorderly Conduct*; Vicinus, *Independent Women*; and Wulf, *Not All Wives*.

20. This approach is based somewhat on the thinking of the social theorist Alfred Schutz. See Natanson, *Phenomenology and Social Reality*, 35–72, and Wagner, *Alfred Schutz on Phenomenology*. For elaboration on "cultural givens" as connective tissue in the formation and functioning of communities, see Habermas, *Theory of Communicative Action*; and C. H. Johnson, "Lifeworld, System, and Communicative Action." For the link between slavery as a cultural given and patriarchy as the prevailing ideology of southern life, see Fields, *Slavery and Freedom*; and Fields, "Slavery, Race, and Ideology."

21. Edwards, *Gendered Strife and Confusion*.

22. Bennett and Froide, *Singlewomen in the European Past*, 259.

CHAPTER ONE. ANTEBELLUM NATCHEZ

1. Audhuy, "Natchez in French Louisiana"; James Barnett Jr., *Natchez Indians*; and Usner, *Indians, Settlers and Slaves*, 32–48, 65–76.

2. Haynes, *Natchez District and the American Revolution*; Holmes, "Spanish Province"; P. Hamilton, "British West Florida"; Howard, "Colonial Natchez"; Howell, "French Period"; D. James, *Antebellum Natchez*, 3–100; F. Riley, "Transition from Spanish to American Control"; and Siebert, " Loyalists in West Florida."

3. Coker, "Spanish Regulation"; Cummins, "Enduring Community"; Elliott, "City and Empire"; Holmes, "Cotton Gins"; Ingmire and Erickson, *First Settlers of the Mississippi Territory*; J. Moore, *Emergence of the Cotton Kingdom*, 1–11, 39; Rothstein, "Natchez Nabobs"; Rothstein, "Remotest Corner"; William Banks Taylor, "Southern Yankees"; W. Scarborough, "Lords or Capitalists"; and W. Scarborough, *Masters of the Big House*, 22–25, 128.

4. For the early history of Natchez and its place in the Old Southwest, see Box, "Antebellum Travelers in Mississippi"; T. Clark and Guice, *Frontiers in Conflict*; W. Davis, *Way through the Wilderness*; and Matthias, "Natchez-under-the-Hill"; E. Moore, *Natchez Under-the-Hill*, 7–13; and Phelps and Ross, "Names Please."

5. McElligott, "1787 Census of Natchez"; and U.S. Manuscript Census (1860), Natchez, Adams County, Miss., and Concordia Parish, La., NARA.

6. Calhoun, "History of Concordia Parish, Louisiana"; and Rothstein, " Natchez Nabobs."

7. Brazy, *American Planter*, 17–158; R. Davis, *Black Experience*, 17–24; D. James, *Antebellum Natchez*, 131–61; Rothstein, "Acquisitive Pursuits in a Slaveholding Society"; W. Scarborough, *Masters of the Big House*, 7–9, 22–25, 30, 128, 155; William Banks Taylor, "Southern Yankees"; and Shade, "In re Those 'Prebourgeois' Planters."

8. Harrell, "Horse Racing in the Old Natchez District"; Harrell, "Jockey Clubs and Race Tracks" ; Keller, "Horse Racing Madness"; D. James, *Antebellum Natchez*, 217–93; Jenkins, "Next of Kin," 1–18; S. Johnson, "From Wilderness to Society," 16; and T. Scarborough, "Cotton Planters and Plantations."

9. D. James, *Antebellum Natchez*, 181–237; Miller and Miller, *Great Houses of Natchez*; and Power, *The Memento*, 1:7–16, 25–26.

10. See household and population data for Natchez in U.S. Manuscript Census (1840, 1850, and 1860), Natchez, Adams County, Miss., NARA. See also Gleeson, *Irish in the South*, 29–30, 36–50; D. James, *Antebellum Natchez*, 162–82; Ingraham, *The South West*, 18–190; and E. Moore, *Natchez Under-the-Hill*, 35–52, 85–89.

11. Broussard, "Stepping Lively in Place"; R. Davis, *Black Experience*, 47–61; Hogan and Davis, *William Johnson's Natchez*; and Ribianszky, "She Appeared to Be Mistress."

12. For more on the free-black population of antebellum Natchez, see Alford, *Prince among Slaves*; Buchanan, "Levees of Hope"; R. Davis, *Black Experience*, 21–44; D. James, *Antebellum Natchez*, 87,163, 170–80, 184, 255–62; and Sydnor, *Slavery in Mississippi*, 5–7, 124, 150–69.

13. R. Davis, *Black Experience*, 67–92. For examples of antebellum slave traders, their stalls, and slaves at the Forks, see *Mississippi Free Trader*, November 12, 1851; January 3, 1852; and April 3, 1852. For the isolated but distinctive neighborhood character of the city's enslaved hinterland, see Kaye, *Joining Places*.

14. For scholarship on Natchez slave markets, see Jim Barnett and Burkett, " Forks of the Road Slave Market"; R. Davis, *Black Experience*, 67–92; Deyle, *Carry Me Back*, 38, 147–48, 100, 105, 153, 155; Doolittle, "Forks of Road"; Gudmestad, *Troublesome Commerce*, 17, 23–25, 93–95, 107–8, 161–62; W. Johnson, *Soul by Soul*, 7, 41, 47, 50, 161, 173–74, 181; Gross, *Double Character*, 22–46; Kaye, "Neighborhoods and Solidarity"; Stephenson, *Isaac Franklin*; Rosenblum, "Driving Out the Slave Traders"; and Usner, "Frontier Exchange and Cotton Production."

15. See the various surveyor maps of Natchez located in the deed and mortgage record books housed in ORAC: "Plan of the City of Natchez," June 26, 1829, in Adams County Township Plats; John Girault, Deed Book K (1818); Deed Book Z, "Map of Natchez Streets" (1838); "Map of Levee Street running Under-the-Hill" (1839); Deed Book RR, "Map of Canal & State Streets" (1860); and Deed Book RR, "Map of Brown's Gardens" (1872). See also various subject files of the Mississippi Department of Archives and History (MDAH): "Institute Hall," "Natchez Bluffs," "Natchez Cemetery Bluff District," "Natchez Churches," "Natchez Opera House," "Natchez Spanish Market," and "Trinity

Parish." Also see D. James, *Antebellum Natchez*; Ingraham, *The South West*, 2–134; and Wang and Provin, "Mapping the Historic Natchez District."

16. D. James, *Antebellum Natchez*, 183–293; Ingraham, *The South West*, 57, 72; E. Moore, *Natchez Under-the-Hill*, 14–28, 104–11; and Sydnor, *Slavery in Mississippi*, 82.

17. "Magnolia Vale (Natchez)," subject file, MDAH; Ingraham, *The South West*, 52–61; D. James, *Antebellum Natchez*, 36, 168–96, 225–73; Kibler, "Natchez Landing," 1–21; and J. Moore, *Andrew Brown and Cyprus Lumbering*.

18. H. Davis, "Tornado of 1840 Hits Mississippi"; J. Moore, *Andrew Brown and Cyprus Lumbering*, 37–38; and "Natchez Tornado, 1840," subject files, MDAH.

19. This perspective on the city's gendered spaces reflects a close reading of Natchez newspapers from the 1820s through the 1850s as well as readings of numerous travel accounts and personal papers, especially the letters of Rebecca Mandeville and the 1848 diary of Rebecca Mandeville (hereafter cited as Mandeville 1848 Diary), Henry D. Mandeville Family Papers (hereafter cited as MFP), LSU.

20. The gendered character of the courthouse grounds and buildings was a common aspect of small-town life everywhere in colonial and antebellum America, but the presence of enslaved and free blacks, both as onlookers and as criminals, principally captured runaways, rendered southern courthouses especially off limits to the more respectable free white women. See Dayton, *Women before the Bar*, 1–328; Gross, *Double Character*, 22–46; and Hogan and Davis, *William Johnson's Natchez*, 130, 137, 211, 235, 313, 333–37, 362, 385–86, 471–72, 492, 526, 547, 556, 567, 593, 623, 721–23, 757–59. For Mississippi ordinances that limited the appearance of women in court, see A. Hutchinson, *Code of Mississippi*.

21. Mandeville 1848 Diary, MFP, LSU.

22. For discussion of the importance of place, landscape, architecture, and the built environment in shaping and reflecting the gendered experiences of city and town dwellers, see Tolbert, *Constructing Landscapes*; and Spain, *Gendered Spaces*, 1–30, 81–108.

23. Anderson, *Builders of the New South*; Broussard, "Occupied Natchez"; R. Davis, *Good and Faithful Labor*, 58–152; Dresser, "Kate and John Minor"; Greenberg, "Civil War and the Redistribution of Land"; Smithers, "Profit and Corruption"; Behrend, "Freedpeople's Democracy," and Behrend, *Reconstructing Democracy*.

CHAPTER TWO. STEPPING LIVELY AMID THEIR SHADOWS

1. Theodosia L. Griffith to Miss Margaret Biggs, September 14, 1828, Edward Turner Family Papers, LSU. The letter speaks candidly and confidentially about relatives, friends, and Biggs's handling of Theodosia's "personal affairs" at her father's house in Natchez.

2. Historian Joan Cashin writes about how lonely life could be on the plantations of rural Mississippi for wives and mothers when their husbands traveled on business or for other reasons. It is not difficult to understand why the widow Theodosia Griffith would look to Biggs's companionship as a saving grace, necessary perhaps to preserve her sanity. J. Cashin, *Family Venture*, 3–8, 53–98.

3. Biggs appears to have resided some of the time in a small house near the First Presbyterian Church, to which she belonged, when not living at the Turner family estate

just outside of town. When Biggs died in 1853, she left $1,000 to Elizabeth Turner as a "token of gratued [sic] for her kindness and attention" and bequeathed $100 to Judge Edward Turner, who was, in her words, the "best friend" to whom she was especially grateful for his "Gentlemanly and brotherly deport and Kindness." Margaret Biggs, Will, November 28, 1853, ORAC; and Margaret Biggs, Probate Inventory, April 11, 1856, CCAC, ORAC. See also the manuscript diaries of Rev. Joseph B. Stratton, 1843, 1847–1903, especially the August 12, 1853, entry, in Joseph B. Stratton Papers, LSU. For Turner's legal career, see Landon, "Mississippi State Bar Association"; May, *John A. Quitman*, 25–27, 33, 40, 98, 204, 303, 372, 374, 433; and Rosenblum, "John T. McMurran of Old Natchez," NNHP.

4. Most of the information on Biggs is found in an array of public records, especially several court cases involving her brother and the final settlement of her estate, CCAC, ORAC. See Ann Biggs to Francis Surget, Deed, January 15, 1828, Deed and Mortgage Records, ORAC; Ann Biggs, Will, October 5, 1822, ORAC; *Francis Surget v. Ann Biggs*, January 14, 1828, Superior Court of the Western District, Natchez, Adams County, Miss., MDAH; Guardianship of Minor Children of William and Ann Biggs, December 22, 1832, Orphan Court Minutes, ORAC; *Margaret Biggs v. James Berthe*, April 13, 1833, ORAC; *Margaret Biggs v. State of Mississippi*, November 28, 1853, CHCAC, ORAC; Guardianship of Minor Children of William and Ann Biggs, December 22, 1832, Orphan Court Minutes, ORAC; *George M. Davis v. William H. Biggs*, July 13, 1858, CHCAC, ORAC; William Biggs, Division of Estate to Heirs, January 13, 1833, CHCAC, ORAC; and William H. Biggs (nephew of Margaret Biggs) to Delia Parker and daughter, Deed of Manumission, June 6, 1836, Deed and Mortgage Records, ORAC. See also Elizabeth B. Turner to Miss Margaret Biggs, August 28, 1838, and January 17, 1841, Edward Turner Family Papers, LSU; and "Obituary of Mary Helm nee Biggs" (niece of Margaret Biggs), *Weekly Mississippi Pilot*, April 8, 1875. For information on William Biggs's property and wealthy neighbors, see *Natchez Weekly Democrat*, January 4, 1833; and W. Scarborough, *Masters of the Big House*, 11–12, 23–27, 67, 100, 128, 148, 235, 252.

5. Jane Mayes, Tax Rolls, Adams County, Miss., 1851, ORAC; Jail Docket Books, Adams County, Miss., 1830–60, HNF; U.S. Manuscript Census (1850, 1860), Natchez, Adams County, Miss., NARA; Miles Kelly to Jane Mayes, Bill of Sale, January 9, 1842; and John Johnston to Jane Mayes, Deed, December 17, 1847, Deed and Mortgage Records, ORAC.

6. Mary Ann Simmons to Jane Mayes, Agreement, February 25, 1853, Deed and Mortgage Records, ORAC. Just the year before, Mary Ann had bound out her other, two-year-old, daughter under a similar arrangement to one of the other reigning madams in town, Malvina Matthews. For a fuller discussion of antebellum Natchez as a fun-loving town teeming with whores, gamblers, and saloons, see Broussard, "Malvina Matthews"; D. James, *Antebellum Natchez*, 36–37, 88–89, 99, 168–69, 174, 260–61; and Kibler, "Natchez Landing."

7. Adams, "Murder, Madness, Corpses, and Confusions"; Adams, "Natchez District Women"; W. A. Evans, "Sarah Ann Ellis Dorsey"; and E. James, J. James, and Boyer, *Notable American Women*, 533–35. For information on the Dahlgren family and more on Sarah Ann (Ellis) Dorsey's relationship with Jefferson Davis, see Gower, *Charles Dahlgren of Natchez*, 16–26, 31, 86–87, 104, 138, 189–97, 205.

8. Ibid. Historian Michael O'Brien discusses an unnamed Natchez District spinster who also worked as a governess; see O'Brien, *An Evening When Alone*, 15–22, 187–53.

9. To arrive at the number of white, spinster-age women, each female member of a white household in Natchez and Adams County was traced through available public records to determine marital status, wealth, occupation, and family relationships. The data is drawn from the U.S. Census (manuscript schedules) and an array of public records for Natchez and Adams County, Mississippi, for the years 1820–70. These city and county records include circuit and chancery court records, county and municipal death records, deed and mortgage records, jail dockets, justice court dockets, marriage records, probate and will records, superior and supreme court records, and city and county tax rolls. Although some white spinsters were undoubtedly missed in the above investigation, the number is probably small because of the extensive cross-checking involved. On the other hand, twenty-seven single white women living in Natchez during the 1850s according to noncensus public records do not show up in the U.S. manuscript census records for 1850 or 1860. They most likely had died during the 1850s, left town before 1860, or simply had avoided the census enumerators.

10. A few nonelite white spinsters in Natchez, about 11 percent of the spinster population, appear in the public records without occupations; these women were elderly and probably too old to work for wages or at a trade or enterprise and most likely were sustained by relatives and friends. About a dozen white spinsters located in assorted public records appear nowhere in the federal census records.

11. Many of the city's white female criminals were single women in their twenties throughout the period examined; the city's older female criminals were almost always married, divorced, or widowed women. The criminal records consulted for this study are housed in the Historic Natchez Foundation and include an array of justice and jail dockets as well as city and county court minutes.

12. For a theoretical discussion of the constraining impact on women of the "male gaze," see Berger, *Ways of Seeing*, 7–33, 45–64.

13. *Margaret Biggs v. James Berthe*, April 13, 1833, CCAC, ORAC; and Margaret Biggs, Probate Inventory, April 11, 1856, CHCAC, ORAC. For amendments to the 1839 Married Women's Property Law, passed in 1848, which removed restrictions on a married woman's managerial control of her property, including slaves, see Hutchinson, *Code of Mississippi*, 496–98.

14. Sources for Lydia Dowell come from public records in the main, especially the numerous court cases involving her as a plaintiff and defendant during the 1830s and 1840s. I first came across Lydia Dowell one summer while working with Mississippi Supreme Court and High Court of Errors and Appeals cases (HCEA), MDAH, and later when leading a graduate history student internship program in Natchez for the California State University, Northridge, Natchez Court House Records Project. At that time Susan Falck, then a graduate student but now a PhD historian, did yeoman work locating many of the Dowell cases. During a subsequent student research trip, one of my graduate students, Cai Hamilton, began doing further research on Dowell, presenting her findings in a conference session in 2009; since then, Hamilton has continued to work

on Dowell, and much of what follows here is based on her meticulous research. See C. Hamilton, "Illuminating Lydia Dowell."

Court cases involving Dowell for Natchez and Adams County are currently archived at HNF. Dowell cases appealed to the state's High Court of Errors and Appeals can be found at MDAH. In addition to these sources, information on Dowell and her family and associates turns up in county death and manuscript tax records for Natchez and Adams County, Mississippi, and Vicksburg, Warren County, Mississippi. Additionally, material on Dowell is recorded in the deed and mortgage records for Adams and Warren County housed at the Adams County Office of Records and the Warren County Office of Records in Vicksburg, as well as in various Natchez and Vicksburg newspapers and the U.S. manuscript census schedules (1830 and 1840), Adams and Warren Counties, Miss., NARA. She also is mentioned in the diary of William Johnson, the free-black barber of Natchez, reproduced in Hogan and Davis, *William Johnson's Natchez*, 365, 368.

15. See *Nathanial M. Ricker v. Alexander Dowell, Jr.*, November Term, 1831, CCAC, ORAC.

16. Christian McClure and Ruth Dowell, Marriage Records, 1835–50, ORAC; and Manuscript Tax Rolls for Adams County, 1820–50, MDAH.

17. *Lydia Dowell v. Daniel G. Benbrook*, March 10, 1836; and *Lydia Dowell v. Mary Rowan*, May 6, 1843, CCAC, HNF.

18. For discussion of shopping by women and men in antebellum Mississippi and the larger South, see Atherton, *Southern Country Store*; Ownby, *American Dreams in Mississippi*, 1–60; and Woodman, *King Cotton and His Retainers*, 74–84. Although no historians have focused specifically on the female merchant in the nineteenth-century U.S. South, the above books make it clear that most women avoided shopping in general merchandise stores and that specialty shopping by women for women was a relatively late development in the region's mercantile history.

19. See *Lydia Dowell v. Mary McGuire*, April 11, 1836; and *Lydia Dowell v. George Carradine*, September 28, 1840, CCAC, HNF. For discussion of the place of sewing and fashions in the lives of women in the antebellum South, see Jabour, *Scarlett's Sisters*, 23, 96, 181, 204, 198–200.

20. The free-black barber William Johnson identified Dowell in his diary as the only female merchant in the community in 1836, but at least forty-eight male merchants of one sort or another crossed her path in the city's mercantile arena during the 1840s. Hogan and Davis, *William Johnson's Natchez*, 365, 368. In time, other female entrepreneurs entered the millinery business, obviously modeling their operations after Dowell's pioneering store. Wilhelmina Kohncke, widowed in 1856, for example, operated her millinery and fancy goods store on Main Street (perhaps the same establishment once owned by Dowell) for most of the 1850s. One of Kohncke's competitors, Madame Sardin Benoist, whose shop was also located on Main Street, offered fancy goods that she personally selected on her buying trips to New Orleans. She proudly differentiated her wares as European in origin rather than from Philadelphia suppliers, declaring in her advertisements that she carried the latest Parisian fashions and the finest materials required in the millinery and dressmaking line. Not to be outdone, ten years later, a Mrs. De La Hunt announced that she had engaged a dressmaker recently arrived from the North, a woman "thoroughly

acquainted with all the newest and most fashionable styles of the season." See *Natchez Courier*, March 26, May 8, 1850; and March 15, 1861.

21. U.S. Manuscript Census (1840), Natchez, Adams County, Miss., NARA; Hogan and Davis, *William Johnson's Natchez*, 368; *Lydia Dowell v. Richard Abby*, April 18, 1837, CCAC, HNF; and R. C. Randolph to Lydia Dowell, January 3, 1833, Indenture, Deed and Mortgage Record Books, ORAC.

22. *Lydia Dowell v. Adolph Agmee*, December 1, 1865; *Lydia Dowell v. William Collins*, June 18, 1840; and *Lydia Dowell v. Samuel W. Speer*, October 8, 1844, CCAC, HNF.

23. Hogan and Davis, *William Johnson's Natchez*, 368.

24. *Mary Ann Stanton v. Lydia Dowell*, March 16, 1847; and *Dowell v. Abby*, April 18, 1837, CCAC, HNF.

25. See details on this Vicksburg land transaction in *Wood, Johnston, et al. v. Lydia Dowell*, 1838, CCAC, HNF; and *Dowell v. Wood, Johnston et al.*, June 11, 1845, Supreme Court of Mississippi, MDAH. In the latter case, it is noted that Dowell had purchased a Natchez lot from the wealthy slaveholder Stephen Duncan. See also Brazy, *American Planter*, 189.

26. Brazy, *American Planter*, 189; and *George Yerger et al. v. Lydia Dowell*, January 7, 1846, Supreme Court of Mississippi, MDAH.

27. Ann Mix to P. B. Harrison and Lydia Dowell, October 11, 1845, Deed and Mortgage Record Books, ORAC.

28. William M. Gwin to Lydia Dowell, March 14, 1840, Deed and Mortgage Record Books, ORAC.

29. For the tendency of Natchez lawyers, merchants, and doctors to move as quickly as possible into slavery and planting cotton, see Brazy, *American Planter*, 4–68; and R. Davis, *Good and Faithful Labor*, 24–57.

30. For the jurisdiction and functioning of the Mississippi courts in Mississippi and the larger South, see Gross, *Double Character*, 24–25, 159–60, 183n74; Hoffheimer, "Mississippi Courts"; Hutchinson, *Code of Mississippi*; J. Moore, "Local and State Governments"; Sharkey, Harris, and Elliot, *Revised Code of Mississippi*; and Wooster, *People in Power*.

31. Broussard, "Career of John T. McMurran."

32. Because Dowell's cases usually involved sums of less than $500, the Adams County Circuit Court heard the bulk of them. For examples, see *Isaac Swain v. Lydia Dowell*, May 10, 1845; *Baylor Winn v. Lydia Dowell*, May 15, 1845; *Mary Ann Stanton v. Lydia Dowell*, March 12, 1847; and *Thomas Gaw v. Lydia Dowell*, May 10, 1844, CCAC, HNF.

33. *Lydia Dowell v. Shepard Brown and Joseph H. Johnston*, November 10, 1848; *Lydia Dowell v. Samuel S. Boyd*, 1844; *Planters' Bank of Mississippi v. Lydia Dowell*, April 15, 1843; and *John D. James v. Lydia Dowell*, August 5, 1845, HCEA, MDAH.

34. C. Hamilton, "Illuminating Lydia Dowell," 33–35.

35. *S. J. Levy and Co. v. Lydia Dowell*, May 18, 1856, CCAC, HNF.

36. See the deposition of Christopher McClure, May 19, 1842, in *Lydia Dowell v. Silas Wood, Robert Johnston et al.*, June 11, 1845, Supreme Court of Mississippi, MDAH.

37. Dowell had used Harring in other land transactions, including some in Natchez. See Samuel Newman to Lydia Dowell, Deed, March 7, 1842, Deed and Mortgage Record Books, ORAC.

38. Hutchinson, *Code of Mississippi*, sec. 136; ch. 61, art. 9, sec. 14; and Alden and Van Hosen, *Digest*, sec. 133, p. 150; sec. 138, p. 150; sec. 142, p. 151.

39. Women typically avoided appearing in court if possible, instead giving depositions in their homes or attorney offices. See Gross, *Double Character*, 37.

40. Hogan and Davis, *William Johnson's Natchez*, 368.

41. C. Hamilton, "Illuminating Lydia Dowell," 14n36; and *Vicksburg Weekly Whig*, August 21, 1850. For discussion of antimerchant attitudes among the general public in the premodern South, see R. Davis, "Southern Merchant."

42. H. Carter, *Lower Mississippi*, 234–46. Carter wrote his book at the beginning of his career as the acclaimed editor of the *Delta Democrat Times*, which championed racial tolerance in opposition to state-supported segregation in Mississippi. His editorials won a Pulitzer Prize in 1946. There is some uncertainty about Rebecca Mandeville's exact age in 1848, because public death records give her age as eighty-nine in 1911, but family records suggest that she was born in 1826 rather than 1822. See Mandeville 1848 Diary, MFP, LSU; and Hogan and Davis, *William Johnson's Natchez*, 84, 220n, 255, 286n, 292, 295, 300, 420, 571, 612n, 689, 737.

43. Except for Carter's passing words, almost nothing has been published about Rebecca Mandeville, a Natchez spinster whose life spanned three generations of Natchez history, from when she arrived in 1835 as a young girl from Philadelphia with her parents and eight siblings until her death in 1911. In recent years, however, students of Natchez history have taken a fresh look at the Mandeville family. See especially Broussard, "Female Solitaires," 78–92; Rowe, "Brothers and Sisters"; and Tripp, "Affair of the Heart."

44. The largest collection of Mandeville correspondence is in the Henry D. Mandeville Family Papers (MFP), LSU). Most of these letters were written to Rebecca Mandeville, but the collection also includes her father's numerous business records. Among these are 135 letters sent from, or received by, Rebecca prior to the Civil War, 84 letters written during the Civil War, and 657 letters written after the Civil War. Additional Mandeville materials are located in the Adams County Office of Records in Natchez and in the Mississippi Chancery and Supreme Court Records housed at MDAH. We meet Rebecca Mandeville in her first diary, written in 1848; she was almost certainly aware that it might someday be read, perhaps even as she wrote it, by her sister Josephine as well as other family members. Because she most likely wrote it as a "second-gaze" document with readers in mind, it is precisely written and a carefully crafted script. See especially Berger, *Ways of Seeing*, 7–33, 45–64, for insight on journals as "second-gaze" musings rather than spontaneous writings with no readers in mind. But the diary is also a private expression of her personal emotions and feelings about family, friends, and the world in which she lived. See Mandeville 1848 Diary, February 24–August 9, 1848, MFP, LSU.

45. Cornelia Naomi Mandeville, born in 1811, the oldest child of Henry Sr. and Charlotte Mandeville, married James D. Oakley in 1839. The couple lived in Natchez and briefly in Tallahassee, Florida, until her death at age thirty in 1841. In 1851, Rebecca's older brother Henry Jr., born in 1815, was left a widower with the death of his wife, Julie. Educated at Princeton University, he had given up his legal practice in Natchez for health reasons and turned to managing the family's Westwood plantation, located

west of Natchez on the Tensas River in Catahoula Parish, Louisiana. Although his three children (Constance, Cornelia, and George) appear to have remained with their father in Louisiana after their mother's death, they lived there off and on and visited frequently with the Mandeville family in Natchez, most likely supervised by Rebecca and Josephine. Charlotte Augustus Mandeville, born in 1818, married sometime after 1841 and thereafter lived with her husband, whose name is unknown, on a plantation near the Mandeville family property in Louisiana, probably the one referred to in family letters as the Bayou Louis Tract. She died of unknown causes in 1844, at age twenty-six. There is no record of her husband or any offspring. Rebecca's brother George Mandeville, born in 1821, married Amelia Postlethwaite, the granddaughter of a prosperous Natchez merchant, in 1842; thereafter, he lived with his wife and three children (Annie, Charles, and George Jr.), first in Natchez and then in Woodville, Mississippi, a few miles south of Natchez, before moving to New Orleans in the late 1840s. He, too, may have lived briefly on the family plantations in Louisiana. Rebecca's three other brothers—Augustus, born in 1824; Theodore, born in 1830; and Ellwyn, born in 1833—lived at various times as adults during the 1850s in New Orleans, Natchez, and with their older brother Henry Jr. on the Westwood plantation. They had tried their hands at clerking and as merchants before joining the Confederate army with the outbreak of the Civil War. In 1858, Josephine Mandeville, born in 1828, married George H. Rozet, and the couple moved to New Orleans for a few years before moving to Philadelphia and then Chicago, where he prospered for a time in real estate. MFP, LSU.

46. For details of Mandeville Sr.'s responsibilities as trustee of the Planters' Bank, see "Assignment, Planters' Bank to Mandeville, et als, Assignees," Probate Court, Adams County, Mississippi, June 25, 1863, ORAC. The assignment was affirmed by the Mississippi High Court of Errors and Appeals, Planters' Bank, Case #6497, HCEA, 1843, ser. 208, box 5827, MDAH. Although cash poor when it collapsed, the bank held substantial claims to real estate and slaves mortgaged to it by debtors for loans. Hundreds of debtors owed the bank $2,061,049 when it closed its doors, including $266,689 owed by Natchez residents. Mandeville served as trustee along with his good friend Henry P. Walworth, a prominent slaveholder and banker, and Eli Montgomery, also a wealthy planter and merchant in the city. For information on Mississippi banking, the Planters' Bank of Mississippi, and Mississippi's financial collapse and recovery during the years 1837 through 1845, see Brazy, *American Planter*, 68–82; Rowland, *History of Mississippi*, 1:636–37; Schweikart, *Banking in the American South*, 27, 52, 175–82, 203–5; and Weems, "Mississippi's First Banking System." For a public accounting of the Planters' Bank's assets and liabilities, see *Mississippi Free Trader*, Mach 16, 17, 1838.

47. U.S. Manuscript Census (1850 and 1860), Natchez, Adams County, Miss., NARA. It appears that Henry Jr. benefited from his father's position as the principal trustee with the Planters' Bank by acquiring real estate mortgaged to the bank for loans in default. For examples of such transactions, see Sheriff's Sale, Sheriff Samuel B. Newman, Sheriff of Adams County, to Henry D. Mandeville Jr.; and Henry Mandeville Jr. to John P. Walworth, Henry Mandeville Sr., and Eli Montgomery, trustees of Planters' Bank, December 12, 1855, Deed and Mortgage Record Books, ORAC.

48. George's wife, Amelia, was the granddaughter of Samuel Postlethwaite, a pioneer merchant, large slaveholder in Natchez, and founding member of the Bank of Mississippi. See D. James, *Antebellum Natchez*, 84, 95, 150, 153, 159, 193, 198, 245.

49. Planters' Bank, Case #6497, 1843, ser. 208, box 5827, HCEA, MDAH.

50. The ice cream parlor, Stanwood, advertised a "Ladies Ice Cream Saloon," assuring its female customers that "they need be in no apprehension of being interrupted by gentlemen." See *Mississippi Free Trader*, April 12, 1848.

51. See Rebecca Mandeville to Henry Mandeville Jr., June 1, 1854, MFP, LSU.

52. Her sister-in-law Julia Mandeville once thanked Rebecca for the worn but repaired clothes sent to the slaves at Westwood: "The old clothes you sent in the barrel will delight more than one black heart. I have put them up until next winter. Tell Sissy [Carlie] that Con and Mary and Nina went with me to the quarter Sunday and carried the little frocks and apron which once adorned her little person and dressed up some little black girls— they looked very nice indeed—and I told them they came all the way from Natchez for them, which quite delighted them." Julia Mandeville to Rebecca Mandeville, June 28, 1845, MFP, LSU. In another letter, Charlotte Mandeville congratulated Rebecca on finally getting rid of a troublesome carriage driver: "and then you have got rid of that plague, Black George, you know, he used to worry my life out of me almost, but how do you do when you go a visiting, who drives the carriage?" Charlotte Mandeville to Rebecca Mandeville, May 23, 1841, MFP, LSU.

53. Mandeville 1848 Diary, July 17, 1848, MFP, LSU.

54. For the importance of letter writing as a revelatory routine and ritual among elite southerners in the nineteenth century, see Stowe, "Rhetoric of Authority."

55. Rebecca typically signed her letters to Julia and Amelia Mandeville with the affectionate words "Your Affectionate Sister," and they signed their letters to her using the same words. See Josephine Mandeville to Rebecca Mandeville, February 25, July 5, August 9, 21, 23, 26, October 6, November, December 10, 1850; February 22, 25, 1851; August 19, 1852; February 8, 19, 26, April 23, 11, June 19, 1853; March 1, 9, 11, 14, 17, 21, 28, 1854; October 24, 1855; March 8, 26, April 9, 19, 1856; November 1857; and August 27, 1858, MFP, LSU. See also Julia Mandeville to Charlotte Mandeville, May 24, November 5, 1844; and to Rebecca Mandeville, June 28, 1845, MFP, LSU.

56. Mandeville 1848 Diary, March 6, 1848, MFP, LSU.

57. Ibid., March 13, 1848.

58. Rebecca Mandeville to Henry Mandeville Jr., June 1, 1854, MFP, LSU. For other examples of letters that suggest a more introverted Rebecca, see Josephine Mandeville to Rebecca Mandeville, March, 11, 14, April 14, 26, 1854; and Theodore Mandeville to Rebecca Mandeville, May 22, 1856, MFP, LSU.

59. Josephine Mandeville to Rebecca Mandeville, October 12, 1851, MFP, LSU.

60. Ibid.

61. Josephine Mandeville to Rebecca Mandeville, August 19, 1852, MFP, LSU.

62. Josephine Mandeville to Rebecca Mandeville, February 22, October 12, 1851, MFP, LSU.

63. See Augustus Mandeville to Sisters, November 2, 1844; Josephine Mandeville to Rebecca Mandeville, February 21, 1851; December 10, 1852, MFP, LSU.

64. Augustus Mandeville, for example, having taken a job in New Orleans, asks Rebecca to seek assistance from their father for their brother Theodore, who was also working as a clerk in New Orleans. Theodore apparently had a drinking problem, much to the dismay of and stern rebuke from his father, who apparently banished him to New Orleans without any means of support. Augustus writes, "I implore you Dear Sisters by all the love you bear for Theo to try to see if you can't persuade him [the senior Mandeville] to extend forth his helping hand." He asks his sisters to plead Theodore's case so that their father will "forget his [Theodore's] past follies, or at least forgive them & help him to retain his place." Augustus Mandeville to Sisters, November 29, 1844, MFP, LSU. For other examples of correspondence in which her brothers seek Rebecca's advice and assistance, see Augustus Mandeville to Rebecca Mandeville, December 3, 1844; February 25, November 9, 21, 30, 1850; May 14, 1851; Ellwyn Mandeville to Rebecca Mandeville, December 10, 1850; May 20, 1851; December 30, 1856; August 5, 1857; Henry Mandeville Sr. to Rebecca Mandeville, February 16, 1856; Rebecca Mandeville to Ellwyn Mandeville, June 13, 1854; and Rebecca Mandeville to Henry Mandeville Jr., June 1, 13, 19, July 22, 1854; Theodore Mandeville to Rebecca Mandeville, October 15, 1850; April 15, 1851; May 13, September 10, 1852; May 22, 1856 and July 9, 1857, MFP, LSU.

65. Henry Mandeville Jr. to Rebecca Mandeville, June 6, June 13, August 24, 1854, MFP, LSU.

66. Rebecca Mandeville to Henry Mandeville Sr., June 1, 1854, MFP, LSU.

67. Cornelia Oakley to Henry Mandeville Sr., June 12, 1839, MFP, LSU. See also Mandeville 1848 Diary, March 9, 10, 1848; and Rebecca Mandeville to Henry Mandeville Jr., July 22, 1854, MFP, LSU.

68. Rebecca Mandeville to Henry Mandeville Sr., June 2, 1854, MFP, LSU.

69. Henry Mandeville Jr. to Rebecca Mandeville, May 20, 1854, MFP, LSU.

70. Henry Mandeville Sr. to Rebecca Mandeville, May 24, 1854, MFP, LSU.

71. Mandeville 1848 Diary, May 11, 1848, MFP, LSU.

72. Mandeville 1848 Diary, June 24, 27, July 3, 1848, MFP, LSU.

73. Mandeville 1848 Diary, March 10, 1848, MFP, LSU.

74. Henry Mandeville Jr. to Rebecca Mandeville, July 21, 1851, MFP, LSU.

75. Ibid.

76. Ibid.

77. Henry Mandeville Jr. to Rebecca Mandeville, March 1, 1852, MFP, LSU.

78. Historian Jean Friedman discusses the hold of community, family, and evangelical religion on southern women as an enclosed garden within which they struggle to embrace the often conflicting commitments to matronly duty and personal independence. See Friedman, *Enclosed Garden*, 3–127. For insight into Rebecca's involvement, or noninvolvement, with religion, see Joseph B. Stratton Diary, June 2, 3, 1860, Joseph B. Stratton Papers, LSU.

79. See especially the second diary of Rebecca Mandeville, 1864–65; family correspondence, 1865–1911, MFP, LSU; Broussard, "Female Solitaires," 78–92; and Tripp, "Affair of the Heart."

80. Family correspondence, 1865–1911, MFP, LSU; Death Records, Sexton Reports, April 15, 1911, Natchez, Adams County, Miss., HNF; Cause #676, Chancery Court Case, Estate

of Henry D. Mandeville, April 4, 1879; Will, Henry D. Mandeville, April 4, 1879, bk. 4, p. 142; Cause #2661, Chancery Court Case, Estate of Rebecca Mandeville, April 29, 1911; and Will of Miss Rebecca Mandeville, April 29, 1911, bk. 6, pp. 126–28, ORAC.

81. H., "Old Maids."

82. Josephine Mandeville to Rebecca Mandeville, n.d., MFP, LSU. For Rebecca Mandeville's wartime work on the home front as a volunteer doing sewing and helping support Confederate soldiers, see Mandeville family correspondence for the war years, 1862–64, MFP, LSU.

CHAPTER THREE. STEPPING OUT ON THEIR OWN

1. *Wilhelmina Aubaye v. Joseph Aubaye*, 1805, Divorce Petitions, Legislative Papers, Territorial Legislature of Mississippi, MDAH.

2. For territorial and state statutes covering divorce as well as related topics, see Hutchinson, *Code of Mississippi*, 495–97; *Laws of the State of Mississippi*, 1830, ch. 18, p. 67; *Laws of the State of Mississippi*, 1850, 118; *Statutes of the Mississippi Territory*; Alden and Van Hosen, *Digest*; and Sharkey, Harris, and Elliott, *Revised Code of Mississippi*, 333–35. For judicial decisions and cases, see *Mississippi Digest Annotated*; George, *Digest*; Humphreys and Owen, *Index of Mississippi Session Acts*, 74–75; and Smedes, *Digest*.

3. *Laura McGill v. John McGill*, 1856, CHCAC, HNF.

4. See An Act Concerning Divorces and Alimony, June 14, 1822, in Hutchinson, *Code of Mississippi*, 394; An Act Amendatory of the Laws Relative to Divorce, *Laws of the State of Mississippi*, 1850, 118–19; Sharkey, Harris, and Elliott, *Revised Code of Mississippi*, 334.

5. *Margaret O'Conner v. Luke O'Conner*, 1849, CHCAC, HNF.

6. *Louisa Holmes v. William Holmes*, 1837, CHCAC, HNF; and Hutchinson, *Code of Mississippi*, 394–97.

7. The 110 cases surveyed are not all of the divorces filed in the county during this period because some have been lost from the public record, although a careful gleaning of newspapers, church records, and private manuscripts indicates that the missing cases number no more than a dozen or two, if that many. The examined divorces are drawn principally from the following judicial records: the chancery court and circuit court records for the Natchez area (1800–1870) housed in HNF and ORAC; the divorce decrees of the territorial legislature and records of the Mississippi Supreme Court and the High Court of Error and Appeals, which succeeded the Supreme Court in 1833, in MDAH. Chancery records include docket books and records of judgment books as well as actual court manuscript cases containing briefs, depositions, testimonies, subpoenas, published notices, decrees, and so on. In addition, court cases heard by the Superior Court of Chancery, or appealed to the Mississippi Supreme Court or the High Court of Errors and Appeals, can be found in annotated versions in George, *Digest*; *Mississippi Digest Annotated*; and Smedes, *Digest*. Finally, because divorces granted by the various chancery and appellant courts required legislative approval prior to 1841, these legislative actions can be found in Humphreys and Owen, *Index of Mississippi Session Acts*. In 1857 the legislature abolished the chancery court system, giving total chancery authority to county circuit courts.

8. Another two hundred divorces sampled were filed by residents in other counties throughout Mississippi, and many of these were also heard in the Adams County courthouse in Natchez, especially for residents of counties immediately adjacent to Adams County. The Adams County Court served as the chancery court for divorces within the Western District (1822–39), the Third Chancery District (1839–46), and the Southern Vice-Chancery District (1846–56), although the Adams County Circuit Court also heard divorce appeals sitting in chancery throughout these years. This means that many of the two hundred discovered divorces filed by residents living beyond Adams County and Natchez were heard, nevertheless, in the Adams County courthouse. Because the 110 divorces of Adams County residents studied herein occurred in a small urban enclave or its immediate environs, at least some of the experiences of the divorcing women who lived in or immediately around Natchez might have differed somewhat from the experiences of women in other parts of the state. For example, in the two hundred non–Adams County divorces heard in Natchez courts, female plaintiffs brought suit or petitioned the legislature in 59 percent of the cases, compared to more than 70 percent for Adams County residents.

9. For more on how the antebellum court system worked in Mississippi, see Gross, *Double Character*, 22–46; Hoffheimer, "Mississippi Courts"; J. Moore, "Local and State Governments," 104–35; and Wooster, *People in Power*, 64–80.

10. Among the most important secondary sources on the history of divorce in the United States, including the nineteenth-century South, are the following: Bardaglio, *Reconstructing the Household*, 32–34, 63, 80–81, 92, 95, 100, 107, 117–20, 134, 142–48, 225–27, 281; Basch, *Framing American Divorce*; Buckley, *Great Catastrophe of My Life*; Bynum, *Unruly Women*, 59–87; Censer, "Smiling through Her Tears"; Chused, "Married Women's Property Law"; Chused, *Private Acts in Public Places*; Grossberg, *Governing the Hearth*, 85, 238, 240, 250–53, 344; Hartog, *Man and Wife in America*, 1–4, 9–14, 20–27, 36, 64–73, 211–16, 242–86; Lebsock, *Free Women of Petersburg*, 15–86; G. Riley, *Divorce*, 34–84; Schweninger, *Families in Crisis in the Old South*; Sedevie, "Prospect of Happiness"; and Ziff, "No Longer under Cover(ture)."

11. Historian Loren Schweninger discusses the English and ecclesiastical influences on state statutes and judicial decisions regarding divorce in *Families in Crisis in the Old South*, 2–16.

12. *Rachael Mitchell v. John Mitchell*, 1842, CHCAC, HNF.

13. Appeals to the High Court of Errors and Appeals could be advanced on the basis of an error in a lower-court ruling or for any reason deemed valid for review. See *Ophelia Carter v. David Carter*, 1853; *McGill v. McGill*, 1856; and *Martha Tewkesbury v. Timothy Tewkesbury*, 1839, HCEA, MDAH.

14. See *Susan Foster v. Thomas Foster*, 1827; *Mirabella Henry v. Oliver Henry*, 1850; and *Melinda Brice v. Nelson Brice*, 1841, CHCAC, HNF. According to Schweninger, 65 percent of the divorces he surveyed in the entire antebellum South listed violent behavior among the charges lodged against husbands. See Schweninger, *Families in Crisis in the Old South*, 47.

15. *Sylvia Anne Stutson v. John S. Stutson*, 1824; and *Adeline Witherspoon v. Charles Witherspoon*, 1824, CHCAC, HNF.

16. See *Aubaye v. Aubaye*, 1805, Divorce Petitions, Legislative Papers, Territorial Legislature of Mississippi, MDAH; *Witherspoon v. Witherspoon*, 1824; *Sally Pryor v. William Pryor*, 1825; and *Eliza Powell v. Garston Powell*, 1829, CHCAC, HNF.

17. *Ann Jean Singleton v. Richard Singleton*, 1807; *Lydia Bradley v. Calvin Bradley*, 1824; and *Eliza Spenser v. Robert B. Spenser*, 1844, CHCAC, HNF.

18. *Witherspoon v. Witherspoon*, 1824; *Sarah Dye v. John Dye*, 1829; *O'Conner v. O'Conner*, 1849; and *Alzomuth Whitehead v. James Whitehead*, 1854, CHCAC, HNF.

19. *Kenley v. Kenley*, 1838; and *Waskam v. Waskam*, 1854, as cited in *Mississippi Digest Annotated*, 910; and *Lydia Jane Ireson v. Lansford Ireson*, 1856, CHCAC, HNF.

20. *Elizabeth (Eliza) Hutchins v. John Hutchins*, 1799, Territorial Petitions, Legislative Papers of the Mississippi Territory and Subject File, MDAH; and *O'Conner v. O'Conner*, 1849, CHCAC, HNF.

21. *Elizabeth Ducay v. William Ducay*, 1839, CHCAC, HNF.

22. *Jane Howard v. Edward Howard*, 1807; *Ann Marie Ventress v. Edward L. Ventress*, 1846; *Henry v. Henry*, 1850; *Anne Tebo v. William Tebo*, 1854; and *Mary Elizabeth McAlister v. Samuel T. McAlister*, 1856, CHCAC, HNF.

23. *Jane Carson v. William Carson*, 1830, CHCAC, HNF.

24. *McGill v. McGill*, 1856, CHCAC, HNF.

25. *O'Conner v. O'Conner*, 1849, CHCAC, HNF.

26. Ibid.

27. Ibid.

28. Schweninger, *Families in Crisis in the Old South*, 44.

29. *Wesley Rourk v. Sarah Rourk*, 1850; *Lydia Flynn v. Alexander Flynn*, 1850; *Henry v. Henry*, 1850; and *Susannah Sessions v. William B. Sessions*, 1839, CHCAC, HNF.

30. *Flynn v. Flynn*, 1850; and *Laurinda Griffin v. Young F. Griffin*, 1851, CHCAC, HNF.

31. *James Smith v. Ruth Smith*, 1809, Territorial Petitions, Legislative Papers of the Mississippi Territory, MDAH.

32. *Mary Rowena Russell v. James Russell*, 1849 and 1850, CHCAC, HNF.

33. *Flynn v. Flynn*, 1850, CHCAC, HNF.

34. *Valentine C. Groom v. Louisa A. Groom*, 1853; *John Renton v. Anna M. Renton*, 1854; *Richard L. Smith v. Mary Smith*, 1825; and *Felix Winsch v. Magdalena Winsch*, 1842, CHCAC, HNF.

35. Schweninger, *Families in Crisis in the Old South*, 23–29.

36. *Dye v. Dye*, 1829, CHCAC, HNF. For examples of other such cases, see *Griffin v. Griffin*, 1851; *Mitchell v. Mitchell*, 1842; and *Mary Yates v. James W. Yates*, 1851, CHCAC, HNF.

37. Box, "Antebellum Travelers in Mississippi"; T. Clark and Guice, *Frontiers in Conflict*, 84, 93–94, 198, 203; W. Davis, *Way through the Wilderness*, 112–13, 242–52; D. James, *Antebellum Natchez*, 183–216; Ingraham, *The South-West*, 9–96; and E. Moore, *Natchez Under-the-Hill*, 7–70. (A word of caution is in order regarding Edith Wyatt Moore as a source: although it is one of the most colorful portraits of Under-the-Hill Natchez and truly captures the temper of the times, Moore's account is filled with inaccuracies and must be taken with more than a little skepticism and carefully double checked.)

38. See *Foster v. Foster*, 1827; *Ventress v. Ventress*, 1846; and *Witherspoon v. Witherspoon*, 1824, CHCAC, HNF.

39. See, for example, *McAlister v. McAlister*, 1856, CHCAC, HNF.

40. See, for example, *Asher Ezekiel v. Italia Ezekiel*, 1854; and *John Kingwell v. Rhoda Ann Kingwell*, 1853, CHCAC, HNF.

41. John Farr accused his wife, Catherine, of fathering two children by other men, one of whom was black. *John Farr v. Catherine Farr*, 1834, CHCAC, HNF. For the lager South, see Schweninger, *Families in Crisis in the Old South*, 27–29.

42. *Sessions v. Sessions*, 1839; *Brice v. Brice*, 1841; *Amelia Brown v. Harrison W. Brown*, 1850; *Whitehead v. Whitehead*, 1854; and *McAlister v. McAlister*, 1856, CHCAC, HNF.

43. McGehee, *Record of the Descendants of Bisland and Rucker*.

44. *Sessions v. Sessions*, 1839, CHCAC, HNF.

45. *Mississippi Digest Annotated*, 119.

46. *Nancy Bankston v. Thomas Bankston*, 1854, HCEA, MDAH. Although this case originated in Scott County, Mississippi, it summarized existing judicial opinion and served thereafter as precedent. For all court decisions affecting alimony in Mississippi prior to 1860, see *Mississippi Digest Annotated*, 908–17.

47. *George Armstrong v. Phoebe Ann Armstrong*, 1856, HCEA, MDAH.

48. see *Mississippi Digest Annotated*, 914–15.

49. Ibid. See also the lower court's decision dismissing the divorce suit of Martha Tewkesbury because of her adultery. The case was overturned, however, on appeal to the High Court of Errors and Appeals. *Tewkesbury v. Tewkesbury*, 1839, CHCAC, HNF; and *Tewkesbury v. Tewkesbury*, 1839, record group 32, HCEA, MDAH.

50. See Sharkey, Harris, and Elliott, *Revised Code of Mississippi*, 33–35; and *Cocke v. Hannum*, 1860, in *Mississippi Digest Annotated*, 916.

51. For discussions of the Mississippi courts and child custody as well as the more general history of child custody in the nation, see Grossberg, *Governing the Hearth*, 207–11, 225–26, 234–288; Mason, *From Father's Property to Children's Rights*, 49–84; and McCarthy, "Cautious, Conservative, and Raced." See also specific references to guardianship in Hutchinson, *Code of Mississippi*, 495–97; and Sharkey, Harris, and Elliott, *Revised Code of Mississippi*, 334–35.

52. *Spenser v. Spenser*, 1844; *Ventress v. Ventress*, 1846; *Carson v. Carson*, 1830; *Bradley v. Bradley*, 1824; and *Brice v. Brice*, 1841, CHCAC, HNF.

53. For a discussion of divorce, prenuptial contracts, and separate estates in Adams County prior to and after passage of the Married Women's Property Law, see Broussard, "Naked before the Law."

54. Chused, "Late Nineteenth Century Married Women's Property Law"; Chused, "Married Women's Property Law"; Hoff, *Law, Gender, and Injustice*, 104, 116, 120–35; Lebsock, "Radical Reconstruction"; Lebsock, *Free Women of Petersburg*, 54–86, 112–43; Moncrief, "Mississippi Married Women's Property Act"; Shammas, "Re-Assessing the Married Women's Property Acts," 9–30; and Warbasse, *Changing Legal Rights of Married Women*.

55. Chused, "Married Women's Property Law."

56. Twenty-seven marriage contracts were registered in the Adams County Deed and Mortgage Record Books for the years 1798–1860. Deed, Liens, and Mortgage Record Books, 1798–1860, Adams County, Mississippi, ORAC.

57. *Whitehead v. Whitehead*, 1854; and *Louisa Holmes v. William Holmes*, 1837, CHCAC, HNF. For other examples, see *Elizabeth Hawley v. Quinton Hawley*, 1849; and *O'Conner v. O'Conner*, 1849, CHCAC, HNF.

58. A Gentleman of the Bar, *Clerk's Assistant*.

59. *McGill v. McGill*, 1856, HCEA, MDAH.

60. *Tewkesbury v. Tewkesbury*, 1838, CHCAC, HNF.

61. Ibid. The Newcomer estate held substantial obligations for lumber purchased from the merchant Brown, in settlement of which Martha transferred to him a piece of land in Under-the-Hill Natchez valued at $11,000.

62. *Tewkesbury v. Tewkesbury*, 5 Miss. 1839, RG 32, HCEA, MDAH.

63. *Lydia Jane Ireson v. Lansford Ireson*, December 13, 1853; April 4 and November 14, 1856; September 17 and November 12, 1857, CHCAC, HNF; and Probate, Euphemia Lassley, January 27, 1858, HNF. The High Court of Errors and Appeals affirmed the lower court's ruling on February 28, 1859, as attested in *Ireson v. Ireson*, May 24, 1859, CCAC, HNF.

64. For biographical information on the Lassley and Ireson families, see Henry B. Eaton to Ernst O. Guenther, January 12, 1948; and Imogene Ireson Guenther to Sally and Dan Farrar, May 14, 1952, Daniel S. Farrar Jr. and Family Papers, MDAH.

65. For the Jersey Settlement in Mississippi, see Claiborne, *Mississippi*, 106–7; Drake, "Note on the Jersey Settlers"; H. Eaton, *Descendants of the Jersey Settlers*, 21–22; D. James, *Antebellum Natchez*, 16–17; Mills, *History of the Descendants*, 1:25; and Rowland, *History of Mississippi*, 1:264–65.

66. Information on Lydia Ireson's inheritance from her mother and father can be found in Deed of Partition, Heirs of Matthew Lassley, January 26, 1853; and Lydia Jane and Lansford O. Ireson to Ann Lambert, April 21, 1853, Deed and Mortgage Record Books, ORAC. See also Probate, Matthew Lassley, January 21, 1853; Agreement, James G. Lassley, Lydia Jane Ireson, and Lansford O. Ireson, December 18, 1854; and Probate, Euphemia Lassley, January 27, 1858, HNF.

67. Depositions of James Carpenter, Susan Livesay, and Carolina Mahala Phipps, *Ireson v. Ireson*, November 24, 1857, CHCAC, HNF.

68. Depositions of Caleb Farrar and Charles N. Vaughan, *Ireson v. Ireson*, November 24, 1857, CHCAC, HNF.

69. Depositions of Robert J. Lassley and James Lassley, *Ireson v. Ireson*, November 24, 1857, CHCAC, HNF.

70. Depositions of Farrar, Vaughn, Robert Bixby, and John Baird, *Ireson v. Ireson*, November 24, 1857, CHCAC, HNF.

71. The court also ordered the receiver of Lydia's properties to pay Lydia $1,500 in temporary spousal and child support until Lansford's appeal to the High Court was settled.

72. See Lansford Ireson's answer in his deposition of November 24, 1857, CHCAC, HNF.

73. Marriage Records, 1858, Adams County, Miss., ORAC.

74. For biographical information on the Phipps family, see Imogene Ireson Guenther to Sally and Dan Farrar, May 14, 1852, Farrar Family Papers, MDAH; and H. Eaton, *Descendants of the Jersey Settlers*, 21–22. Details about these family connections are somewhat sorted out in the Farrar Family Papers, MDAH. Caroline M. Ireson Phipps, who was Lansford Ireson's sister, lived with the Farrar family after her mother's death (Hannah Swayze Ireson) in 1832, when she was nine years old, and she was raised essentially as Daniel Farrar's daughter. Her father, James H. Ireson, had died in 1823. Marriage Records, 1835–50, Adams County, Miss., ORAC.

75. *Lydia Jane Phipps vs. Henry M. Phipps*, 1867, CCAC, HNF.

76. Stanton, "Marriage and Divorce." See also Hartog, "Lawyering Husbands' Rights"; Basch, *In the Eyes of the Law*; and Grossberg, *Governing the Hearth*, 85, 238–53, 344.

CHAPTER FOUR. STEPPING BEYOND THEIR HUSBANDS' GRAVES

1. Catherine Moore, Petition for Writ of Habeas Corpus, November 16, 1857, CCAC, HNF.

2. For information on Sister Mary Thomas McSwiggan and St. Mary's Orphanage, see Gerow, *Cradle Days of St. Mary's*, 205–7, 233–38, and 245–53; Natchez Orphanages, WPA Files, MDAH; Nolan, *St. Mary's of Natchez*, 305–11; and U.S. Manuscript Census (1850, 1860), Natchez, Adams County, Miss., NARA. For the Natchez Protestant Orphanage, see Groen, "Emancipation and Education"; and Sparks, "Good Sisters."

3. Moore, Petition for Writ of Habeas Corpus, November 16, 1857, CCAC, HNF.

4. *State vs. Catherine Moore*, April 8, 1854; November 3, 1854; March 29, 1856, CCAC, HNF.

5. Death Records, Sexton Reports (1800–1920), Adams County, Miss., HNF.

6. Information on the composition and character of the widows depicted here is drawn from the U.S. Manuscript Census (1820–1860), Natchez, Adams County, Miss., NARA, as well as marriage and death records and numerous municipal and county public records, including court records, housed in HNF, MDAH, and ORAC.

For pertinent scholarship on widows, see Boswell, *Her Act and Deed*, 34–44, 68–72, 98–101, 120–23, 130; Froide, "Marital Status"; Gonzalez, "Widowed Women of Santa Fe"; Keyssar, "Widowhood in Eighteenth-Century Massachusetts"; Salmon, *Women and the Law of Property*, 141–85; L. Wilson, *Life after Death*; and Wulf, *Not All Wives*, 6, 8–9, 12, 14, 17, 30, 44, 49, 52, 88, 90, 92–93, 95–101, 116, 119, 124, 128, 130–33, 135, 149–51, 153, 166, 178, 204.

7. On Mississippi's Married Women's Property Law and prenuptial contracts see W. Scarborough, *Masters of the Big House*, 107–8. For an example of a wealthy widow who relied on trusted males and overseers to handle the daily management of her plantation and slaves, see the case of Clarissa Sharp, as detailed in Wayne, *Death of an Overseer*, 24–26.

8. Bynum, *Unruly Women*, 34–37; C. Carter, *Southern Single Blessedness*, 1–4; Edwards, "Law, Domestic Violence"; Fox-Genovese, *Within the Plantation Household*, 256–57; C. Kennedy, *Braided Relations, Entwined Lives*, 77–110; Stevenson, *Life in Black and White*, 37–158; Bennett and Froide, *Singlewomen in the European Past*; and Dubler, "In the Shadow of Marriage."

9. For discussion of the widow's dower as an extension of the dead husband's hold on his living spouse, see Dubler, "In the Shadow of Marriage"; and Salmon, *Women and the Law of Property*, 147–84.

10. For the laws of dower in antebellum Mississippi, see Hutchinson, *Code of Mississippi*, 617–22; and Sharkey, Harris, and Elliott, *Revised Code of Mississippi*, 313, 332, 337, 375, 410, 467–70.

11. Inventories of Estates (1803–90); Probate Records (1800–1900); and Will Books, ORAC.

12. Will of Susan E. Conner, probated December 1858, Will Books, ORAC.

13. Will of Lavinia Ford, probated January Term 1853, Will Books, ORAC.

14. Lebsock, *Free Women of Petersburg*, 55–56.

15. Will of James Green, probated January Term 1832; Will of Eliza C. Wood, probated April Term 1851, Will Books, ORAC.

16. This evaluation of the differences in the manumission behavior of white men and women is based on an examination of manumission documents for the years 1820–60, found in the Deed and Mortgage Record Books, Inventories of Estates, Probate Records, and Will Books for Adams County, 1798–1860, ORAC. For secondary sources dealing with the behavior and practices of slaveholding women regarding their enslaved servants and workers, see Fox-Genovese, *Within the Plantation Household*, 308–71; and Weiner, *Mistresses and Slaves*, 72–132.

17. *Mississippi Free Trader* (Natchez), February 4, 1852.

18. Information about Mary Wattles is principally drawn from various public records, especially probate files related to the estate of her first husband, John Forsyth, death and marriage records, federal and local manuscript census schedules, and the numerous court cases in which she was involved. See U.S. Manuscript Census (1830, 1840, 1850, 1860), Natchez, Adams County, Miss., NARA. See also John Forsyth Papers, Natchez Trace Collection, Center for American History, University of Texas at Austin.

19. Marriage Records, Adams County, Miss.; and John Forsyth Sr., Probate Record File, Final Settlement, January 16, 1854, ORAC. According to the death records recorded by the city sexton, Alonzo Wattles died of consumption on May 2, 1843. Death Records, Sexton Reports (1800–1920), Adams County, Miss., HNF.

20. Deposition of Samuel Cotton, June 30, 1848, John Forsyth Probate Record File, ORAC.

21. *Abijah Hull v. John Forsyth's Heirs and Administrators*, Petition for Assignment of Dower, December 13, 1829, Superior Court of Chancery, MDAH.

22. John Forsyth's five children, from a previous marriage or with a woman other than Wattles, inherited various shares of the remaining Forsyth property, including the enslaved people not sold to satisfy creditors. All of Forsyth's personal property, including enslaved people, was inventoried and sold to satisfy his creditors, leaving only portions of his real estate to be passed on to his heirs and as his widow's dower. See John Forsyth Probate File, Probate Records, ORAC. For evidence pertaining to Alonzo Wattles' financial circumstances, see Alonzo Wattles and Mary Ann Wattles to William L. Cullen, Deed, October 15, 1834; Alonzo Wattles to Samuel Cotton, March 18, 1840, Deed of Trust;

Alonzo Wattles to Charles E. Bentley and James Johnston, Deed of Mortgage, April 17, 1841, Deed and Mortgage Records, ORAC; and *Murchesian & Doyal v. Mary Wattles, Executrix*, April 4, 1845, CHCAC, HNF.

23. John Forsyth to Dempsey P. Jackson, Power of Attorney, June 27, 1828, Deed and Mortgage Records, ORAC.

24. See the final settlement of the Forsyth probate accounts, which occurred in 1854, in the John Forsyth Probate Record File, ORAC. For a description of Dempsey P. Jackson, see Wayne, *Death of an Overseer*, 21–22.

25. For evidence of Mary Wattles's numerous dealings in real estate linked to her Forsyth dower, see *American Life Insurance and Trust Co. v. Wood Pentecost and Co., Noah Barlow, and Alonzo Wattles*, 1842, HCEA, MDAH; John Wells, Dempsey P. Jackson, and Mary Ann Wattles, June 16, 1851, Deed of Partition; Mary Ann Wattles to William B. Quigley, April 19, 1856, Lease; and Mary Wattles to William Quigley, April 19, 1859, Lease, Deed and Mortgage Record Books, ORAC.

26. John Forsyth to George Smith, July 21, 1822, John Forsyth Papers.

27. Elizabeth Smith and Children, License to Remain in State as a Free Person of Color, July Term, 1844, Board of Police Minutes, HNF.

28. Mary Ann Wattles to Charles Green and Co., July 2, 1860, Deed and Mortgage Record Books; and Will of Mary Ann Wattles, March 21, 1867, Will Books, ORAC.

29. Mary Ann Wattles to Richard Carkeet, September 1, 1846, Deed of Dower, Deed and Mortgage Records, ORAC.

30. Elder came to Natchez in 1857 after ministering to the poor and teaching for a decade at St. Mary's College in Maryland, his home state. Sister Mary Thomas had arrived with six Daughters of Charity years earlier. Both would achieve notoriety during the Civil War for their outspoken activism in defense of the city's orphans, in the case of Sister Mary Thomas, and the Confederacy, in the case of Bishop Elder. Bishop Elder was banished for a time from the city because of his refusal to offer a prayer for President Lincoln. See Nolan, *St. Mary's of Natchez*, 116, 132–33, 149, 369; and Pillar, *Catholic Church in Mississippi*, 82–347. For more on the involvement of Natchez women in community charities, see Sparks, "Good Sisters."

31. The Gireaudeau name is found under several spellings in the records, including Gireadeau and Girodeux. Death Records, Sexton Reports, January 12, 1862, Adams County, Miss., HNF. Accounts of her funeral procession can be found in "Announcements in Church," February 19, 1860–January 19, 1868, St. Mary's Cathedral Archives, St. Mary's Catholic Church, Natchez, Miss. (SMA). Evidence of public esteem for Gireaudeau as a woman committed to the spiritual life of her parish can be found in the church eulogy hailing her as a "benefactress of the church, of the orphans, and of all in need, according to her means." "Announcements," January 12, 1862, SMA. For more on Gireaudeau's reputation, see Broussard, "Female Solitaires," 51–59; and E. Clark, "Felicite Girodeau."

32. Will of Felicite Gireaudeau, January 6, 1862, Will Books, ORAC. Madame Gireaudeau also owned two lots adjoining her residence. See also Gerow, *Cradle Days of St. Mary's*, 35–38, 68–69; Nolan, *St. Mary's of Natchez*, 97; and Register of Baptisms and Sacramental Records (1820–65), SMA.

33. See Family Histories File, SMA; and Felicite Gireaudeau, "Personal Memoirs and Recollections" (1859), Henry Elder Files and Letter Books, Catholic Diocese of Jackson Archives, Jackson, Miss. (CDJA).

34. Much of the information on the Gireaudeau family genealogy comes from research notes compiled by historian Charles E. Nolan, provided by historian Emily Clark, Natchez Project Archives, California State University, Northridge. See also Clark, "Felicite Girodeau," 7–8; and Nolan, *St. Mary's of Natchez*, 96–97.

35. Gerow, *Cradle Days of St. Mary's*, 19–20; and Nolan, *St. Mary's of Natchez*, 97.

36. Gabriel Gireaudeau and Felicite Gireaudeau to Peter M. Lapice, November 29, 1827, Deed and Mortgage Record Books, ORAC; and Nolan research notes, Natchez Project Archives, California State University, Northridge.

37. U.S. Manuscript Census (1850, 1860), Natchez, Adams County, Miss., NARA. Madame Gireaudeau's younger sister, Delphine, married Felicite's husband's brother, Antonio Edmundo Gireaudeau, a New Orleans merchant who assisted Felicite with her financial affairs after her husband's death.

38. Nolan research notes, Natchez Project Archives, California State University, Northridge.

39. Register of Baptisms and Sacramental Records (1820–65), SMA. Serving "as a godmother to infants of slaves" was well within a Catholic tradition "of women evangelizing women and then serving as godmothers to their infants." See Gould and Nolan, "Mother Henriette Delille."

40. Deeds of Emancipation, Rosalie Gireaudeau, Sophia Gireaudeau, and Sally McFadden, June 9, 1835; Deeds of Sale, Leonard Pomet to Gabriel and Felicite Girardeau, July 6, 1825; Felicite Gireaudeau to George W. Smyth, August 25, 1830, Deed and Mortgage Record Books, ORAC.

41. R. Davis, *Black Experience*, 46–60; and Sydnor, "Free Negro in Mississippi."

42. Buchanan, *Black Life on the Mississippi*, 39; Libby, *Slavery and Frontier Mississippi*, 101–21; and R. Welch, "Family Affair." For laws governing manumission, see Sharkey, Harris, and Elliot, *Revised Code of Mississippi*, 237–38.

43. Nolan, *St. Mary's of Natchez*, 97; Henry Elder Files, CDJA; and E. Clark, "Felicite Girodeau."

44. Bell, *Revolution, Romanticism, and the Afro-Creole Protest*; Brasseaux, *French, Cajun, Creole, Houma*; E. Clark, *Strange History of the American Quadroon*; Force, "House on Bayou Road"; Hanger, "Origins of New Orleans's Free Creoles"; Long, *Great Southern Babylon*, 6–20; J. Martin, "*Plaçage* and the Louisiana *Gens de Couleur Libre*"; Schafer, *Brothels, Depravity, and Abandoned Women*, 31–32, 35–36; Spear, *Race, Sex, and Social Order*; and S. Thompson, *Exiles at Home*.

45. In 1933, church historian Richard O. Gerow interviewed an elderly Natchez woman who spoke fondly about her memories of the white Madame Felicite Gireaudeau. See *Natchez Democrat*, September 19, 1933.

46. E. Clark, "Felicite Girodeau," 17–18.

47. Historian Jean Friedman found similar female associations in other towns and cities of the urban South prior to the Civil War. See Friedman, *Enclosed Garden*, 19;

and Nguyen, "Active Faith." For information on Natchez orphanages and the women who supported them, see Shiells, "Orphanages of Ante-bellum Natchez"; and Stites, "Expanded Bonds of Womanhood."

48. Gerow, *Cradle Days of St. Mary's*, 205–7, 233–38, 245–53; and D. James, *Antebellum Natchez*, 218–19.

49. Sparks, *Religion in Mississippi*, 55–73.

50. In his history of the Catholic Church in Natchez, *Cradle Days of St. Mary's*, historian Richard O. Gerow mistakenly claims that Gireaudeau had freed four of her enslaved women (Angel Victorine, Ann or Nanny, Mary Elizabeth or Betty, and Andrenette) sometime just before her death and that the women continued to live with Gireaudeau as free women. In fact, the women were bequeathed at Gireaudeau's death to her good friend Mary David, with no instructions for their emancipation. Gireaudeau owned seven enslaved people at the time of her death, although her will mentions only four bequeathed to others. See Felicite Gireaudeau Probate Record File, January Term, 1862, ORAC.

51. Historians Elizabeth Fox-Genovese and Robert May find little evidence of any so-called sisterhood sentiments toward their female slaves by slaveholding women; they also argue that slaveholding women accepted slavery because of the class privileges that followed from owning humans as chattel. Fox-Genovese, *Within the Plantation Household*, 20–22, 96–97, 242–45; and May, "Southern Elite Women."

52. See Knowlton, "Only a Woman Like Yourself"; and Hunt, "Sapphic Strain."

53. Judith Kelleher to George Smith, February 27 [no year], Deed of Manumission, Deed and Mortgage Record Books, ORAC; and R. Welch, "Family Affair," 51.

54. On the other hand, the George Smith Forsyth referred to as a neighbor may have been a white man unrelated to the person emancipated by Kelleher. See John Forsyth to George Smith, May 29, 1819, Deed and Mortgage Record Books, ORAC.

55. John Forsyth Probate Files, ORAC.

56. For a detailed discussion of the petty mercantile economy in the Natchez hinterland as it was linked to a more global national and international market for cotton and slaves, see David, "In Pursuit of their Livelihood," 217–248; and David, "Role of Credit and Debt."

57. See Bieber, "Making the Most of Freedom," 75–83. Mary Miller, director of the Historic Natchez Foundation, has created a Natchez Trails Project, which shows that Eliza Smith purchased property on St. Catherine Street in Natchez sometime during the mid-1850s and this property remained in Smith family hands into the twentieth century. See M. W. Miller, "History of St. Catherine Street."

58. On slaveholding women in other parts of the plantation South and how they related to black women, see Weiner, *Mistresses and Slaves*, 72–154.

CHAPTER FIVE. STEPPING LIVELY IN PLACE

1. U.S. Manuscript Census (1860), Natchez, Adams County, Miss., NARA.

2. Will of Allan Davis, 1861, Will Books, ORAC; Death Records, Sexton Reports, 1861, Adams County, Miss. HNF; Marriage Records, Adams County, Miss. ORAC; and U.S.

Manuscript Census (1860), Natchez, Adams County, Miss., NARA. Historian Richard M. Tristano discusses Margaret Dent and her descendants in "Holy Family Parish."

3. Slave manumissions can be found in an array of public records housed in the Office of Records for Adams County and the Historic Natchez Foundation in Natchez. See Board of Police Minutes for Adams County, Mississippi, 1820–60, HNF; City Council Minutes, 1820–60, HNF; Criminal and Justice Docket Books, 1820–60, HNF; Deeds and Mortgage Record Books, 1800–1860, ORAC; Grand and Petite Jury Docket Books, 1820–60, HNF; Probate Records, 1800–1860, ORAC; and Will Books, 1800–1860, ORAC.

4. Claiborne, *Mississippi*, 215, 320, 328. See also Jane Dent's claim with the Southern Claims Commission for compensation for damages done to her property by Union troops: Jane Dent, December 1877, Claim No. 6616, SCC, NARA.

5. R. Davis, *Black Experience*, 49–50; Sydnor, "Free Negro in Mississippi." For the efforts of local whites to drive free blacks from the state during Dent's lifetime, see Hogan and Davis, *William Johnson's Natchez*, 12–13, 340–46.

6. *Harriet Johnson v. L. H. Corey and L. M. Benbrook*, 1860, CCAC, HNF.

7. For the common practice among antebellum blacks in Mississippi and Louisiana of claiming Native American heritage to challenge their alleged African ancestry, see Spear, *Race, Sex, and Social Order*, 17–52, 54–55, 157–58, 169–77.

8. *Johnson v. Corey and Benbrook*, 1860, CCAC, HNF.

9. William Cullen to Harriett Johnson, June 10, 1829, Deeds and Mortgage Record Books, ORAC. Historian Nichole S. Ribianszky, building on the work of historians Joyce L. Broussard, Ronald Davis, Ariela Gross, and Rosanne Welch, discusses Johnson's petition in her dissertation, suggesting that Johnson's deportment and behavior established her whiteness and were more important than her actual African heritage. This perspective fails to consider, however, the possibility that the court purposefully buried Johnson's obviously enslaved background due to community pressure or for reasons not revealed in the records. See Ribianszky, "To Find Shelter She Knows Not Where," 233–35. For how the Adams County courts handled cases involving free blacks and slaves, see Broussard, "Stepping Lively in Place"; Gross, *What Blood Will Tell*; and R. Welch, "Family Affair." For the importance of proper decorum and submissive behavior among free blacks in antebellum Natchez, see R. Davis, *Black Experience*, 46–59.

10. For the hysteria that overwhelmed some Natchez whites with the onset of the Civil War and the fear of slave rebellion, see Berlin, *Slaves without Masters*, 375–77; and Jordan, *Tumult and Silence at Second Creek*, 11–19.

11. For Warner McCary's life as the Indian Okah Tubbee, see Littlefield, *Life of Okah Tubbee*. For Winn, see Hogan and Davis, *William Johnson's Natchez*, 55–64.

12. For Ann Johnson's life as a widow and the lives of her children, see Gould, *Chained to the Rock of Adversity*; and Shulman, "Bingamans of Natchez."

13. For discussion of how William Johnson coped with life as a free man of color who was more prosperous than most whites in Natchez yet deemed inferior because of his race, see Berlin, "Southern Free People of Color"; and R. Davis, *Black Experience*, 46–59.

14. The residency data for 1860 is somewhat misleading because some free blacks may have lived in servant quarters or dependency buildings linked to but separate from

the white household that employed them. See R. Davis, *Black Experience*, 35–36, 46–59; Libby, *Slavery and Frontier Mississippi*, 101–19; and U.S. Manuscript Population Census (1820–60), Natchez, Adams County, Miss., NARA.

15. See Berlin, *Slaves without Masters*, 375–77; R. Davis, *Black Experience*, 46–59; and Jordan, *Tumult and Silence at Second Creek*, 11–19. For more on the impact of alleged slave-conspiracy scares and actual uprisings by slaves, such as the Nat Turner rebellion, see Kolchin, *American Slavery*, 155–60, 296–97.

16. This list of sixty-four free women of color is drawn principally from the following public records. For those at HNF, see Board of Police Minutes, Adams County; City Council Minutes, Natchez, 1820–60; Death Records, Sexton Reports for Natchez and Adams County, 1800–1920. For those at ORAC, see Deeds and Mortgage Records Books, 1795–1910; Inventories of Estates, 1803–90; Probate Records, 1800–1900; and Will Books, 1800–1860. Invaluable as well is the manuscript census data for Mississippi: U.S. Manuscript Census (1840, 1850, 1860), Natchez, Adams County, Miss., NARA.

17. U.S. Manuscript Census (1860), Natchez, Adams County, Miss., NARA.

18. *Natchez Tri-Weekly Democrat*, September 17, 1872.

19. U.S. Manuscript Census (1860), Natchez, Adams County, Miss., NARA. See also Lebsock, *Free Women of Petersburg*, 87–111; and Roark and Johnson, "Strategies of Survival."

20. R. Davis, *Black Experience*, 46–59; Ribianszky, "She Appeared to Be Mistress"; and R. Welch, "Family Affair," 56–72.

21. These rules of behavior are spelled out in various legislative acts and local ordinances passed by the Natchez City Council and the Adams County Board of Police, which served as the county governing board of elected officials. See especially City Council Minutes, Natchez, 1830–60, HNF; Board of Police Minutes, Adams County, 1820–60, HNF; Hutchinson, *Code of Mississippi*, 510–42; and Sharkey, Harris, and Elliot, *Revised Code of Mississippi*, 234–56. The so-called unwritten and written rules of behavior for free blacks are discussed in R. Davis, *Black Experience*, 46–59; Sydnor, "Free Negro in Mississippi"; and R. Welch, "Family Affair," 56–72. For free blacks working on Mississippi River steamboats, see Buchanan, *Black Life on the Mississippi*, 11, 13, 15, 23–25, 35–36, 66, 69, 70, 182–83, 188.

22. Hogan and Davis, *William Johnson's Natchez*, 12–13. This notion that whites considered a black person's freedom as a gift bestowed for faithful service or due to parental affection is more fully discussed in R. Davis, *Black Experience*, 46–59. But it should also be pointed out that some Natchez blacks were manumitted by owners opposed to slavery in principle rather than as a reward for good conduct or familial affection. See the following manumission document that articulates opposition to slavery as the reason for freeing slaves: Samuel Terrell to Mary Ann, July 10, 1837, Deeds and Mortgage Record Books, ORAC.

23. For more on sexual images of black women in the white mind, see Bynum, *Unruly Women*, 36–37; Clinton, "Southern Dishonor," 52–68; Fox-Genovese, *Within the Plantation Household*, 292; Jones, *Labor of Love, Labor of Sorrow*, 27; C. Kennedy, *Braided Relations, Entwined Lives*, 111–26; Sommerville, *Rape and Race*, 157–58; and White, *Ar'n't I a Woman?*, 35, 41.

24. Petition of Agnes Earhart, n.d., folder 1850–59, RG 47, vols. 26, 27, Legislative Records, MDAH; Marriage Records, 1835–50, Natchez and Adams County, Miss., ORAC; U.S. Manuscript Census (1850), Natchez, Adams County, Miss., NARA.

25. Death Records, Sexton Reports, 1800–1910, Adams County, Miss., HNF.

26. Will of David Earhart, January 23, 1860, Will Books, ORAC.

27. U.S. Manuscript Census (1850), Natchez, Adams County, Miss., NARA; and Petition of Agnes Earhart, n.d., folder 1850–59, RG 47, vols. 26, 27, Legislative Records, MDAH.

28. David Earhart to Agnes Gordon (aka Earhart, f.w.c.), November 5, 1841, Deeds, Liens, and Mortgage Record Books, ORAC.

29. E. Moore, *Natchez Under-the-Hill*, 53–60.

30. James Hoggatt, for James Bosley, "claiming a slave," April 28, 1795, Book E, Spanish Records, ORAC; and Jacob Earhart to Cassandra Bosley (a slave), August 11, 1803, Deeds, Liens, and Mortgage Record Books, ORAC.

31. Elizabeth Earhart to Isaac House, July 12, 1808, Deeds and Mortgage Record Books, ORAC.

32. Jacob and Cassandra Earhart to Walter Irwin, July 1, 1809, Deeds and Mortgage Record Books, ORAC.

33. Jacob Earhart and wife Cassandra to James J. Rowan, Trustee for David Earhart, et al., Deed of Trust, September 6, 1824, Deeds, Liens, and Mortgage Record Books, ORAC.

34. Jacob Earhart and wife Cassandra to James J. Rowan, Trustee for David Earhart, et al., September 6, 1824; William Shupan for John and Christiana Zeigline to Cassandra Earhart, March 22, 1836, Deeds, Liens, and Mortgage Record Books; and Marriage Records, 1826–45, ORAC; U.S. Manuscript Census (1820–60), Natchez, Adams County, Miss., NARA; Alford, "Some Manumissions."

35. *Leiper v. Huffman et al.* (1851), 26 Miss. 622, HCEA, MDAH.

36. John R. Wells to Malvina Huffman, February 27, 1834; Malvina J. Hoffman to Alfred Bemiss and Oliver L. Bemiss, April 29, 1841; and Joseph Winscot to Malvina Hoffman, September 27, 1845, Deeds and Mortgage Record Books, ORAC. See also Criminal Justice Docket Books, 1800–1870, Adams County, Miss., HNF; *State v. Malvina J. Matthews (alias Malvina J. Huffman)*, May 26, 1868, CCAC, HNF; and U.S. Manuscript Census (1850, 1860), Natchez, Adams County, Miss., NARA. See also Broussard, "Malvina Matthews."

37. *Leiper v. Huffman et al.* (1851), 26 Miss. 622, HCEA, MDAH. See also E. A. Davis, "William Johnson," 65.

38. See Hogan and Davis, *William Johnson's Natchez*, 33, 70, and 115; and E. A. Davis and Hogan, *Barber of Natchez*, 27–28.

39. Emancipation Papers, Maria, Mary, Martha, and William Parker, December 23, 1843, Deed and Mortgage Record Books, ORAC.

40. U.S. Manuscript Census (1850, 1860), Natchez, Adams County, Miss., NARA. See also Kyle House Files, HNF.

41. Ibid.; D. James, *Antebellum Natchez*, 156–57; and Arnold, "Frederick Stanton."

42. Davis and Hogan, *William Johnson's Natchez*, 345; Deeds of Manumission, March 18, 1819; March 22, 1825; July 24, 1825; September 1826; and June 5, 1827, Deeds, Liens, and

Mortgage Record Books, ORAC; Kyle House Files, HNF; and Will of Christopher H. Kyle, 1827, Will Books, ORAC.

43. R. Davis, *Black Experience*, 46–60; and Jordan, *Tumult and Silence at Second Creek*, 206–10.

44. Hogan and Davis, *William Johnson's Natchez*, 345.

45. Board of Police Minutes, March 1832, August 1838, January 1839, and September 1841, Adams County, HNF and MDAH.

46. Hogan and Davis, *William Johnson's Natchez*, 345.

47. *Thomas Smith v. Woodson Wren*, 1821, CCAC, HNF.

48. Hogan and Davis, *William Johnson's Natchez*, 345, 453.

49. Death Records, Sexton Reports, 1820–1910, Adams County, Miss., HNF. It is important to note that the Natchez cemetery's all-black burial section was more a product of the city's postwar era of Jim Crow segregation than its antebellum racial environment.

50. *State v. Eliza Cotton alias Eliza Holden, alias Eliza Bossack*, August 1, October 10, 1841; and March 9, 1842, CCAC, HNF.

51. Eliza Cotton, Board of Police Minutes, June 1832, Adams County, Miss.; and *State v. John Holden*, May Term, 1832, Justice Court Docket Books, Adams County, Miss., HNF.

52. Account Journal—Rent Book, April 1841–68, Pullen-Carson Family Papers, MDAH; and U.S. Manuscript Census (1840, 1850), Natchez, Adams County, Miss., NARA.

53. Eliza Bossack, September 6, 1841, Board of Police Minutes, Adams County, Miss., HNF; *Eliza Bossack v. Henry S. Conner*, December 1, 1841, CCAC, HNF; and *State v. Eliza Bossack, a free negro*, October 1, 1841, CCAC, HNF.

54. Probate of William Cotton, November 27, 1843, Probate Box 94, ORAC.

55. Ibid. For information on Ballard, see Tadman, *Speculators and Slaves*, 89.

56. Death Records, Sexton Reports, 1820–1910, Adams County, Miss., HNF; and *State v. Elizabeth Smith and Eliza Cotton*, July 19, 1867, CCAC, HNF.

57. R. Davis, *Black Experience*, 46–59; Hogan and Davis, *William Johnson's Natchez*, ix–xxv, 1–64, 115, 468; Pletcher, "In between Two Worlds," 1–29; Pletcher, "Horrors of the Inquisition," 1–30; Nomelli, "Jim Crow, Louis J. Winston"; and R. Welch, "Family Affair," 36–72.

58. Shulman, "Bingamans of Natchez"; Hogan and Davis, *William Johnson's Natchez*, 597; and Gould, *Chained to the Rock of Adversity*, 36.

59. See Hodes, *White Women, Black Men*, 1–125; C. Kennedy, *Braided Relations, Entwined Lives*, 111–26; and Stevenson, *Life in Black and White*, 159–330.

60. For the Barland family, see R. Davis, *Black Experience*, 53; Hogan and Davis, *William Johnson's Natchez*, 334, 514; Pletcher, "In between Two Worlds," 1–29; and R. Welch, "Family Affair," 25–27.

61. Hogan and Davis, *William Johnson's Natchez*, 262–72.

62. *Natchez Courier*, June 2, 1858. This view is elaborated on in R. Davis, *Black Experience*, 53–59.

63. On free blacks obtaining and profiting from the support of white men, see chapter 6 of this book; Broussard, "Female Solitaires," 226–55, 474–80; and K. Welch, "Black Litigiousness and White Accountability," 374–79.

64. Hogan and Davis, *William Johnson's Natchez*, 15, 18–19, 44–45, 71, 76, 86, 89, 90, 102, 175, 183, 187, 189, 203, 211, 354, 641–42. See also *Amy Johnston, f.w.c. v. Arthur Mitchum, f.m.c.*, April 19, 1819; and *State v. Arthur Mitchum, f.m.c.*, May 25, 1819, CCAC, HNF.

65. For examples of municipal officials disciplining the enslaved, see R. Davis, *Black Experience*, 86–109.

CHAPTER SIX. STEPPING LIVELY AT THE EDGE

1. See *State v. Hiram Simmons and Sally Clarke*, November 7, 1822, CCAC, HNF; and Death Records, Sexton Reports, Adams County, Miss., 1800–1920, HNF.

2. *State v. James Way and Elizabeth Claravagal*, April 5, 1821, CCAC, HNF; Criminal Justice Docket Books, 1821, CCAC, HNF; and Sharkey et al, Harris, and Elliot, *Revised Code of Mississippi*, 573–74.

3. *Alexander H. Pettits v. Lydia Pettits*, 1834, CCAC, HNF. See also Natchez Criminal Justice Docket Books, 1830–60, and State Justice Docket Books, 1830–60, Adams County, Miss., HNF. For laws defining vagrancy and punishing vagrants, see Sharkey, Harris, and Elliot, *Revised Code of Mississippi*, 628–29.

4. *State of Mississippi v. Elizabeth Payne*, December 24, 1840, CCAC, HNF; Petition of Elizabeth Stansel (alias Elizabeth Payne), January 22, 1841; and Petition of Mississippi Residents to Governor Alexander G. McNutt, January 1841, Legislative Records, RG 47, vol. 1, MDAH. For more on Governor McNutt's political ambitions, see May, *John A. Quitman*, 119–20.

5. *John Tretwell v. Catherine Johnson*, January 10, 1859; and *State v. Catherine Johnson*, April 1, May 1, 1857, CCAC, HNF. For other sources on Tuomey and Johnson in various public records, see Criminal Justice Docket Books, 1830–63, 1865–80, Adams County, Miss.; *Elila Tuomey v. John Tuomey*, 1835; *John Tuomey v. Bridget Tuomey*, 1838; and State Justice Dockets, 1830–63, 1866–80, Adams County, Miss., HNF. See also Marriage Records, 1835–50, Adams County, Miss.; and Will of Catherine Johnson, October 23, 1865, Will Books, ORAC; and U.S. Manuscript Census (1850, 1860), Natchez, Adams County, Miss., NARA. The descendants of the free-black barber William Johnson began using the name Johnston in local deed and mortgage records, tax records, wills, and family correspondence during the 1870s, and in some cases even earlier. The free-black Catherine Johnson (Johnston) also began signing her name as Katherine, perhaps to distance herself from the white Catherine Johnson. See Gould, *Chained to the Rock of Adversity*, 42–66.

6. Unless otherwise indicated, information on the criminal women used in this study comes from an array of manuscript and original arrest ledgers and court records housed at the Historic Natchez Foundation. These sources, which are hereafter cited as Natchez Criminal Records, include Board of Police Minutes, Adams County, 1820–63; Circuit Court Minutes and Criminal Justice Dockets, Adams County, 1820–63; City Council (Selectmen) Minutes for Natchez, 1818–63; Criminal Judgment Dockets, Superior Court, Adams County, 1810–33; Jail Dockets for Natchez and Adams County, 1859–63; Justice Court Minutes for Adams County, 1851–61; Magistrate Criminal Dockets, 1808–38; Record of Judgment Books for Adams County, 1800–63; and State Justice Dockets for Adams County, 1830–63, 1866–80.

7. *Melissa Ayles v. Peter Southworth*, May 13, 1822, CCAC, HNF. For white and black sexual activities, see chapter 5. State laws on fornication also forbade adultery between unmarried or married couples, but actions for violation of adultery ordinances almost never show up in arrest or jail dockets. Typically, adultery came before the court in suits for divorce, and in those cases no criminal offenses were ever lodged against anyone. For more on adultery in divorce, see chapter 3.

8. *Territory v. Francis Surget*, October 1808, CCAC, HNF. Regarding the alleged rape of Mary Ellis by Frances Surget, the records do not provide any detail about the alleged assault, nor do they clearly identify which Frances Surget was the alleged male, Frances Sr. or Frances Jr. For more on the Ellis and Surget families, see Butler, *Unhurried Years*, 1–16; and W. Scarborough, *Masters of the Big House*, 12–13, 23, 100, 153, 180–84.

9. See Magistrate Criminal Dockets, 1820–25, Natchez, HNF.

10. For the "Inquisition" and its impact on Natchez, see R. Davis, *Black Experience*, 84, 96, 97, 104; and D. James, *Antebellum Natchez*, 163–78.

11. See Broussard, "Female Solitaires," 474–80.

12. *Natchez Cutter*, April 2, 1841.

13. Bynum, *Unruly Women*, 88–110.

14. Beard, "Frontier Port on the Mississippi"; Beard, "Natchez Under-the-Hill"; W. Davis, *Way through the Wilderness*, 242–57; D. James, *Antebellum Natchez*, 254–73; Kibler, "Natchez Landing"; Marshall and Evans, *They Found It in Natchez*, 98–116; Ingraham, *The South West*, 52–61; Matthias, "Natchez Under-the-Hill"; E. Moore, *Natchez Under-the Hill*, 38–43; and May, *John A. Quitman*, 67–69. Regarding the interplay in other nineteenth-century cities between public spaces, community tolerance of vice, demographics, law, and prostitution, see Shumsky and Stringer, "San Francisco's Zone of Prostitution."

15. For Natchez and Adams County's peacekeeping apparatus, see *Code of the Ordinances of the City of Natchez*, 15–19, 72, 94, 98, 109–12, 124–32, 149–54, 183; and Sharkey, Harris, and Elliot, *Revised Code of Mississippi*, 120–26, 134, 629–31.

16. For members of the Natchez patrol, see Minutes, Natchez Board of Selectmen, 1818–63, HNF; and Mayor's Office, Natchez, Mississippi.

17. *Natchez Democrat*, May 30, 1868; *State v. Malvina (alias Lavina or Lavinia) J. Matthews*, transcript, 1868–69, CCAC, HNF. The manuscript proceedings for this case include testimony, military orders, assorted communications, and relevant miscellaneous documents. See also the correspondence between the commander of the Natchez Post and military personnel at the headquarters of the Fourth Military District of Mississippi in Vicksburg, most notably Col. N. A. M. Dudley to Bvt. Maj. Gen. John Tyler, acting adjutant general, Fourth Military District of Mississippi, May 30, June 9, October 20, and November 6, 1868, U.S. Army Continental Commands, Letters Sent, Post Natchez, RG 393, NARA; and Death Records, Sexton Reports, Adams County, Mississippi, HNF.

18. Will of Eliza Perry, September 24, 1833, Will Books, ORAC. Perry may have operated a brothel in Louisville, Kentucky, prior to moving to New Orleans. See U.S. Manuscript Census (1830), Louisville, Jefferson County, Ky., NARA. See also Dudley to Tyler, June 9, 1868, in which the Natchez military commandant describes Matthews as a "notorious prostitute of thirty-five years standing" (U.S. Army Continental Commands, Letters Sent, Post Natchez, RG 393, NARA); and Death Records, Sexton Reports, Adams County,

Miss., HNF. The Lavinia Mitchell alias that Matthews sometimes used, as indicated in the sexton notes reporting her death, remains a mystery because there is no record of her having been related to or married to anyone by that name. Register of Baptisms and Sacramental Records, January 20, 1869, SMA.

19. For discussion of New Orleans' interracial sexual reputation, see Long, *Great Southern Babylon*, 6–20; J. Martin, "*Plaçage* and the Louisiana *Gens de Couleur Libre*"; and Spear, *Race, Sex, and Social Order*. For antebellum Natchez's reputation for sexual vices, see Beard, "Frontier Port on the Mississippi"; Herring, "Natchez, 1795–1830," 102–38, 276–314; Kellar, "Journey through the South in 1836"; and Shulman, "Bingamans of Natchez."

20. The following deeds are cited in their order of appearance in the records: John R. Wells to Melvina Jane Huffman, February 27, 1834; Joseph Winscot to Malvina J. Huffman, September 27, 1845; Malvina J. Huffman to Edward J. Matthews, May 10, 1852; Edward J. Matthews to John Liddell, James Hardie, and G. Malin Davis, January 19, 1854; Edward J. Matthews and Wife Malvina J. Matthews to Joseph Buntura, August 12, 1857; and Edward J. Matthews to Malvina J. Matthews, December 24, 1868, Deed and Mortgage Record Books, ORAC. Matthews's property is described by Colonel Dudley in his correspondence about the case: Dudley to Tyler, May 30, 1868, U.S. Army Continental Commands, Letters Sent, Post Natchez, RG 393, NARA.

21. Hogan and Davis, *William Johnson's Natchez*, 12–13. See also Buchanan, *Black Life on the Mississippi*, 145–46.

22. Ordinance to Suppress Disorderly Houses, February 8, 1843; and Ordinance for the Preservation of Good Order and Morality within the City of Natchez, January 17, 1866, Municipal Ordinance Books, HNF. In the 1843 ordinance, the law focused on "dance houses" in which immoral conduct occurred. No mention was made of bawdy houses or prostitution. Matthews's house never met the specific description of a disorderly house as defined by the law. See D. James, *Antebellum Natchez*, 260, for a brief but misleading comment on municipal efforts to limit prostitution to Under-the-Hill Natchez. On New Orleans prostitution, see Schafer, *Brothels, Depravity, and Abandoned Women*, 1–30, 40–137, 145–59, 180.

23. See Broussard, "Stepping Lively in Place," 29–30; and Hogan and Davis, *William Johnson's Natchez*, 345.

24. *Elizabeth Ducay v. William Ducay*, Divorce, January 14, 1839, CHCAC, HNF.

25. *State v. Lavinia Mitchell* (alias Malvina Huffman), November 1, 1841, CCAC, HNF.

26. Malvina J. Hoffman to Alfred Bemiss, Deed of Trust, April 29, 1841, Deed and Mortgage Record Books, ORAC.

27. For discussion of the legal meaning of the terms *feme sole* and *feme covert*, see Blackstone, *Commentaries on the Laws of England*, 430; Broussard, "Naked before the Law," 64–65; and Wulf, *Not All Wives*, 3–5.

28. *Walter J. Sexton v. Malvina J. Huffman*, February 23, 1841; *Robert Stewart v. Malvina Hoffman (alias Malvina Mitchell)*, May 14, 1841; *Charles F. Thomas and wife Cecelia v. Malvina J. Matthews*, Mortgage, March 30, 1857; *Malvina J. Matthews v. Benjamin F. Womack*, September 29, 1858; *Edward J. Matthews and wife Malvina J. Matthews v. Amasa Davis et al.*, April 23, 1859, CCAC, HNF; Malvina J. Hoffman to Charles Reynolds,

Mortgage, May 7, 1841; Amasa Davis and wife Ann E. Davis to Malvina J. Matthews, Mortgage, April 6, 1857; Edward J. Matthews and wife Malvina J. Matthews to Joseph Buntura, Deed, August 12, 1857; Joseph Buntura and wife Frances Buntura to Edward J. Matthews, Deed, January 14, 1858; Stephen and Jane Ellis to Edward J. Matthews, Mortgage, March 5, 1858; and Edward J. Matthews and wife Malvina J. Matthews to Martha B. Benbrook, Deed, January 4, 1860, Deed and Mortgage Record Books, ORAC.

29. See *Edward J. Matthews and wife Malvina J. Matthews v. Amasa Davis and Anne E. Davis*, April 23, 1859, CCAC, HNF.

30. William H. Simmons and wife Mary with Melvina J. Huffman, Agreement, May 8, 1852, Deed and Mortgage Record Books, ORAC.

31. *Malvina J. Matthews v. Edwin [sic] J. Matthews*, Divorce, January 6, 1860, CHCAC, HNF.

32. For divorce in antebellum Natchez, see chapter 3 of this book and Broussard, "Naked before the Law."

33. *Matthews v. Matthews*, Divorce, January 6, 1860, CHCAC, HNF.

34. *Matthews v. Matthews*, Divorce, September 17, 1866, CHCAC, HNF; and Edward J. Matthews to Malvina J. Matthews, Deed, December 24, 1868; William T. Martin and wife to M. J. Matthews, Deed, December 24, 1868; and Malvina J. Matthews to James Orr and Joshua Curtain, Mortgage, December 25, 1868, Deed and Mortgage Record Books, ORAC. Edward and Malvina's story did not end with their divorce. Edward held legal title to Malvina's residence on the bluffs even as she continued to live there after their divorce. When Malvina went on trial for the murder of Private Moffatt in 1868, Edward deeded his share of the house and property to Malvina, which she then mortgaged to James Orr and Joshua Curtain as collateral for her bail.

35. For more on Matthews's murder trial in the context of Reconstruction-era Natchez, see Broussard, "Malvina Matthews."

36. Will of Catherine Johnson, October 23, 1868, Will Books, ORAC. For John B. Nevitt's prominence in antebellum Natchez, see D. James, *Antebellum Natchez*, 131, 171–74, 219, 243, 284.

37. Gleeson, *Irish in the South*, 166; and Vaughan, "Natchez during the Civil War," 302.

38. *Natchez Cutter*, April 5, 1841.

39. *Natchez Cutter*, April 6, 1841.

CHAPTER SEVEN. STEPPING THROUGH THE TUMULT

1. In the ensuing trial, handled in the Adams County Circuit Court rather than before a military commission, Leonard pleaded self-defense. When Private Carr mysteriously disappeared in a military transfer to Tennessee, the Adams County district attorney had no choice but to continue the case until the witness could be produced, which never happened. *State vs. Charles Leonard*, January 29, 1868, CCAC, HNF; see also *Natchez Democrat*, May 25, June 1, 1867; January 6, 30, 1868. The case is also discussed in Broussard, "Malvina Matthews," 33–34.

2. On prostitution in Natchez during the war, see William Burnet, assistant special agent, to William Mellen, supervising special agent, March 12, 1864, Letters Sent,

Records of Civil War Special Agencies of the Treasury Department, Records of Field Offices, RG 366, NARA; *Natchez Courier*, September 29, 1863; February 19, 1864; Frankel, *Freedom's Women*, 39–40; and Smithers, "Profit and Corruption," 21–22. The three soldiers caught up in the McCrudden killing were among fewer than one hundred Union troops remaining in Natchez during the summer of 1867, and all black federal soldiers stationed in Mississippi had been mustered out a year earlier. Many of the mustered-out black veterans continued to wear their uniforms on the streets of Natchez, and they could be called up by the state government for emergency service as a black militia force at any time. See Harris, *Presidential Reconstruction in Mississippi*, 37–141, 228–46; Slay, "New Masters on the Mississippi"; and Wharton, *Negro in Mississippi*, 138–56.

3. Brig. Gen. Thomas E. G. Ransom to Lt. Col. W. T. Clark, July 13, 1863, *War of the Rebellion* (hereafter cited as *OR*), ser. 1, vol. 24, pt. 2, pp. 681–83. See also Bigelow, "Freedmen of the Mississippi Valley"; Berlin et al., *Wartime Genesis of Free Labor*, 611–50; R. Davis, *Black Experience*, 129–57; J. Eaton, *Grant, Lincoln and the Freedmen*, 1–29, 142–66; Frankel, *Freedom's Women*, 28–55; and Yeatman, *Report on the Condition of the Freedmen*, 1–16.

4. R. Davis, *Black Experience*, 140–57; and Frankel, *Freedom's Women*, 39–40.

5. Mollie Matthews appears in Natchez death records as a thirty-five-year-old black woman who died of syphilis in 1895; it is likely that the sexton records mistakenly noted her age as thirty-five instead of fifty-five. Death Records, Sexton Reports, Natchez, 1800–1920, HNF.

6. Information on the experience of the Dunbar women during the war principally comes from Martha Dunbar Claiborne's testimony in support of her claim for compensation as a Unionist for properties taken by Union soldiers from her family. Martha W. Dunbar, Claim No. 57481, March 1880, Allowed Claims, SCC, NARA. For the Dunbar family genealogies, see Daniel S. Farrar Jr. and Family Papers and Ellen Shields, "Genealogical Memoir of Ellen Shields," 1903, MDAH; and Murray, *My Mother Used to Say*, 186–91.

7. John F. H. Claiborne believed that his wife, in-laws, and children would be safer at Dunbarton then with him on the Mississippi coast, in view of his known Union sympathies and suspected collaboration with the Yankees. He had served until 1862 as a U.S. government official in charge of federal timber lands in the Mississippi Delta. For more on his Civil War activities, see Lang, "J. F. H. Claiborne at 'Laurel Hill' Plantation"; and Cain, "Letter from J. F. H. Claiborne."

8. Testimony of Mary Washington, Dunbar Claim No. 57481, SCC, NARA. For guerilla warfare in the "no-man's land" adjacent to Union-controlled areas, see Ash, *When the Yankees Came*, 76–107; and Whites and Long, *Occupied Women*, 5–6.

9. Testimony of John F. H. Claiborne and Martha Claiborne, Dunbar Claim No. 57481, SCC, NARA.

10. Testimonies of Oliver Jackson and George Washington, ibid.

11. Testimony of John F. H. Claiborne, ibid.

12. Testimonies of Martha Dunbar Claiborne, Oliver Jackson, and Harrison Lucky, ibid.

13. Testimonies of Martha Dunbar Claiborne, Matilda B. Dunbar, Nancy Farrar, and Mary Washington, ibid.

14. For more on the alleged insurrection of 1861 and its brutal suppression by a special Natchez vigilance group, see the pathbreaking study Jordan, *Tumult and Silence at Second Creek*; Behrend, "Rebellious Talk and Conspiratorial Plots"; Haviland, *Woman's Life-Work*, 251–55; Kaye, *Joining Places*, 183–86; and Sydnor, *Gentleman of the Old Natchez Region*, 295–97. Jordan mistakenly identifies several Dunbarton slaves among those hanged. In fact, the executed slaves belonged to a separate Dunbar family unrelated to Martha and her family. The Dunbar family mistakenly identified by Jordan (headed by Mary Dunbar) lived on the nearby Forest plantation. It is likely, however, that Martha's slaves personally knew the executed slaves because Martha often hosted social occasions for her enslaved workers that included neighborhood slaves. And certainly the Dunbarton women and their black and white neighbors knew about the alleged insurrection and the threat it posed to them as unprotected women once the Yankees occupied Natchez.

15. Information about the Yankee attack on the Shields family home is taken from Ellen Shields, "Genealogical Memoir of Ellen Shields," 1903, photocopy provided by Katherine Blakenstein of Natchez and also archived at MDAH; and the report of 1st.Lt. I. N. Earl to Lt. R. F. Smith, August 30, 1864, *OR*, ser. 1, vol. 39, pp. 350–52.

The Shields family, headed by the patriarch Gabriel Shields, owned extensive lands and numerous slaves in Adams County, Mississippi, and Concordia Parish, Louisiana, prior to 1860, including 444 slaves when Mississippi seceded from the United States. Gabriel was closely tied through marriage to two of the wealthiest planters in the area, Alfred V. Davis and Francis Surget Jr., who owned 651 and 456 slaves, respectively. Davis and Shields had married the sisters of Francis Surget, one of the five largest slaveholders in the lower South during the 1850s. The Shieldses, Davises, and Surgets were part of a group of approximately forty slaveholding families in the area known collectively as "nabobs" because of their immense wealth. For more on Shields's status among the South's wealthiest planters, see W. Scarborough, *Masters of the Big House*, 12, 20, 100, 260. For more on the elite Natchez-area slaveholders, see R. Davis, *Good and Faithful Labor*, 24–57; D. James, *Antebellum Natchez*, 136–61; and Wayne, *Reshaping of Plantation Society*, 5–30.

16. For Earl's role as a Union scout and special agent, see Culver, "Brevet Major Isaac N. Earl."

17. Telling Shields that he was exposing his family to unspeakable atrocities at the hands of the furious Yankee scouts, Rivers arranged surrender terms. See "Genealogical Memoir of Ellen Shields," MDAH.

The versions of the raid reported in military records and in a memoir written years later by one of the Union scouts in the raiding party play down the strong-arm tactics used in capturing Shields, emphasizing instead the old man's probable collaboration with rebels in the area. Culver, "Brevet Major Isaac N. Earl," 323, 362–63; Earl to Smith, August 30, 1864, *OR*, ser. 1, vol. 39, pp. 350–52; and M. Martin, *History of the 4th Wisconsin Infantry*, 373–91.

18. The summer of 1864 witnessed an increasing crackdown on Natchez residents by

the army with the arrival of a new post commander, Brig. Gen. Mason Brayman, who replaced several notably lax if not corrupt commanders. As a result, Natchez jails filled up with assorted misfits and unruly characters during the summer of 1864. See Maj. Gen. N. J. T. Dana to Maj. C. T. Christensen, July 20, 1864, *OR*, ser. 1, vol. 39, pp. 186–93; and Col. B. G. Farrar to Capt. J. H. Odlin, July 20, 1864, *OR*, ser. 1, vol. 39, pp. 196–97.

19. Quote from "Genealogical Memoir of Ellen Shields," MDAH. On the black soldiers stationed in Vidalia, Louisiana, see Maj. Gen. N. J. T. Dana to Brig. Gen. Mason Brayman, July 19, 1964, *OR*, ser. 1, vol. 39, pp. 194–95.

20. In their search of Montebello, Earl turned up a few weapons, two hundred rounds of cartridges, and molds for making bullets and Minnie balls. See Earl to Smith, August 30, 1864, *OR*, ser. 1, vol. 39, pp. 350–52.

21. Caroline C. Lovell authored a vivid description of the ruins of Montebello sometime after it was abandoned, probably in the 1890s. Lovell describes the place as "a ruin so beautiful, I catch my breath." She also tells of the still standing "twenty-four creamy pink columns, with Doric capitals, sun-flocked and garlanded with vines." See Lowell, "Natchez Notes," Quitman Family Papers, Southern Historical Collection, University of North Carolina at Chapel Hill (hereafter UNC-CH); and Estes, *Legends of the Natchez City Cemetery*, 86–87; see also Broussard, "Occupied Natchez," 201–5; and Cook, "Practical Ladies of Occupied Natchez," 128–29.

22. The principal source for Jane Dent is her compensation claim as a Unionist during the war for property taken by the Union army in Natchez: Jane Dent, Claim No. 6616, SCC, NARA.

23. Testimony of Charles Smith, ibid.

24. The sources are unclear about what happened to Jane's husband. No witness testified to seeing Thomas Dent during the war, and several said that he had died during or shortly after the war; Jane claimed in her testimony supporting her claim to compensation that her terrified "husband went deranged on account of the war." Ibid.

25. Testimonies of Jane Dent, Robert W. Fitzhugh, John Pryer, and J. J. Maine, ibid.

26. R. Davis, *Black Experience*, 129–47.

27. Dent Claim No. 6616, SCC, NARA.

28. Ibid. See also Joseph B. Stratton Diary, March 9, 1900, Joseph B. Stratton Papers, LSU.

29. In the national election for president in 1860, Adams County voted nearly two to one for the Unionist candidates Stephen Douglas (158) and John Bell (448) over the secessionist John C. Breckinridge (376). When the state convention on secession was called on January 7, 1861, Adams County sent two prominent Unionists, Josiah Winchester and Alex K. Farrar, as delegates. Natchez Unionists tended to be wealthy former Whigs who feared, among other things, that a southern Confederate state would resort to income taxes as opposed to tariffs to raise revenue. *Natchez Courier*, September 19, 1860; January 4, 1861; *Natchez Free Trader*, November 12, December 24, 1860; Rainwater, "Analysis of the Secession Controversy"; William Banks Taylor, "Southern Yankees"; and Vaughan, "Natchez during the Civil War," 24–35.

30. Scholarship on the Civil War in Mississippi and the Natchez District includes

Bearss, *Decision in Mississippi*; Behrend, "Freedpeople's Democracy"; Bettersworth, *Confederate Mississippi*; Cook, "Practical Ladies of Occupied Natchez"; R. Davis, *Black Experience*, 125–57; R. Davis, *Good and Faithful Labor*, 58–89; Greenberg, "Civil War and the Redistribution of Land"; Jordan, *Tumult and Silence at Second Creek*; Wilcox, "War Times in Natchez"; and Vaughan, "Natchez during the Civil War."

Among the most important works on the impact of the Civil War on southern women are E. Campbell and Rice, *Woman's War*; Clinton, *Battle Scars*; Clinton and Silber, *Divided Houses*; Edwards, *Scarlett Doesn't Live Here Anymore*; Faust, *Mothers of Invention*, 30–65; Rable, *Civil Wars*; Roberts, *Confederate Belle*; W. Scarborough, *Masters of the Big House*, 90–121; Whites, *Civil War as a Crisis in Gender*; Whites and Long, *Occupied Women*; and Wood, *Masterful Women*, 159–91.

31. At the start of the Civil War, Natchez served as the official staging point for all volunteer companies in southwestern Mississippi. *Natchez Free Trader*, September 8, 1860.

32. Mary McMurran to Mr. & Mrs. George Austen, Addison Papers, Natchez National Historic Park, Natchez, Mississippi (NNHP). For the Natchez Fencibles, see Gates, "Ornament of the City"; Dresser, "Kate and John Minor," 198; and Vaughan, "Natchez during the Civil War," 189–216.

33. B. L. C. Wailes Diary, August 24, 1861, B. L. C. Wailes Papers, 1762–1862, MDAH; Deen, *Annie Harper's Journal*, 9–11, 20–21; and Peltier, "Confederate Natchez," 19–27, 78–82.

34. *Natchez Courier*, January 17, 1863; and Joseph B. Stratton Diary, December 12, 1861, Stratton Papers, LSU.

35. John Sanderson Foster to Kate Foster, November 29, 1861, Isaac G. and John S. Foster Papers, 1861–66, LSU.

36. *Natchez Courier*, June 11, 1863.

37. Elizabeth Christie Brown Diary, February 27, 1863, Department of Archives and Special Collections, J. D. Williams Library, University of Mississippi, Oxford.

38. Charlotte "Carlie" Mandeville lived, as discussed in chapter 2, with her upper-class planter-banker grandfather and two aunts, Rebecca and Josephine, in Natchez following the demise of her mother when she was a young girl. The two aunts raised Carlie like their own daughter. Carlie (Charlotte) Mandeville to Rebecca Mandeville, May 19, 1861; April 14, 1864; August 18, September 19, 1865; Henry S. Mandeville to George Rozet, February 12, March 17, 1863; and Jose Rozet to Rebecca Mandeville, January 25, 31, March 8, 25, 1862; August 22, 1865, MFP, LSU. See also Tripp, "Affair of the Heart."

39. Elizabeth Christie Brown Diary, January 21, 22, 30, February 19, and March 14, 1863, Department of Archives and Special Collections, J. D. Williams Library, University of Mississippi, Oxford.

40. At least 240 Natchez-area women were identified as participants in the Military Aid Society. See *Natchez Courier*, September 27, November 13, 27, December 4, 1861; April 5, November 29, 1862; and Wailes Diary, June 10, 1861, Wailes Papers, MDAH.

41. Emily Caroline Douglass manuscript autobiography, 124, 126, Emily Caroline Douglas Papers, 1855–68, 1913, LSU; and Vaughan, "Natchez during the Civil War," 236.

42. Deen, *Annie Harper's Journal*, 11.

43. Ibid, 14. Two free markets operated in Natchez prior to the arrival of Federal troops, one providing food for the needy families of Confederate soldiers and a second to help feed the city's poor who did not qualify for soldiers' benefits, but neither had enough donated food to fully meet the needs of the city's poor and hungry, especially as more sick and wounded soldiers arrived, along with growing numbers of white refugees from the countryside. See Board of Aldermen Minutes, Natchez, March 18, 1863, and Board of Police Minutes for Adams County, Miss., April 6, 1863, HNF; John S. Foster to Dr. James Foster, May 21, 1863, Isaac G. and John S. Foster Papers, LSU; *Natchez Courier*, March 18, April 18, May 9, July 4, 1863; and Joseph B. Stratton Diary, April 19, 1863, Stratton Papers, LSU.

44. Broussard, "Occupied Natchez," 182–87.

45. For the battle of Shiloh and its aftermath at Corinth, Illinois, see Welcher, *Union Army, 1861–1865*, 187–99, 559–65; and Woodworth, *Nothing but Victory*, 225–42.

46. Natchez nurses also ministered in hospitals at Brookhaven and Jackson, Mississippi. *Natchez Courier*, April 8, 9, May, 1, 3, 13, September 16, 18, 1862; and Vaughn, "Natchez during the Civil War," 238–40. Southern white women nursed wounded soldiers inside Confederate lines for the duration of the war, and the physical intimacies in nursing created tensions as elite women mixed not only with the men whom they nursed but also with women from all classes of life. See Faust, Glymph, and Rable, "Women's War," 5; and Schultz, *Woman at the Front*.

47. Vaughn, "Natchez during the Civil War," 245–46.

48. Ibid. The Catholic orphanage increased the number of children in its care by about 10 percent, peaking at one hundred wards prior to the city's conquest by the Yankees. Vaughn, "Natchez during the Civil War," 242–47. Vaughn quotes Catholic Bishop Elder's speech, "The Collection at the Cemetery," given on November 5–11, 1862, as found in Elder's Letter Books, CDJA.

49. See Bynum, *Unruly Women*, 111–29.

50. Deen, *Annie Harper's Journal*, 10.

51. Ibid., entry for May 1, 1863.

52. Biddle, *Reminiscences of a Soldier's Wife*, 11–17; Coussons, "Federal Occupation of Natchez"; R. Davis, *Black Experience*, 125–29; Estes, *Legends of the Natchez City Cemetery*, 146–47; Gresham, *Life of Walter Quintin Gresham*, 239–64; *New York Times*, August 2, 16, 1863, as cited in Garner, *Reconstruction in Mississippi*, 53; and Peltier, "Confederate Natchez," 315.

53. Not all Natchez residents complied. Frank Shields, a member of the wealthy Shields family, complained in a letter to a relative who had fled Natchez that he could not "conceive what would induce anyone to take the oath to the U. S." Frank Shields to Joseph D. Shields Sr., October 2, 1863, Joseph D. Shields Papers, 1802–97, LSU. In general, the military confiscated little real estate in town outright but it did assign officers to live in private residences, take over larger homes and buildings for hospitals and barracks, including the Forks-of-the-Road slave market, and acquire horses, wagons, and lumber for military use.

54. The most notorious incident involving Natchez clergy occurred when Bishop

William Henry Elder refused the Union order for the city's clergy and ministers to offer prayers at Sunday services for Lincoln. He was placed for a time under house arrest in Vidalia, Louisiana. Elder Diary, June 4, 25; July 6, 13, 16, 18, 19, 26, 1864, CDJA; see also the letter from Margarette Martin to William T. Martin, August 26, 1863, quoted in Murray, *Early Romances of Natchez*, 78–79.

55. A friend of Louisa Jenkins complained that Natchez residents were forced to attend a "Yankee ball" thrown by the post commandant or suffer the consequences. Unknown author to Louisa Jenkins, December 11, 1864, John C. Jenkins Family Papers, 1840–1900, LSU.

56. Lt. Col. James B. McPherson to Brig. Gen. Thomas E. G. Ransom, July 17, 1863, *OR*, ser. 1, vol. 24, p. 521. See also Bigelow, "Freedmen of the Mississippi Valley"; and R. Davis, *Good and Faithful Labor*, 59–84.

57. According to historian Kirsten E. Wood, women in many urban areas throughout the South typically evoked traditional ideals of chivalry and feminine dependency conventions to shame and then coax Yankee officers into treating them like ladies. Wood, *Masterful Women*, 176–83. To better understand the complexities of the Union occupation of the South overall, and particularly as a "distinctive experience," especially for women, see Ash, *When the Yankees Came*, 28–31, 38–75. Ash elaborates on the conflict felt by Federal soldiers during the Union occupation of southern states as they tried to uphold a Victorian ethos that protected and respected southern women while also dealing with them as potentially hostile enemies. See also Grimsley, *Hard Hand of War*.

58. Gresham, *Life of Walter Quinton Gresham*, 262–23.

59. Murray quotes Special Order No. 49, issued by General Ransom on July 22, 1863, in *Early Romances of Natchez*, 51–57. This action, coupled with the infamous "Woman Order" issued in New Orleans a year earlier by the Union general Benjamin Butler, stood as a stern warning to the elite women of Natchez. See Hearn, *When the Devil Came Down to Dixie*, 101–9; and Long, "(Mis)Remembering General Order No. 28."

60. Gresham, *Life of Walter Quinton Gresham*, 250. Historian Giselle Roberts adds the important point that much of the flirtation and socializing done by southern women of the upper class with Yankee soldiers masked a profound sense of rage and a desire for retribution that conflicted with their gendered upbringing. See Roberts, *Confederate Belle*, 138–39.

61. Faust, *Mothers of Invention*, 207.

62. Annie Harper married William L. Harper in 1864 and lived thereafter for the duration of the war on a plantation a day's ride from Natchez. Deen, *Annie Harper's Journal*, 20–21. Historian Cita Cook generally agrees with Harper and Faust, documenting persuasively the extent to which some elite Natchez women charmed Yankee soldiers and officers into doing their bidding, even to the point of overlooking the women's smuggling escapades. See Cook, "Practical Ladies of Occupied Natchez," 130; and J. T. Davidson to C. T. Christensen, January 17, 1865, *OR*, ser. 1, vol. 48, p. 562.

63. Historian Michael Fellman quotes Lee on the dangers posed by persuasive Yankees over southern women: "I know the Yankees will get out of them all they know. I hope they know nothing to injure us, but the Yankees have a very coaxing & insidious manner,

that our Southern women in their artlessness cannot resist, no matter how favorable they may be to our cause or how full of good works for our men." See Robert E. Lee to Mary Lee, February 16, 1863, quoted in Fellman, *Making of Robert E. Lee*, 239.

64. *Natchez Daily Courier*, October 9, 1863.

65. John R. Metcalfe to Mary Susan Ker, December 27, 1863; Col. Loren Kent to unknown, June 21, 1864; Col. Loren Kent to Mary Susan Ker, May 25, July 1, October 27, 1864, Mary Susan Ker Papers, UNC-CH.

66. Richard A. Hall to parents, November 26, 1864, Richard Alexander Hall Letters, 1862–67, LSU.

67. Gresham, *Life of Walter Quinton Grisham*, 261–62. For other examples of the many times Natchez women socialized with their Yankee conquerors at military balls, dinner parties, and regimental parades and reviews, see *Natchez Courier*, October 9, 13, 20, 30, 1863; February 14, 1864; January 6, 10, 1865.

68. Isaac Gaillard Foster to Kate Foster, April 17, 1864, Isaac G. and John S. Foster Papers, LSU.

69. Culver, "Brevet Major Isaac N. Earl," 325.

70. *Natchez Courier*, October 27, December 22, 1863.

71. Kate Foster's brother, serving in Georgia with the Natchez Southrons, praised what he called the "spirit of some of the people in and near Natchez" but also wondered if the contraband carried on by "many of the ladies of N[atchez]" benefited them rather than his brothers in arms. Isaac Gaillard Foster to Kate Foster, April 17, 1864, Isaac G. and John S. Foster Papers, LSU.

72. Deen, *Annie Harper's Journal*, 21–23.

73. Marshall and Evans, *They Found It in Natchez*, 170–71. In this story the "charming lady" was the not-married Ruth Britton, the sister of the Natchez banker Audley Britton, in town visiting from New York when the war broke out.

74. Kate D. Foster Diary, September 20, 1863, Perkins Library, Duke University.

75. Ibid., August 16, 1863.

76. Ibid., July 17, 24, 25, 1863; November 26, 1865.

77. Cook, "Practical Ladies of Occupied Natchez," 128–30; Maj. Gen. N. J. T. Dana, special inspector, to Maj. C. T. Christensen, assistant adjutant general, Military Division of West Mississippi, July 20, 1864, *OR*, ser. 1, vol. 39, pp. 186–93; and B. G. Farrar, colonel, Commanding Natchez Post, to Capt. J. H. Odlin, assistant adjutant general, July 20, 1864, *OR*, ser. 1, vol. 39, pp. 196–97.

78. Brig. Gen. Mason Brayman to Lt. Col. H. C. Rodgers, August 20, 1864; Brayman to Christensen, August 20, 1864, General Records of the Department of the Treasury, Natchez, Adams County, Mississippi, RG 576, NARA.

79. Cook, "Practical Ladies of Occupied Natchez," 128; and Deen, *Annie Harper's Journal*, 21.

80. William Burnet to Garrett Davis, *Natchez Daily Courier*, March 26, 1866; and Special Orders No. 126, November 24, 1864, Brig. Gen. Mason Brayman, pt. 2, 293, U.S. Army Continental Commands, RG 393, NARA.

81. For more on Brayman's career and subsequent removal from command in Natchez,

see Smithers, "Profit and Corruption"; William Burnett, assistant special agent, Treasury Department, to William Mellon, supervising special agent, Treasury Department, March 12, 1864, RG 366, NARA; and charges filed against Brayman by Colonel Bernard G. Farrar, "Charges and Specifications Against Brayman," September 13 and November 7, 1864, Bailhache-Brayman Papers, Chicago Historical Society.

82. J. T. Davidson to C. T. Christensen, January 17, 1865, *OR*, ser. 1, vol. 48, p. 562. See also Cook, "Practical Ladies of Occupied Natchez," 130.

83. The transformation of enslaved households into free-labor households throughout much of the Confederate South is best described in Glymph, *Out of the House of Bondage*.

84. As quoted in Marshall and Evans, *They Found It in Natchez*, 169–70.

85. Kate Foster Diary, July 30, November 15, 1863, Perkins Library, Duke University.

86. Ibid., March 12, 1868.

87. Deen, *Annie Harper's Journal*, 31.

88. Kate Foster Diary, July 25, 1863, Perkins Library, Duke University. For insight into the southern slaveholding male as a gentleman patriarch, see William R. Taylor, *Cavalier and Yankee*.

89. This rationalization for the South's defeat would emerge fully in the so-called Lost Cause memorialization efforts that swept over the former Confederacy in the 1890s. On the Lost Cause, see especially Foster, *Ghosts of the Confederacy*.

90. Louisa Russell Conner Memoirs, n.d., MDAH.

91. "Genealogical Memoir of Ellen Shields," 35–40, MDAH.

92. The Natchez Nabob and antebellum lawyer William Martin, who opposed secession but organized a company of wealthy Natchez volunteers and went on to become a distinguished Confederate general, recalled in testimony given after the war the energized efforts of white militia groups to control Natchez-area slaves. See Testimony of William T. Martin, December 12, 1877, Katherine S. Minor, Claim No. 78960 SCC, NARA; and Louisa Lovell to Joseph Lovell, September 21, 1861, Quitman Family Papers, UNC-CH.

93. This slave insurrection (or the hysteria associated with it) is most fully discussed in Behrend, "Rebellious Talk and Conspiratorial Plots"; Haviland, *Woman's Life-Work*, 251–55; Jordan, *Tumult and Silence at Second Creek*, 1–261; Kaye, *Joining Places*, 183–86; and Sydnor, *Gentleman of the Old Natchez Region*, 295–306.

94. For scholarship on enslaved refugees in Mississippi during the Civil War, see Berlin et al., *Wartime Genesis of Free Labor*, 77–80; R. Davis, *Black Experience*, 125–58; and Frankel, *Freedom's Women*, 15–55. For the larger South, see Faust, *Mothers of Invention*, 60–61; Glymph, *Out of the House of Bondage*, 97–38; Massey, *Refugee Life in the Confederacy*; Rable, *Civil Wars*, 116–20; Schwalm, "Between Slavery and Freedom"; and Whites, *Civil War as a Crisis in Gender*, 6–9.

95. Brig. Gen. Thomas E. G. Ransom to Lt. Col. W. T. Clark, assistant adjutant general, 17th Army Corps, July 13, 1863, *OR*, ser. 1, vol. 24, pt. 2, pp. 681–83. See also Joseph B. Stratton Diary, July 16, 1863, Stratton Papers, LSU.

96. Deen, *Annie Harper's Journal*, 31.

97. *Natchez Courier*, September 25, 1863.

98. A. G. Howell to [unknown], February 6, 1864, American Missionary Association Papers, Amistad Research Center, Tulane University, New Orleans (AMA).

99. Emily Caroline Douglas autobiography, 168–70, Emily Caroline Douglas Papers, LSU.

100. Deen, *Annie Harper's Journal*, 30–31.

101. R. Davis, *Black Experience*, 158–59; J. Eaton, *Grant, Lincoln, and the Freedmen*, 1–251; Gresham, *Life of Walter Quintin Gresham*, 256–57; and Yeatman, *Report on the Condition of the Freedmen*, 1–16.

102. R. Davis, *Black Experience*, 161–65; Deen, *Annie Harper's Journal*, 30–2; Elder, *Civil War Diary*, 62–63; Gresham, *Life of Walter Quintin Gresham*, 256–57; and Yeatman, *Report on the Condition of the Freedmen*, 13. For the number of female refugees who died in the freedmen camps in Natchez, see Register of Baptisms, May 9, 1861–December 26, 1865, SMA.

103. Special Order No. 8, October 26, 1863, and Special Order No 15, Order Books for Sixth Regiment, U.S. Colored Heavy Artillery, Records of the Adjutant General's Office, RG 94, NARA.

104. Farrar to Odlin, July 20, 1864, *OR*, ser. 1, vol. 39, pp. 196–97.

105. This order by health officer Kelly is enclosed in a report from Maj. George W. Young, superintendent of freedmen in the District of Natchez, to Gen. Lorenzo Thomas, adjutant general of the U.S. Army, March 31, 1864, Letters Received, Bureau for Colored Troops, Records of the Adjutant General's Office, RG 94, NARA, also cited in Berlin et al., *Wartime Genesis of Free Labor*, 814–15. See also Haviland, *Woman's Life-Work*, 294.

106. The dire circumstances, which bordered on mutiny among the black soldiers and wholesale resistance by the city's female refugees, is revealed in a series of letters that passed back and forth between members of the American Missionary Society in Natchez and their superiors: Mattie W. Childs to Rev. George Whipple, June 20; S. G. Wright to Rev. George Whipple, April 7; and [unidentified correspondent] to Rev. George Whipple, April 7, 1864, AMA.

107. Protest of Missionaries to General Tuttle, April 1, 1864, as cited in Berlin et al., *Wartime Genesis of Free Labor*, 817–18.

108. Farrar to Odlin, July 20, 1864, *OR*, ser. 1, vol. 39, pp. 196–97. Opposition to the health order resulted in a resolution to investigate the order by the U.S. House of Representatives and General Tuttle's resignation as post commander. Berlin et al., *Wartime Genesis of Free Labor*, 819.

109. R. Davis, *Good and Faithful Labor*, 177–78.

110. See Coussons, "Federal Occupation of Natchez," 44, 88; and *Natchez Courier*, September 29, 1863. On February 19, 1864, the city's military health officer called attention to the numerous prostitutes in Natchez when he ordered the "inmates of all houses of ill repute [to] disperse forthwith" or be dealt with in the "most summary manner." *Natchez Courier*, February 19, 1864. In an earlier incident, a white woman, probably a prostitute, was banished beyond Union lines for cohabitating with a black man in open "amalgamation." *Natchez Courier*, September 29, 1863. For more on prostitution during the Civil War in Natchez and Mississippi, see General Order No. 30, Col. Ed D. Townsend,

assistant adjutant general, January 15, 1864, *OR*, ser. 3, vol. 4, pp. 44–45; Frankel, *Freedom's Women*, 39–44; and Yeatman, *Report on the Condition of the Freedmen*, 1–16. For incidents of reported larceny, brawling, drunkenness, and disturbing the peace by black women, see *Natchez Courier*, October 16, 23, 30, 1863; February 7, 28, 1865.

111. General Order No. 30, Col. Ed D. Townsend, assistant adjutant general, January 15, 1864, *OR*, ser. 3, vol. 4, pp. 44–45; Frankel, *Freedom's Women*, 39–44; and Yeatman, *Report on the Condition of the Freedmen*, 1–16.

112. The four spinster daughters of William Johnson (Anna, Alice, Josephine, and Katherine) all carved out careers for themselves after the war in the Natchez public schools. See Gould, *Chained to the Rock of Adversity*, xlvii–xlix, 4, 25; Behrend, "Freedpeople's Democracy," 123–42; Bieber, "Making the Most of Freedom," 92–95; Haviland, *Woman's Life-Work*, 254–56; and James Yeatman to Maj. Gen. O. O. Howard, May 25, 1865, Bureau of Refugees, Freedmen and Abandoned Lands, RG 105, NARA.

113. See Behrend, "Freedpeople's Democracy," 125–26; Bieber, "Making the Most of Freedom," 92–95; Freedman, "African American Schooling," 21; Haviland, *Woman's Life-Work*, 255–56; J. P. Mardwell to M. E. Strieby, January 5, 1865, AMA; Register of Teachers and Pay Certificates, Adams County, Miss., 1873–1900, HNF; Teachers' Monthly Report, Natchez, 1866–77, AMA; Union School and Institute Payroll Ledger, 1874–1905, HNF; and Will of Lilly Ann Gunderson, 1889, Will Books, ORAC.

CHAPTER EIGHT. STEPPING INTO THE BREACH

1. Information on the Foster sisters, their relatives and friends, and their financial and business affairs can be found in the following archival sources and public records: Assessment of Lands in Adams County, Miss., 1866–72, HNF; Death Records, Sexton Reports, 1800–1920, Adams County, Miss., HNF; Foster Genealogy File, HNF; Inventory of Estates, Miss Kate O. Foster, March 25, 1905, CHCAC, ORAC; Kate D. Foster Diary (1863–72), Foster Family Papers, Duke University; James Foster Papers, LSU; U.S. Manuscript Census, (1860, 1870, 1880), Natchez, Adams County, Miss., NARA; Will of James Foster, January 6, 1862, probated in 1882, Probate Records, ORAC; Will of Elizabeth (Lizzy) J. Foster, July 6, 1898, Will Books, ORAC; and Will of Kate O. Foster, July 6, 1898, Will Books, ORAC. For information on the Natchez business community after the Civil War, see *Directory of the City of Natchez*, 24–25; Lowenburg, *Census of Inhabitants*; Power, *The Memento*; and *Natchez Business Directory for 1877–76*. See also the lien contract for leasing Hermitage plantation: Kate Foster with Thomas R. Shields and Freedmen, Lien, August 28, 1868, CCAC, HNF.

2. Kate Foster Diary, February 5, 1872, Foster Family Papers, Duke University.

3. See E. D. Farrar to Kate Foster, March 23, 1874, and rent receipts for February 5, 1880, James Foster Papers, LSU. In 1887, the bankruptcy liquidators appointed to administer the cotton factorage firm of S. D. Stockman and Company successfully sued Kate Foster to recover advances secured by a lien on her cotton crop; her delivered cotton fell short of advances by $665. See *S. D. Stockman v. Kate Foster*, February 22, 1887, Supreme Court of Mississippi, MDAH. It is unclear whether the Foster sisters lived on the city lots they purchased or inherited because there is no mention in Kate's

final estate to that effect. It is likely that these were undeveloped lots without houses or other buildings or perhaps lots with shanty houses rented to blacks. See Inventory of Estates, Miss Kate O. Foster, March 25, 1905, CHCAC, ORAC; Will of Kate O. Foster, July 6, 1898, Will Books, ORAC; and Will of Elizabeth (Lizzy) J. Foster, July 6, 1898, Will Books, ORAC.

4. See J. Floyd King to Lemuel P. Conner Sr., April 15, 1868; and Notice of Bankruptcy, December 4, 1869, Lemuel P. Conner Family Papers, LSU; see also "Lemuel Parker Conner, Sr.," in *Goodspeed's Biographical and Historical Memoirs*, 1:581. For the senior Conner's role in the murder of at least forty enslaved men in the spring and summer of 1861, see Jordan, *Tumult and Silence at Second Creek*, 49, 83–126, 169, 139–47, 238, 265–84. For Conner Jr., see *Goodspeed's Biographical and Historical Memoirs*, 1:583; and the following manuscript letters: George F. Dean to Lemuel P. Conner Jr., April 10, 1909; J. D. Barkdull to William A. Dicksen, April 24, 1909; A. J. McLaurin to L. P. Conner Jr., April 26, 1909; Lemuel P. Conner Jr. to Audley Britton, December 16, 1919; and Lemuel P. Conner Jr. to Gaillard Conner, December 19, 1925, Conner Family Papers, LSU. Conner Jr.'s widowed grandmother, Jane E. B. Conner, seems to have been the force that held the family together, sustaining both her son and grandson with gifts of money and purchasing their foreclosed lands and household furnishings, which she deeded back to her son Lemuel Conner Sr. Jane Conner used her plantation lands as the family's main source of income, leasing them out in sharecropping arrangements and eventually selling off acres in small batches to sustain her extended family. See Jane E. B. Conner to Lemuel P. Conner Sr., October 22, December 22, 1862; January 1, 1863; and December 12, 1883, Conner Family Papers, LSU. On the relationship of Kate Foster and her friend Mary Britton Conner, see Mary B. Conner to Kate Foster, n.d., and Kate Foster to Mary B. Conner, July 23, no year, James Foster Papers, LSU.

5. Kate kept a series of verse notebooks throughout her life in which she copied especially meaningful poems and sayings, many of which spoke of lost love and the sacrifice southern women bore with the death of their loved ones in the Civil War. See Kate Foster Notebook of Verses, 1857–1904, James Foster Papers, LSU; and Kate D. Foster Diary, November 26, 1865; April 8, 1866; December 7, 1871, Foster Family Papers, Duke University.

6. Kate Foster Diary, November 26, 1865, Foster Family Papers, Duke University; and Mary M. Gaillard to Sinah Foster, April 27, 1886, James Foster Papers, LSU.

7. For details on Kate's work with the Confederate Memorial Association of Natchez and the Daughters of the Confederacy, see Confederate Memorial Association Record Books, 1888–89, James Foster Papers, LSU. For more on the Lost Cause in Natchez and Mississippi, see Bercaw, *Gendered Freedoms*, 88; Cook, "Growing Up White, Genteel, and Female," 237–47, 335–37, 370, 393n41; Falck, "Black and White Memory Making," 176–82; and Kubassek, "Ask Us Not to Forget," 161–62.

8. For scholarship on the Lost Cause in the larger South and the conflicting interpretations about what motivated southern women to embrace it, see Brundage, *Southern Past*; Censer, *Reconstruction of White Southern Womanhood*, 191–206; Faust, *Mothers of Invention*, 187–95; Hale, *Making Whiteness*, 84–88; Janney, *Burying the Dead*;

McWhite, "Echoes of the Lost Cause," 181–88; Whites, *Civil War as a Crisis in Gender*, 181–88; and C. Wilson, *Baptized in Blood*.

9. R. Davis, *Black Experience*, 158–83.

10. For the politics of Reconstruction in Natchez and Mississippi, see Behrend, "Freedpeople's Democracy," 165–425; Behrend, *Reconstructing Democracy*; Bond, *Political Culture in the Nineteenth-Century South*, 151–82, 215–51; R. Davis, *Black Experience*, 158–83; Garner, *Reconstruction in Mississippi*; Harris, *Presidential Reconstruction in Mississippi*, 37–251; Harris, *Day of the Carpetbagger*; and Wharton, *Negro in Mississippi*, 138–215. For the larger South, see Woodward, *Origins of the New South*, 321–50.

11. For the postbellum economy of Natchez and Mississippi, see Anderson, *Builders of the New South*; R. Davis, *Good and Faithful Labor*, 121–51; and Wayne, *Reshaping of Plantation Society*, 150–96. For the larger South, see Woodman, *King Cotton and His Retainers*, 243–60; Woodman, *New South—New Law*; and G. Wright, *Old South, New South*, 3–53, 81–123, 239–75.

12. For the role merchants played in the creation and implementation of Jim Crowism in Natchez and its hinterland, see Anderson, *Builders of the New South*, 40–220; and R. Davis, *Good and Faithful Labor*, 121–51. For the rise in Mississippi of the Jim Crow disfranchisement of black males and the creation of a caste system based on race and segregation as white males reasserted mastery over their households and dependents, namely, women as well as all blacks, see Bercaw, *Gendered Freedoms*, 95–187; Bolton, *Hardest Deal of All*, 3–20; Frankel, *Freedom's Women*, 57–180; McMillen, *Dark Journey*, 3–154; 197–256; and Wharton, *Negro in Mississippi*, 181–276. For the emergence of "whiteness" as a new-but-old political economy aimed at resurrecting the dominance of white males in the larger South during the late nineteenth century, see Bardaglio, *Reconstructing the Household*, 115–228; Gilmore, *Gender and Jim Crow*; Hale, *Making Whiteness*; and Williamson, *Rage for Order*, 36–61.

13. Scholarship on the impact of the Civil War on southern women has flourished in recent years, and most of it either supports or opposes Anne Firor Scott's argument that the Civil War ushered in an era of significant change for southern women because it forced them to assume new responsibilities in new ways. See Scott, *Southern Lady*. For the perspective of historians who doubt that the Civil War represented a fundamental watershed for southern women, see Faust, *Mothers of Invention*; Rable, *Civil Wars*; and Whites, *Civil War as a Crisis in Gender*. In addition, there are a number of important works that inform this debate: Bercaw, *Gendered Freedoms*; Clinton and Silber, *Divided Houses*; Edwards, *Gendered Strife and Confusion*; Edwards, *Scarlett Doesn't Live Here Anymore*; W. Scarborough, *Masters of the Big House*, 90–121; and Wood, *Masterful Women*, 159–191. For the changes in gender relationships among Mississippi blacks during Reconstruction, see Frankel, *Freedom's Women*, 8–122.

14. Censer, *Reconstruction of White Southern Womanhood*.

15. See Bieber, "Making the Most of Freedom"; and Hale, *Making Whiteness*, 31–35.

16. Behrend, "Freedpeople's Democracy," 98–99; Behrend, *Reconstructing Democracy*; Bercaw, *Gendered Freedoms*, 110–16, 151; Edwards, *Gendered Strife and Confusion*, 144–83; and Hale, *Making Whiteness*, 32–33.

17. Bercaw, *Gendered Freedoms*, 159–87; Edwards, *Gendered Strife and Confusion*, 185–254; and May, "Southern Elite Women," 251–52, 276–85.

18. I use the term "single women" to refer to not-married women aged thirty and older, including in some cases women who may have been divorced or were married but abandoned women. In determining the number of single women, I have excluded female-headed households that appear to have included adult males who might have been nonlegal husbands or common-law spouses. For household living arrangements, see *Directory of the City of Natchez*, 24–25; Lowenburg, *Census of Inhabitants*; Marriage Record Books, Natchez and Adams County, Miss., White (1820–1900) and Black (1865–1900), ORAC; *Natchez Business Directory for 1877–76*; and U.S. Manuscript Census (1860, 1870, 1880), Natchez, Adams County, Miss., NARA.

19. See Marriage Record Books, Natchez and Adams County, Miss., White (1820–1900), ORAC. For scholarship on postbellum marriage patterns in the larger South, see Bardaglio, *Reconstructing the Household*, 130–31.

20. R. Davis, *Black Experience*, 125–57; Faust, *This Republic of Suffering*, 137–249; U.S. Manuscript Census (1860, 1880), Natchez, Adams County, Miss., NARA; and Vaughan, "Natchez during the Civil War," 378–85.

21. Historian William K. Scarborough documents how commonly Natchez men-on-the-make such as John Quitman, a noted lawyer/planter/politician, married affluent spouses during the antebellum era. Many of these marriages included marriage contracts that protected a wife's family properties. W. Scarborough, *Masters of the Big House*, 18–174. For discussion of the war's impact on Natchez elites, see Anderson, *Builders of the New South*, 11–142; R. Davis, "Plantation Lifeworld of the Old Natchez District"; Kaye, *Joining Places*, 210–20; and Wayne, *Reshaping of Plantation Society*, 75–111.

22. Jabour, *Scarlett's Sisters*, 276–80. For analysis of the diminished power of males over their households after the war, see Bercaw, *Gendered Freedoms*, 52–94.

23. See the voluminous correspondence between Alice Jenkins and her lawyer, Josiah Winchester, various family members, and several of her suitors and friends in the John Carmichael Jenkins Family Papers and the Winchester Family Papers, Natchez Trace Collection, Center for American History, University of Texas at Austin. For Alice's sister's marital difficulties with her less-than-successful husband, see Mary Jenkins Johnstone to John F. Jenkins, January 4, 1879, Jenkins Family Papers, Natchez Trace Collection, Center for American History, University of Texas at Austin. See also Sadler, "Yellow Plague," 68–87; E. Thompson, "Southern Women, Gender Roles"; and Alice G. Jenkins, Will, April 1, 1927; and John C. Jenkins, Will, October 23, 1855, Will Books, ORAC.

24. Cook, "Growing Up White, Genteel, and Female," 205.

25. Rebecca Mandeville's continued spinsterhood after the war probably stemmed from her devotion to her elderly father, with whom no suitor apparently could compare, as well as her ongoing care for her dead sister's child, Carlie. The same most likely could be said for Anna Johnson, profiled briefly in chapter 5. See chapter 2 for more on Rebecca Mandeville's relationship with her father, brothers, and sisters.

26. See Marriage Record Books, Natchez and Adams County, Miss., Black (1865–1900), ORAC. For a careful and insightful discussion of the pressure to legally marry and the plight

black women faced in freedom in Mississippi, see Frankel, *Freedom's Women*, 79–122; and Bercaw, *Gendered Freedoms*, 99–134. Historian Laura Edwards sees a somewhat different dynamic at work regarding the value some African Americans, especially men, placed on legal marriage as a means to solidify their claims to citizenship and to establish, especially for women, a measure of security for themselves and their families. See Edwards, *Scarlett Doesn't Live Here Anymore*, 61.

27. Cook, "Growing Up White, Genteel, and Female," 183; and Nguyen, "Laying the Foundations," 49–58.

28. Edwards, *Gendered Strife and Confusion*, 145–84.

29. Aguilar, "Boarding House Women." The city's large commercial hotels closed during the war and no similarly sized hotels serviced the community until the Natchez Hotel began business in 1892. Power, *The Memento*, 1:73. For an informed discussion of the distinction between keeping house and running a boardinghouse in nineteenth-century America, see Gamber, *Boarding House in Nineteenth-Century America*, 54–59. For households that served as licensed boardinghouses in Natchez, see U.S. Manuscript Census (1850, 1860, 1870, 1880), Natchez, Adams County, Miss., NARA.

30. Adams County Teacher Register and Teacher Pay Certificates, 1873–1900, HNF; Bieber, "Making the Most of Freedom," 60–82; Union School and Institute Payroll Ledger, 1874–1905, HNF; and Censer, *Reconstruction of White Southern Womanhood*, 153–83.

31. Mary Susan Ker Diary, May 1886–1899, Mary Susan Ker Papers, UNC-CH. Ker's situation also is discussed in Nguyen, "Laying the Foundations," 61.

32. Nguyen, "Laying the Foundations," 47; and U.S. Manuscript Census (1870, 1880), Natchez, Adams County, Miss., NARA.

33. As before the war, female shopkeepers hired single and married women to work as clerks and salespersons, but most clerking women worked for male storeowners. See, for example, the clerking experiences of the married woman Josephine Thomas, who testified in her divorce suit that she had sustained herself independent of her husband by clerking in a millinery store owned by Miss Ronina Solari and by sewing on her own. *Henry A Thomas v. Josephine Thomas*, July 1870, CHCAC, HNF; and U.S. Manuscript Census (1870, 1880), Natchez, Adams County, Miss., NARA. For examples of specific advertisements by female shopkeepers and merchants as well as information on Natchez businesswomen, see *Directory of the City of Natchez*; Lowenburg, *Census of Inhabitants*; *Natchez Business Directory for 1877–76*; *Natchez Daily Democrat*, November 3, 1873; June 19, 1881; and *Natchez Tri-Weekly Courier*, April 20, 1870. For the business community in Natchez and Mississippi after the war, see Anderson, *Builders of the New South*, 40–71, 142–79; R. Davis, *Good and Faithful Labor*, 121–51; Ownby, *American Dreams in Mississippi*, 61–97; and Wayne, *Reshaping of Plantation Society*, 150–96. For scholarship on the rise of the new mercantile class and furnishing stores in the larger South, see Ayers, *Promise of the New South*, 13–19, 81–103; T. Clark, *Pills, Petticoats, and Plows*; Hale, *Making Whiteness*, 151–99; and Woodman, *King Cotton and His Retainers*, 295–334.

34. U.S. Manuscript Census (1870, 1880), Natchez, Adams County, Miss., NARA, and Nguyen, "Laying the Foundations," 51–53.

35. U.S. Manuscript Census (1870, 1880), Natchez, Adams County, Miss., NARA.

36. Ibid. For postwar Natchez and Adams County schools and teachers, see note 30; Behrend, "Freedpeople's Democracy," 121–42; and Bieber, "Making the Most of Freedom." For secondary literature on the education of blacks in the postwar South, see Buchart, *Northern Schools, Southern Blacks, and Reconstruction*; Jones, *Soldiers of Light and Love*; Morris, *Reading, 'Riting, and Reconstruction*; Richardson, *Christian Reconstruction*; and Williams, *Self-Taught*.

37. Although more divorces may have occurred than cited here, the extant records surveyed include complete case files largely undisturbed in their original containers, chancery record books, and published divorce announcements in Natchez newspapers, as required by state law. See the following newspapers for divorce notices: *Natchez Democrat*, 1867–74; *Natchez Daily Democrat*, 1869–74, 1875–98; *Natchez Tri-Weekly Courier*, 1870–71; and *Natchez Weekly Democrat*, 1865–86. For the one woman arrested and sent to jail for adultery, see *Andrew J. Ramsey v. Marinda Ramsey*, October 26, 1882, CHCAC, ORAC.

38. For state laws on divorce from 1857 to 1890, see Sharkey, Harris, and Elliot, *Revised Code of Mississippi*, 331–38; Johnston, *Revised Code*, 371–80; and J. Campbell, *Revised Code*, 335–42. For examples of divorces in which the spouse alleged desertion after three years while noting abuse, adultery, and drunkenness as contextual evidence, see *Rosalie Kelly v. William B. Kelly*, March 1, 1875; *Jacob Miller Jr. v. Lavinia Miller*, September 29, 1877; *Samuel Pickering v. Delia Pickering*, June 26, 1879; and *Minerva Ashley v. Robert Ashley*, April 17, 1880, CHCAC, ORAC.

39. Sharkey, Harris, and Elliot, *Revised Code of Mississippi*, 334; Johnston, *Revised Code*, 374; and J. Campbell, *Revised Code*, 337. See also *Crutcher v. Crutcher* 38 So. 337, 86 (1905), and *Pierce v. Pierce* 38 So. 46 (1905), cited in *Mississippi Digest Annotated*, 1:911.

40. For black-white marriage being punishable as a crime of incest and as grounds for divorce in postbellum Mississippi, see Campbell, *Revised Code*, 33, 38, 791; *James L. Newbell v. Katie Newbell*, July 22, 1885, CHCAC, ORAC; and *Samuel Pickering v. Delia Pickering*, June 26, 1879, CHCAC, ORAC. For discussion of antimiscegenation laws and practices in Mississippi and other states, see Bardaglio, *Reconstructing the Household*, 177–88; Bercaw, *Gendered Freedoms*, 158–84, Frankel, *Freedom's Women*, 113–16; Hodes, *White Women, Black Men*, 146–75; Litwack, *Been in the Storm So Long*, 260–66, 555; McMillen, *Dark Journey*, 14–23; Wharton, *Negro in Mississippi*, 87; and Williamson, *Rage for Order*, 187–88.

41. For an example of a divorce in which a female plaintiff accused her husband of committing adultery with black women, see *Marial Ketteringham v. John Ketteringham*, February 28, 1882, CHCAC, ORAC. For an example of Natchez whites terrorizing a white male teacher married to a black woman, see Broussard, "Malvina Matthews," 36–37; *Natchez Democrat*, January 1, 20, February 3, 20, April 6, 18, May 4, 18, and 22, July 7, 21, August 1, 1868; and Ward, "William T. Hewett."

42. See Mimi Miller's discussion of a well-known interracial couple in a common law marriage who nevertheless lived in separate residences: M. W. Miller, "Historic St Catherine Street Marker." For the sociological study of Natchez caste, class, and interracial relationships in the 1930s, sees A. Davis, Gardner, and Gardner, *Deep South*, 15–58.

43. For more on the emergence of a prosperous and relatively conservative but race-conscious black elite in postwar Natchez as well as in other cities of the larger South, see

Behrend," Freedpeople's Democracy," 93–165; Bieber, "Making the Most of Freedom," 106–26; R. Davis, *Black Experience*, 158–92; Gatewood, *Aristocrats of Color*; Gilmore, *Gender and Jim Crow*; and McMillen, *Dark Journey*, 22–23. For elite black men and women as a class within a caste system in early twentieth-century Natchez, see A. Davis, Gardner, and Gardner, *Deep South*, 208–55, 422–53; J. Davis, *Race against Time*, 83–147; and Falck, "Black and White Memory Making," 51–67. For the Victorian-era service ideal and the adoption of middle-class values as motivating behavior among many educated, professional, and elite black women after the Civil War and into the twentieth century, see E. L. Davis, *Lifting as They Climb*; Hine and Thompson, *Shining Thread of Hope*, 177–83; Higginbotham, *Righteous Discontent*; Neverdon-Morton, *Afro-American Women of the South*; Shaw, *What a Woman Ought to Be*; and Wesley, *History of the National Association of Colored Women's Clubs*.

44. For examples of divorces involving relatively affluent spouses (listed in chronological order), see *Elizabeth Brennan v. Lawrence Brennan*, July 24, 1866; *Malvina J. Matthews v. Edwin J. Matthews*, September 17, 1866; *Emma M. Railey v. Charles R. Railey*, October 2, 1866; *Lydia Jane Phipps v. Henry M. Phipps*, 1867; *Elizabeth Austin v. John H. Austin*, August 4, 1869; *Susan Balance v. Charles W. Balance*, July 6, 1870; *George D. Farrar v. Elizabeth Farrar*, July 6, 1870; *Rachel Marsh v. Campbell Marsh*, July 20, 1870; *Emma Sutherland v. James Sutherland*, December 16, 1870; and *Peter C. Rucker v. Emma Lewis Rucker*, October 21, 1887, CHCAC, ORAC.

45. See Johnston, *Revised Code*, 376–77; and Campbell, *Revised Code*, 339. Historian Nancy Bercaw notes the limitations to a married woman's control over her wages, especially for sharecropping women paid wages in cotton, and over other assets in Mississippi despite revisions in the Married Women's Property Law passed during Reconstruction and shortly after. See Bercaw, *Gendered Freedoms*, 173–74, 182–83.

46. *Natchez Weekly Democrat*, September 27, 1871.

47. As with white divorces, although the total number of black divorces is unknown for the years 1865–90, the extant records surveyed include complete case files largely undisturbed in their original containers housed in the chancery court documents of the Office of Records for Adams County, Mississippi. Although it is clear that some divorce documents were pilfered or removed over the years, most likely by relatives of the involved parties or by document seekers, the number appears to have been relatively small. Also, Mississippi law required divorce notices to be published in Natchez newspapers, which were carefully surveyed for this study. See Chancery Court Records, Adams County, Miss., ORAC; and the following newspapers surveyed for divorce announcements: *Natchez Daily Democrat*, 1869–74, 1875–98; *Natchez Democrat*, 1867–74; *Natchez Tri-Weekly Courier*, 1870–71; and *Natchez Weekly Democrat*, 1865–86. See Lowenburg, *Census of Inhabitants*, for population data.

CHAPTER NINE. STEPPING THROUGH THE RUINS

1. *Natchez Weekly Democrat*, December 14, 1868; and *State v. Malvina J. Matthews*, CCAC, HNF. For a full discussion of Matthews's murder trial in the context of Reconstruction-era Natchez, see Broussard, "Malvina Matthews."

2. Matthews posted a $1,500 bail by taking out a mortgage on some of her real estate. N. A. M. Dudley to B. H. Hunter, sheriff of Adams County, June 21, 1868, Deed and Mortgage Records, ORAC.

3. See General Orders Nos. 1–30, issued by Brig. Gen. E. O. C. Ord, commanding general, Fourth Military District, Vicksburg, Miss., March 26, 1867, MDAH. On the use of military commissions in Mississippi and the South during Reconstruction, see Garner, *Reconstruction in Mississippi*, 180–83, 213–16; Sefton, *United States Army and Reconstruction*, 29–31, 90–113; and Waldrep, *Roots of Disorder*, 41–48, 106–11.

4. See Dudley to Bvt. Maj. Gen. John Tyler, acting adjutant general, Fourth Military District of Mississippi, November 6, 1868, U.S. Army Continental Commands, Letters Sent, Post Natchez, RG 393, NARA; and Dudley to Bvt. Maj. Gen. S. C. Greene, November 21, 1868, Report of Inspection of Post of Natchez, RG 393, NARA.

5. All black soldiers in Mississippi had been mustered out of service two years earlier, although some black veterans continued to wear their uniforms on the city's streets as a potential militia force ready to be called up for emergency service if the need arose. For military orders issued to govern Natchez during Military Reconstruction, see U.S. Army Commands, Fourth Military District Orders, 1867–70, Microfilm Roll No. 2585, MDAH. For scholarship on Reconstruction in Natchez and Mississippi, see Behrend, "Freedpeople's Democracy," 165–434; R. Davis, *Black Experience*, 140–51; R. Davis, *Good and Faithful Labor*, 58–199; Frankel, *Freedom's Women*, 56–180; Garner, *Reconstruction in Mississippi*, 51–414; Harris, *Presidential Reconstruction in Mississippi*, 37–141, 228–46; Harris, *Day of the Carpetbagger*, 1–311; McNeily, "War and Reconstruction in Mississippi"; Rowland, *History of Mississippi*, 2:105–206; Sansing, "Congressional Reconstruction"; and Wharton, *Negro in Mississippi*, 138–56.

6. See *Natchez Democrat*, October 21, 1869; *State v. Malvina J. Matthews*, CCAC, HNF; and Sharkey, Harris, and Elliot, *Revised Code of Mississippi*, 620–21.

7. For more on Martin, see Behrend, "Freedpeople's Democracy," 205–6, 220; Broussard, "Malvina Matthews"; and Lenowski, "William T. Martin."

8. Black Union soldiers allegedly had killed Gibson's brother-in-law, Elias Julian Rogillio, and Sargent's father, George Sargent Jr. For the Rogillio murder, see Pvt. Richard H. Burr et al., Court Martial Trial, Murder, 1866, Records of the Office of the Judge Advocate General, Court Martial Proceedings, RG 153, NARA; and Col. H. A. McCaleb, Sixth U.S. Colored Infantry, to Bvt. Col. M. P. Beston, assistant acting adjutant general, Fourth Military District, April 1, 1866; and McCaleb to Lt. Col. A. S. Gilson, judge advocate general, Department of Mississippi, n.d., both in RG 393, NARA.

For the Sargent case, see Pvts. David Geer, Alexander McBride, William Thomas et al., Court Martial Trial, Murder, August 24, 1864, RG 153, NARA; George Sargent Jr. to Gen. A. C. Gillem, Commander, Fourth Military District, Mississippi, October 28, 1868, Governor's Papers, MDAH; J. M. Smiley, judge, First Judicial District, Mississippi, to John Tyler, acting adjutant general, Fourth Military District, Mississippi, November 23, 1868, Governors' Papers, MDAH; Mary Duncan to Maj. Gen. Henry W. Halleck, July 25, 1864, RG 393, NARA; and Maj. Gen. Henry W. Halleck to Mary Duncan, October 3, 1864, RG 393, NARA.

9. For the Hewett episode and numerous ongoing confrontations between Union soldiers and Natchez whites in the years preceding and following Matthews's trial, see Broussard, "Malvina Matthews," 48–58; General Court Martial Orders, No. 37, Headquarters, Fourth Military District, Department of Mississippi, Vicksburg, Miss., November 1, 1868, RG 393, NARA; Col. N. A. M. Dudley to Governor Adelbert Ames, January 7, 14, 1869, Governor's Papers, MDAH; *Natchez Democrat*, August 1, October 12, December 26, 1868; U.S. Congress, House, *Condition of Affairs in Mississippi*, 267, NARA; and the following letters sent by Colonel Dudley, located in RG 393, NARA: Dudley to Col. Samuel Green, acting adjutant general, Subdistrict Mississippi, July 22, 30, 1868; Dudley to Bvt. Maj. John Tyler, acting adjutant general, Fourth Military District, September 21, December 26, 28, 29, 30, 1868; Dudley to James Gillespie, sheriff, Tensas Parish, Louisiana, January 3; Dudley to W. Harris, sheriff, Concordia Parish, Louisiana, January 7; Dudley to Governor Adelbert Ames, January 21, 1869.

10. Broussard, "Malvina Matthews," 45–46; *State v. Malvina J. Matthews*, CCAC, HNF; and *Natchez Weekly Courier*, May 30, 1868.

11. Malvina J. Matthews to William T. Martin, Mortgage, December 10, 1872; Malvina J. Matthews to Natchez, Jackson, and Columbus Railroad, Deed, December 10, 1872; Robert H. Wood, sheriff, to Margaret D. Martin, Tax Collector Deed, March 7, 1881; and Robert H. Wood, sheriff, to Margaret D. Martin, Tax Collector Deed, March 7, 1881, Deed and Mortgage Record Books, ORAC.

12. Broussard, "Malvina Matthews," 52–53.

13. For scholarship on the interplay of class, gender, and race in the postbellum South, see Bardaglio, *Reconstructing the Household*; Edwards, *Gendered Strife and Confusion*; and Fields, *Slavery and Freedom*.

14. M. L. McMurran to James T. Thompson, March 26, 1868, Addison Family Papers, NNHP. Fortunately, a substantial body of information on the McMurran family has been researched and preserved by the Natchez National Historic Park, which owns the McMurran estate house, Melrose, located on the outskirts of Natchez.

15. See the *Baton Rouge Weekly Advocate*, December 29, 1866; *Baton Rouge Weekly Gazette and Comet*, December 29, 1866; January 5, 12, 19, 1867; and *New Orleans Daily Picayune*, January 4, 1867, for accounts of the burning of the steamboat *Fashion* and related details. See also Testimonial for John T. McMurran, Mississippi State Bar, June 4, 1867, John T. McMurran Family Papers, LSU; Broussard, "Profile: John T. McMurran"; and Broussard, "Career of John T. McMurran."

16. M. L. McMurran to James T. Thompson, March 26, 1868, Addison Family Papers, NNHP. Analysis of the McMurran family history is drawn from the extensive accounts, correspondence, and manuscripts found in several archival collections, including the Addison Family Papers, NNHP; Alice Austen McMurran Journal, typescript copy, HNF; Lemuel P. Conner Family Papers, John T. McMurran Family Papers, McMurran-Austen Family Papers, John Anthony Quitman Papers, and Edward Turner Family Papers, LSU; Leverich Papers, Manuscript Department, New York Historical Society; McMurran Letters and Papers, Special Collections, University of Louisiana at Monroe, ; Quitman Family Papers, UNC-CH; and various public records, such as Deeds, Liens, and Mortgage

Record Books; Inventories of Estates; Marriage Records; Probate Records; Tax Rolls; and Records of Wills, 1800–1900, ORAC. The following secondary sources were also helpful: Broussard, "Profile: John T. McMurran"; May, *John A. Quitman*, 12, 22–27, 33, 38–40, 78, 98, 109, 114–15, 141, 150, 180, 204, 251, 303, 372–74, 387, 391, 432–33; and Rosenblum, *John McMurran of Melrose*.

17. M. L. McMurran to James T. Thompson, March 26, 1868, Addison Family Papers, NNHP.

18. Administrator's Records of Accounts, John T. McMurran Probate, 1855–71, Probate Records, ORAC. Although the records are unclear, it seems that John T. McMurran managed to hide and sell cotton during the Civil War, amassing large sums of money that he left on account with the New York banking firm owned and operated by the Leverich brothers or invested in various industrial and railroad stocks held by the Leverich brothers. Evidence suggests that McMurran may have tried to put these cotton funds aside rather than pay off his substantial debts, in the hope of selling his Mississippi properties after the war and moving his family to the Eastern Seaboard, where his son and daughter-in-law lived with their family in Maryland. See Rosenblum, *John McMurran of Melrose*, 89–97.

19. John T. and Mary L. McMurran to Elizabeth S. Davis, December 8, 1865, Deeds, Liens, and Mortgage Record Books, ORAC. John also sold his law office to Elizabeth's husband, George Malin Davis, on the same date as the Melrose sale. See John T. McMurran and Wife to G. Malin Davis, December 8, 1865, Deeds, Liens, and Mortgage Record Books, ORAC.

20. Edward Turner had migrated to Natchez in 1802, where he married a daughter of Cato West, a wealthy planter and the acting territorial governor of the Mississippi Territory in 1803–4. He parlayed this family position into a brilliant career in law, authoring a detailed digest of Mississippi laws and serving as the first president of the Mississippi Bar Association in 1821. After his first wife's death, Turner married Eliza B. Baker in 1812, who survived him. Turner held numerous other prestigious positions within the state before his death in 1860, including chief justice of the Mississippi Supreme Court, state attorney general, chancellor of the state, and Speaker of the Mississippi House of Representatives. See the Edward Turner Subject File, MDAH; and the Edward Turner Family Papers, LSU. Turner's substantial plantation holdings were lost during and after the Civil War, leaving his widow with little more than their suburban villa, Woodlands. See also *Goodspeed's Biographical and Historical Memoirs*, 1:109, 2:928–29; Claiborne, *Mississippi*, 213, 228, 231, 242, 263, 379, 390, 468, 470; Landon, "Mississippi State Bar Association," 222–42; James Lynch, *Bench and Bar of Mississippi*, 84–87; and Rowland, *Courts, Judges and Lawyers of Mississippi*, 48, 68, 72, 77, 79, 87, 248, 256.

21. Lemuel P. Conner Sr. attended Yale University and studied law under John T. McMurran in Natchez as a young man, but instead of practicing law he turned his attention to managing his several plantations and numerous enslaved workers as well as those plantations and slaves owned by his mother, Jane E. B. Conner, widowed in 1843. After the Civil War, Conner lost his lands to creditors and his mother's property depreciated drastically. To survive, Lemuel Sr. turned to law once again but with little success, until he was joined by his son, Lemuel P. Conner Jr. See Conner Family Papers,

LSU. Mary McMurran also talked about the hard times the Conner family experienced: "My sister Fanny has been much out of health in the past year or so. The cares of a large family and the anxieties in regard to their present & future provision weighs heavily upon her, who never knew before what want was. Her Husband has lost all his property and is using all his energy to care for his family the best way he can, often with not much success. It is a sad, sad time to everyone, calling for great humility & submission & trust in a merciful God!" See M. L. McMurran to James T. Thompson, March 26, 1868, Addison Family Papers, NNHP.

22. Mary L. McMurran to Alice Austen McMurran, April 7, 1864; John T. McMurran Jr. to Alice Austen McMurran, June 10, 1864; and Antonia Quitman Lovell to Alice Austen McMurran, October 18, 1865, Addison Family Papers, NNHP. See also Alice Austin McMurran Diary, June 8, 1864; June 5, 1865, HNF.

23. Farrar Conner eventually married the spinster Maria Chotard in 1889, daughter of Henry Chotard, a wealthy planter who died in 1870 leaving his family land-rich, owning several plantations, but cash-poor, as were so many of the district's surviving antebellum planters. Henry's wife, Frances Minor Chotard, had died in 1864. Mary McMurran once commented that three of the five Chotard daughters seemed destined for spinsterhood, in contrast to her own daughter, Mary Elizabeth, who was happily married to Farrar Conner at the time. The Chotard daughters, "verging up to the thirties, [are] still alone"; they lived at Somerset, a plantation on the outskirts of town, for their entire lives, dying between 1895 and 1912. M. L. McMurran to J. T. McMurran Jr., August 26, 1856, Addison Family Papers, NNHP. See also Chotard Family Genealogy, HNF.

24. Lemuel P. Conner Jr. to Fanny Conner, June 17, 1891, Conner Family Papers, LSU. In a later note to Fanny, her husband commented thusly about Fazee: "We see but little of Fazee; he prefers the cats, horses and Negroes." June 3, 1892, Conner Family Papers, LSU. Six weeks later, Lemuel wrote to Fanny about the animosity between Mary McMurran's son, John Jr., and Fazee (July 24, 1892, Addison Family Papers, NNHP): "I was out at Woodlands a few days ago, and saw only cousin John, Fazee having gone up to the 'Island' which is beginning to emerge from the water. The former is terribly out and disgusted with the latter; says he can't get one word of explanation as to what was done with all the money for which the estate is now so heavily in debt, and that he wants to know and must know how it was spent. Also that the young man is 'good for nothing except to raise cats.' I told him he had had excellent opportunities for 15 months to judge the young man's character, and it seemed he had not wasted the opportunities. If Fazee had the least particle of spirit, there would certainly be a row; but he has not the gumption of a toad; so nothing will come of it."

25. For the McMurran family's numerous legal and financial transactions, including those of Mary Louisa McMurran, see Case Dockets, 1820–1900, HNF; and Deeds, Liens, and Mortgage Record Books; Inventories of Estates; Marriage Records; Probate Records; Tax Rolls; and Records of Wills, 1800–1900, ORAC. Also see Deeds, Liens, and Mortgage Record Books, 1820–1900, Office of Records for Concordia Parish, Vidalia, La.; and Deeds, Liens, and Mortgage Record Books, Wilkinson County Office of Records, Woodville, Miss.

26. See the extensive correspondence (444 letters) between James Carson and Mary L. McMurran that lasted until his death in January 1889: McMurran Letters and Papers, Special Collections, University of Louisiana at Monroe; and Last Will and Testament of James Carson, February 8, 1889, Will Books, ORAC.

27. Most of these letters between Carson and McMurran were hand carried by trusted family servants, much as had been the case prior to the Civil War. The content of these Carson-McMurran letters falls into four overlapping categories: (1) financial affairs—88 percent; (2) nonbusiness and personal matters—48 percent; (3) expressions of absolute trust in Carson's judgment—25 percent; and (4) mutual interests as business partners—10 percent.

28. Rosenblum, *John McMurran of Melrose*, 105.

29. The analysis herein is based principally on the Nutt Family Papers, 1805–1937, MDAH; and public records located in ORAC and HNF. The following secondary sources were also helpful: Hawks, "Julia A. Nutt of Longwood"; R. Kennedy, "Postscripts to History"; Nutt, *Nutt Family through the Years*; and Whitewell, *Heritage of Longwood*.

30. Hawks, "Julia A. Nutt of Longwood," 294–95; and Haller Nutt to Julia Nutt, February 2, 1863, Nutt Family Papers, MDAH.

31. See the following unpublished manuscripts: Cooledge Jr., "A Stately Pleasure Dome," and author unknown, "Longwood," Nutt Family File, HNF. Also see R. Kennedy, "Postscripts to History."

32. G. W. Williams (coexecutor of Haller Nutt's estate), to Julia Nutt, n.d., Nutt Family Papers, MDAH.

33. Testimony of Julia A. Nutt, November 21, 1883, RG 217, SCC, and RG 123, Records of the Judiciary, NARA. For a history of the Southern Claims Commission, see Klingberg, *Southern Claims Commission*.

34. Haller Nutt died insolvent, and his estate remained in debt some thirty-nine years after his death. See Inventories and Appraisements Ledger, 1866–99, ORAC; Will of Haller Nutt, April 26, 1866, Will Books, ORAC; and Petition with Exhibits of Julian Nutt (claiming insolvency), May 30, 1867, and Petition of Julia Nutt for Dower, July 29, 1871, Probate Records and Probate Real Estate Record Books, ORAC. Included in the probate records is a register of claims by Haller Nutt's creditors and Julia Nutt's original claim against the U.S. government for $858,386.04 in damages, dated May 18, 1874. See also "On Petition of Julia A. Nutt for Dower," *Natchez Weekly Courier*, April 1, 1872.

35. Julia Nutt's daughter Carrie married, in 1866, a New Orleans lawyer with family in Chicago, but she died shortly after giving birth to a baby girl in 1867. The child was raised by her father's family in Chicago. Diary of Joseph B. Stratton, January 3, 1867, Stratton Papers, LSU; and Hawks, "Julia A. Nutt of Longwood," 299.

36. Julia Nutt's tumultuous relationship with her family is detailed in the numerous family letters found in the Nutt Family Papers, MDAH. See also Hawks, "Julia A. Nutt of Longwood," 301–7.

37. Will of Haller Nutt, April 26, 1866, Will Books, ORAC. Haller Nutt's will named Julia Nutt as the "first executor" of the coexecutors of his estate, which, along with her dower claim to one-third of the property, enabled her to maneuver in the interests

of her children as Haller's heirs. The county records are replete with Julia's financial manipulations. Over the years she mortgaged Longwood and Cloverdale plantation at least a dozen times, sold three plantations (Evergreen, Winter Quarters, and Lochland), and borrowed funds from local bankers and supply merchants, giving liens on her crops for collateral. At her death she owed thousands of dollars in unpaid claims to the Philadelphia builder of Longwood; her brother-in-law, Joseph B. Stratton; the longtime head of the First Presbyterian Church of Natchez; and the heirs of Andrew Brown, a local lumber-mill owner, for timber used in constructing Longwood. See the mortgage and lien transactions (too numerous to list here) in the Adams County public records, especially in the Deeds, Liens, and Mortgage Record Books, 1865–1900, ORAC, as well as a list of debts submitted by Sargeant Prentiss Knut, 1901, Nutt Family Papers, MDAH. See also Hawks, "Julia A. Nutt of Longwood," 298–99.

38. See Julia A. Nutt to S. Prentiss Nutt, April 26, 1878, and Julia A Nutt to S. Prentiss Knut, February 24, 1893, Nutt Family Papers, MDAH. (S. P. Nutt changed his name to Knut sometime in the 1880s.)

39. Ibid.

40. Julia Nutt Estate, Probate File, Chancery Court, ORAC.

41. Among the important manuscript collections documenting the Minor family are the following: Katherine Minor Papers, William L. Clements Library, University of Michigan, Ann Arbor; William J. Minor Family Papers, LSU; and Surget Family Papers and Surget-McKitrick-MacNeil Family Papers, MDAH. In addition, important secondary scholarship includes Dresser, "Kate and John Minor"; Holmes, "Stephen Minor"; Keller, "Horse Racing Madness,"; Klingberg, *Southern Claims Commission*, 12n26, 108n55, 112n71; and Sitterson, "William J. Minor Plantations." For the Surget Family, see especially Marest, "The Surgets"; and W .Scarborough, *Masters of the Big House*, 9–12, 23, 33, 65, 100, 109, 123, 128, 144, 153, 156, 158–59, 161, 180, 183–84, 200, 204, 209, 213, 220, 235, 260, 267, 332, 334–35, 347–48, 361, 377, 394.

42. Testimony of Katherine S. Minor, October 5, 1872, Claim No. 7960, Katherine S. Minor, SCC, NARA.

43. Testimony of Julia A. Nutt, March 19, 1874, ibid.

44. Testimony of William T. Martin, December 12, 1877, ibid.

45. Rebecca Ann Gustine Minor, Southdown Plantation, to Frances Wilkins Chotard, August 20, 1869, Minor Family Papers, MDAH.

46. Much of the information on John Minor and family is drawn from the Minor Family Papers, MDAH; Dresser, "Kate and John Minor"; and Dresser, "Minor Family of Natchez." See also W. Scarborough, *Masters of the Big House*, 11, 23, 30, 33, 56, 67, 133, 145, 156–58, 224, 251, 254–58, 340, 348–49.

47. See the Surget Family Papers, MDAH; and W. Scarborough, *Masters of the Big House*, 9–12, 348.

48. Dresser, "Kate and John Minor," 195–200, 210–12; Dresser, "Minor Family of Natchez," 93–110; and Kate Minor's obituary in the *Natchez Democrat*, February 18, 1926.

49. Dresser, "Minor Family of Natchez," 63–112; and John Minor and Kate Minor to Leverich & Co. of New York, April 1, 1867, Deeds, Liens, and Mortgage Record Books,

ORAC. For the hold of furnishing merchants on landlords and sharecroppers in the Natchez District, see Anderson, *Builders of the New South*, 4–38, 50–62, 71–155, 180–219, 221, 223n17; and R. Davis, *Good and Faithful Labor*, 124.

50. R. Davis, *Good and Faithful Labor*, 124; Dresser, "Minor Family of Natchez," 79–81; James Surget Jr., John Minor, and Kate Minor to William J. Minor, January 1, 1869, and John Minor to Charles and Edward Leverich, April 11, 1867, Deed and Mortgage Record Books, ORAC; and John Minor to Leverich & Co., December 16, 1865, and John Minor to Julius Le Blanc, April 26, 1867, Deed and Mortgage Record Books, Office of Records for Concordia Parish, Vidalia, La.

51. For a discussion of the Married Women's Property Law in Mississippi, see chapter 3 of this study and Broussard, "Naked before the Law."

52. John Minor to James Surget and Kate Minor, September 10, 1867, and John Minor to Julius Le Blanc, president, Louisiana State Bank, April 25, 1867, Deed and Mortgage Record Books, ORAC; and Dresser, "Minor Family of Natchez," 79–81.

53. See Katherine S. Minor to Edward Leverich, October 22, 1866, Leverich Family Papers, Manuscript Department, New York Historical Society; R. Davis, *Good and Faithful Labor*, 58–120; and Dresser, "Minor Family of Natchez," 75–88.

54. Jacob Surget, Will, March 16, 1869, Surget Family Papers, MDAH; and John J. Brower to Kate Surget Minor, June 11, 1878, Deed and Mortgage Record Books, ORAC.

55. *Natchez New Era*, February 11, 1882; and Dresser, "Minor Family of Natchez," 106–10.

56. Report of Orange Ferriss, judge, Southern Claims Commission, November 22, 1879, Claim No. 7960, Katherine S. Minor, SCC, NARA. See also Dresser, "Minor Family of Natchez," 103, 116; and Klingberg, "Case of the Minors."

57. Dresser, "Minor Family of Natchez," 108–10.

58. Callon and Smith, *Goat Castle Murder*; biography and history section of the Minor Family Papers, MDAH; and Dresser, "Minor Family of Natchez," 11–12.

59. Blodgett, "Enigmatic William T. Martin"; and Hesseltine and Gara, "Mississippi's Confederate Leaders after the War," 95.

60. Analysis of the Sessions family household is based on public records located in ORAC; the Office of Records for Concordia Parish, Vidalia, La.; and the Death Records and Sexton Records, Adams County, Mississippi, 1840–1940, HNF. Pertinent manuscript collections include extensive correspondence located in the Lemuel P. Conner Family Papers, LSU; and the Session Family Subject Files, MDAH.

61. Alonzo Blanchard, master of the steamship U.S. *New York*, to Mrs. Joseph W. Sessions, July 3, 1870, Conner Family Papers, LSU.

62. Will of John F. Gillespie, November 26, 1855, Will Books, ORAC.

63. Maria P. Sessions to Britton & Koontz, Promissory Notes, July 27, September 22, 1881; March 11, May 3, May 13, 1882; and March 9, 1883, Conner Family Papers, LSU.

64. Maria P. Sessions to Annie M. Sessions et al., Deed, July 9, 1881, Deed and Mortgage Record Books, ORAC. See also the undated testimony of Maria P. Sessions, given sometime in the mid-1880s, when she was sixty years old. Maria P. Sessions, Testimony, n.d., Conner Family Papers, LSU.

65. Maria P. Sessions, Last Will and Testament and three codicils, November 14, 1884; October 15, 1887; February 26, 1898; July 16, 1898; and October 10, 1904, Will Books, ORAC. See also Annie M. Sessions to Susan McConnell, January 29, 1912, Conner Family Papers, LSU.

66. City death records note that Maria P. Sessions had "accidentally burned to death." Death and Sexton Records, Adams County, Mississippi, HNF. According to Annie Sessions, her mother's will made it nearly impossible for her to lease the family plantations on a long-term basis or to use them as collateral for advances or loans. Annie claimed, in an embittered letter sent to her sister in 1912, that this limited lifetime legacy greatly undermined her ability to negotiate agreements to her advantage because few would accept arrangements for more than a year at a time. Annie Sessions to Susan McConnell, January 29, 1912, Conner Family Papers, LSU.

67. John G. Sessions to Lemuel P. Conner Jr., February 29, 1908; Lemuel P. Conner Jr. to John G. Sessions, March 3, 1908; J. D. Jos. Curry to L. P. Conner Jr., March 19, 1908; and Jos. Curry to L. P. Conner, March 22, 1908; Conner Family Papers, LSU. See also Annie M. Sessions to Lemuel P. Conner Jr., March 9, 1908, Probate Records, ORAC; and the brief biography of Lemuel P. Conner Jr. in Rowland, *Mississippi*, 15. See also Jane E. B. Conner to Lemuel P. Conner Sr., October 22, December 22, 1862; January 1, 1863; *Jane E. B. Conner v. Lemuel P. Conner Sr.*, legal notice dated 1864; and Jane E. B. Conner to Lemuel P. Conner Sr., December 1883, Conner Family Papers, LSU.

68. See Will of Annie Sessions, March 9, 1908; and Codicil, September 15, 1913, Conner Family Papers, LSU, wherein she explains in detail her relations with the Gillespie family, her siblings, and her attorney, Lemuel P. Conner Jr.

69. Ibid.

70. Annie M. Sessions to Lemuel P. Conner, March 9, 1908, Probate Records, ORAC.

71. Mr. John G. Sessions, Tallulah, Louisiana, to Lemuel P. Conner, Natchez, Mississippi, February 29, 1908; Lemuel P. Conner, Natchez, to Mr. John G. Sessions, Tallulah, Louisiana, March 3, 1908; J. D. Jos. Curry, St. Joseph, to L. P. Conner, Natchez, March 19, 1908; Jos. Curry, St. Joseph, to Mr. L. P. Conner, Natchez, March 22, 1908, Conner Family Papers, LSU.

72. See correspondence between Annie Sessions and Mary Conner, April 2, 1916; September 7, October 7, 1917; May 16, July 28, December 27, 1919; May 16, 1923; July 15, 1924; April 22 (year not given), Conner Family Papers, LSU; and J. P. Barkdull to Wm. A. Dicksen, April 24, 1909; A. J. McLaurin to Lemuel P. Conner Jr., April 26, 1909; and Lemuel P. Conner Jr., to Audley Britton Conner, December 16, 1919, Conner Family Papers, LSU.

73. Johnson family member ages in 1866: William Jr., 30; Richard, 29; Byron, 27; Anna L., 25; Katherine G., 24; Alice, 19; Josephine, 17; and Clarence, 16. See Anna Johnson's Notebook, 1870–72; and Catherine Johnson's Diary, 1864–74, William T. Johnson and Family Papers, LSU. See also Register of Teachers and Pay Certificates, Adams County, 1873–80; and Union School and Natchez Institute Payroll Ledgers, 1874–1905, HNF. For Anna Johnson and her sisters, see Bieber, "Making the Most of Freedom," 60–66; Broussard, "Female Solitaires," 392–98; R. Davis, *Black Experience*, 186–91; Gould, *Chained*

to the Rock of Adversity, xxii, xlii–xlix, 39–93; and Hogan and Davis, *William Johnson's Natchez*, 44, 63, 419, 714.

74. For more on the city's propertied and educated blacks during the Reconstruction years and their "blue-vein" descendants into the twentieth century, see Behrend, "Freedpeople's Democracy," 93–274; Bieber, "Making the Most of Freedom," 119–25; A. Davis, Gardner, and Gardner, *Deep South*, 39, 214–17, 245–47; R. Davis, *Black Experience*, 158–92; and J. Davis, *Race against Time*, 91.

75. On the murders of William Johnson and his son, see *Mississippi Free Trader* (Natchez), April 8, 24; May 5, 1852; and the *Natchez Democrat*, January 17, 1872. See also Gould, *Chained to the Rock of Adversity*, xi–liv; and Hogan and Davis, *William Johnson's Natchez*, 58–62. For Anna Johnson's family, see R. Davis, *Black Experience*, 186–200; and J. Davis, *Race against Time*, 91.

76. Gould, *Chained to the Rock of Adversity*, 36, 43–47; Hogan and Davis, *William Johnson's Natchez*, 41, 58, 63, 549, 551, 597; Shulman, "Bingamans of Natchez"; and Shulman, "Adam Lewis Bingaman."

77. Blodgett, "Enigmatic William T. Martin"; Broussard, "Malvina Matthews," 49–56; Lenowski, "William T. Martin"; and Hesseltine and Gara, "Mississippi's Confederate Leaders after the War," 95.

78. See Behrend, "Facts and Memories"; R. Davis, *Black Experience*, 172–79; numerous documents showing Lynch's involvement with the Johnson family in court manuscript cases, HNF; and multiple property entries in Deed, Liens, and Mortgage Records, 1865–98, ORAC. For details on Lynch's personal and political life, see John Lynch, *Reminiscences of an Active Life*.

79. Bieber, "Making the Most of Freedom," 84–87; R. Davis, *Black Experience*, 172–73, 176, 180–83; and Nomelli, "Jim Crow, Louis J. Winston."

80. Bieber, "Making the Most of Freedom," 61–105; Register of Teachers and Pay Certificates, Adams County, 1873–80, HNF; and Union School and Natchez Institute Payroll Ledgers, 1874–1905, HNF.

81. R. Davis, *Black Experience*, 188–89. See also Anna Johnson et al. to Duncan Minor and James Surget, February 16, 1885, Deed and Mortgage Record Books, ORAC.

82. For more on the behavior expected of the Union School teachers by prominent Natchez whites as well as by the female educators themselves, see Bieber "Making the Most of Freedom," 106–33. For scholarship that discusses African American female teachers and educated black women professionals as agents of "racial uplift" in the postbellum South, see Fairclough, *Teaching Equality*, 9, 25–174; Gilmore, *Gender and Jim Crow*, 75–78; Harley, "Beyond the Classroom"; Higginbotham, *Righteous Discontent*, 21–44; Hine and Thompson, *Shining Thread of Hope*, 182–83; Jones, "Women Who Were More Than Men"; Neverdon-Morton, *Afro-American Women of the South*, 1–9, 78–104; Rabinowitz, "Half a Loaf"; and Shaw, *What a Woman Ought to Be*, 7–11.

83. Edwards, *Gendered Strife and Confusion*, 1–106, 145–217.

EPILOGUE

1. Death Records, Sexton Reports, HNF; *Natchez Democrat,* January 6, 1894; and Joseph B. Stratton Diary, Joseph B. Stratton Papers, LSU.

2. For examples, see Stratton Diary, December 22, 1848, and November 16, 1852, Stratton Papers, LSU.

3. A woman named Louisa LeRoy is listed in the city's death records as having died on May 26, 1849, from a "disorganization of the lung." Death Records, Sexton Reports, May 29, 1849, HNF.

4. Stratton Diary, Stratton Papers, LSU.

5. Stratton Diary, February 24, June 5, 10, 1851; May 28, 1852; August 3, 1858; June 2, 1860, Stratton Papers, LSU.

6. Susan B. Conner to Alexander Farrar, 1852, quoted in Wayne, *Death of an Overseer,* 125–26.

BIBLIOGRAPHY

ABBREVIATIONS

Archives and Public Records

AMA   American Missionary Association Papers, Amistad Research Center, Tulane University, New Orleans

CCAC   Circuit Court Records for Adams County, Natchez, Mississippi

CDJA   Catholic Diocese of Jackson Archives, Jackson, Mississippi

CHCAC   Chancery Court Records for Adams County, Natchez, Mississippi

HCEA   High Court of Errors and Appeals Records, MDAH, Jackson, Mississippi

HNF   Historic Natchez Foundation, Natchez, Mississippi

LSU   Louisiana and Lower Mississippi Valley Collections, Louisiana State University, Baton Rouge

MDAH   Mississippi Department of Archives and History, Jackson, Mississippi

MFP   Henry D. Mandeville Family Papers, Louisiana and Lower Mississippi Valley Collections, Louisiana State University, Baton Rouge

NARA   National Archives and Records Administration, Washington, D.C.

NNHP   Natchez National Historical Park, Natchez, Mississippi

OR   *War of the Rebellion: A Compilation of the Official Records of the Union and Confederate Armies*. 128 vols. Washington, D.C.: U.S. Government Printing Office, 1880–1901.

ORAC   Office of Records for Adams County, Natchez, Mississippi

RG   Record Group

SCC   Records of the Southern Claims Commission, Records of the General Accounting Office, Department of the Treasure, Record Group 217, NARA.

SMA   St. Mary's Cathedral Archives, St. Mary's Catholic Church, Natchez, Mississippi

UNC-CH   Southern Historical Collection, University of North Carolina at Chapel Hill

MANUSCRIPT MATERIALS

Adams County Office of Records, Natchez, Mississippi.

Chancery Court Records.

Circuit Court Records.

Deeds, Liens, and Mortgage Records.

Inventories and Appraisements Ledger (1866–99).
Inventories of Estates.
Marriage Records.
Orphan Court Minute Books.
"Plan of the City of Natchez," June 26, 1829. Thomas Freeman, Surveyor.
Probate Real Estate Record Books.
Probate Records.
Records of the General Land Office, Mississippi Local Office Plat Book, No. 35,
    National Archives, Washington D.C., in the "Township Plats."
Records of Wills.
Spanish Records.
Superior Court Records.
Tax Rolls.

Amistad Research Center, Tulane University, New Orleans.
American Missionary Association Papers.

Catholic Diocese of Jackson Archives, Jackson, Mississippi.
Henry Elder Files and Letter Books.

Chicago Historical Society.
Bailhache-Brayman Papers.

Concordia Parish Office of Records, Vidalia, Louisiana.
Deeds, Liens, and Mortgage Records.

Duke University, Perkins Library, Durham, North Carolina.
Kate D. Foster Diary, Foster Family Papers.

Historic Natchez Foundation, Natchez, Mississippi.
Alma Carpenter Papers.
Assessment of Lands in Adams County, Mississippi, 1866–72.
Board of Aldermen Minutes.
Board of Police Minutes.
Chancery Court Records.
Chotard Family Genealogy.
Circuit Court Case Records.
Circuit Court Minutes.
City Council (Selectmen) Minutes.
County and Municipal Death Records.
Court Manuscript Cases.
Criminal Judgment Dockets, Superior Court.

Criminal Justice Docket Books.
Death Records, Sexton Reports.
Foster Family Genealogy File.
Grand and Petite Jury Docket Books.
Jail Docket Books.
Justice Court Dockets.
Justice Court Minutes.
Kyle House Files.
Lighthouse Files.
Magistrate Criminal Dockets.
Map of Natchez, U.S. Military Corps, 1864.
Mayor's Docket.
Minutes, Natchez Board of Selectmen.
Minutes of the Adams County Board of Supervisors.
Municipal Ordinance Books.
Natchez Trails Exhibit.
Nutt Family File.
Probate Records.
Record of Judgment Books.
Register of Teachers and Pay Certificates.
State Justice Docket Books.
Tax Records.
Union School and Natchez Institute Payroll Ledgers, 1874–1905.

Louisiana State University, Louisiana and Lower
Mississippi Valley Collections, Baton Rouge.

Conner, Lemuel P., Family Papers.
Douglas, Emily Caroline, Papers.
Foster, Isaac G. and John S., Papers.
Foster, James, Papers.
Hall, Richard Alexander, Letters.
Jenkins, John C., Family Papers.
Johnson, William T., and Family Papers.
Mandeville, Henry D., Family Papers.
McMurran, Alice Austen, Journal (typescript copy).
McMurran, John T., Family Papers.
McMurran-Austen Family Papers.
Minor, William J., Family Papers.
Quitman, John Anthony, Papers.
Shields, Joseph D., Papers.
Stratton, Joseph B., Papers.
Turner, Edward, Family Papers.

Mayor's Office, Natchez, Mississippi.

Minutes, Natchez Board of Selectmen.

Mississippi Department of Archives and History, Jackson.

Board of Police Minutes, Adams County, Mississippi.
Conner, Louisa Russell, Memoirs.
Farrar, Daniel S., Jr. and Family Papers.
Genealogical Memoir of Ellen Shields (typescript).
General Orders, Brigadier General E. O. C. Ord, Commanding General, Fourth
    Military District, Vicksburg, Mississippi, 1867.
Governors' Papers (Adelbert Ames).
High Court of Errors and Appeals.
Legislative Records.
Minor Family Papers.
Nutt Family Papers.
Probate Records, Adams County, Mississippi.
Pullen-Carson Family Papers.
Subject Files.
Superior Court of Chancery Records, Natchez, Adams County, Mississippi.
Supreme Court of Mississippi Records.
Superior Court of the Western District Records, Natchez, Adams County, Mississippi.
Surget Family Papers.
Surget-McKitrick-McNeil Family Papers.
Territorial Petitions, Legislative Papers of the Mississippi Territory.
U.S. Army Commands, Fourth Military District Orders, 1867–70, Microfilm Roll
    No. 2585.
Wailes, B. L. C., Papers.
Wailes-Covington Family Papers.
WPA Files.

Natchez National Historic Park, Melrose Archives, Natchez, Mississippi.

Addison Family Papers.
Rosenblum, Thom. "John T. McMurran of Old Natchez." Special history study for the
    Natchez National Historical Park. 1996.

Natchez Project Archives, California State University–Northridge.

Nolan, Charles E. Compiled notes on Felicite Gireaudeau. Typescript by Emily Clark.
    2004.

National Archives and Records Administration, Washington, D.C.

Bureau of Refugees, Freedmen, and Abandoned Lands, Record Group 105.
General Records of the Department of the Treasury, Record Group 576.

Letters Received, Bureau for Colored Troops, Records of the Adjutant General's Office, Record Group 94.

Letters Sent, Records of Civil War Special Agencies of the Treasury Department, Records of Field Offices, Record Group 366.

Order Books for Sixth Regiment, U.S. Colored Heavy Artillery, Records of the Adjutant General's Office, Record Group 94.

Records of the Office of the Judge Advocate General, Court Martial Proceedings, Record Group 153.

Records of the Southern Claims Commission, Records of the General Accounting Office, Department of the Treasury, Record Group 217.

Records of the United States Court of Claims, Records of the Judiciary, Record Group 123.

U.S. Army Continental Commands, Letters Sent, Post Natchez, Adams County, Mississippi, Record Group 393.

U.S. CENSUS.

Adams County, Mississippi. Manuscript Agricultural, Manufacturing, Population, and Slave Schedules. 1810, 1820, 1830, 1840, 1850, 1860, 1870, 1880.

Concordia Parish, Louisiana. Manuscript Agricultural, Manufacturing, Population and Slave Schedules. 1810, 1820, 1830, 1840, 1850, 1860.

Louisville, Jefferson, County, Kentucky. Manuscript Population Schedules. 1830.

Vicksburg, Warren County, Mississippi. Manuscript Agricultural, Manufacturing, and Population Schedules. 1830, 1840.

U.S. Congress. House. *Condition of Affairs in Mississippi.* 40th Cong., 3d sess.(1868). H. Misc. Doc. 53.

New York Historical Society, Manuscript Department.

Leverich Family Papers.

St. Mary's Cathedral Archives, St. Mary's Catholic Church, Natchez, Mississippi.

"Announcements in Church," February 19, 1860–January 19, 1868.

Family Histories File.

Register of Baptisms and Sacramental Records, 1820–65.

University of Louisiana at Monroe, Special Collections.

McMurran Letters and Papers.

University of Michigan, William L. Clements Library, Ann Arbor.

Katherine Minor Papers.

University of Mississippi, Department of Archives and Special Collections, J. D. Williams Library, Oxford.

Elizabeth Christie Brown Diary.

University of North Carolina at Chapel Hill, Southern Historical Collection.
Ker, Mary Susan, Papers, 1785–1958.
Quitman Family Papers, 1784–1940.

University of Texas at Austin, Natchez Trace Collection, Center for American History.
Forsyth, John, Papers.
Jenkins, John Carmichael, Family Papers.
Winchester Family Papers.

Warren County Office of Records, Vicksburg, Mississippi.
Deeds, Liens, and Mortgage Records.

Wilkinson County Office of Records, Woodville, Mississippi.
Deeds, Liens, and Mortgage Records.

PUBLIC DOCUMENTS

Ingmire, Frances Terry, and Carolyn Reeves Erickson. *First Settlers of the Mississippi Territory: Grants Taken from the American State Papers, Class VIII, Public Lands.* Vol. 1, *1789–1809.* St. Louis: Ingmire, 1982.
War of the Rebellion: A Compilation of the Official Records of the Union and Confederate Armies. 128 vols. Washington, D.C.: U.S. Government Printing Office, 1880–1901.

LEGAL CODES, DIGESTS, DIRECTORIES, INDEXES, AND STATUTES

Alden, T. J., and J. A. Van Hosen. *A Digest of the Laws of Mississippi.* New York: Alexander S. Gould, 1839.
Blackstone, William. *Commentaries on the Laws of England: A Facsimile of the First Edition of 1765–1769.* Vol. 1. Chicago: University of Chicago Press, 1979.
Campbell, J. A. P. *The Revised Code of the State of Mississippi.* Jackson, Miss.: J. L. Power, 1880.
Code of the Ordinances of the City of Natchez. Natchez, Miss.: Giles M. Hillyer, 1854.
DeVille, Winston. *Mississippi Land Papers and Secret Militia Rolls of 1788: Anglo-American Settlers in the Spanish Gulf South.* Ville Platte, La.: Smith Publications, 1995.
Directory of the City of Natchez. Natchez, Miss.: Banner, 1892.
George, James Z. *A Digest of the Reports of the Decisions of the Supreme Court and of the High Court of Errors and Appeals, of the State of Mississippi, from the Organization of the State, to the Present Time.* Philadelphia: J. & J. W. Johnson, 1872.
Humphreys, Rena, and Mamie Owen. *Index of Mississippi Session Acts, 1817–1865.* Jackson, Miss.: Tucker Publishing House, 1937.
Hutchinson, A. *Code of Mississippi: Analytical Compilation of the Public and General Statutes of the Territory and State with Tabular References to the Local and Private Acts from 1798 to 1848.* Jackson, Miss.: Price and Fall, 1848.
Johnston, Amos R. *The Revised Code of the Statute Laws of the State of Mississippi.* Jackson, Miss.: Alcorn & Fisher, 1871.

Laws of the State of Mississippi. Jackson, Miss.: B. D. Howard, 1839.

Laws of the State of Mississippi. Jackson, Miss.: Fall and Marshall, 1850.

Lowenburg, Isaac. *Census of Inhabitants of Natchez, Mississippi, 1886.* Natchez, Miss.: City of Natchez, 1886.

Mississippi Digest Annotated: A Complete Digest of All Reported Mississippi Decisions from the Earliest Times to September 2, 1911. Vol. 1. Indianapolis: Bobbs-Merrill, 1911.

Natchez Business Directory for 1877–76. Vicksburg, Miss.: Rogers & Groome, 1877.

Sharkey, William, William Harris, and Henry T. Elliot. *The Revised Code of the Statute Laws of the State of Mississippi.* Jackson, Miss.: E. Barksdale, 1857.

Smedes, William C. *A Digest of the Cases Decided and Reported in the High Court of Errors and Appeals and the Superior Court of Chancery of the State of Mississippi from 1818 to 1847.* Boston: C. C. Little and J. Brown, 1847.

Statutes of the Mississippi Territory. Natchez, Miss.: P. Isler, 1816.

NEWSPAPERS

Daily Picayune, 1867.

DeBow's Review, 1845–60.

Mississippi Free Trader (Natchez), 1838–63.

Natchez Courier, 1850–65.

Natchez Cutter, 1841.

Natchez Daily Courier, 1863–66.

Natchez Daily Democrat, 1869–98.

Natchez Democrat, 1867–1933.

Natchez Tri-Weekly Courier, 1870–71.

Natchez Weekly Courier, 1868–72.

Natchez Weekly Democrat, 1833, 1865–86.

New York Times, 1863.

Weekly Advocate, 1866.

Weekly Gazette and Comet, 1866–67.

Weekly Mississippi Pilot, 1875.

Vicksburg Weekly Whig, 1850.

PUBLISHED REMINISCENCES AND CONTEMPORARY ACCOUNTS

Biddle, Ellen McGowan. *Reminiscences of a Soldier's Wife.* Charleston, S.C.: Bibliolife, 2009. Originally published by Press of J. B. Lippincott, 1907.

Chestnut, Mary Boykin. *A Diary from Dixie.* Edited by Ben Ames Williams. Cambridge, Mass.: Harvard University Press, 1980.

Claiborne, J. F. H. *Mississippi, as a Province, Territory and State, with Biographical Notices of Eminent Citizens,* Vol. 1. Jackson, Miss.: Power & Barksdale, 1880.

Cox, Margaret. *The Young Lady's Companion: In a Series of Letters.* Columbus, Oh.: I. N. Whiting, 1839.

Deen, Jeannie Marie, ed. *Annie Harper's Journal: A Southern Mother's Legacy.* Denton, Miss.: Flower Mound Writing Company, 1983.

Eaton, Henry Blackburn. *Descendants of the Jersey Settlers: Kingston, Adams County, Mississippi.* Jackson, Miss.: Dixie Bookbinding, 1950.

Eaton, John. *Grant, Lincoln and the Freedmen: Reminiscences of the Civil War with Special References to the Contrabands and Freedmen of the Mississippi Valley.* New York: Longmans, Green, 1907.

Elder, Bishop William Henry. *Civil War Diary: 1862–1865.* Jackson, Miss.: R. O. Gerow, 1980.

"From a Discourse on Marriage." *Godey's Magazine and Lady's Book* 35 (July 1847): 1–3.

Fuller, Margaret S. "The Great Lawsuit. Man versus Men. Woman versus Women." *Dial,* July 1843.

———. *Women in the Nineteenth Century.* New York: Greeley & McElrath, 1845.

A Gentleman of the Bar. *The Clerk's Assistant: Revised and Greatly Improved.* Poughkeepsie, N.Y.: P. & S. Potter, 1814.

Goodspeed's Biographical and Historical Memoirs of Mississippi, Embracing an Authentic and Comprehensive Account of the Chief Events in the History of the State and a Record of the Lives of Many of the Most Worthy and Illustrious Families and Individuals. Vols. 1–2. Chicago: Goodspeed, 1891.

Gresham, Matilda. *Life of Walter Quintin Gresham, 1832–1895.* Vols. 1–2. 1919. Reprint, Freeport, N.Y.: Books for Libraries Press, 1970.

H. "Old Maids." *Southern Literary Messenger,* August 1857, 473–74.

Haviland, Laura S. *A Woman's Life-Work: Labors and Experiences of Laura S. Haviland.* 1881. Reprint, n.p.: BiblioBazaar, 2006.

Hogan, William Ransom, and Edwin Adams Davis, eds. *William Johnson's Natchez: The Antebellum Diary of a Free Negro.* Baton Rouge: Louisiana State University Press, 1993.

Ingraham, Joseph Holt. *The South West: By a Yankee.* New York: Harper & Brothers, 1835.

J. A. M. "Thoughts on Married Life: 'To My Wife.'" *Godey's Magazine and Lady's Book* 34 (January 1847): 1–5.

Kellar, Herbert A., ed. "A Journey through the South in 1836: Diary of James D. Davidson." *Journal of Southern History* 1 (August 1935): 345–77.

Lynch, James D. *The Bench and Bar of Mississippi.* New York: E. J. Hale and Son, 1881.

Lynch, John R. *Reminiscences of an Active Life: The Autobiography of John Roy Lynch.* Edited by John Hope Franklin. Chicago: University of Chicago Press, 1970.

M. "Spoiling a Husband." *Southern and Western Literary Messenger and Review* 13 (February 1847): 114–19.

"Married Life as a Theme for Poets." *Southern Literary Messenger* 23, no. 6 (December 1856): 443.

"Moral and Natural Law Contradistinguished." *DeBow's Review,* March 1, 1862, 286–95.

Murray, Elizabeth Dunbar. *Early Romances of Natchez.* Natchez, Miss.: Natchez Printing and Stationary, 1950.

———. *My Mother Used to Say: A Natchez Belle of the Sixties.* Boston: Christopher Publishing House, 1959.

"Plantation Life—Duties and Responsibilities." *DeBow's Review,* September 1860, 357–68.

Power, Major Steve. *The Memento: Old and New Natchez, 1700–1897*. Vols. 1–2. 1897.
Reprint, Natchez, Miss.: Myrtle Bank, 1984.

Stanton, Elizabeth Cady. "Marriage and Divorce." *Liberator*, June 1, 1860.

Thompson, John. R. "Woman's True Mission." *Southern Literary Messenger* 19 (May
1853): 303–6.

Wilcox, S. Griffing. "War Times in Natchez." *Southern Historical Papers* 30 (1902): 36–58.

Yeatman, James E. *A Report on the Condition of the Freedmen of the Mississippi River
Valley*. St. Louis: Western Sanitary Commission Reports, 1864.

BOOKS

Alexander, Logan. *Ambiguous Lives: Free Women of Color in Rural Georgia, 1789–1879*.
Fayetteville: University of Arkansas Press, 1991.

Alford, Terry. *Prince among Slaves: The True Story of an African Prince Sold into Slavery in
the American South*. New York: Oxford University Press, 1977.

Anderson, Aaron. *Builders of the New South: Merchants, Capital, and the Remaking of
Natchez, 1865–1914*. Jackson: University Press of Mississippi, 2013.

Ash, Stephen B. *When the Yankees Came: Conflict and Chaos in the Occupied South*.
Chapel Hill: University of North Carolina Press, 1995.

Atherton, Lewis. *The Southern Country Store, 1800–1866*. Baton Rouge: Louisiana State
University Press, 1949.

Ayers, Edward I. *The Promise of the New South: Life after Reconstruction*. New York:
Oxford University Press, 1984.

Bardaglio, Peter. *Reconstructing the Household: Families, Sex, and the Law in the
Nineteenth-Century South*. Chapel Hill: University of North Carolina Press, 1995.

Barnett, James F., Jr. *The Natchez Indians: A History to 1735*. Jackson: University Press of
Mississippi, 2007.

Basch, Norma. *Framing American Divorce: From the Revolutionary Generation to the
Victorians*. Berkeley: University of California Press, 2001.

———. *In the Eyes of the Law: Women, Marriage, and Property in Nineteenth-Century
New York*. Ithaca, N.Y.: Cornell University Press, 1982.

Bearss, Edwin C. *Decision in Mississippi: Mississippi's Important Role in the War between
the States*. Little Rock: University of Arkansas Press, 1962.

Behrend, Justin. *Reconstructing Democracy: Grassroots Black Politics in the Deep South after
the Civil War*. Athens: University of Georgia Press, 2015.

Bell, Caryn C. *Revolution, Romanticism, and the Afro-Creole Protest Tradition in
Louisiana, 1718–1868*. Baton Rouge: Louisiana State University Press, 1997.

Benjamin, Jessica. *The Bonds of Love: Psychoanalysis, Feminism, and the Problem of
Domination*. New York: Pantheon Books, 1988.

Bennett, Judith, and Amy Froide. *Singlewomen in the European Past, 1250–1800*.
Philadelphia: University of Pennsylvania Press, 1999.

Bercaw, Nancy, ed. *Gender and the Southern Body Politic*. Jackson: University Press of
Mississippi, 2000.

———. *Gendered Freedoms: Race, Rights, and the Politics of Household in the Delta, 1861–1875.* Gainesville: University Press of Florida, 2003.

Berger, John. *Ways of Seeing.* New York: Penguin Books, 1977.

Berlin, Ira. *Slaves without Masters: The Free Negro in the Antebellum South.* New York: Vintage Books, 1976.

Berlin, Ira, Thavolia Glymph, Steven F. Miller, Joseph P. Reidy, Leslie S. Rowland, and Julie Saville, eds. *The Wartime Genesis of Free Labor: The Lower South.* Ser. 1, vol. 3 of *Freedom: A Documentary History of Emancipation, 1861–1867.* New York: Cambridge University Press, 1990.

Bettersworth, John K. *Confederate Mississippi: The People and Policies of a Cotton State in Wartime.* Baton Rouge: Louisiana State University Press, 1944.

Billingsley, Carolyn Earle. *Communities of Kinship: Antebellum Families and the Settlement of the Cotton Frontier.* Athens: University of Georgia Press, 2004.

Bolton, Charles C. *The Hardest Deal of All: The Battle over School Integration in Mississippi, 1870–1980.* Jackson: University Press of Mississippi, 2005.

Bond, Bradley G. *Political Culture in the Nineteenth-Century South: Mississippi, 1830–1900.* Baton Rouge: Louisiana State University Press, 1995.

Boswell, Angela. *Her Act and Deed: Women's Lives in a Rural Southern County, 1837–1873.* College Station: Texas A & M University Press, 2001.

Brasseaux, Carl A. *French, Cajun, Creole, Houma: A Primer in Francophone Louisiana.* Baton Rouge: Louisiana State University Press, 2005.

Brazy, Martha Jane. *An American Planter: Stephen Duncan of Antebellum Natchez and New York.* Baton Rouge: Louisiana State University Press, 2006.

Brundage, W. Fitzhugh. *The Southern Past: A Clash of Race and Memory.* Cambridge, Mass.: Belknap Press of Harvard University Press, 2005.

Buchanan, Thomas C. *Black Life on the Mississippi: Slaves, Free Blacks, and the Western Steamboat World.* Chapel Hill: University of North Carolina Press, 2004.

Buchart, Ronald E. *Northern Schools, Southern Blacks, and Reconstruction: Freedmen's Education, 1862–1875.* Westport, Conn.: Greenwood Press, 1980.

Buckley, Thomas E. *The Great Catastrophe of My Life: Divorce in the Old Dominion.* Chapel Hill: University of North Carolina Press, 2002.

Burton, Vernon. *In My Father's House Are Many Mansions: Family and Community in Edgefield, South Carolina.* Chapel Hill: University of North Carolina Press, 1985.

Butler, Pierce. *The Unhurried Years: Memories of the Old Natchez Region.* Baton Rouge: Louisiana State University Press, 1948.

Bynum, Victoria E. *Unruly Women: The Politics of Social and Sexual Control in the Old South.* Chapel Hill: University of North Carolina Press, 1992.

Callon, Sim C., and Carolyn Vance Smith. *The Goat Castle Murder: A True Natchez Story That Shocked the World.* Natchez, Miss.: Plantation Publishing, 1985.

Campbell, Edward D. C., Jr. and Kym S. Rice, eds. *A Woman's War: Southern Women, Civil War, and the Confederate Legacy.* Richmond: University Press of Virginia, 1996.

Carter, Christine Jacobson. *Southern Single Blessedness: Unmarried Women in the Urban South, 1800–1865.* Urbana: University of Illinois Press, 2006.

Carter, Hodding. *Lower Mississippi*. New York: Rinehart, 1942.

Cashin, Joan. *A Family Venture: Men and Women on the Southern Frontier*. New York: Oxford University Press, 1991.

Censer, Jane Turner. *North Carolina Planters and their Children: 1800–1860*. Baton Rouge: Louisiana State University Press, 1984.

———. *The Reconstruction of White Southern Womanhood, 1865–1895*. Baton Rouge: Louisiana State University Press, 2003.

Chambers-Schiller, Lee Virginia. *Liberty, a Better Husband: Single Women in America: The Generations of 1780–1840*. New Haven, Conn.: Yale University Press, 1984.

Chused, Richard H. *Private Acts in Public Places: A Social History of Divorce in the Formative Era of American Family Law*. Philadelphia: University of Pennsylvania Press, 1994.

Cipra, David L. *Lighthouses, Lightships, and the Gulf of Mexico*. Alexandria, Va.: Cypress Communications, 1997.

Clark, Emily. *The New Orleans Ursulines and the Development of a New World Society, 1727–1834*. Chapel Hill: University of North Carolina Press, 2007.

———. *The Strange History of the American Quadroon: Free Women of Color in the Revolutionary Atlantic World*. Chapel Hill: University of North Carolina Press, 2013.

Clark, Thomas D. *Pills, Petticoats, and Plows: The Southern Country Store*. New York: Bobbs-Merrill, 1944.

Clark, Thomas D., and John D. W. Guice. *Frontiers in Conflict: The Old Southwest, 1795–1830*. Albuquerque: University of New Mexico Press, 1989.

Clinton, Catherine. *Battle Scars: Gender and Sexuality in the Civil War*. New York: Oxford University Press, 2006.

———. *The Plantation Mistress: Woman's World in the Old South*. New York: Pantheon Press, 1983.

Clinton, Catherine, and Nina Silber, eds. *Divided Houses: Gender and the Civil War*. New York: Oxford University Press, 1992.

Davis, Allison, Burleigh B. Gardner, and Mary R. Gardner. *Deep South: A Social Anthropological Study of Caste and Class*. Chicago: University of Chicago Press, 1941.

Davis, Edwin Adams, and William Ransom Hogan. *The Barber of Natchez*. 1954. Reprint, Baton Rouge: Louisiana State University Press, 1990.

Davis, Elizabeth L. *Lifting as They Climb: The National Association of Colored Women*. Washington, D.C.: National Association of Colored Women, 1933.

Davis, Jack E. *Race against Time: Culture and Separation in Natchez since 1930*. Baton Rouge: Louisiana State University Press, 2001.

Davis, Ronald L. F. *The Black Experience in Natchez, 1720–1880*. Denver: Eastman, 1992.

———. *Good and Faithful Labor: From Slavery to Sharecropping in the Natchez District, 1860–1890*. Westport, Conn.: Greenwood Press, 1982.

Davis, William C. *A Way through the Wilderness: The Natchez Trace and the Civilization of the Southern Frontier*. New York: Harper Collins, 1995.

Dayton, Cornelia Hughes. *Women before the Bar: Gender, Law, and Society in Connecticut, 1639–1789*. Chapel Hill: University of North Carolina Press, 1995.

Deyle, Steven. *Carry Me Back: The Domestic Slave Trade in American Life*. New York: Oxford University Press, 2005.

Edwards, Laura F. *Gendered Strife and Confusion: The Political Culture of Reconstruction*. Urbana: University of Illinois Press, 1997.

———. *Scarlett Doesn't Live Here Anymore: Southern Women in the Civil War Era*. Urbana: University of Illinois Press, 2000.

Estes, Don. *Legends of the Natchez City Cemetery: The Most Interesting Cemetery in the South*. Natchez, Miss.: GraveDigger, 2009.

Evans, Sarah M. *Born for Liberty: A History of Women in America*. 1989. Reprint, New York: Free Press, 1997.

Fairclough, Adam. *Teaching Equality: Black Schools in the Age of Jim Crow*. Athens: University of Georgia Press, 2001.

Faust, Drew Gilpin. *Mothers of Invention: Women of the Slaveholding South in the American Civil War*. Chapel Hill: University of North Carolina Press, 1996.

———. *This Republic of Suffering: Death and the American Civil War*. New York: Alfred A. Knopf, 2008.

Fellman, Michael. *The Making of Robert E. Lee*. New York: Random House, 2000.

Fields, Barbara J. *Slavery and Freedom on the Middle Ground: Maryland during the Nineteenth Century*. New Haven, Conn.: Yale University Press, 1985.

Foster, Gaines M. *Ghosts of the Confederacy: Defeat, the Lost Cause, and the Emergence of the New South*. New York: Oxford University Press, 1987.

Fox-Genovese, Elizabeth. *Within the Plantation Household: Black and White Women of the Old South*. Chapel Hill: University of North Carolina Press, 1988.

Frankel, Noralee. *Freedom's Women: Black Women and Families in Civil War–Era Mississippi*. Bloomington: Indiana University Press, 1999.

Frederickson, George M. *White Supremacy: A Comparative Study in American and South African History*. New York: Oxford University Press, 1981.

Friedman, Jean E. *The Enclosed Garden: Women and Community in the Evangelical South, 1830–1900*. Chapel Hill: University of North Carolina Press, 1985.

Froide, Amy M. *Never Married: Singlewomen in Early Modern England*. New York: Oxford University Press, 2005.

Gamber, Wendy. *The Boarding House in Nineteenth-Century America*. Baltimore: Johns Hopkins University Press, 2007.

Garner, James Wilford. *Reconstruction in Mississippi*. New York: Macmillan, 1901.

Gatewood, Willard B. *Aristocrats of Color: The Black Elite, 1880–1920*. Bloomington: Indiana University Press, 1990.

Genovese, Eugene D. *The Political Economy of Slavery: Studies in the Economy and Society of the Slave South*. New York: Pantheon Books, 1965.

———. *Roll, Jordan, Roll: The World the Slaves Made*. New York: Pantheon Books, 1974.

———. *The World the Slaveholders Made: Two Essays in Interpretation*. New York: Pantheon Books, 1974.

Genovese, Eugene, and Elizabeth Fox-Genovese. *The Mind of the Master Class: History and Faith in the Southern Slaveholder's Worldview*. Cambridge: Cambridge University Press, 2005.

Gerow, R. O. *Cradle Days of St. Mary's at Natchez*. 1941. Reprint, Natchez, Miss., 1985.

Gilmore, Glenda Elizabeth. *Gender and Jim Crow: Women and the Politics of White Supremacy in North Carolina, 1896–1920*. Chapel Hill: University of North Carolina Press, 1996.

Gleeson, David T. *The Irish in the South: 1815–1877*. Chapel Hill: University of North Carolina Press, 2001.

Glover, Lori. *All Our Relations: Blood Ties and Emotional Bonds among the Early South Carolina Gentry*. Baltimore: Johns Hopkins University Press, 2000.

Glymph, Thavolia. *Out of the House of Bondage: The Transformation of the Plantation Household*. Cambridge: Cambridge University Press, 2008.

Gould, Virginia Meacham, ed. *Chained to the Rock of Adversity: To Be Free, Black, and Female in the Old South*. Athens: University of Georgia Press, 1998.

Gower, Herschel. *Charles Dahlgren of Natchez: The Civil War and Dynastic Decline*. Dulles, Va.: Brassey's, 2002.

Grimsley, Mark. *The Hard Hand of War: Union Military Policy toward Southern Civilians, 1861–1865*. Cambridge: Cambridge University Press, 1995.

Gross, Ariela. *Double Character: Slavery and Mastery in the Antebellum Southern Courtroom*. Princeton, N.J.: Princeton University Press, 2000.

———. *What Blood Will Tell: A History of Race on Trial in America*. Cambridge, Mass.: Harvard University Press, 2008.

Grossberg, Michael. *Governing the Hearth: Law and the Family in Nineteenth-Century America*. Chapel Hill: University of North Carolina Press, 1985.

Gudmestad, Robert H. *A Troublesome Commerce: The Transformation of the Interstate Slave Trade*. Baton Rouge: Louisiana State University Press, 2003.

Habermas, Jürgen. *The Theory of Communicative Action: Lifeworld and System: A Critique of Functionalist Reason*. Vol. 2. Translated by Thomas McCarthy. Boston: Beacon Press, 1987.

Hale, Grace Elizabeth. *Making Whiteness: The Culture of Segregation in the South, 1890–1940*. New York: Pantheon Books, 1998.

Hall, Jacquelyn Dowd, James LeLoudis, Robert Korstad, Mary Murphy, Lu Ann Jones, and Christopher B. Daly. *Like a Family: The Making of a Southern Cotton Mill World*. Chapel Hill: University of North Carolina Press, 2000.

Harris, William C. *The Day of the Carpetbagger: Republican Reconstruction in Mississippi*. Baton Rouge: Louisiana State University Press, 1979.

———. *Presidential Reconstruction in Mississippi*. Baton Rouge: Louisiana State University Press, 1967.

Hartog, Hendrik. *Man and Wife in America*. Cambridge: Harvard University Press, 2000.

Haynes, Robert. *The Natchez District and the American Revolution*. Jackson: University Press of Mississippi, 1976.

Hearn, Chester G. *When the Devil Came Down to Dixie: Ben Butler in New Orleans*. Baton Rouge: Louisiana State University Press, 1997.

Higginbotham, Evelyn Brooks. *Righteous Discontent: The Women's Movement in the Black Baptist Church, 1880–1920*. Cambridge, Mass.: Harvard University Press, 1994.

Hine, Darlene Clark, and Kathleen Thompson. *A Shining Thread of Hope: The History of Black Women in America*. New York: Broadway Books, 1998.

Hodes, Martha. *White Women, Black Men: Illicit Sex in the Nineteenth-Century South*. New Haven, Conn.: Yale University Press, 1997.

Hoff, Joan. *Law, Gender and Injustice: A Legal History of U.S. Women*. New York: New York University Press, 1991.

Jabour, Anya. *Scarlett's Sisters: Young Women in the Old South*. Chapel Hill: University of North Carolina Press, 2007.

James, D. Clayton. *Antebellum Natchez*. Baton Rouge: Louisiana State University Press, 1968.

James, Edward T., Janet Wilson James, and Paul S. Boyer, eds. *Notable American Women, 1607–1950*. Vol. 1. Cambridge, Mass.: Belknap Press of Harvard University Press, 1971.

Janney, Caroline E. *Burying the Dead but Not the Past: Ladies' Memorial Associations and the Lost Cause*. Chapel Hill: University of North Carolina Press, 2008.

Johnson, Charles Owen. *The Order of the First Families of Mississippi, 1699–1817*. Dexter, Mich.: Thomas-Shore, 1991.

Johnson, Walter. *Soul by Soul: Life Inside the Antebellum Slave Market*. Cambridge, Mass.: Harvard University Press, 1999.

Jones, Jacquelyn. *Labor of Love, Labor of Sorrow: Black Women, Work, and the Family from Slavery to the Present*. New York: Basic Books, 1985.

———. *Soldiers of Light and Love: Northern Teachers and Georgia Blacks, 1865–1873*. Chapel Hill: University of North Carolina Press, 1980.

Jordan, Winthrop. *Tumult and Silence at Second Creek: An Inquiry into a Civil War Slave Conspiracy*. Baton Rouge: Louisiana State University Press, 1993.

Kane, Harnett T. *Natchez on the Mississippi*. New York: William Morrow, 1947.

Karsten, Peter. *Heart versus Head: Judge-Made Law in Nineteenth-Century America*. Chapel Hill: University of North Carolina Press, 1997.

Kaye, Anthony E. *Joining Places: Slave Neighborhoods in the Old South*. Chapel Hill: University of North Carolina Press, 2007.

Kennedy, Cynthia M. *Braided Relations, Entwined Lives: The Women of Charleston's Urban Slave Society*. Bloomington: Indiana University Press, 2005.

Klingberg, Frank W. *The Southern Claims Commission*. Berkeley: University of California Press, 1955.

Kolchin, Peter. *American Slavery, 1819–1877*. 1993. Reprint, New York: Hill and Wang, 2003.

Lebsock, Suzanne. *The Free Women of Petersburg: Status and Culture in a Southern Town, 1784–1860*. New York: Norton, 1985.

Lerner, Gerda. *The Grimke Sisters from South Carolina: Pioneers for Women's Rights and Abolition*. 1967. Reprint, Chapel Hill: University of North Carolina Press, 2004.

Libby, David J. *Slavery and Frontier Mississippi, 1720–1835*. Jackson: University Press of Mississippi, 2004.

Littlefield, Daniel F., Jr., ed. *The Life of Okah Tubbee*. Lincoln: University of Nebraska Press, 1988.

Litwack, Leon F. *Been in the Storm So Long: The Aftermath of Slavery*. New York: Alfred A. Knopf, 1979.

Long, Alecia P. *Great Southern Babylon: Sex, Race, and Respectability in New Orleans, 1865–1920*. Baton Rouge: Louisiana State University Press, 2004.

Marshall, Theodore Britton, and Gladys Crail Evans. *They Found It in Natchez*. New Orleans: Pelican, 1939.

Martin, Michael J. *A History of the 4th Wisconsin Infantry and Cavalry in the Civil War*. New York: Sevas Beatie, 2006.

Mason, Mary Ann. *From Father's Property to Children's Rights: The History of Child Custody in the United States*. New York: Columbia University Press, 1994.

Massey, Mary Elizabeth. *Refugee Life in the Confederacy*. Baton Rouge: Louisiana State University Press, 1964.

May, Robert E. *John A. Quitman, Old South Crusader*. Baton Rouge: Louisiana State University Press, 1985.

McGehee, Elizabeth "Betty" Shields, comp. *A Record of the Descendants of John Bisland and Susannah Rucker, with Emphasis on the Family of Their Son, William Bisland*. 1990. Reprint, San Bernardino, Calif.: Borgo Press, 2010.

McMillen, Neil R. *Dark Journey: Black Mississippians in the Age of Jim Crow*. Champaign: University of Illinois Press, 1990.

Miller, Mary Warren, and Ronald W. Miller. *The Great Houses of Natchez*. Jackson: University Press of Mississippi, 1986.

Mills, Frances Preston, ed. *The History of the Descendants of the Jersey Settlers of Adams County, Mississippi*. Vol. 1. Jackson, Miss.: Hederman Brothers, 1981.

Mitchell, Brodus. *The Rise of the Cotton Mills in the South*. Baltimore: Johns Hopkins University Press, 1921.

Moore, Edith Wyatt. *Natchez Under-the-Hill*. Natchez: Southern Historical Publication, 1958.

Moore, John Hebron. *Agriculture in Antebellum Mississippi*. New York: Bookman Associates, 1958.

——. *Andrew Brown and Cypress Lumbering in the Old Southwest*. Baton Rouge: Louisiana State University Press, 1967.

——. *The Emergence of the Cotton Kingdom in the Old Southwest*. Baton Rouge: Louisiana State University Press, 1988.

Morgan, Edmund S. *American Slavery, American Freedom*. New York: W.W. Norton, 1975.

Morris, Robert C. *Reading, 'Riting, and Reconstruction: The Education of Freedmen in the South*. Chicago: University of Chicago Press, 1976.

Natason, Maurice, ed. *Phenomenology and Social Reality: Essays in Memory of Alfred Schutz*. The Hague: Martinus Nijhoff, 1970.

Neverdon-Morton, Cynthia. *Afro-American Women of the South and the Advancement of the Race, 1895–1925*. Knoxville: University of Tennessee Press, 1989.

Nolan, Charles E. *St. Mary's of Natchez: The History of a Southern Catholic Congregation, 1716–1988*. Vol. 1. Natchez: St. Mary's Parish, 1992.

Nutt, Merle C. *The Nutt Family through the Years, 1635–1973*. Phoenix: Merle C. Nutt, 1973.

Oakes, James. *The Ruling Race: A History of American Slaveholders*. New York: Alfred A. Knopf, 1982.

O'Brien, Michael, ed. *An Evening When Alone: Four Journals of Single Women in the South, 1827–1867*. Charlottesville: University Press of Virginia, 1994.

Ownby, Ted. *American Dreams in Mississippi: Consumers, Poverty, & Culture, 1830–1938*. Chapel Hill: University of North Carolina Press, 1999.

Pagan, John Ruston. *Anne Orthwood's Bastard: Sex and Law in Early Virginia*. New York: Oxford University Press, 2003.

Parish, Peter J. *Slavery: History and Historians*. New York: Harper and Row, 1989.

Pease, Jane H., and William H. Pease. *Ladies, Women and Wenches: Choice and Constraint in Antebellum Charleston and Boston*. Chapel Hill: University of North Carolina Press, 1990.

Pillar, James J. *The Catholic Church in Mississippi, 1837–1865*. New Orleans: Hauser Press, 1964.

Powell, Lawrence N. *New Masters: Northern Planters during the Civil War and Reconstruction*. New Haven, Conn.: Yale University Press, 1980.

Rable, George C. *Civil Wars: Women and the Crisis of Southern Nationalism*. Urbana: University of Illinois Press, 1989.

Richardson, Joe M. *Christian Reconstruction: The American Missionary Association and Southern Blacks, 1861–1890*. Athens: University of Georgia Press, 1986.

Riley, Glenda. *Divorce: An American Tradition*. New York: Oxford University Press, 1991.

Roberts, Giselle. *The Confederate Belle*. Columbia: University of Missouri Press, 2003.

Rowland, Dunbar. *Courts, Judges and Lawyers of Mississippi, 1798–1935*. Vol. 1. Jackson, Miss.: Hederman Bros., 1935.

———. *History of Mississippi: Heart of the South*. Vols. 1–2. Chicago: J. Clarke, 1925.

———. *Mississippi*. Vol. 3. Atlanta: Southern Historical Publishing Association, 1907.

Rosenblum, Thom. *John McMurran of Melrose*. Denver: Eastern National, 2001.

Salmon, Marylynn. *Women and the Law of Property in Early America*. Chapel Hill: University of North Carolina Press, 1986.

Scarborough, William K. *Masters of the Big House: Elite Slaveholders of the Mid-Nineteenth-Century South*. Baton Rouge: Louisiana State University Press, 2003.

Schafer, Judith Kelleher. *Brothels, Depravity, and Abandoned Women: Illegal Sex in Antebellum New Orleans*. Baton Rouge: Louisiana State University Press, 2011.

Schultz, Jane E. *Woman at the Front: Hospital Workers in Civil War America*. Chapel Hill: University of North Carolina Press, 2004.

Schweber, Howard. *The Creation of American Common Law, 1850–1880: Technology, Politics, and the Construction of Citizenship*. New York: Cambridge University Press, 2004.

Schweikart, Larry. *Banking in the American South: From the Age of Jackson to Reconstruction*. Baton Rouge: Louisiana State University Press, 2000.

Schweninger, Loren. *Families in Crisis in the Old South: Divorce, Slavery, and the Law.* Chapel Hill: University of North Carolina Press, 2012.

Scott, Anne Firor. *The Southern Lady: From Pedestal to Politics, 1830–1930.* Chicago: University of Chicago Press, 1970.

Sefton, James E. *The United States Army and Reconstruction, 1865–1877.* Baton Rouge: Louisiana State University Press, 1967.

Shammas, Carole, Marylynn Salmon, and Michel Dahlin. *Inheritance in America: From Colonial Times to the Present.* New Brunswick, N.J.: Rutgers University Press, 1987.

Shaw, Stephanie J. *What a Woman Ought to Be and to Do: Black Professional Women Workers during the Jim Crow Era.* Chicago: University of Chicago Press, 1996.

Simon, Barbara Levy. *Never Married Women.* Philadelphia: Temple University Press, 1987.

Smith-Rosenberg, Carroll. *Disorderly Conduct: Visions of Gender in Victorian America.* New York: Knopf Press, 1985.

Sommerville, Diane Miller. *Rape and Race in the Nineteenth-Century South.* Chapel Hill: University of North Carolina Press, 2004.

Spain, Daniel. *Gendered Spaces.* Chapel Hill: University of North Carolina Press, 1992.

Sparks, Randy. *Religion in Mississippi.* Jackson: University Press of Mississippi, 2001.

Spear, Jennifer M. *Race, Sex, and Social Order in Early New Orleans.* Baltimore: Johns Hopkins University Press, 2009.

Stephenson, Wendell Holmes. *Isaac Franklin: Slave Trader and Planter of the Old South.* Baton Rouge: Louisiana State University Press, 1998.

Stevenson, Brenda E. *Life in Black and White: Family and Community in the Slave South.* New York: Oxford University Press, 1996.

Stowe, Steven M. *Intimacy and Power in the Old South: Ritual in the Lives of Planters.* Baltimore: John Hopkins University Press, 1987.

Sydnor, Charles S. *A Gentleman of the Old Natchez Region: Benjamin L. C. Wailes.* Durham, N.C.: Duke University Press, 1938.

———. *Slavery in Mississippi.* 1933. Reprint, Gloucester, Mass.: Peter Smith, 1965.

Tadman, Michael. *Speculators and Slaves: Masters, Traders, and Slaves in the Old South.* Madison: University of Wisconsin Press, 1989.

Taylor, William R. *Cavalier and Yankee: The Old South and American National Character.* 1957. Reprint, New York: Oxford University Press, 1993.

Thompson, Shirley Elizabeth. *Exiles at Home: The Struggle to Become American in Creole New Orleans.* Cambridge, Mass.: Oxford University Press, 2009.

Tolbert, Lisa C. *Constructing Landscapes: Space and Society in Antebellum Tennessee.* Chapel Hill: University of North Carolina Press, 1999.

Ulrich, Laurel Thatcher. *Good Wives: Image and Reality in the Lives of Women in Northern New England, 1650–1750.* New York: Alfred A. Knopf, 1982.

Usner, Daniel H., Jr. *Indians, Settlers and Slaves in a Frontier Exchange Economy: The Lower Mississippi Valley before 1783.* Chapel Hill: University of North Carolina Press, 1992.

Vicinus, Martha. *Independent Women: Work and Community for Single Women, 1850–1920.* Chicago: University of Chicago Press, 1985.

Wagner, Helmut R., ed. *Alfred Schutz on Phenomenology and Social Relations.* Chicago: University of Chicago Press, 1970.

Waldrep, Christopher. *Roots of Disorder: Race and Criminal Justice in the American South.* Urbana: University of Illinois Press, 1998.

Warbasse, Elizabeth Bowles. *The Changing Legal Rights of Married Women.* New York: Garland Press, 1987.

Wayne, Michael. *Death of an Overseer: Reopening a Murder Investigation from the Plantation South.* Oxford: Oxford University Press, 2001.

———. *The Reshaping of Plantation Society: The Natchez District, 1860–1880.* Baton Rouge: Louisiana State University Press, 1982.

Weiner, Marli F. *Mistresses and Slaves: Plantation Women in South Carolina, 1830–80.* Urbana: University of Illinois Press, 1998.

Welcher, Frank J. *The Union Army, 1861–1865: Organizations and Operations, The Western Theater.* Vol. 2. Bloomington: Indiana University Press, 1993.

Wesley, Charles Harris. *The History of the National Association of Colored Women's Clubs: A Legacy of Service.* Washington, D.C.: Association of Colored Women's Clubs, 1984.

Wharton, Vernon Lane. *The Negro in Mississippi.* New York: Harper & Row, 1947.

White, Deborah Gray. *Ar'n't I a Woman?: Female Slaves in the Plantation South.* New York: Norton, 1985.

Whites, LeeAnn. *The Civil War as a Crisis in Gender: Augusta, Georgia, 1860–1890.* Athens: University of Georgia Press, 1995.

Whites, LeeAnn, and Alecia P. Long, eds. *Occupied Women: Gender, Military Occupation and the American Civil War.* Baton Rouge: Louisiana State University Press, 2009.

Whitewell, William L. *The Heritage of Longwood.* Jackson: University Press of Mississippi, 1975.

Williams, Heather Andres. *Self-Taught: African American Education in Slavery and Freedom.* Chapel Hill: University of North Carolina Press, 2005.

Williamson, Joel. *A Rage for Order: Black-White Relations in the American South since Emancipation.* New York: Oxford University Press, 1986.

Wilson, Charles Reagan. *Baptized in Blood: The Religion of the Lost Cause, 1865–1920.* Athens: University of Georgia Press, 1980.

Wilson, Lisa. *Life after Death: Widows in Pennsylvania, 1750–1850.* Philadelphia: Temple University Press, 1992.

Wood, Kirsten E. *Masterful Women: Slaveholding Widows from the American Revolution through the Civil War.* Chapel Hill: University of North Carolina Press, 2004.

Woodman, Harold D. *King Cotton and His Retainers: Financing the Marketing of the Cotton Crop of the South, 1800–1925.* 1968. Reprint, Columbia: University of South Carolina Press, 1990.

———. *New South—New Law: The Legal Foundations of Credit and Labor Relations in the Postbellum Agricultural South.* Baton Rouge: Louisiana State University Press, 1995.

Woodward, C. Vann. *Origins of the New South, 1877–1913*. 1951. Reprint, Baton Rouge: Louisiana State University Press, 1971.

Woodworth, Steven E. *Nothing but Victory: The Army of the Tennessee, 1861–1865*. New York: Alfred A. Knopf, 2003.

Wooster, Ralph A. *The People in Power: Courthouse and Statehouse in the Lower South, 1850–1860*. Knoxville: University of Tennessee Press, 1969.

Wright, Gavin. *Old South, New South: Revolutions in the Southern Economy since the Civil War*. New York: Basic Books, 1986.

Wulf, Karen. *Not All Wives: Women of Colonial Philadelphia*. Ithaca, N.Y.: Cornell University Press, 2000.

Wyatt-Brown, Bertram. *Southern Honor: Ethics and Behavior in the Old South*. New York: Oxford University Press, 1982.

ARTICLES AND ESSAYS

Adams, Katherine J. "Natchez District Women: Voices of Southern Women in the Natchez Trace Collection." In *Inside the Natchez Trace Collection: New Sources for Southern History*, edited by Katherine J. Adams and Lewis L. Gould, 58–93. Baton Rouge: Louisiana State University Press, 1999.

Alford, Terry L. "Some Manumissions Recorded in the Adams County Deed Books in Chancery Clerk's Office, Natchez, Mississippi, 1795–1835." *Journal of Mississippi History* 33 (February 1971): 39–50.

Audhuy, Letha Wood. "Natchez in French Louisiana and Chateaubriand's Epic, The Natchez." In *Natchez before 1830*, edited by Noel Polk, 29–42. Jackson: University Press of Mississippi, 1989.

Bardaglio, Peter W. "Rape and the Law in the Old South: 'Calculated to excite indignation in every heart.'" *Journal of Southern History* 40 (November 1994): 749–72.

Barnett, Jim, and H. Clark Burkett. "The Forks of the Road Slave Market at Natchez." *Journal of Mississippi History* 63 (Fall 2001): 169–87.

Bartlett, Irving H., and C. Glenn Cambor. "The History and Psychodynamics of Southern Womanhood." *Women's Studies* 2 (1974): 9–24.

Beard, Michael F. "Natchez Under-the-Hill: Reform and Retribution in Early Natchez." *Gulf Coast Historical Review* 8 (1993): 29–44.

Behrend, Justin. "Facts and Memories: John R. Lynch and the Revising of Reconstruction History in the Era of Jim Crow." *Journal of African American History* 97 (September 2012): 427–48.

———. "Rebellious Talk and Conspiratorial Plots: The Making of a Slave Insurrection in Civil War Natchez." *Journal of Southern History* (February 2011): 17–52.

Berlin, Ira. "Southern Free People of Color in the Age of William Johnson." *Southern Quarterly* 42 (Winter 2006): 9–17.

Bigelow, Martha Mitchell. "Freedmen of the Mississippi Valley, 1862–1865." *Civil War History* (March 1962): 38–47.

Box, Mrs. Eugene. "Antebellum Travelers in Mississippi." *Journal of Mississippi History* 17 (February 1955): 110–26.

Broussard, Joyce L. "Malvina Matthews: The Murderess Madam of Civil War–Era Natchez." *Journal of Mississippi History* 73 (Spring 2011): 23–58.

———. "Naked before the Law: Married Women and the Servant Ideal in Antebellum Natchez." In *Mississippi Women: Their Histories, Their Lives*, vol. 2, edited by Elizabeth Anne Payne, Martha H. Swain, and Marjorie Julian Spruill, 57–76. Athens: University of Georgia Press, 2010.

———. "Occupied Natchez, Elite Women, and the Feminization of the Civil War." *Journal of Mississippi History* 70 (Summer 2008): 179–207.

———. "Stepping Lively in Place: The Free Black Women of Antebellum Natchez." In *Mississippi Women: Their Histories, Their Lives*, vol. 2, edited by Elizabeth Anne Payne, Martha H. Swain, and Marjorie Julian Spruill, 23–38. Athens: University of Georgia Press, 2010.

Brown, Elizabeth Gaspar. "Husband and Wife—Memorandum on the Mississippi Woman's Law of 1839." *Michigan Law Review* 42 (April 1944): 1110–21.

Buchanan, Thomas C. "Levees of Hope: African American Steamboat Workers, Cities, and Slave Escapes on the Antebellum Mississippi." *Journal of Urban History* 30 (2003): 360–77.

Cain, C. E., ed. "Letter from J. F. H. Claiborne to Richard Abbey." *Journal of Mississippi History* 6 (January 1944): 48–50.

Calhoun, Robert Dabney. "A History of Concordia Parish, Louisiana, 1768–1931." *Louisiana Historical Quarterly* 15 (January 1932): 44–67; 15 (April 1932): 214–33; 15 (July 1932): 428–52; 15 (October 1932): 618–45; 16 (January 1933): 92–124.

Cashin, Edward J. "Paternalism in Augusta: The Impact of the Plantation Ethic upon an Urban Society." In *Paternalism in a Southern City: Race, Religion, and Gender in Augusta, Georgia*, edited by Edward J. Cashin and Glenn T. Eskew, 1–41. Athens: University of Georgia Press, 2001.

Censer, Jane Turner. "'Smiling through Her Tears:' Antebellum Southern Women and Divorce." *American Journal of Legal History* 25 (January 1981): 24–47.

Chesebrough, David B. "Dissenting Clergy in Confederate Mississippi." *Journal of Mississippi History* 55 (May 1993): 115–32.

Chused, Richard. "Late Nineteenth Century Married Women's Property Law: Reception of the Early Married Women's Property Acts by Courts and Legislatures." *American Journal of Legal History* 29 (January 1985): 3–35.

———. "Married Women's Property Law: 1800–1850." *Georgetown Law Journal* 71 (June 1983): 1359–425.

Clark, Emily. "Felicite Girodeau: "Racial and Religious Identity in Antebellum Natchez." In *Mississippi Women: Their Histories, Their Lives*, vol. 1, edited by Martha H. Swain, Elizabeth Anne Payne, Marjorie Julian Spruill, and Susan Ditto, 4–20. Athens: University of Georgia Press, 2003.

Clinton, Catherine. "'Southern Dishonor': Flesh, Blood, Race, and Bondage." In *In Joy and in Sorrow: Women, Family, and Marriage in the Victorian South, 1830–1900*, edited by Carol Bleser, 52–68. New York: Oxford University Press, 1983.

Coker, William S. "Spanish Regulation of the Natchez Indigo Industry, 1793–1794: The South's First Antipollution Laws?" *Technology and Culture* 13 (January 1972): 55–58.

Cook, Cita. "The Practical Ladies of Occupied Natchez." In Whites and Long, *Occupied Women*, 117–34.

Crowley, John. "The Importance of Kinship: Testamentary Evidence from South Carolina." *Journal of Interdisciplinary History* 16 (Spring 1986): 559–77.

Crowther, Edward R. "Mississippi Baptists, Slavery, and Secession, 1806–1861." *Journal of Mississippi History* 56 (May 1994): 129–48.

Culver, Newton. "Brevet Major Isaac N. Earl: A Noted Scout of the Department of the Gulf." *Proceedings of the State Historical Society of Wisconsin* 64 (1917): 319–63.

Cummins, Light Townsend. "An Enduring Community: Anglo-American Settlers at Colonial Natchez and the Felicianas, 1774–1810." *Journal of Mississippi History* 55 (May 1993): 133–54.

David, Elbra. "'In Pursuit of Their Livelihood:' Credit and Debt Relations among Natchez Planters in the 1820s." In *Southern Society and Its Transformation, 1790–1860*, edited by Susanna Delfino, Michiele Gillespie, and Louis M. Kyriakoudes, 217–48. Columbia: University of Missouri Press, 2011.

Davis, Edwin Adams. "William Johnson: Free Negro Citizen of Ante-bellum Mississippi." *Journal of Mississippi History* 15 (April 1953): 57–72.

Davis, H. Bruce. "The Tornado of 1840 Hits Mississippi." *Journal of Mississippi History* 36 (February 1974): 43–52.

Davis, Ronald L. F. "The Plantation Lifeworld of the Old Natchez District, 1840–1880." In *Plantation Society and Race Relations: The Origins of Inequality*, edited by Thomas J. Durant Jr. and J. David Knottenerus, 165–81. Westport, Conn.: Prager, 1999.

———. "The Southern Merchant: A Perennial Source of Discontent." In *The Southern Enigma: Essays on Race, Class, and Folk Culture*, edited by Walter J. Fraser Jr. and Winfred B. Moore Jr., 131–43. Westport, Conn.: Greenwood Press, 1983.

Doolittle, Jason. "Forks of Road: The Old Slave Market of Natchez." In *Natchez on the Mississippi: A Journey through Southern History, 1870–1920*, edited by Ronald L. F. Davis and Joyce L. Broussard, 22. Los Angeles: Norstel Press, 1995.

Drake, W. Magruder. "A Note on the Jersey Settlers of Adams County." *Journal of Mississippi History* 15 (October 1953): 274–75.

Dresser, Rebecca M. "Kate and John Minor: Confederate Unionists of Natchez." *Journal of Mississippi History* 64 (Fall 2002): 189–216.

Dubler, Ariela R. "In the Shadow of Marriage: Single Women and the Legal Construction of the Family and the State." *Yale Law Journal* 112 (May 2003): 1641–1715.

Edwards, Laura. "Law, Domestic Violence, and the Limits of Patriarchal Authority in the Antebellum South." In Bercaw, *Gender and the Southern Body Politic*, 63–94.

Elliott, Jack D., Jr. "City and Empire: The Spanish Origins of Natchez." *Journal of Mississippi History* 59 (Winter 1997): 271–322.

Evans, W. A. "Sarah Ann Ellis Dorsey, Donor of Beauvoir." *Journal of Mississippi History* 6 (April 1944): 67–88.

Faust, Drew Gilpin, Thavolia Glymph, and George C. Rable. "A Women's War: Southern Women in the Civil War." In Campbell and Rice, *Woman's War* 1–27.

Fields, Barbara J. "Slavery, Race, and Ideology in the United States of America." *New Left Review*, no. 181 (May–June 1990): 95–118.

Force, Pierre. "The House on Bayou Road: Atlantic Creole Networks in the Eighteenth and Nineteenth Centuries." *Journal of American History* (June 2013): 21–45.

Freedman, David. "African American Schooling in the South Prior to 1861." *Journal of Negro History* 84 (Winter 1999): 1–47.

Froide, Amy M. "Marital Status as a Category of Difference: Singlewomen and Widows in Early Modern England." In *Singlewomen in the European Past, 1250–1800*, edited by Judith M. Bennett and Amy M. Froide, 236–79. Philadelphia: University of Pennsylvania Press, 1999.

Genovese, Eugene D. "Our Family, White and Black: Family and Household in the Southern Slaveholder's World View." In *In Joy and in Sorrow: Women, Family, and Marriage in the Victorian South, 1830–1900*, edited by Carol Bleser, 69–87. New York: Oxford University Press, 1991.

Getman, Karen A. "Sexual Control in the Slaveholding South: The Implementation and Maintenance of a Racial Caste System." *Harvard Women's Law Journal* 7 (Spring 1984): 115–52.

Gonzalez, Deena J. "The Widowed Women of Santa Fe: Assessments on the Lives of an Unmarried Population, 1850–1880." In *On Their Own: Widows and Widowhood in the American Southwest, 1848–1839*, edited by Arlene Scadron, 65–91. Urbana: University of Illinois Press, 1988.

Gould, Virginia Meacham, and Charles E. Nolan. "Mother Henriette Delille (1812–1862): Servant of Slaves." In *Religious Pioneers: Building the Faith in the Archdiocese of New Orleans*, edited by Dorothy Dawes and Charles Nolan, 25–36. New Orleans: Archdiocese of New Orleans, 2004.

Greenberg, Kenneth S. "The Civil War and the Redistribution of Land: Adams County, Mississippi, 1860–1870." *Agricultural History* 52 (April 1878): 69–90.

Hamilton, Peter J. "British West Florida." *Publications of the Mississippi Historical Society* 7 (1903): 399–426.

Hanger, Kimberly S. "Origins of New Orleans's Free Creoles of Color." In *Creoles of Color of the Gulf South*, edited by James H. Dorman, 1–27. Knoxville: University of Tennessee Press, 1996.

Harley, Sharon. "Beyond the Classroom: The Organizational Lives of Black Female Educators in the District of Columbia, 1890–1930." *Journal of Negro Education* 51 (Summer 1982): 254–65.

Harrell, Laura. "Horse Racing in the Old Natchez District, 1783–1830." *Journal of Mississippi History* 13 (July 1951): 123 37.

———. "Jockey Clubs and Race Tracks in Antebellum Mississippi, 1795–1861." *Journal of Mississippi History* 28 (November 1966): 304–18.

Hartog, Hendrik. "Lawyering Husbands' Rights and 'the Unwritten Law' in Nineteenth-Century America." *Journal of American History* (June 1997): 67–96.

Hawks, Joanne V. "Julia A. Nutt of Longwood." *Journal of Mississippi History* 56, no. 4 (November 1994): 291–308.

Hesseltine, William B., and Larry Gara. "Mississippi's Confederate Leaders after the War." *Journal of Mississippi History* 13 (1951): 88–100.

Hoffheimer, Michael H. "Mississippi Courts: 1790–1868." *Mississippi Law Journal* 65 (Fall 1995): 99–170.

Holmes, Jack D. L. "Cotton Gins in the Spanish Natchez District, 1795–1800." *Journal of Mississippi History* 31 (August 1969): 159–71.

———. "A Spanish Province: 1779–1798." In *A History of Mississippi*, edited by Richard A. McLemore, 1:158–73. Hattiesburg: Southern Mississippi University Press, 1973.

———. "Stephen Minor: Natchez Pioneer." *Journal of Mississippi History* 42 (February 1980): 17–26.

Howard, C. N. "Colonial Natchez: The Early British Period." *Journal of Mississippi History* 7 (February 1945): 37–53.

Howell, Walter G. "The French Period, 1699–1763." In *A History of Mississippi*, edited by Richard A. McLemore, 1:110–33. Hattiesburg: Southern Mississippi University Press, 1973.

Hunt, Margaret R. "The Sapphic Strain: English Lesbians in the Long Eighteenth Century." In *Singlewomen in the European Past, 1250–1800*, edited by Judith M. Bennett and Any M. Froide, 271–96. Philadelphia: University of Pennsylvania Press, 1999.

Johnson, Christopher H. "Lifeworld, System, and Communicative Action: The Habermasian Alternative in Social History." In *Essays on Discourse and Class Analysis: Rethinking Labor History*, edited by Leonard R. Berlanstein, 34–89. Urbana: University of Illinois Press, 1993.

Johnson, Michael P., and James L Roark. "A Middle Ground: Free Mulattos and the Friendly Moralist Society of Antebellum Charleston." *Southern Studies* 21 (Fall 1982): 246–65.

Johnson, Suni. "From Wilderness to Society: Socializing the Natchez Frontier." In *Natchez on the Mississippi: A Journey through Southern History, 1870–1920*, edited by Ronald L. F. Davis and Joyce L. Broussard, 16. Los Angeles: Norstel Press, 1995.

Jones, Jacqueline. "Women Who Were More Than Men: Sex and Status in Freedmen's Teaching." *History of Education Quarterly* 19 (Spring 1979): 47–59.

Kaye, Anthony E. "Neighborhoods and Solidarity in the Natchez District of Mississippi: Rethinking the Antebellum Slave Community." *Slavery & Abolition* 23 (2002): 1–24.

Keller, Mark A. "Horse Racing Madness in the Old South: The Sporting Epistles of William J. Minor of Natchez, 1837–1860." *Journal of Mississippi History* 47 (August 1985): 165–86.

Kennedy, Roger G. "Postscripts to History: Longwood: The Untimely Octagon." *American Heritage* (Society of American Historians) 36 (October 1985): 100–106.

Keyssar, Alexander. "Widowhood in Eighteenth-Century Massachusetts: A Problem in the History of the Family." *Perspectives in American History* 8 (1974): 83–119.

Klingberg, Frank W. "The Case of the Minors: A Unionist Family within the Confederacy." *Journal of Southern History* 13 (February 1947): 27–45.

Knowlton, Elizabeth W. "'Only a Woman Like Yourself'—Rebecca Alice Baldy: Dutiful Daughter, Stalwart Sister, and Lesbian Lover of Nineteenth-Century Georgia." In *Carrying' On in the Lesbian and Gay South*, edited by John Howard, 34–53. New York: New York University Press, 1997.

Kubassek, Melody. "Ask Us Not to Forget: The Lost Cause in Natchez, Mississippi." *Southern Studies* 3 (1992): 155–70.

Landon, Michael D. L. "The Mississippi State Bar Association, 1821–1825: The First in the Nation." *Journal of Mississippi History* 42 (August 1980): 222–42.

Lang, Herbert H. "J. F. H. Claiborne at 'Laurel Hill' Plantation, 1853–1870." *Journal of Mississippi History* 18 (January 1956): 1–17.

Lebsock, Suzanne. "Radical Reconstruction and the Property Rights of Southern Women." *Journal of Southern History* 43 (May 1977): 195–216.

Long, Alicia P. "(Mis) Remembering General Order No. 28: Benjamin Butler, the Woman Order, and Historical Memory." In Whites and Long, *Occupied Women*, 17–32.

Martin, Joan. "*Plaçage* and the Louisiana *Gens de Couleur Libre*: How Race and Sex Defined the Lifestyles of Free Women of Color." In *Creole: The History and Legacy of Louisiana's Free People of Color*, edited by Sybil Kein, 57–70. Baton Rouge: Louisiana State University Press, 2002.

Matthias, Virginia Park. "Natchez-Under-the-Hill as It Developed under the Influence of the Mississippi River and the Natchez Trace." *Journal of Mississippi History* 7 (October 1945): 201–21.

May, Robert E. "Southern Elite Women, Sectional Extremism, and the Male Political Sphere: The Case of John A. Quitman's Wife and Female Descendants, 1847–1931. *Journal of Mississippi History* 50 (November 1988): 251–87.

McCarthy, Kevin D. "Cautious, Conservative, and Raced: The Maternal Presumption in Mississippi Child Custody Law, 1830–1920." In *Mississippi Women: Their Histories, Their Lives*, vol. 2, edited by Elizabeth Anne Payne, Martha H. Swain, and Marjorie Julian Spruill, 77–96. Athens: University of Georgia Press, 2010.

McNeily, J. S. "War and Reconstruction in Mississippi, 1863–1890." *Publications of the Mississippi Historical Society, Centenary Series* 2 (1918): 165–535.

Moncrief, Sandra. "The Mississippi Married Women's Property Act of 1839." *Journal of Mississippi History* 67 (May 1985): 110–25.

Moore, John Hebron. "Local and State Governments of Antebellum Mississippi." *Journal of Mississippi History* 45 (May 1982): 104–35.

Morgan, Edmund S. "Slavery and Freedom: The American Paradox." *Journal of American History* 59 (June 1972): 5–29.

Nguyen, Julia Huston. "Active Faith: The Participation of Louisiana Women in Antebellum Religious Services." In *Searching for Their Places: Women in the South across Four Centuries*, edited by Thomas H. Appleton Jr. and Angela Boswell, 101–21. Columbia: University of Missouri Press, 2003.

———. "Laying the Foundations: Domestic Service in Natchez, 1862–1877." *Journal of Mississippi History* (Spring 2001): 35–62.

Phelps, Dawson A., and Edward Hunter Ross. "Names Please: Place Names along the Natchez Trace." *Journal of Mississippi History* 13 (August 1951): 217–56.

Rabinowitz, Howard N. "Half a Loaf: The Shift from White to Black Teachers in the Negro Schools of the Urban South, 1865–1890." *Journal of Southern History* 40 (November 1974): 565–94.

Rainwater, Percy. "An Analysis of the Secession Controversy in Mississippi, 1854–1861." *Mississippi Valley Historical Review* 24 (June 1937): 35–42.

Ribianszky, Nichole. "'She Appeared to Be Mistress of Her Own Actions, Free from the Control of Anyone': Property Holding Free Women of Color in Natchez, Mississippi, 1779–1865." *Journal of Mississippi History* 67 (Fall 2005): 217–25.

Riley, Franklin L. "Transition from Spanish to American Control in Mississippi." *Publications of the Mississippi Historical Society* 3 (1900): 261–312.

Roark, James, and Michael Johnson. "Strategies of Survival: Free Negro Families and the Problem of Slavery." In *In Joy and in Sorrow: Women, Family, and Marriage in the Victorian South*, edited by Carol Bleser, 88–103. New York: Oxford University Press, 1991.

Rosenblum, Thom. "Driving Out the Slave Traders: The Natchez Uprising of 1833." *Journal of Mississippi History* 67 (2005): 45–68.

Rothstein, Morton. "Acquisitive Pursuits in a Slaveholding Society: Business History in the Natchez Trace Collection." In *Inside the Natchez Trace Collection: New Sources for Southern History*, edited by Katherine J. Adams and Lewis L. Gould, 93–114. Baton Rouge: Louisiana State University Press, 1999.

———. "The Changing Social Networks and Investment Behavior of a Slaveholding Elite in the Antebellum South: Some Natchez 'Nabobs,' 1800–1860." In *Entrepreneurs in Cultural Context*, edited by Sidney M. Greenfield, Arnold Strickon, and Robert T. Aubey, 65–84. Albuquerque: University of New Mexico Press, 1979.

———. "The Natchez Nabobs: Kinship and Friendship in an Economic Elite." In *Toward a New View of America: Essays in Honor of Arthur C. Cole*, edited by Hans Trefousse, 97–111. New York: Columbia University Press, 1977.

———. "'The Remotest Corner': Natchez on the American Frontier." In *Natchez before 1830*, edited by Noel Polk, 98–109. Jackson: University Press of Mississippi, 1989.

Sansing, David G. "Congressional Reconstruction." In *A History of Mississippi*, edited by Richard A. McLemore, 1:571–89. Hattiesburg: University Press of Mississippi, 1973.

Scarborough, Thomas. "Cotton Planters and Plantations in the Natchez District, 1760–1880." In *Natchez on the Mississippi: A Journey through Southern History, 1870–1920*, edited by Ronald L. F. Davis and Joyce L. Broussard, 14–15. Los Angeles: Norstel Press, 1995.

Scarborough, William K. "Lords or Capitalists: The Natchez Nabobs in Comparative Perspective." *Journal of Mississippi History* 54 (August 1992): 239–68.

Schwalm, Leslie. "Between Slavery and Freedom: African American Woman and Occupation in the Slave South." In Whites and Long, *Occupied Women*, 137–55.

Sedevie, Donna Elizabeth. "The Prospect of Happiness: Women, Divorce, and Property in the Mississippi Territory, 1798–1817." *Journal of Mississippi History* 47 (Fall 1995): 189–206.

Shade, William G. "In re Those 'Prebourgeois' Planters: The Political Economy of Flush Times in Mississippi." In *Inside the Natchez Trace Collection: New Sources for Southern History*, edited by Katherine J. Adams and Lewis L. Gould, 146–84. Baton Rouge: Louisiana State University Press, 1999.

Shammas, Carole. "Reassessing the Married Women's Property Acts." *Journal of Women's History* 6 (Spring 1994): 1–38.

Shulman, Cecilia M. "Adam Lewis Bingaman: A Southern Aristocrat of a Different Kind." In *Natchez on the Mississippi: A Journey through Southern History, 1870–1920*, edited by Ronald L. F. Davis and Joyce L. Broussard, 25. Los Angeles: Norstel Press, 1995.

———. "The Bingamans of Natchez." *Journal of Mississippi History* 63 (Winter 2001): 285–316.

Shumsky, Neil Larry, and Larry M. Stringer. "San Francisco's Zone of Prostitution, 1880–1934." *Journal of Historical Geography* 7 (1981): 71–89.

Siebert, Wilbur H. "The Loyalists in West Florida and the Natchez District." *Mississippi Valley Historical Review* 2 (August 1930): 553–609.

Sitterson, J. Carlyle. "The William J. Minor Plantations: A Study in Ante-bellum Absentee Ownership." *Journal of Southern History* 9 (February 1943): 59–74.

Smithers, Leslie. "Profit and Corruption in Civil War Natchez: A Case History of Union Occupation Government." *Journal of Mississippi History* 64 (Spring 2002): 17–33.

Sparks, Randy. "The Good Sisters: White Protestant Women and Institution Building in Antebellum Mississippi." In *Mississippi Women: Their Histories, Their Lives*, vol. 2, edited by Elizabeth Anne Payne, Martha H. Swain, and Marjorie Julian Spruill, 39–56. Athens: University of Georgia Press, 2010.

Stowe, Steven M. "The Rhetoric of Authority: The Making of Social Values in Planter Family Correspondence." *Journal of American History* 73 (March 1987): 916–33.

Sydnor, Charles S. "The Free Negro in Mississippi before the Civil War." *American Historical Review* 32 (July 1927): 769–88.

Taylor, William Banks. "Southern Yankees: Wealth, High Society, and Political Economy in the Late Antebellum Natchez Region." *Journal of Mississippi History* 59 (Summer 1997): 79–122.

Thompson, Elizabeth Lee. "Southern Women, Gender Roles, and the Unconventional Alice Jenkins." *Journal of Mississippi History* 62 (Spring 2000): 21–56.

Tristano, Richard M. "Holy Family Parish: The Genesis of an African-American Catholic Community in Natchez, Mississippi." *Journal of Negro History* 83 (Autumn 1998): 258–83.

Usner, Daniel H., Jr. "Frontier Exchange and Cotton Production: The Slave Economy in Mississippi, 1798–1836." *Slavery & Abolition* 20 (1999): 24–37.

Weems, Robert C., Jr. "Mississippi's First Banking System." *Journal of Mississippi History* 29 (November 1967): 386–408.

Welch, Kimberly. "Black Litigiousness and White Accountability: Free Blacks and the Rhetoric of Reputation in the Antebellum Natchez District." *Journal of the Civil War Era* 5 (September 2015): 372–98.

Welter, Barbara. "The Cult of True Womanhood: 1820–1860." *American Quarterly* 18 (Summer 1966): 151–74.

Wright, Willard E. "Bishop Elder and the Civil War." *Catholic History Review* 44 (1958): 290–306.

Ziff, Karen. "No Longer under Cover(ture): Marriage, Divorce, and Gender in the 1868 Constitutional Convention." In *North Carolinians in the Era of the Civil War and Reconstruction*, edited by Paul D. Escott, 193–219. Chapel Hill: University of North Carolina Press, 2008.

UNPUBLISHED DISSERTATIONS, CONFERENCE PAPERS, AND THESES

Adams, Katherine J. "Murder, Madness, Corpses, and Confusions: Natchez Author Eliza Ann Dupuy." Paper presented at the Fifth Biennial Historic Natchez Conference, Natchez, Miss., 2002.

Aguilar, Janet. "Boarding-House Women of 19th-Century Natchez." Paper presented at the Fourth Biennial Historic Natchez Conference, Natchez, Miss., 2000.

Arnold, Kashia. "Frederick Stanton: Cotton Factor, Super Planter, and the Natchez Nabobs." Paper presented at the Ninth Biennial Historic Natchez Conference, Natchez, Miss., 2013.

Beard, Michael F. "Frontier Port on the Mississippi: A History of the Legend of Natchez Under-the-Hill, 1800–1900." Master's thesis, Louisiana State University, 1981.

Behrend, Justin J. "Freedpeople's Democracy: African-American Politics and Community in the Postemancipation Natchez District." PhD diss., Northwestern University, 2006.

Bieber, Darcy. "Making the Most of Freedom: Black Female School Teachers in Postbellum Natchez Mississippi, 1865–1910." Master's thesis, California State University, Northridge, 2005.

Blodgett, Jim. "The Enigmatic William T. Martin: The Survival of an Old Southern Aristocrat." Paper presented at the Third Biennial Historic Natchez Conference, Natchez, Miss., 1998.

Broussard, Joyce L. "The Career of John T. McMurran: From Yankee Lawyer to Planter Elite in the Natchez District, 1823–1866." Unpublished manuscript. Mississippi Department of Archives and History, Jackson.

———. "Female Solitaires: Women Alone in the Lifeworld of Mid-Century Natchez, Mississippi, 1850–1880." PhD diss., University of Southern California, 1998.

———. "Profile: John T. McMurran: The Economic and Sociopolitical Life Cycle of a Lawyer and Planter in the Old South." Unpublished manuscript. Mississippi Department of Archives and History, Jackson.

Carvill, Caroline. "The Stereotype of Spinsters in Southern Fiction." PhD diss., University of Arkansas, 1989.

Cook, Cita. "Growing Up White, Genteel, and Female in Natchez, Mississippi." PhD diss., University of California, Berkeley, 1992.

Coussons, John S. "The Federal Occupation of Natchez." Master's thesis, Louisiana College, 1951.

David, Elbra. "The Role of Credit and Debt in 1826 Natchez, Mississippi." Master's thesis, California State University, Northridge, 2007.

Dresser, Rebecca. "The Minor Family of Natchez: A Case of Southern Unionism." Master's thesis, California State University, Northridge, 2000.

Everett, Donald. "Free Persons of Color in New Orleans, 1803–1865." PhD diss., Tulane University, 1954.

Falck, Susan Thorston. "Black and White Memory Making in Postwar Natchez, Mississippi, 1865–1935." PhD diss., University of California, Santa Barbara, 2012.

Gates, Randall D. "An Ornament of the City: The Fencibles of Natchez." Paper presented at the Second Biennial Historic Natchez Conference, Natchez, Miss., 1996.

Groen, Mark. "Emancipation and Education in Civil War Era Natchez." Paper presented at the Fourth Biennial Historic Natchez Conference, Natchez, Miss., 2000.

Guillory, Monique. "Some Enchanted Evening on the Auction Block: The Cultural Legacy of the New Orleans Quadroon Balls." PhD diss., New York University, 1999.

Hamilton, Cai. "Illuminating Lydia Dowell: The Extraordinary Life of Lydia Dowell in Antebellum Natchez, Mississippi." Paper presented at the Eighth Biennial Historic Natchez Conference, Natchez, Miss., 2009.

Herring, Todd A. "Natchez, 1795–1830: Life and Death on the Slavery Frontier." PhD diss., Mississippi State University, 2000.

Jenkins, Kathleen. "Next of Kin—the Turners, Quitmans, McMurrans, and Conners: An Intimate Glimpse into the Households of Four Historically Prominent Natchez Families." Paper presented at the Natchez Literary Celebration, Natchez, Miss., 1997.

Kibler, David. "The Natchez Landing." Paper presented at the First Biennial Historic Natchez Conference, Natchez, Miss., 1994.

Lenowski, Jaime. "William T. Martin: A Pillar of Southern Honor." Paper presented at the Fifth Biennial Historic Natchez Conference, Natchez, Miss., 2002.

Marest, Laure. "The Surgets: A French Family in the South, 1780–1870." Paper presented at the Seventh Biennial Historic Natchez Conference, Natchez, Miss., 2006.

McElligott, Carroll Ainsworth. "1787 Census of Natchez." Unpublished manuscript. Historic Natchez Foundation, Natchez, Miss.

McWhite, Sally Leigh. "Echoes of the Lost Cause: Civil War Reverberations in Mississippi from 1865–2001." PhD diss., University of Mississippi, 2002.

Miller, Mary Warren. "History of St. Catherine Street." Unpublished manuscript. Natchez Trails Project, Historic Natchez Foundation, Natchez, Mississippi.

Nomelli, Sheryl. "Jim Crow, Louis J. Winston, and the Survival of Black Politicos in Post-bellum Natchez, Mississippi." Master's thesis, California State University, Northridge, 2004.

Peltier, Corbett James. "Confederate Natchez." Master's thesis, Louisiana State University, Baton Rouge, 1948.

Pletcher, Cody. "'The Horrors of the Inquisition': The Hoggatt Family, White vs. Mulatto." Unpublished student paper in author's possession, 2012.

———. "In between Two Worlds: The Barland Family and a 'Caste of Intermediate Status' in Natchez." Unpublished student paper in author's possession, 2010.

Ribianszky, Nichole S. "'To Find Shelter She Knows Not Where:' Freedom, Movement, and Gendered Violence among Free People of Color in Natchez, Mississippi, 1779–1863." PhD diss., Michigan State University, 2011.

Rowe, Julie. "Brothers and Sisters in the Old Natchez District: The Character of Sibling Relations within a Planter Patriarchy, Natchez, Mississippi, 1820–1860." Paper presented at the Southwestern Historical Association Conference, New Orleans, 1996.

Sadler, Elizabeth. "Yellow Plague: Yellow Fever in Natchez, 1853–1855." Master's thesis, California State University, Northridge, 2013.

Shiells, Dan. "The Orphanages of Ante-bellum Natchez." Paper presented at the Fifth Biennial Historic Natchez Conference, Natchez, Miss., 2002.

Slay, David Henson. "New Masters on the Mississippi: The United States Colored Troops of the Middle Mississippi Valley." PhD diss., Texas Christian University, 2009.

Stites, Barbara. "Expanded Bonds of Womanhood: Female Associations in Antebellum Natchez." Paper presented at the Third Biennial Historic Natchez Conference, Natchez, Miss., 1998.

Tripp, Connie. "An Affair of the Heart: A Natchez Scandal in the Midst of War." Paper presented at the Fifth Biennial Historic Natchez Conference, Natchez, Miss., 2002.

Vaughan, William Ashley. "Natchez during the Civil War." PhD diss., University of Southern Mississippi, 2001.

Wang, I-Shou, and Robert Provin. "Mapping the Historic Natchez District in Its Regional Context, Based on the United States Census of 1860." Charts and maps exhibited at the Second Biennial Historic Natchez Conference, Natchez, Miss.,1996.

Ward, Derrick S. "William T. Hewett and the Role of Violence in Reconstruction Era Adams County, Mississippi." Paper presented at the First Biennial Historic Natchez Conference, Natchez, Miss., 1994.

Welch, Rosanne. "A Family Affair: Emancipation and Slavery in the Old Natchez District, 1795–1860." Master's thesis, California State University, Northridge, 2004.

INDEX

abandonment: after the Civil War, 196; by women, 2, 68–69, 138, 199
Above-the-Hill Natchez, 19, 20, 25
Adams County: courts, Dowell's cases heard in, 249n32; courts, marital disputes heard in, 2–3; slaves and whites in (1787), 17. *See also* courts
Adams Troop, 163
adultery: alimony and, 72–73; black-white cohabitation as, 197; charges of, 269n7; divorce petitions and, 69–72, 89, 196, 257n41; Iresons and, 85, 86; slavery and, 1; Tewkesburys and, 79, 80. *See also* fornication
African Americans. *See* blacks
African ancestry suspicions, Native American heritage and, 116–17
alimony, 72–73, 81, 196
American Missionary Association, 178, 180
Ames, Adelbert, 188, 228
Anderson, William, 129
Andre, Jacques, 2–3
Andre, Jane, 2–3, 142
Anglo-American settlers, land grants for, 16
Armat and Rawlings (lawyers), 39
Army, U.S., 157. *See also* Union occupation
Attaway, Elizabeth, 140
Aubaye, Joseph, 60, 61
Aubaye, Wilhelmina, 60, 61
Ayles, Melissa, 142

Balance, Emily, 129
Ballard, Rice C., 132
Barland, William, 134–35
Battles, Harriet, 117, 128
Bell, John, 274n29
Bemiss, Alfred, 150
Bemiss, Oliver L., 126, 127
Benbrook, Daniel G., 35
Benoist, Madame Sardin, 248n20
Bercaw, Nancy, 4, 190, 287n45

Biggs, Ann, 29–30
Biggs, Margaret, 29, 30, 33, 56, 57, 245–46n3
Biggs, William, 29, 30
Bilo, Phillip, 147, 201
Bingaman, Adam L., Jr., 29, 117, 134, 218, 227, 231
Bingaman, Charlotte, 134
Bingaman, Eleanora Lucille, 134
Bingaman, James A., 134
Bisland, William, 72
Black, Delia, 136
Black, Mary, 70
Black Codes, 202
black federal soldiers, after the Civil War, 272n2, 288n5, 288n8
black men, 190, 204–5. *See also* free people of color
black women: as entrepreneurs, 179–80, 195; freed, as refugees into Natchez, 176–78, 238; marriages/cohabitation with whites and, 197–98; nondependence on men and, 190; postbellum challenges for, 189; single, after the Civil War, 193, 225–32; Union occupation and, 181–82. *See also* free people of color; free-black women; *plaçage*
blacks: adultery charges involving, 70–71; divorce among, 199, 287n47; Jim Crow disfranchisement of, 188–89, 228, 229, 239, 283n12; in Natchez (1787), 17; "not employed by responsible white person" order and, 178–79, 280n106, 280n108; postbellum elite, 198, 225, 286–87n43
bluffs, Natchez, 24, 25, 26
boardinghouses, postbellum, 194, 285n29
Bosley, Cassandra, 125
Bossack, Eliza, 132. *See also* Cotton, Eliza
Bowser, Jim, 153–54
Boyd, Samuel S., 132
Brayman, Mason, 173, 274n18
Breckinridge, John C., 163, 274n29
Britton, Audley, 185